HISTORY AND DERIVATION
OF
EDINBURGH STREET NAMES

Edinburgh Corporation
City Engineers Department
Edinburgh
MAY 1975

FOREWORD

A great amount of the history of Edinburgh is contained in the street names, and in the past considerable care has been taken in the choice of these names.

Charles B. Boog-Watson had completed a substantial history of the derivation of the street names in the city by 1920 and his work forms Part I of this publication.

Subsequently the City Engineer has kept the history up to date and this forms Part II of the publication.

The Highways and Road Safety Committee have authorised the publication of this information at the time of the termination of Edinburgh Corporation, and as Chairman of the Committee I welcome the opportunity of acknowledging the effort which has been made in the compilation of this book. I am sure that it will be of interest and value to many Edinburgh citizens.

JAMES McINALLY
Chairman
Highways and Road Safety Committee
Edinburgh Corporation

May 1975

PREFACE

HISTORY AND DERIVATION
OF EDINBURGH STREET NAMES

IN TWO PARTS

PART I   Page 1

This part consists of the notes of Charles B. Boog Watson, FRSE, FSA (Scotland), one of Edinburgh's most noted historians and antiquarians. An engineer by profession, he was a former vice president of the Old Edinburgh Club contributing frequently to their proceedings and he was also, for many years, a member of the Edinburgh Public Libraries Committee.

For 24 years he carried out voluntary research into the city records working in an office provided for him in the City Chambers. He died on 16 January 1947 in his 89th year.

He provided 15 volumes of notes on the history of Edinburgh and a supplementary volume dealing specifically with the derivation of street names which existed up until about 1920 and which were contained within the city boundary at that time. It is the notes contained in this volume that form Part I of this publication.

PART II   Page 113

This section contains notes on the history and derivation of streets named between about 1920 and the date of the termination of Edinburgh Corporation on 15th May 1975. Research was carried out under the direction of the City Engineer by Mr. W.G. Park, the assistant concerned with street names.

The notes in this part show the date of naming, where known, and the derivation of names of streets in districts which were brought within the city boundary since 1920 such as Cramond, Davidson's Mains, Corstorphine, Juniper Green, Colinton, Fairmilehead, Liberton, Gilmerton and Craigmillar.

Derivations were established by contact with factors of estates, consultation of the files on applications for an order to construct a street, reference to minutes of the various committees of the Town Council, examination of warrants granted by the Dean of Guild Court and City Assessor's survey books dating from 1843. Research was also carried out in the Edinburgh City Libraries and the help of the staff is acknowledged.

A.S. CROCKETT, BSc CEng FICE FIMunE FIStructE
City Engineer, Edinburgh.

May 1975

PART I

The notes of Charles B. Boog Watson

AUTHORITIES QUOTED

Ainslie	Ainslie's plans of Edinburgh, 1780 and 1804. When 'Ainslie' is given, and no date, *both* maps are quoted.
Anderson	John Anderson's 'History of Edinburgh', 1856.
a.o.e.	'Ancient Old Edinburgh', Alison Dunlop, 1890.
Arnot	Hugo Arnot's 'History of Edinburgh', 1788.
B. Bell	Life of Benjamin Bell—surgeon 1868.
Baird	'Annals of Portobello and Duddingston', Wm. Baird, 1898.
Brown, Greyfriars	'Epitaphs and Monumental Inscriptions in Greyfriars' Churchyard', James Brown, 1867.
Burke	Burke's peerage and landed Gentry.
B. & H.	History of Burke & Hare. Geo. Macgregor 1884.
b.b.	'History of the Barony of Broughton', John Mackay, 1869.
Burghmuir	Old Edinburgh Club Book vol. x.
Bruce, J. Home	'Old Houses in Edinburgh', Bruce J. Home.
Chambers' fires	Fires in Edinburgh by Robert Chambers 1824.
c.h.i.	Charter House Inventory, City of Edinburgh.
Chambers	Robert Chambers's 'Traditions of Edinburgh', 1825.
c.c.	Calendar of Charters, Register House.
Can. Chart.	Canongate Chartulary, vol. and date, City Chambers.
D. and date	Directory of Edinburgh.
Denovan	New Picture of Edinburgh printed for Denovan 1806.
D. Map	Postal Directory Map.
D.W. Map	Map of north side of Castlehill in Sir Daniel Wilson's portfolio, in Library of Soc. Ant. Scot.
e.a.	Edinburgh Advertiser.
Edr. Almk.	Edinburgh Almanack.
e.s.s.	'Edinburgh Street Studies', Edinburgh Evening News, N.D.
e.o.t.	'Edinburgh in the Olden Times,' T.G. Stevenson, 1880.
e.c.b.c.ld.	Edinburgh Co-op Building Co. Ltd. Information given by secretary.
Edgar	Edgar's map of Edinburgh 1742 & 1765.
e.e.c.	Edinburgh Evening Courant.
Fires	Robert Chambers's 'Fires in Edinburgh', 1824.
g.l.b.	George Lennox Beattie, F.R.I.B.A. Lauriston House 1921.
Greyfriar's	Moir Bryce's History of Old Greyfriars' Church.
Gilbert	Edinburgh in the 19th century. Wm. M. Gilbert 1901.
Gordon	Plan of Edinburgh in 1647 by James Gordon of Rothiemay. Often called 'De Wit's'.
Holyrood	Moir Bryce's Holyrood, its palace and its abbey.
Home, Bruce J.	See Bruce.
i.w.c.h.	Inventory of the Writings in the Charter house of the City of Edinburgh.
Irons	Leith and its Antiquities. Campbell Irons, 1897.
Imp Map	Maps in "Improvement Scheme" 1866.
j.r.	John Russell, Duke St. School, Leith.
j.r.s.l.	'The Story of Leith', John Russell 1922.
John Knox	'John Knox and the Town Council of Edinburgh', Rt. Miller, 1895.
John Foular	Protocol book of John Foular 1501-1503.
j.s.	John Smith. Author of the Old Scottish Clockmakers.
Kay	Kay's Portraits (A. & C. Black), 1877.
Kerr	Map of Edinburgh in 18th Century, by Henry F. Kerr, A.R.I.B.A., in Old Edinburgh Club, Vol. xi.
Kincaid	'History of Edinburgh', Alex. Kincaid, 1787.
Kirkwood	Robert Kirkwood's plans of Edinburgh, with list of closes, 1817.
l.c.	David Laing, LL.D., Charters.
Littlejohn	Dr. Henry Littlejohn's Report on Sanitary Condition of Edinburgh, 1865.
Mackinlay	'Ancient Church Dedications in Scotland, Unscriptural', Jas. Mackinlay, 1914.
m.h.c.	'History of the Burgh of the Canongate', John Mackay, 1879.

M.	Maitland's 'History of Edinburgh', 1753.
m.b.	'Municipal Buildings of Edinburgh', Robert Miller, 1895.
McDowall	McDowall's new guide in Edinburgh 1850.
McK.	Jas. McKenzie, chemist. Forrest Road.
Mackay	See m.h.c.
m.t.c.	Minutes of the Town Council of Edinburgh.
m.m.s.	'Master Masons to the Crown of Scotland', Rev. R. Scott Mylne, 1893.
New Lights	'New Lights on Old Edinburgh', John Reid, 1894.
o. & n.e.	'Old and New Edinburgh', James Grant, N.D.
o.e.c.	Old Edinburgh Club, volume and page.
o.s.	Ordnance Survey maps, 1852.
Prot.	Protocols, City of Edinburgh, City Chambers, viz:— A.W., Adam Watt. J.T., James Tait. G.H., George Home, J.W., Joseph Williamson. G.I., George Irving. W.F., William Forbes. G.L., George Lindsay. J.H. Canong., James Hamilton, Clerk of Canongate. There are four MS. volumes of condensed translations of John Foular's protocols, vol. iv., 18th April 1528—3rd October 1534, made by Mr. Alex. Buchanan.
Pict. Bits	Picturesque bits from Old Edinburgh. Burns & Henderson, 1868.
p.w.	Peter Williamson's Edinburgh Directories.
r.o.s.	Roll of the Superiorities of the City.
Rev. J.S.	Note book of Rev. Jas. Stevenson, Newgreyfriars 1745-60. Municipal Museum.
r.c.g.	Report on the Common Good, City of Edinburgh, 1905.
Reek.	Reekiana, Robert Chambers's 'Minor Antiquities of Edinburgh', 1833.
Reg.	Burgh Registers, City Chambers.
Rom. Edinr.	'Romantic Edinburgh', John Geddie, 1900.
Speedy	Craigmillar & its environs by Tom Speedy, 1892.
Stewart Chambers	Jas. Stewart in Chambers' Journal 13/8/1904. "Ravelston Dykes".
Soc. Ant. S.	Proceedings of the Society of Antiquaries of Scotland.
Shepherd	Modern Athens. Thos. Shepherd, London, 1829.
Sir John Scott	Sir John Scott of Scotstarvet, "The staggering state of Scottish Statesmen", 1745.
s.s.l.	Sculptured stones of Leith. D.H. Robertson, M.D., 1851.
St. G.	St. Giles, Edinburgh. Rev. J. Cameron Lees, D.D., 1889.
St. C.H.	'St. Cecilia's Hall', David F. Harris, 1911.
St. Matthews	About St. Matthews Morningside, 1908.
St. L.	History & Antiquities of St. Leonard's. Geo. Forrest, 1898.
St. Giles	'The Grange of St. Giles', Mrs. J. Stewart Smith, 1898.
Storer	'Views in Edinburgh and its Vicinity', J. & H.S. Storer, 1820 (Plates alphabetical).
Stothert	'The Christian and Religious Antiquities of Edinburgh', Rev. J.A. Stothert, 1856.
Stockbridge	Historic memorials etc. of Stockbridge. Cumberland Hill, 1889.
Stranger's Guide	The Stranger's Guide to Edinburgh, 1820.
Skinner	From the Castle to Holyrood. R.T. Skinner, 1920.
Stark	Stark's Picture of Edinburgh, different dates.
St. C.	History of the Church & Parish of St. Cuthbert's or West Kirk of Edinburgh, 1829.
t.c.	'The Tolbooth Church', Wm. Brown, 1867.
t.b.	'The Trained Bands of Edinburgh', Wm. Skinner, 1889.
t.o.e.	'Traditions of Edinburgh', Anon., Wm. Rutherford, 1848.
Trad.	'Traditions of Edinburgh', Robert Chambers, 1848.
t.t.l.	'Tales, Traditions, and Antiquities of Leith' (Wm. Hutchison), 1865.
Tron Kirk	'The Tron Kirk of Edinburgh', Rev. D. Butler, 1906.
v.r.	Valuation Roll, brought up to date from 1726 to 1811.
w.c.	Wm. Cowan, prest. Old Edinb. Club.
Wilson	Sir Daniel Wilson's 'Memorials of Edinburgh', 1891.
Walks in Edinr.	Chambers's Walks in Edinburgh', 1825.
w.o.l.	Water of Leith. John Seddie, 1896.
w.s.b.	Writs for building of the South Bridge, City Chambers.

A ABBEYHILL

"A suburban village", *Walks, 16)*. Abbeyhill house and grounds for sale *29/7/1776 eec.j.s.* Occupied by Hon. Mrs. Norton, *D.1827*.
See also Abbeyhill Crescent—Part II).

ABBEY MOUNT
> **STRAND**
> **STREET**
> **LANE**

All derived from the neighbouring Abbey of Holyrood.

ABBOTSFORD PARK
> **CRESCENT**

Both Abbotsford Place, *Littlejohn*. From the same enthusiasm as named Marmion Ter. and Banner Pl. q.v. *After D.1855/6*.
Marmion Ter. and Banner Place now part of Morningside Road.

ABERCORN AVENUE
> **CRESCENT**
> **GARDENS**
> **TERRACE**
> **ROAD**

From the Marquis of Abercorn, superior of the ground. The lands of Duddingston were acquired by the Marquis of Abercorn from the Argyle family in 1745. *Baird 83.*
See also Abercorn Drive, Grove—Part II.

ABERCROMBY PLACE

Abercrombie D. 1809. From Sir Ralph Abercrombie who fell at Aboukir Bay, 1801. *o.e.c. IX. 97.* Correspondence anent shape etc., no name mentioned. *m.t.c. 14/3/1804.* Both forms are given *m.t.c. 17/6/1807* and allusion made from the original plan under which feus were granted in 1803. *See Ainslie, 1804.* "South Crescent" *m.t.c. 16/10/1808.*

ABINGER GARDENS

So named on plan when the Murrayfield Real Estate Co. Ltd. acquired the property from the late Mr. Lockhart Thomson.

ADAM STREET EAST
> **WEST**

From the architect Robert Adam, who designed much in the New Town. He was the King's architect. Born 1728, died 1792. Buried in Westminster Abbey. In Ainslie's map 1804 the street is named Edinburgh St. In Arnot's map 1816, and Kirkwood's 1817, it is Eldin St. In Knox's map 1822, Adam St.

ADMIRAL TERRACE

Built on the grounds of the house long occupied by Admiral Peat, *D.M. 1883.* Captain Peat, R.N. Viewforth House *D. 1846/7—1855/6.* Admiral Peat of Seggie, lived for long in Viewforth House, which was removed when Boroughmuir Secondary School was erected in its grounds. He died 1879, aged 86. Buried New Calton. Married Miss Pratt of Seggie. *"Silences that speak", p. 645.*

ADMIRALTY STREET

Natural in a sea port. Named after 1812, just when first docks were constructed, towards with it ran. This the source of the name, *j.r.*

THE ADVOCATE'S CLOSE

From the house of Sir James Stewart of Goodtrees, Lord Advocate of Scotland, 1692-1709 and 1711-13. *Reek. Index: Sir James Stewart of Gutters, Queen's Advocate. Prot. A.W. 2, 25/3/1704.* It stood on the west side of the close, at the foot thereof, and was occupied later by Andrew Crosbie, the accepted original of Counsellor Pleydell in 'Guy Mannering'. *'Men of the Covenant', 144.* Sir James returned from exile on the landing of the Prince of Orange, 1688; he was hated by the Jacobites, who attacked him in lampoons, and nicknamed him James Wylie.

He inherited the house from his father, Sir James Stewart of Coltness, Provost of Edinburgh 1648-49, at the time of Cromwell's first visit to the city, and again 1658-59. It was rebuilt by the Lord Advocate soon after the Revolution.

In 1769 his grandson, another Sir James, sold the house to David Dalrymple, Lord Westhall. The Rev. Hugh McKail, so miserably caricatured as Ephraim Macbriar in 'Old Mortality' was at one time tutor in the family of Provost Sir James Stewart, and was almost caught by the hunters in the house at Goodtrees, now Moredun, but escaped for the time to Holland; '*Men of Covenant*', *144*.

Edgar. Ainslie. Kirkwood. Kerr .

The close was also known as Stewart's Close, *Prot. W.F.7, 25/4/1748.* Sir James Stewart's Close, *Prot. W.F. 7, 27/5/1755,* **and** Provost Stewart's Close, *Prot. A.W. 3, 21/3/1711,* from the Lord Advocate and his father.

Its original name was Cant's Close, *Prot. A.W. 3, 21/3/1711,* from the property of Henry Cant of Over Libbertoun, *Prot. G.H. 12, 26/7/1737.* It was one of the bewildering closes of this name.

The Advocate's Close was formerly Home's Close, *Reg. 17/11/1760.* A tenement in Home's close, owned in succession by Adam Rae of Piteddie: Sir Wm. Dick of Brade: his creditors: Mr. John Mitchelson of Midleton: John Spotswood of that Ilk: Sir Jas. Stewart senior: Mr. Henry Barclay, looked into Home's Close on the east and Byres' Close on the west. Henry Home of Kaims, Senator of the College of Justice, possessed a house in the Advocate's Close, *Reg. 17/11/1760.* He died 1782, aged 87, living latterly in New Street, Canongate, *Kay, i. 14, 323; P.W. 1773, 1780.*

AGNEW TERRACE	Shown as Ferry Road, *D.1905.* Possibly from Lt. Col. G. Agnew, resident in East Warriston House.
A INSLIE PLACE	Built on the estate of the Earl of Moray, feued 1822-3. Named from maiden name of Lord Moray's second wife. (He was Francis 10th Earl born 1771, died 1848, married 1801. Margaret Jane, 2nd daughter of Sir Philip Ainslie of Pilton. She died 1837. Edmund Archibald, 15th Earl lived in No. 7 Ainslie Place).
AIRLIE PLACE	David, 6th Earl of A. representative peer 1833/49, as also the 7th Earl, 1850/1881.
AITCHISON'S PLACE	From Mr. Aitchison, who owned it. He was a confectioner in Edinburgh, and was locally known as "Sweetie Mill", *w.b.*
ALBANY STREET LANE	So called because the neighbouring York Place preserved the title of the King's second son in England (Duke of York). In Scotland the King's second son is Duke of Albany. It was first called Abany Row, *m.t.c. 13/2/1799, 9/4/1800, 11/6/1800 Albany St. m.t.c. 7/5/1800, Denovan 1804, and Stark 1806, Albion Row. Directory 1807 Albany Row, also Arnot 1816. Kirkwood 1817 Albany St., Albany St. 5/9/1801, eec.j.s. To be called Albion 17/10/1801 eec.j.s.* There may have been some confusion.
	Ainslie 1804 the eastern part is Albany St., the Western Albion Row.
	Late act anent height of houses, n.s. Albany St. rescinded, owing to failure of feuars to carry out scheme, *m.t.c. 1/1/1802.*
ALBERT DOCKS ROAD **ALBERT PLACE STREET**	Dock opened 1869. All from Albert, Prince Consort, husband of Queen Victoria. Married 1840. Born 1819. Died 1861.
ALBERT TERRACE	*D.M. 1870,* formerly Dow Lane. Derivation as above.
ALBION PLACE ROAD TERRACE	Shown as Easter Road, *D.M. 1899.* Fanciful—compliment to Scotland.
ALBYN PLACE	*Lothian Map 1825, Stark 1825.* Probably in connection with the Highland Society of Scotland, whose Hall was in No. 6 , *D.1827.* On Lord Alva's land, *Charles Erskine, m.t.c. 3/1/1827.* There is a building plan & evaluation (not carried out) of David Scott in Register House.

Hist. Dept. 1818. Albyn Pl., the central part of which is appropriated to the use of the Highland Society" *Walks in Edr. 200.*
Albany, Albion or Albinn—the ancient Gaelic name of Scotland.

ALDERBANK GARDENS
PLACE
TERRACE

1885-1900. Fanciful, after the tree, *e.c.b.c.ltd.*

ALFRED PLACE

1865-66 Albert Place—probably changed in 1867 to avoid confusion. Perhaps from Duke of Edinburgh.

ALISON'S CLOSE
WYND

Prot. W.F. 9, 22/6/1759. Ainslie. Kirkwood. Kerr. Also known as Wardlaw's Close, *Prot. G.L. 3, 5/11/1766.*

An Alison's Close, probably this, is mentioned in 1708, *Prot. G.H. 3, 6/12/1708.* It is named from the property on the north side of the Cowgate, opposite the Magdalen Chapel, acquired by Mr. Alexr. Alison, deputy receiver of Excise of Scotland. A house there was owned by Margaret Alison, who received it from James Alison, merchant, burgess. She married Andrew Cheyne, or Chene, or Skeyn, and had a son, Robert, minister, *Prot. A.W. 5, 6/4/1714; W.F. 9, 22/6/1759.* The alias is clearly given.

The older name, Wardlaw's Close, was derived from James Wardlaw, to whom the Temple lands on the south side of the Castlehill, east side of the West Bow, were disponed by Wm. Rankeillour, and who was succeeded therein by his son John, *Prot. W.F. 5, 3/6/1751; J.W. 3, 15/7/1756.* **James Wardlaw owned a tenem**ent bounded on the west by Wardlaw's Close, near the Upper Bow, *Prot. G.H. 11, 1/2/1737.* The lands of the late James Wardlaw lay on the east of those of the late Ninian M'Morran, *Prot. G.H. 3, 19/11/1706.* The close opened to the south side of the Lawnmarket, *Reg. 28/6/1767; Prot. G.I.2, 24/5/1734.* James Riddell owned a tenement in it. This suggests its entering through Riddell's Court, and giving the name to the entry. See Kerr; also 'Riddell's Court'.

ALLAN STREET

From the same proprietor as Allan St., Leith. *For sale 20/11/1824, eec.j.s.* From local proprietor, Mr. Allan of Allanfield. *Kirkwood 1817, D. 1827. Stranger's Guide, 265.* For sale apply to Thomas Allan of Allanfield, *20/11/1824 eec.j.s.* Thomas Allan cooperage and cellars 12 Timberbush, house 9 Wellington Place *D.1827, 209.*
Allan St., Leith renamed Dudley Ave. South 4/5/66.

ALLAN'S CLOSE

Also known as Leith's, Leithe's, or Leitch's Close, Dunlop's Close, Duell's, Doul's, or Dowel's, or Dougal's or Douglas' Close, Abernethy's Close.

No derivation has appeared for Allan's Close.

Leitch's Close (the variants are many), now Allan's Close, *Prot. W.F.2, 30/7/1747,* owes its name to David Leche, *Prot. 20/3/1528.* His son Archibald, *Prot. 17/7/1534,* had lands there, *Prot. W.F. 1, 14/1/1747.* and a cross-house, *Prot. A.W. 5, 6/5/1715.*

The name Duell's Close appears in several forms as above. It is **derived** from the tenement of Simon Dowell in the close, *Prot. W.F. 1, 14/1/1747.* The form Dougal's is due to the tenement of John Dougal and (later) of his brother James, *Prot. A.W..6, 29/6/1719,* apparently descendants of Simon's. Douglas Close, *Prot. W.F.5, 8/3/1753,* seems to be but a variant. Maitland, *M.216,* gives Dugal's Close, but Allan's Close also.

It was also named Dunlop's Close, alias Leitche's Close, from the property therein of Mr. John Dunlop, *Prot. J.W.2, 29/7/1749.*

Another name, whose derivation is unknown, was Abernethy's Close, *Abernethy's or Allan's Close: Prot. W.F.4, 3/10/1750.*

Note:—The endeavour to identify Leich's Close with Hope's Court, north side, Netherbow, made in Soc. Ant. S., 9th February 1891, p. 147, is wholly unsuccessful—several closes are, as one may say, transported.

ALMOND BANK TERRACE

Fanciful, after the almond tree. *e.c.b.c. ld.*

ALVA PLACE

Property near belonging to Johnston of Alva.

ALVA STREET

On the property of James Erskine, Lord Alva. *Ainslie 1804. Kirkwood 1817.* "James Erskine of Alva, Drumsheugh", *p.w.1780/81. D. 1827.* Lord Alva's property acquired 1820. *m.t.c. 3/6/1834.*

ALVANLEY TERRACE

From the sister of Lord Alvanley, wife to Capt. John Warrender of Bruntsfield. *o. & n.e. III, 4b.* See Arden St. Sir John Warrender 5th Bart. married Frances Henrietta, daughter of Richard Pepper, 1st Lord Alvanley.

ANCHOR CLOSE

Also known as Fowlar's or Fuller's Close, Fisher's Close, Fordyce Close.

Named from the 'Anchor Tavern in Fuller's Close' kept by George Cumming, *Prot. G.H.10, 17/10/1734*, where the Lord High Commissioner was long in the habit of holding his levees, *o.e.c. iv. 36*, and where the Crochallan Club met, and entertained Burns, *Wilson, ii.25. Edgar. Ainslie. Kirkwood. Kerr.*

The older name, Fowler's or Foular's Close, is mentioned in 1521, *o. & n.e.ii, 241,* and is attributed to its containing the house of Wm. Fowler, merchant, burgess, supposed author of 'The Triumph of Death', *o. & n.e. i. 236.* The house of Wm. Fowler, merchant, burgess, at the head of former Fowler's, now Anchor Close, was inherited by his son John, and acquired later by Sir Alexr. Ogilvie of Forglen, from whom it took the name of Forglens, *Prot. W.F.5, 28/11/1751,* or Forgulan's *Prot. W.F.2, 24/2/1749* Land.

It is called, misleadingly, Foulis Close, *Prot. W.F.9, 7/9/1759,* but must not be confounded with (north) Foulis Close, which Edgar names Fowler's Close.

It is once *Reg. 14/1/1859* named Fisher's alias Fowler's, now Anchor Close—derivation unknown.

A close, Fordyce Close, may be the same as Anchor Close, but it has no clear alias. It was on the north side of the High Street, and dervied its name from the property of James Fordyce, 'fecialis scriba' in Foullis Close, *Reg. 11/12/1740.* John Fowler owned property in Fordyce Close, *Reg. 20/9/1856; Prot. J.W.3, 29/12/1752.* Wm. Fowler owned property in Fordyce Close, which was inherited by his son and heir John, *Prot. G.H.4, 28/12/1711.* The various bounding lands tend to the identification.

The close seems to have enjoyed other names also, Brown's and Dickson's being on the north side of the High Street, containing the tenement of Agnes, Sibella, and Elizabeth Dickson, *Prot. J.W.8, 7/5/1767; A.W.7, 26/11/1723.* The lands of the late Wm. Fowler were on the east and west: that of Thomas Brown, merchant, on the North, whence Brown's Close: it contained the lands of Thomas Dickson, *Prot. A.W.7, 26/11/1723.* The lands of the late John Dickson were in Dickson's Close, north side of the High Street, *Reg. 10/2/1864.* The tenement of Thomas Dickson was in or close to Fowler's, now

Anchor Close, *Prot. W.F.11, 26/8/1762.* Thomas Dickson's land was on the east side of Fordyce Close, mentioned above, *Prot. J.W.3, 29/12/1752.*

Brown's, now Dickson's Close, *Prot. J.W.8, 7/5/1767; A.W.7, 26/11/1723.*

ANCHORFIELD

Old name. *Kirkwood 1817, D. 1827.* Anchor has a natural connection with a sea port. Ankerfield *m.t.c. 9/2/1814.*

ANDERSON PLACE

From name of builder Thomas Anderson, of 100 Great Junction St. About 1875 or 1880, *j.r.*

ANDERSON'S CLOSE

D. 1827. O.S. Kerr. Also known as Stinking Close, *Kirkwood, Ainslie.* Haunted Close, *Wilson, ii. 161, 165.* 62 West Bow, *D. 1827.*

From John Anderson, deacon of the Hammermen, who built Deacon Anderson's land in the West Bow, *t.b. 77,* in 1678, receiving permission from the Town Council to make an entry thereto in the east end of the putt *buttress* of the pend of the West Bow (clearly the archway) between the north cheik of the putt and the turnpyke or entry to John Moubray, *or Moutray,* his house, *m.t.c. 8/5/1678.* The position is clearly shown by Gordon.

Various Andersons appear in the early directories: William, ironmonger, West Bow, *P.W. 1773;* John, gunsmith, bowhead well, *P.W. 1773;* Henry, shoemaker, Bowhead, *P.W. 1773;* William, stabler, Cowgatehead, *P.W. 1780;* John, coppersmith, west bow, *P.W. 1780.*

This last is probably the John Anderson who acquired property from Gabriel Ranken of Orchyeardhead, previously owned by John McMorran and his heir Ninian, portioner of Kingsbarns, *Prot. J.W.5, 24/5/1760; J.W.7, 5/12/1764.* Deacon Anderson's land was built on ruins on 'the first *were there other unsavoury closes, or is this equivalent to 'first, or Stinking Close'* stinking close, south side of West Bow' beyond the Overbow, by the late John Anderson, *Prot. W.F.1, 26/12/1744; G.L.1, 29/8/1763.*

The Free Church of Scotland acquired, in 1863, property whereon to build a church, on the north side of the Cowgate, bounded on the west by Anderson's Close, on the east by Pollock's Close, and on the north by the lands of the heirs of John Anderson, coppersmith.

Its alias, the Stinking Close, *p.w. list 1779; Ainslie, Kirkwood,* needs no explanation.

Wilson *Wilson, ii. 161, 165* gives it the name of the Haunted Close, from an apparition seen there shortly before Major Weir's confession and execution. Weir's Close was No. 24 West Bow *D. 1825.*

ANGLE PARK TERRACE

From the sharp angle at the corner between the Lanark and Midcalder Roads.
At Angle Park Ter./Ardmillan Ter.

ANN STREET

From Ann, widow of Count Leslie, and wife of Sir Henry Raeburn, who occupied Deanhaugh House. Kirkwood shews Ann, Charlotte and Elizabeth Streets, *Lothian map 1825, Ann, Danube and Carlton,* as if suggesting two British and one English queens. *Built 1825 o.& n.e. III 73.*

ANNANDALE STREET

1826. On ground belonging to the widow of Dr. John Hope, professor of Botany *see Kays portraits,* The Botanic Gardens "Physic garden" there in 1804 *Ainslie.* She was descended from a branch of the Hopetoun family. In 1792 the 3rd Earl of Hopetoun succeeded to the Annandale Estates through his wife, the heiress.

| ANNFIELD | Lady Ann Steuart widow of John Steuart of Blairhaw, thereafter of Annfield *Prot. 1/8/1763 G.L.1.*
See also Annfield St.—Part II. |
|---|---|
| APPIN TERRACE | Built by Bailie Mackenzie of Mackenzie & Moncur, Engineers, who was a native of Appin. |
| ARBORETUM AVENUE ROAD | From the neighbouring Arboretum—the part of the Botanic Gardens devoted to trees. |
| ARCADE NORTH BRIDGE | *Site of Milne's Sq* From someone's belief that an arcade is covered in hall or passage, with booths or stalls on each side. Other arcades existed in Leith Walk (afterwards Croall's Coach Office) and in Princes Street. |
| ARCHIBALD PLACE | From nursery garden of Mr. Archibald *Ainslie 1804.* The place appears in Lothian map 1825 *a.o.e. 81.* Lately Archibald's Nursery, apply to George Archibald, seedsman, 66 Nicolson St. *2/2/1824 eec.j.s.* House at Archibald Place; shop 176 High St.; nursery, Grange Farm *D.1827.* Joseph Archibald, seedsman, *v.r. 47. m.t.c. 22/12/1790 & 7/9/1814.* Perhaps connected with Wm. Archibald, tanner in *Wester* Portsburgh, and his son James, owners in Pocketslieve, *p.w. 1780/81. m.t.c. 2/9/1789.* |
| ARDEN STREET | From family name of the Earl of Haddington, 11th Earl, married 1854 Helen, daughter of Sir John Warrender by Frances, daughter of Lord Chief Justice Alvanley, *Who's Who 1915.* Sir George Bailie Hamilton, Arden, 11th Earl of Haddington. |
| ARDMILLAN PLACE TERRACE | After Lord Ardmillan, judge of session. |
| ARGYLE CRESCENT PLACE | In 1730 the Lands of Duddingston, belonged to the Argyle family: in 1745 they were sold to the Marquis of Abercorn. |
| ARGYLE PARK TERRACE PLACE | On property owned by Mr. Campbell *Ainslie 1804, Kirkwood 1817.* Site of Argyle Park house and grounds *D.1827, 177* owned by Duncan Stevenson, publisher of the notorious "Beacon". In 1800 it was occupied by Gabriel Campbell, spirit dealer, No. 1 West from Meadow Cage *D.1800, 109,* Argyle Park and Place, meadows *D.1800.*

Dwelling house etc. south side of Hope Park *Meadows* on road from Sheens (Sciennes) to Bruntsfield. by enclosure of David Campbell, tailor, thereafter of Mr. John Hope, and Misses Warrender, *Reg. 23/5/1857.* Acquired by David Campbell from John Parkhill of Craiglockhart, merchant, *Reg. 8/7/1857.* A foot entry to the Meadows or Hope Park was granted to certain persons dwelling south thereof. David Campbell, H.M. master tailor for North Britain, *m.t.c. 18/2/1736.* |
| ARTHUR STREET | *Ainslie 1804, 23/3/1822, eec.j.s.* Probably as having a view of Arthur's Seat, *17/2/1819, j.r.* |
| ASHLEY TERRACE | Fancy—from the ash tree, *e.c.b.c. ld.*
See also Ashley Drive etc.—Part II. |
| ASHVILLE TERRACE | From the ash tree, fancy, *e.c.b.c.ld.* |
| ASSEMBLY STREET | Where the Assembly Rooms were and are, *j.r.* Built 1789, *j.r.* |
| AUCHENLECK'S BRAE | Newhaven. From local proprietor. *Kirkwood 1817.*
See also Auchenleck Court—Part II. |
| AVONDALE PLACE | Fancy, *e.c.b.c.ld.* |

B BACK STAIRS

Ainslie. Kirkwood. Shown as Parliament Stairs, *Reek. 298.*

Leading up from the Cowgate to the Back of the Parliament Close. The part known as Henderson's Stairs was demolished in 1828, *o.& n.e.i.179,181.* These were the New Stairs at the west end of the Meal Market, opposite Henderson's land on the north, *Prot. G.L.3, 2/7/1766; Reg. 27/6/1741.* John Henderson, wright, had a lodging at Henderson's Stairs, *Reg. 2/10/1863,* which were bounded on the west by Forrest's *(sic)* Wynd, *Reg. 23/10/1863.* They did not exist in Gordon's days, but are shown by Edgar and named by Ainslie.

These stairs must not be confounded with the President's Stairs, *p.w. 1780, p.16; D.1799, p.160,* which were scale stairs at the east end of the Parliament Close and took their name from Sir Hugh Dalrymple (son of the first Earl of Stair), President of the Court of Session, *Fires, p.13; t.c., p.17; Prot j.w. 3, 3/3/1753.* They were the stairs leading down through, or under, the 'Babel' on the south side of the Parliament Close to the Old Post Office Close below. q.v.

BAILEYFIELD ROAD

From the house built for himself by Wm. Bailey, first Provost of Portobello, 1833, flint glass and bottle manufacturer, *Baird 366/7.*

BAILIE FYFE'S CLOSE

Also known as Barrie's Close, Trotter's Close. *Edgar. Ainslie. Kirkwood. Kerr.*

There are two closes leading into one court, the westermost of which has borne this name certainly since Edgar's map of 1742. It owes its name to the property on the east side of Morrison's Close, **owned by** Gilbert Fyfe, merchant, bailie, *Prot.W.F.3, 14/2/1750. Gilbert Fyfe, 4th bailie 1677, 2nd bailie 1680, and 1st bailie 1686.* There seems to have been some family dispute over the property, for we find mention of action by the executors of the late Patrick, only son of the late David Fyfe, surgeon-apothecary, against Gilbert, merchant, son of the late Gilbert Fyfe, merchant and bailie, *Reg.21/7/1744.*

It was also known as Barry's Close, now Bailie Fyfe's Close, *Prot.J.W. 8, 8/8/1767; G.L. 1, 9/7/1763,* but no derivation given.

Another name was Trotter's Close, *Prot. A.W.6, 21/3/1720,* from the tenement on the east side of Morrison's Close owned by the family of Trotter of Mortonhall, *Prot. A.W.2, 1/3/1706; G.H.7, 20/12/1726. Reg. 21/7/1744.*

There was also a Cockburn's Close near Trotter's Close, *Prot.A.W.2, 1/3/1706; A.W.6, 21/3/1720, possibly going north, but the exact position and origin of its name have not been traced.*

BAIRD AVENUE

From the Bairds of Saughtonhall.
See also Baird Drive etc—Part II.

BAKEHOUSE CLOSE

(o.s.) Shown as Huntly Close or Cordiners' Close, *J. Bruce Home.*

Kirkwood gives Hammermen's or Bakehouse Close. Ainslie gives Hammermen's Close.

The name comes from the bakehouse and property on the west side of the close owned by the Incorporation of Bakers of the Canongate; *Can. Chart. 12/9/1832.*

Its older name, Hammermen's Close, was taken from the lands of Wm. Wilson, writer, on the west of the lands of Sir Patrick Aitchison of Glentourne, *or Glencairne, son of Sir Archibald Aitchison, builder of the Aitchison house in this close,* now of the Hammermen of the Canongate, *Can. Chart. 13/12/1758.* The lands of the Hammermen were on the east of those of the Sugar House, *Can. Chart. 3/6/1767.*

Bruce Home *'Back of Bakehouse Close'* states that the House of Huntly held feudal possession of the entire soil of this close on its western side—'. . . we cannot tell why the close has ceased to bear the name of Huntly, nor when it became successively known as Cordiners' and then as Bakehouse Close'. But neither Huntly nor Cordiners' Close is found elsewhere.

BALFOUR PLACE
STREET

After the Balfours of Pilrig, on whose lands they are built.

BALGREEN ROAD

From old house and property, *m.t.c. 19/6/1811.*
See also Balgreen Avenue etc—Part II.

BALMORAL PLACE

After Queen Victoria's Highland seat, *e.c.b.c.ld.*

BALTIC STREET

Leith has always had much trade with the Baltic ports, *D.1800, 71, m.t.c. 10/8/1825.*

BANGHOLM TERRACE

From "Bangholm Bower, near Trinity", *B.1827,* or Farm of Bangholm to be sublet *eec.j.s. 1789, Ainslie 1804, m.t.c. 19/1/1814.*
See also Bangholm Avenue etc—Part II.

BANGOR ROAD

Messrs. Field & Allan, slate, tile etc. merchants, had great dealings in Welsh slates, *j.r.*
Bangor—a town in N.W. Wales.

BANK LANE

Off Clyde St. From the neighbouring Royal Bank of Scotland, St. Andrew Sq.
Small section on south side of Bus Station remains.

BANK STREET
NORTH

From the adjacent Bank of Scotland. Shewn un-named *Ainslie, 1780.* Named *Ainslie 1804.* Bank opened 1806. Rebuilt 1868. Named *m.t.c. 8/10/1800.* The street leading to the Mound, called Bank St. *m.t.c. 25/3/1801.*

BARCLAY PLACE
TERRACE

From the Barclay United Free Church, built by the Misses Barclay, 1862/3.

BARONSCOURT ROAD
TERRACE

Baronscourt is the Irish residence of the Duke of Abercorn on whose ground the road and terrace are built.

BARONY PLACE
STREET

From the barony of Broughton, *Wilson II, 208/9.*

BATH PLACE
STREET

A fancy name taken from the celebrated English watering place. Compare Mentone Avenue and Brighton Place, *Baird.*

BATH ROAD

From the bathing facilities: bathing coaches first used there in Scotland, 1766, *e.s.s. 250.*

BATHFIELD ROAD

Bathfield house, *Ainslie 1804. D.1827.*

BAXTER'S PLACE

Built by Baxter, architect, *e.e.c. Apr. 1801, j.s.* Feued by him from the Town before 1799, *eec.j.s.,* (he then died). Baxter's Buildings, head of Leith Walk, *D.1800, 166.* Feu applied for by John Baxter, architect 28/6/1780. Feuar 6/9/1780, *r.o.s* Granted 5/7/1780, *m.t.c. 16/11/1803.* "Baxter's Buildings". "Baxter's feu". "Now called Greenside Place", *m.t.c. 23/10/1822.*

BEAUMONT PLACE

D.1827. Shown as Bomond. *Kirkwood, Storer, 1820.* Two tenements built 1812 and 1813, *15/12/1812, 19/6/1819, eec.j.s.* Apparently built by Alex. Thomson. Bomond.*New pict. Edin. 1820,* not shewn in *do. do. 1818.* John, 5th Earl of Roxburgh, created Duke of —— Marquis of Beaumont & Cessford 1707 Beaumont Cottage at Beaumont Place. *D.1855-56.*

BEAVERBANK PLACE

w.o.l. 172. Probably suggested by Beaverhall. In 1683 Captain Thos. Hamilton, merchant in Edinburgh, in a petition to the Privy Council asking for privileges of a **manu**factory, i.e. the importing of the raw material and the exporting of the finished goods free of custom, states that he has a considerable trade with the Plantations in America in Scottish goods, and brings home in return beaver and racoon skins, which serve for making beaver, half-beaver and castor hats, none of which either have been or can be made by any of the natives of the Kingdom. He is bringing from abroad the persons best skilled in the art and craft of making these hats and craves as the first undertaker in the business to have a monopoly for a period of years and to have the other benefits accorded to manufacturers, *j.r.*

BEAVERHALL ROAD

From the old house, *Ainslie 1804*. Built on the lands of Powderhall, for sale. Beside the house is a large building formerly used as a hat manufactury, *10/4/1782, eec.j.s. j.r.s.l. 369.*

BEECHWOOD TERRACE

Off Lochend Road. Fancy, from the beech tree, *e.c.b.c.ld.*

BELFORD PARK
    PLACE
    ROAD
    TERRACE

There must have been a ford, giving access to Bell's Mills, see *Kirkwood*, also anon. map No. 6, where Belford Bridge now spans the Water of Leith. Old Belford Bridge is shown in Hamilton's map of 1827.
      See *also Belford Avenue, Gardens—Part II.*

BELFRAGE LANE

Ord. Surv. 1852. Charter to Andrew Belfrage, farmer at Kingsknows of large back tenement, erected on part of lands of High Riggs, commonly called Circhen's Gardens, with close thereto adjoining, *m.t.c. 30/8/1826.* Subjects at Cowfeeder Row, *m.t.c. 28/3/1827.*

BELL PLACE

Off Glenogle Road. After one of the directors of the *e.c.b.c.ld.*

BELL'S BRAE

Old way to Dean. Leads from south of Dean Bridge to Bell's Mills, named from Walter Bell, miller, tenant there, *circa 1600.* "An old meal mill", Anon. map, *circa 1730*. Lothian map 1825. *o. & n.e. III, 63.* So named 1621 *o.e.c. I. 97,* being corn and waulk mills. Bell's Milns steps. *m.t.c. 21/9/1785.* Bell's brae, near Water of Leith Bridge, *e.a. 3/1/1764.* Bell's Mill alias Dean's Mill, *o.e.c.I.126.* Bell's Mill, *Prot. G.H.4, 21/6/1714.* John Bell, in Water of Leith, elected to serve in the malt mylne and two Wester mylnes, *m.t.c. 11/4/1628.*

BELL'S WYND

Vicus Belli. *Gordon. Edgar. Ainslie. Kirkwood. Kerr.*

This wynd seems to have no alias. It is mentioned in John Fowler's protocols at the beginning of the sixteenth century, and took its name from John Bell, brewer at the foot of the wynd, connected with Bell's Brewery in the Pleasance, *New Lights, 169.* He is mentioned as being in the wynd in 1529, *Prot. 13/4/1529,* as owning a tenement at the head thereof *Prot. A.W.5, 14/6/1714* and as being succeeded in possession by the Bishop of Dunkeld, *Prot. G.H.5, 13/5/1715,* and in a general way in early charters, *C.C. 1550a, 24/2/1551-2; L.C.798, 3/5/1566; 978, 18/2/1579.*

BELLEVUE CRESCENT
    PLACE
    ROAD
    STREET
    TERRACE

From the house and grounds of Genl. Scott of Balcomie, Crail. Bellevue House was built on the site of Drummond Lodge: was purchased by Provost George Drummond 1757. It became later customs and excise office, and was demolished in 1846 when the Scotland St. railway tunnel was made, *Ainslie 1804. Lothian Map 1825.* The property of Bellevue belonged to the Marquis of Titchfield from whom the town bought it, *m.t.c. 30/4/1800,* "from south wall of Bellevue to Albany Row". Feuing plans submitted *m.t.c. 11/2/1800.* House sold for custom house to Government 9/6/1802, *m.t.c.*

Henrietta, daughter of Genl. John Scott of Balcomie, and his heiress, married Wm. Henry Cavendish Bentinck, Marquis of Titchfield, son of the Duke of Portland, who took the name of Scott. The Lands of Bellevue, bought by Genl. Scott from Dr. Archibald Drummond, son to the famous Lord Provost, were feued to the town by his daughter for £1,050 annual feu duty. *m.t.c. specially 7/9/1808.* Genl. John Scott's wife Margaret gave her name to Margaret Scott's Dyke, east side of the property, *m.t.c. 7/9/1808.*

See also Bellevue Gardens, Grove—Part II.

BERESFORD AVENUE GARDENS

From Sir Charles Beresford, R.N. Admiral. A popular and breezy figure early 20th century.

BERNARD STREET

In error St. Bernard's St., *Kirkwood. Also D.1800, 66.* From Bernard Lindsay, of Lochill *Arnot 572* who kept a tavern there about the end of the 16th and beginning of the 17th centuries. He rebuilt the King's Wark, 1613, *t.t.l. 37.* Bernard Nook is shown in Ord. Surv. 1852. Old name Weigh-house Wynd. "Street now called Bernard's Nook", *Arnot 571.* On 26 June 1617 Bernard Lyndsay "cubicularius regius". Royal chamber child or femme de chambre, with many noblemen, clergy, etc., was made honorary burgess and guildbrother on the occasion of the banquet given to James VI when he paid his first and last visit to Scotland, Burgh register, *New pict. Edin.1820-191.* Bernard's Nuke, *m.t.c. 14/6/1770.*

Part of King's Wark *q.v.* sold to Bernard Lindsay, groom of his Majesty's bedchamber, *i.w.c.h., vol. 4, p.54, 17/7/1604.* James VI granted a charter to B.L. allowing him to build a famous piazza, contiguous to his own buildings, having sight of the harbour erected on arches and pillars of hewn stone and set about everywhere with seats of hewn stone, to be the ordinary Burse & walking place for merchants, natural & stranger, *i.w.c.h. vol 4, p. 17/6/ & 7/10/1612.* His wife's name was Barbara Logan, *p.66, 10/12/1614.* He acquired from James Fawsyde of that Ilk that quarter of the Mains of Ballin-crieff called Lochhill, *p.54, 17/7/1604, p.76,* and was known as of Lochhill: he built a tennis court or caitchepell, south of the King's Wark, *p.69, 26/4/1623.* He had two sons, Capt. Thomas, elder, who succeeded him, *p.75 20/1/1632,* and Mr. Robert, *p.76.* He was son to Mr. Robert Lindsay of Tilliehogg, and had a sister, Isobel, who married Mr. Harry McGill, minister, at Dunfermline, *p.82, 19/7/163 .* Also a br. Robert. On 1/3/1643 Capt. Thomas disponed his part of the King's Wark to his brother Mr. Robert, cup bearer to the Prince, *23/6/1632,* and on same day sd. Mr. Robert disponed all his rights to Sir Wm. Dick of Braid, who in his turn, *p.109, 7/4/1647,* disponed the King's Wark to the town of Edinburgh. The waste ground, former-ly called the common closets, being a pendicle of the King's Wark, *i.w.c.h.4, 22/3/1564,* now called the Burs, *do. do. 17/8/1568.* Capt. Bernard Lindsay owned tent. in Broad Wynd, *m.t.c. 15/11/1797.* The Town Council received a decreit from the King, granting to Bernard Lindsay "foure takeins" in the King's Wark in Leith, (connected with the Impost). Margin has "Mister Bernard Lyndsay", *m.t.c. 3/2/1613.* Town agreed to submit the controversy between them and Bernard. Anent the meithing (1) of the King's Wark, specially the n. part thereof to Earle of Dunfermline, great Chancellor of Scotland, *m.t.c. 22/11/1616.* A letter from the King, not offended, anent controversy between the Town and his servant, Bernard L., *m.t.c. 21/2/1617.* Bernard L. one of H.M. grooms of his bedchamber compeared and was with his spouse Barbara Logan infeft in lands, not described in Leith, *m.t.c. 5/12/1617.* Sklaite work between Bernard Lindsay's tower and the Broad Wynd, pertaining to the good toun, *m.t.c. 23/12/1668.* Bernard L. entertained the future Earl of Suffolk in his house, Aug. 1614, *c.d.a.s.i. 455,* also John Taylor, the Water poet, and Ben Jonson, Aug. 1618, *c.d.a.s.i. 455.* St. Bernard's

Street, formerly called the Weigh-house Wynd, *Kincaid 222.* "The old Tower commonly called Bernard's Nook" owned by Patrick Anderson, merchant in Edinburgh, *m.t.c. 7/7/1790.* Barnie's Newck, on the north syd of the way leadding to the weyhous of Leith, *m.t.c. 22/8/1677.* Burnt waste land called Bernard's neuck, owned byGilbert Mathusone, to be rebuilt by him, *m.t.c. 14/2/1711.* Bernard's Nook was an old Tower, commonly called Bernard's Nook, and old waste and burnt lands built into great tenement by late Gilbert Mathieson, *m.t.c. 8/8/1804, Sec. s.s.l. 67.* Tower, (turris) called Bernard's Nuick, beside Weigh-house, *Prot. 8/5/1711, A.W.4, see j.r.s.l. 307-309.* Feu duty due by Alex. Mathieson for Barnie's Wark, *m.t.c. 31/12/1701.* Lands and tenements with Times Courts, yard and stables, close, wells etc. of the King's Wark in Leith pertaining before to Capt. Thos. Lindsay: also dwelling house of old pertaining to Bernard Lindsay, thereafter to Mr. Robt. Lindsay. Tent. of old of B.L. conquist by him from umq.   Thos. Marjoribanks of Ratho.

| BERRY SQUARE | An old name. Supposed to have been from the old proprietor, *Baird.* |
| BISHOP'S CLOSE | Edward Nisbet's, later James Nisbet's *Prot. A.W.3, 31/1/1710* or Patrick Nisbet's Close, *Prot. J.W.1, 24/6/1749.* Alexr. Lindsay's *M.285, c.2* or Lindsay's Close, *Prot.A.W.3, 6/1/1707. Ainslie. Kirkwood. Kerr.* |

The name is certainly derived from the Bishop's land, which stood in the close; the difficulty being to identify the Bishop.

Robert Chambers *Fires, 46* states that the Bishop's land had been the residence of the Bishop of Edinburgh, but gives no authority. Wilson *Wilson, ii.45* states that it was inhabited by John Spottiswoode, Archbishop of St. Andrews, 'as appears from the titles', from his father, Superintendent of Lothian, *Note:It is the Bishop's, not the Archbishop's, land,* but he does not quote the titles.

Grant *o. & n.e. i. 208* quotes and amplifies this, but gives no proof. Chambers, in his Traditions and Reekiana, makes mention of the Bishop's land, but connects no Bishop with it.

From the frequent entries in the protocols it seems clear that the Bishop was Thomas Sydserff or Saintserff, Bishop of Orkney, *Who, as Bishop of Galloway, caused Samuel Rutherford to be removed from Anwoth and confined to Aberdeen, 1636.* In one protocol *J.W.1, 24/6/1749* we find the close of late Edward Nisbet, thereafter of Patrick Nisbet, merchant, west of (North) Gray's Close, where Thomas Sydserff, Bishop of Orkney, having demolished the building, built Bishop's land. In another *Prot. W.F.2, 21/11/1748* it is stated that the Bishop's land was owned of old by George Henderson of Fordell: then by John Saintserff: then by Alexander Saintserff: then by his son James, merchant: then by (his son) Thomas, Bishop of Orkney: then by his son, Mr. (later Sir) John Saintserff, M.D.: then by his daughter Katherine, wife of John Ramsay, advocate, Sheriff-depute of Perth, and their successors.

The Bishop's land was thus built, or rebuilt, by said Thomas Saintserff or Sydserf, Bishop of Orkney, being bounded on the east by the tenement of umquhyle Robert Lindsay, and on the west by the large building of the Bishop of Glasgow, *Prot. G.I.3, between 10/12/1739 and 14/4/1740.*

In another protocol *Prot. G.I.1, 19/2/1731* the boundaries are given, lands of umquhyle John Lindsay (succeeded, it would seem, by

Robert Lindsay) of Covington on the east, and of the former Bishop of Dunkeld on the west. This looks as if the Bishops of Glasgow and Dunkeld had been owners, at different times, of the same mansion.

The Close was also known as Edward Nisbet's, James Nisbet's, *Prot. A.W.2, 20/8/1705,* or Patrick Nisbet's, *Prot J.W.1, 24/6/1749,* from Edward who owned a back-land there, *Prot. A.W.6, 17/1/1723; J.W.2, 21/2/1751,* and who, as eldest son of William Nisbet, burgess and guild brother, was admitted to the same privileges, 9th September 1596. James and Patrick were 'merchants'.

These Nisbets seem to be of the family of the Nisbets of Dirleton. Dirleton's land, owned by Wm. Nisbet of Dirleton, stood at the foot of Hart's Close; it was disponed to the town by his grandson, also Wm. Nisbet of Dirleton, 30th March, 1740, *Prot. J.W.2, 21/2/1751.* Henry Nisbet, provost 1579, owned a tenement in Ballantyne's, now Hart's Close, *Prot. G.H.4, 2/2/1712.*

Lindsay's Close, being the first close west of (North) Gray's Close, *Prot. G.H.7, 12/7/1727,* must be the same as Bishop's Close, although no distinct alias is found. Bishop's land was bounded on the east by the tenement of umquhyle John Lindsay of Coventoun, *Prot. G.H.7, 12/7/1727,* which seems to have been inherited by Robert Lindsay, *Prot. G.I.1, 19/2/1731.* A tenement on the north side of the High Street, on the east side of Lindsay's Close, had been rebuilt by the late Alexr. Lindsay, inherited by Barbara and Margaret Lindsay, and thereafter by Thomas Lindsay. The tenement of Wm. Lindsay of Restalrig lay to the west, *Prot. A.W.4, 13/9/1711.* A tenement, entered by a turnpike from North Gray's Close, pertained sometime to Robert Lindsay, *Reg. 19/10/1860.* It lay on the east side of Bishop's land, *Prot. G.H.4, 15/8/1712.*

Bishop's Close appears lengthened out to Bishop's Land Close, *Reg. 28/4/1742.*

BLACKET PLACE AVENUE	On the grounds of Dr. Benjamin Bell, 1830. From Blacket Castle the ancient seat of the Bell family. He owned Newington House.
BLACKFORD AVENUE ROAD	From Blackford Hill, close by. Lands also known in 1631 as Champunyie, q.v. *See also Blackford—Part II.*
BLACKFRIARS STREET	Formerly Wynd; earlier Preaching friars' vennel, leading to the Monastery of the Black, or Dominican friars, on south side of the Cowgate, *o.& n.e. 1. 258.* Founded by Alexander II, 1230, *Anderson 6, N.1.* "Le frere" or Blackfriars Wynd *John Foular.* Before 1513 "Predicant friars", *m.t.c. 17/1/1821.* Blackfriars' Wynd, *c.c. 506, 3/6/1483.* Wm. Cunninghame's lands on e.s. of the "blak frier" Wynd sometimes pertaining to the blakfriers of this burgh, *m.t.c. 25/7/1601.*
BLACKIE ROAD	From Bailie John Blackie, market gardener there, *j.r. 1890.*
BLACKWOOD CRESCENT	On Blackwood's ground, *Kirkwood.*
BLAIR STREET	Shewn in Ainslie's Map of 1780. Widened later. From Sir James Hunter Blair, provost 1784. His own name was Hunter, he assumed that of his wife on inheriting the estates of Blair of Dunskey, *o. & n.e.* He was King's Printer, and the King's Printing Office was in Blair St. *Kay 1.64, D.1800.*
BLENHEIM PLACE	*D.1827.* From Marlborough's victory in 1704. *Battle of Blenheim.*
BONAR PLACE	From proprietor of the ground, *Kirkwood.* Thomas Bonar, painter, had property in Newhaven, *m.t.c. 31/1/1797.*

BONNINGTON GROVE **ROAD** **TERRACE**	From the mansion house of Bonnytown, evidently flattering. Robt. Logan, sometyme of Bonytown, Burgess Regt. 22/7/1629. Bonytown Mills. *Maitland 58.* Bonytown 1560. *Irons I. 283.* "Pulchella" *Reek. 35.* *See also Bonnington Avenue—Part II.*
BOOTHACRE COTTAGES	At each end of Leith Links booths were erected for the citizens seeking to escape the plague of 1645. Many uncoffined bodies were found at the Boothacre, *j.r.s.l. 334.*
BOROUGHLOCH LANE **SQUARE** **BUILDINGS**	From the Borough or South Loch, now drained, where Meadows are now. "Borrow Loch" *1681, K.50. o.e.c. X.*
BORTHWICK'S CLOSE	*Edgar. Ainslie. Kirkwood. Kerr.* Vicus Borthvici. *Gordon.* **Shown** as Lord Durie's Close, *o.& n.e. 1. 242, but no authority.* From the house built there by Lord Borthwick in the middle of the fifteenth century, on the west side of the close, north of the King's Wall of 1450, *New Lights, 81.* The lands were sometime of Dominus Borthwick *Prot. G.H.4, 28/11/1711* of the family of Borthwick of that Ilk, *Wilson, ii. 31.* Grant says that it was for long called Lord Durie's Close, from the mansion of Lord Durie, President of the Court of Session 1642, *o. & n.e. v.242,* but this seems to be an error arising from a misunderstanding of Wilson's account of the house and story of Lord Durie, *Wilson, ii. 31-33.*
BOSWALL ROAD	On property of Boswall of Blackaders, *Ainslie 1804, Kirkwood.* Capt. Donaldson Boswall of Wardie, *m.t.c. 30/6/1824.* Capt. R.N., *m.t.c. 20/6/1832.* *See also Boswall Avenue etc.—Part II.*
BOSWELL'S COURT	Shown as Boswell's Close, *Ainslie, p.w. list 1779. Kirkwood.* Lothian's Close. It was named from the chief resident, Dr. Boswell, doctor of medicine, dwelling there about the end of the eighteenth century, *o. & n.e. i.90. The name is not given in p.w.1773 or 1780, but see Reg. 7/5/1864.* It has been identified with Ross's Court, *t.c.43,* but this does not tally with D.1827, which gives Boswell's Court as 392 and Ross's Court as 380. It appears, however, to be the same as Lowthian's Close, *Prot. A.W.6, 2/1/1721,* which takes its name from Louthian's land, *Prot. W.F.2, 24/2/1749 and 14/5/1749,* owned by Thomas Lothian, merchant, and situated on the south side of the Castlehill, *Prot.A.W.3, 23/3/1711; Reg. 7/5/1864.*
BOTANIC GARDENS	Originally a square piece of ground at east end of Nor' Loch; *Edgar 1742-1765,* removed to ancient Royal Garden, Holyrood, *Edgar 1742-1765:* again to Westside of Leith Walk, *Ainslie 1804.* Again to Inverleith 1822. *Lothian Map 1825.* Ground acquired there by Horticultural Society from J. Rochead of Inverleith, May 1823, *eec.j.s.* *Not a street name.*
BOWHILL TERRACE	Goldenacre . On ground of the Duke of Buccleuch, who owns Bowhill, near Selkirk, *j.r.*
BOWLING GREEN STREET	From the bowling green there before Queen **Anne's** day, which gave name to Bowling green house, *e.s.s.257.* Street built after 1810, *eec.j.s. 8/2/1810, v.r.31,* in the Lees quarter of Leith, *m.t.c. 3/4/1782. Alias Quilts, m.t.c. 8/8/1821.*
BRAID AVENUE **CRESCENT** **ROAD**	From the Braid hills and Burn/Braidsburn, *m.t.c. 26/11/1786.*

BRAIDBURN CRESCENT **TERRACE**	From the Braid hills and Burn/Braidsburn, *m.t.c. 26/11/1786.*
BRAIDHILLS ROAD	From the Braid hills and Burn/Braidsburn, *m.t.c. 26/11/1786.* *See also Braid—Part II.*
BRAND PLACE	*Littlejohn, App. 26.* James Brand's coach body maker. Ironside Court, Abbeyhill, *D.1827.*
BRANDFIELD STREET	From the house of Sir Alex. Brand, who bought the lands of Dalry from Major Cheislie, *circa 1704, o. & n.e. ii, 217.* Part of Brandsfield, now called Dalry, west side of Dalry lane, running from west end of Maitland St., for sale *21/8/1821.* House & place Ord. Surv. 1852, *place D.1827.* "Sir Alexander Brand of Dalry or Brandsfield", *v.r. 45.* Alex. Brand of Brandfield whose daughter Elizabeth married Alex. Jolly, writer and clerk of Court of Admiralty in Scotland, *2 Reg. 8/2/1744.* Lands of Dalry, sometimes called Brandsfield, now Gardners hall, owned by Wm. Gardner, now dead, *Reg. 16/12/1858.* Purchase of feues belonging to Sir Alex. Brand of Brandfield, in the barony of Dalry, *m.t.c. 12/12/1722.*
BREAD STREET	*D.1825. Orchardfield. Ainslie 1804. Kirkwood.* One baker at least in it ever since 1825, and a Bread Society there at one time. Sugges- ted connection with "Assise on Bread", *m.t.c. 17/11/1830*
BREWERY LANE	Evident.
BRIARBANK TERRACE	Fancy, after the flower, *e.c.b.c.ld.*
BRICKWORK CLOSE	*108 Kirkgate, D.1827.* Evident.
BRIDGE LANE **STREET**	Evident. Old name Tobago St. q.v.
BRIDGE PLACE	Part of Glenogle Road. Evident.
BRIGHT TERRACE	Complimentary to John Bright, M.P. vide infra.
BRIGHT'S CRESCENT	On property of Duncan McLaren, M.P. brother-in-law and admirer of John Bright, M.P., Quaker, freetrader, corn law repealer, etc.
BRIGHTON CRESCENT **PLACE**	Compliment paid by the "Brighton of Scotland" to the older English sister. Built about 1820, *eec.j.s. 25/3/1822, Baird.*
BRISTO PORT **PLACE** **STREET**	From the ancient port in the Flodden wall of 1513. Anciently Gallowgate, *Stark 1806, 96.* Later known as Greyfriars and Society Port, *q.v.* The lands of Bristo mentioned about 1554, *o. & n.e. iii, 29. m.t.c. 12/1/1876.* The name may come from the Brewers or Brew- sters, close by. Reek map gives Briston, an evident error. In one print of Gordon's map of 1647, Bristolb is given—as also olb for row, but the error is consistent, an old form of current w being similar to lb. Bristow St. M. A brother of Touris of Inverleith held the lands there in reign of James IV, *j.r.* In protocol of G.H.13 12/12/1738 Robert Gilmor, ropemaker in Bristol; witnessed deed subscribed at Heriot barns, near Edinburgh. Alias Potterrow, *l.c.1859, 4/4/1621.* The form Bristall occurs *m.t.c. 16/11/1705 and 21/12/1705 and 2/12/1642.* Bristo Place etc. formerly "the calsav leidand fra the Societie port to the Wynd mylne", *m.t.c. 27/12/1635.*
BROAD WYND	Descriptive, *p.w. 1780/81, 105, Irons I. 57.60. Kirkwood Prot 19/12/1699.*
BRODIE'S CLOSE	*Ainslie. Kirkwood. Kerr.* Lord Cullen's Close, *Edgar,* formerly Lord Cullen's Close, *Kirkwood,* Cullen's Close, Little's Close, *o.& n.e.i.111.* South end, 'Entry to Old Bank', *Ainslie,* Bakers' Close, *Reg.21/5/1861.*

This close extended formerly from the Lawnmarket to the Cowgate, till cut through by Victoria Street, *Kerr*. It took its name from Francis Brodie, wright, glass grinder, and burgess, *'Brodie & Son, wrights and undertakers, Lawnmarket,' p.w.1773; 'cabinet-makers', p.w. 1779*, father of and partner with the notorious William Brodie, wright, gambler, burglar, and Deacon of the wrights, who was hanged at the Old Tolbooth, 1st October, 1788, along with his accomplice, George Smith, *See Provost Wm. Creech's account of the trial, published while Brodie lay under sentence of death, also that by Wm. Roughead, W.S., 1906.*

It was from the same family that Brodie's Building and Close, south side of the Canongate foot, took their name, *q.v.*

Edgar names the close Lord Cullen's Close, and Kirkwood, 'Brodie's Close, formerly Lord Cullen's'. It thus perpetuated the name of a former occupant, Sir Francis Grant of Cullen, who joined the Revolution party in 1688, was raised to the bench 1709, and died 1726, *o.& n.e. i. 111.*

An earlier name was Little's Close, from the mansion of William Little of Liberton, which stood in the close, bearing the date 1570, *trad. 74*, but demolished 1836. It seems to be so called in D.1799, pp.6 and 233.

It is also one of the bewildering Cant's Closes, and is described as just east of **Fisher's Close**, *Reg. 9/12/1861*, but no further information given, and this may be a careless slip for Cullen.

The lower end of the close, which was far from being a clear straight thoroughfare, was known as 'Entry to the Old Bank', *Ainslie*, or Bakers' Close, deriving the latter from the property of the Incorporation of the Bakers, *Reg. 21/5/1861*.

BROUGHAM PLACE STREET

From Lord Henry Brougham, statesman, etc. Born in Edinburgh 1778: received freedom of the city 1825. Complimentary banquet Oct. 1859. Lord Chancellor of the University, May 1860. The street was made in 1859, when the Melville Drive was opened. He died May 1868.

BROUGHTON STREET STREET LANE MARKETS PLACE ROAD

From the ancient village and barony of Broughton. "Broughton place to be built", *9/1/1808, eec.j.s.* Broughton St. *m.t.c. 17/6/1807.*

BROWN STREET

Brown's St. D.1827. In Lothian Map 1825, not in Ainslie 1804. In map *New Pict. Edin. 1820, not in do. do. 1818.* Water granted to John Brown, builder; for houses in Brown St. opposite foot of East Richmond St., *m.t.c. 31/5/1815.* "Near Edinburgh", *m.t.c. 17/1/1827.*

BROWN'S CLOSE

D.1827. O.S. Kerr. Sommervile's Close, *Ainslie, Kirkwood.*

John Brown, gardener, owned lands east of those of Mr. John Campbell, *Prot. J.H. Canong. 9/11/1682*, but the name of the close seems to be derived from Joseph Brown, baxter, merchant burgess of Edinburgh, *Can. Chart. 3/6/1845*, who acquired the tenement and close commonly called Paterson's Land and Close.

Joseph Brown *Joseph Brown, baker, head of Rae's Close, Canongate: D.1800* of Anne Mills resided in Chessel's Court; *D.1827*, he had a son John, a farmer at Brunstain, *Can. Chart. 3/6/1745.* Another son was George Bell Brown, brewer. The Rev. Wm. Brown, Free Church, Rayne, and Thos. Carmichael Brown, brewer, North Back of the

Canongate, were of this family, *Can. Chart. 21/5/1887, 20/5/1891.*
John Brown of Annsmills is mentioned in connection with Brown's
formerly Somervell's Close, *Can. Chart. 21/5/1887, 20/5/1891.*

The older name, Sommervile's Close, *Ainslie, Kirkwood,* was named
from the land of the late John Sommerville, now of his son Jack on
the east of Campbell's Close, *Can. Chart. 14 and 19/3/1798.* John
Sommerville was a gunsmith by trade, but failed in business, and his
lands, in part at least, were sold by his creditors. Besides his son Jack,
he had two daughters, Miss Elizabeth, and Jean who married Archd.
Rough, invalid soldier in the Canongate, *Can. Chart. 23/11/1808.*
His widow is probably the Mrs. Somerville in Somerville's Close,
p.w.1780, and his daughter Elizabeth the Miss Somerville in Somerville's land, *D.1799.* He also built a tenement in Little Lochend's
Close, *m.t.c. 25/6/1836.* The alias, 'Somerville's now Brown's
Close', is distinctly given, *Can. Chart. 3/6/1845.*

The name Paterson's Land and Close, mentioned above, is derived from
John Paterson, and is described in a charter granted to Joseph Brown,
baker, Canongate, as lately belonging to John Paterson, merchant,
burgess of Edinburgh, near the foot of the Canongate on the north
side, *m.t.c. 23/10/1808.* The lands and close were bounded on the
west by Campbell's land, *Can. Chart. 23/11/1808.*

Paterson's land is the Golfer's land, traditionally said to have been
built by John Paterson, shoemaker, with his share of the stakes won
by him and the Duke of York, afterward James VII, from two boast-
ful Englishmen, *Wilson, ii, 110; Chambers, i, 197.* The house is now
altered, but Paterson's anagram *'I hate no person'* and Pitcairn's
epigram have been carved at the entrance to the close.

BROWN'S COURT

D.1827, 140. D.1832, 125. Shown as Brown's Close, *Ainslie, Kirkwood.* Wilkie's Close, *Can. Chart. 3/5/1775.* Straton's Close, *Can.
Chart. 3/5/1775.*

The close takes its name from the property therein acquired by
Andrew Brown, late of Greenbank, thereafter by John Straiton,
merchant and burgess of Edinburgh, who had one daughter, Jean, who
conveyed it to Arthur Straiton, wigmaker, and he, in turn, to John
Munro, musician in Edinburgh, and his son John. They conveyed it
to the Earl of Panmuir, and he, 3rd July 1751, to James Ogilvie of
Inchmartine, advocate. Monro's Close was on the east side of the
tenement, *Can. Chart. 22/6/1757, 3/5/1775.* A transe or close led
from the High Street of the Canongate to the lodging and court of
Andrew Brown of Blackford, bounded on the west by Panmure's
Close, *Can. Chart. 28/4/1762, 7/6/1786.* Andrew Brown, brassfounder, was there in 1827, but had probably no connection with the name
of the close or court.

The names, Wilkie's Close or Straton's Close, *Can. Chart. 3/5/1775,*
are derived from Andrew Wilkie, son to Andrew Wilkie, lorimer in the
Canongate, who disponed property in favour of John Straiton,
merchant, *o.e.c. x. 257,* burgess of Edinburgh, from whom it came
to Arthur Straiton, his son, *o.e.c. x. 257, and Can. Chart. 3/5/1775.*
This John Straiton was the man who in 1658 took a nineteen years'
lease of the Broad Meadows, that is, the South Loch, etc., and did
much by draining, etc., to improve the amenity of 'Straiton's Park',
later known as 'Hope Park', and now as 'The Meadows'. Unfortunat-
ely his speculation was so unsuccessful that, falling into arrears with
his rent, he was committed to the Tolbooth, from which he was
released in order to 'maw the grass and dig the stanks', on 19th June

1678 till 1st July 1678, on the petition of his wife, Janet Jamesone, his son-in-law Arthur Straton of Whitehouse becoming cautioner for his re-entering prison. On 28th June the Town accepted the bond of said John Straton and his son-in-law Arthur Straton for 1200 pounds, payable at Martinmas next, and relieved John Straton of his tack.

Arthur Straton had a daughter who married David Steel, tailor, and thus entitled him to be made a burgess, 5th June 1678.

BROWN'S PLACE	Part of Vennel, *D.1827.* James Brown Esq. Brown's Pl. Vennel, *D.1827. 22.* Jas. Brown, resident in Vennal—builder of stables and houses there, *m.t.c. 12/5/1824.*
BRUNSTANE GARDENS **ROAD**	From the old mansion of Brunstane or Gilbertoun. Crichton, Laird of Brunstane, 1545. Both names in 1736, *o.& n.e. iii. 149. Baird 63,* *q.v.* for full information. Brunstane may refer to the local coal seams. *See also Brunstane Bank etc—Part II.*
BRUNSWICK LANE **PLACE** **ROAD** **STREET**	Compliment to Duke of Brunswick, ally of Britain 1809-1815. Killed at Quatre Bras, *D.1827.* Caroline, queen of George IV, of that house of Duke of Brunswick received the freedom of the city, *7/9/1825,* *m.t.c.*
BRUNTSFIELD AVENUE **CRESCENT** **GARDENS** **PLACE** **TERRACE**	From the lands of Brownfield, Brownsfeild, or Bruntsfield, resigned in 1381 by Richard Broune to Alane de Lawdre. Bought by Sir George Warrender 1695. Present house built in 16th century. Called Broomsfield 1738. Brownsfield, *Maitland 178.* "Brantoune Links" Balfour's Annales 1644. *o.& n.e. iii.20, o.e.c. x. for full information.* Not from murder of Stephen Bruntfield, as told *St. G. 97.*
BRYSON ROAD	After Robert Bryson, watchmaker, member of the Merchant Coy. Master of the Merchants Coy. 1874-76. Superiors of the grounds.
BUCCLEUCH STREET **PLACE** **PEND**	Built about 1766 by James Brown, builder of George Sq, *St.L. 44.* Buccleuch St. seems *Ainslie 1780* to have been the street planned opposite to and in a line with Buccleuch Place, where is now an arched pend, marked "Buccleuch St." By 1804 the name had been transferred to a much older part of Causeyside. The Duke of Buccleuch, a prominent nobleman, encourager of Scottish manufactures, cattle breeding, etc. See Scots. Mag. The Duke of Buccleuch made honorary Burgess and Guildbrother along with Duke of Montague for services rendered personally and by ancestors, *m.t.c. 6/6/1770.* Entertained with officers of South Fencible Regt. and Dragoons, *m.t.c. 10/2/1779.*
BUCCLEUGH PLACE	*m.t.c. 1/3/1809 & 12/4/1809.* "The building immediately above the pend or arch leading to Buccleuch Place. This seems to be the pend leading into St. Patrick Square, over which "Buccleugh Street" is cut, as shewn in Ainslie 1804, what is now called Buccleuch St. is there". London road by Carlisle: no sign is given of the future St. Patrick Sq., but a street, planned, not built, is shewn, "Buccleugh Street"—entered by a pend or entry. The west side of Buccleugh St. is mentioned, *D.1800, 224.* Bugcleuch Place, *D.1800, 204.* Buccleuch Place called Buccleuch St, *Kincaid, 108, 126.*
BUCHANAN'S COURT	Shown as Close, *Ainslie. Kerr.* Walter Willie's Close, *Edgar.* Buchanan's, formerly Walter Willie's, *Kirkwood.* Hunter's Close. Named from Buchanan's land, which stood between the close and the Old Bank Close. It is mentioned in the Town Council Minutes, *especially 13/2/1771 in connection with the great fire there,* but not in the protocols examined. Chambers *Fires* states that Buchanan's land took the place of the ancient timber tenement of the Abbot of

Cambuskenneth, burned 1725.

Peter Williamson *1773, p.5* mentions Buchan's Court—probably the same.

The old name was Walter Willie's Close, *Edgar; Kirkwood.* It may be derived from 'Water' Willie, the last waterman plying his vocation, *Kay, ii, 36.*

It seems also to have been called Hunter's Close.

There was a James Hunter, physician, close by in the Old Bank Close, *p.w. 1780, p.46.*

BULL'S CLOSE

o.s. Kerr. Shown as May Drummond's Close, *p.w. list 1779.* Drummond's Close, *Ainslie.* Drummond's or Bull's Close, *Kirkwood.* Ford's Row, *Can. Chart. 26/8/1868, 22/1/1904.*

It was named from the property of Robert Bull, wright, burgess of Edinburgh, husband of Jean or Joanna, second daughter of John Wright, former owner. Robert Bull and his wife resigned the property, 11th April 1701, *Can. Chart. 31/10/1821.* Bull's land was bought by Peter Lamont, lint manufacturer, husband of Agnes Henderson, at the sale of the estate of the late Mrs. Marion Drummond, *Can. Chart. 16/10/1860.* It was known in consequence as Lamont's land, *m.t.c. 18/1/1832.*

The name Drummond's, or May Drummond's Close, was derived from the above Marion Drummond. John Carfrae, coach-maker, acquired property, including two small houses, entering from Bull's Close, owned by the late Miss Mary Drummond, sister of the late George Drummond, late Provost of Edinburgh, *Can. Chart. 27/3/1799.* She was the preaching Quakeress celebrated by Pope, Spence, and others, *Chambers, ii. 50.* Her name varies a little: May, Marion, *Can. Chart. 11/6/1861,* or Mariana, *Can. Chart. 12/6/1833.* She owned the tenement in the close, *m.t.c. 29/11/1815,* as well as other land on the north side of the Canongate, below the church, *m.t.c. 5/3/1800, 1/8/1804.*

A very modern name is Ford's Row, *Can. Chart. 26/8/1868, 22/1/1904,* from the houses there owned by Wm. Ford, Holyrood glassworks.

BURGESS STREET TERRACE

Formerly Burgess Close, a little beneath Tolbooth Wynd, Leith, *Maitland 485 c.2,* granted by Sir Robt. Logan of Restalrig to the burgesses of Edinburgh to gain access to the harbour, *o.& n.e. iii. 166, 167, 235. D.1827. Wilson ii. 192.* Burges Cl., Leith, *Prot. 7/8/1717. p.w.5.*

BURNET'S CLOSE

Edgar. Ainslie. Kirkwood. Kerr. Shown as Johnston's Close, *New Lights, 145: 'Burnet's, formerly Johnston's Close; Prot. G.L.1, 17/2/1764.*

Named from Samuel Burnet, a wealthy brewer and prominent citizen about 1600, *New Lights, 103, 145,* the owner of a tenement on the south side of the High Street at the head of Burnet's Close, *Prot.J.W.4, 12/5/1758.* He was a merchant and burgess, *Prot.J.W.4, 24/4/1758,* having been made burgess and guild brother, 9th March 1591, as being son to the late Alexander Burnet.

Before the close took his name it was known as Johnston's Close, from Edward Johnston, one of the Scottish adventurers for the plantation of Ulster under James VI, 1610, *New Lights, 145: 'Burnet's, formerly Johnston's Close'; Prot. G.L.1, 17/2/1764.* But the name is older. Alexr. Guthrie resigned a tenement in Johnston's Close on the south side of the High Street in 1564: it was bounded on the north by lands of John Marjoribanks, and of James Johnston on the south, *c.c.1968, 3/11/1564.*

Edward Johnston owned property in Johnston's, now Burnet's Close, owned later by Peter Mories, and still later by Mr. Robert Windram, W.S., *Prot. G.L.1, 21/3/1764; W.F.1, 16/7/1746,* which still exists, occupied by Smith, Fletcher & Co., wireworkers, *New Lights, 146.* Wm. Johnston owned a house in the close built by Wm. Stevenson, *Prot.G.I.2, 18/2/1736,* and Sir Daniel Wilson speaks of the house of Sir Patrick Johnston, *see p. 55,* member of parliament for the city at the date of the Union in 1707, as standing at the head of this Johnston's Close, *Wilson, i. 237.*

A tenement of land on the south side of the High Street, pertaining to Mr. Andrew Burnet of Waristoune, had been wadsett by him to John Ewing, merchant, London, for 6877 lib. Scots. Ewing entered into possession, *m.t.c. 30/10/1678.* This may relate to Burnet's Close.

BURN'S LAND

Probably from Wm. Burns, mason, Greenside Well, *D.1827,* or rather from "Robert Burns feu" now called Greenside Place, *m.t.c. 28/12/1803.* Robt. Burns, marble cutter, Leith Walk. East side, *D.1800, m.t.c. 29/4/1807.*
Not a street.

BURNS STREET

D.1827. Named after proprietor, *j.r.*

BYRES' CLOSE

Shown as Byers', *o.s. and Kerr.* Lauder's Close. Malcome's Close.

This close contained the town house of Sir John Byres of Coats, Bart, *o.e.c. i. 6; o.& n.e. i. 153.* His father, John Byres, was 2nd bailie 1617, Treasurer 1612-1615, and Dean of Guild 1619-24. The inscription on his tomb in Greyfriars' churchyard, *see Epitaphs and Monumental Inscriptions in Greyfriars' Churchyard, Edinburgh, by James Brown, 1867,* states that John Byres of Coittes was for six years thesaurer of this city; two years city bailie and suburban bailie; six years Dean of Guild; and two years Old Provost, *'Old Provost' does not imply that the owner of the title had been Provost: it seems to have been equivalent to 'Vice' or 'Depute', and many bailies were elected as Old Provosts who had never been 'Provost' or 'Lord Provost'.* He died 24th November 1629, aged 60.

Sir John Byres inherited more than one tenement in the close from his father, John Byres, merchant. He disponed his property, in part at least, to Archibald Paton, merchant; from whom it passed to his son John Paton, and later to John Malcolm. It belonged formerly to Gilbert Lauder, son and heir of Mr. Henry Lauder, and was inherited from him by his sons—first by James, and after him by Gilbert—from whom it was acquired by John Byres mentioned above; from these former owners the close took the name of Lauder's Close, *Prot.G.I.2, 31/7/1735.* 'Byres' or Lauder's Close' (*Prot.J.W.6, 1/4/1763*). The property of Coates came ultimately into the possession of William Walker, *Ainslie 1804,* and it was feued early in the nineteenth century for streets, bearing such family names as William Street, Walker Street, and Coates Crescent, *Lothian's map 1825.* East Coates House, which was built by Sir John Byres in 1615, and contains lintels and other carved stones of the old family mansion in Byres' Close, *Rom. Edinr. 264,* has fortunately not only escaped the hand of the improver or destroyer, but is appreciatively preserved where its quaint beauty can be seen and enjoyed.

The close, it seems, bore also the name of Malcolm's Close, which is described as being on the north side of the High Street, and contained the tenement of John, son and heir of William Malcolme, *Prot.*

16/12/1532. As stated above, John Malcolm acquired the tenement once owned by Sir John Byres; an adjacent tenement was owned in succession by Alexr. Reith, merchant: John Reith: Jeanna Reith, spouse of Mr. Alexr. Malcolm, minister in Edinburgh: *Greyfriars' 1681; Tron 1687; deprived 1689:* the said Mr. Alexr. Malcolm: Jeanna Malcolm: William Gray: the said Jeanna Malcolm: and lastly by Andrew Purdie, merchant, 4th bailie in 1718, *Prot. G.I.2, 31/7/1735.*

C

CABLES WYND

Probably from Henry Capell, a **Fleming who** lived in Leith and owned property there in the time of Charles I, Cromwell, and Charles II, *j.s.* The suggestion of "Cable" in a seaport is obvious, *M.486.C.2.* Henry Capill to be free maltman of Leith, *m.t.c. 5/12/1660. D.1799, 77.* Cable Wynd, *D.1827.* Originally Kapple's Wynd, *o.& n.e. iii. 226.* Kappel's Wynd in map of 1850 in Robertson's Sculptured Stones of Leith, *Irons 1.297.* From a Dutch or Flemish resident, *m.t.c. 18/8/1802, 6/3/1816.* Alias Mathieson's Wynd, *m.t.c. 7/2/1821, 6/3/1838.* Among streets in Leith to be repaired is Caple Wynd leading to the Water of Leith, *m.t.c. 13/4/1743.*

CADIZ STREET

Trade connection.

CALEDONIAN CRESCENT
PLACE
ROAD

From Caledonian Railway closeby.

CALLENDER'S ENTRY

D.1827. o.s. Shown as Callender's Close, *Ainslie, Kirkwood,* which gave access to the house of Mr. Callender, *Edgar 1765, inserted.*

Callender House in the Canongate, *m.t.c. 10/9/1823,* was built by John Callender of Craigforth, the grandson and heir of John Callender of Craigforth, former deacon of the Blacksmiths, whose wife was Jonnet Taylor, *Prot.W.F.1, 25/6/1745; A.W.7, 25/1/1725.* John Callender, advocate, acquired the land from Gilbert Duncan, mason, 15th September 1768, *but it is inserted in Edgar 1765,* and built the house, *Can. Chart. 18/7/1769 and 23/10/1782.* He sold it later to Sir Ludovick Grant of Grant, *Can. Chart. 30/4/1901.* It now forms part of the Veterans' Residence.

It is said that the ancestral blacksmith acquired the family wealth through having received in pounds sterling payment of an account which he had rendered in pounds Scots for work done by him as farrier in Scotland to James VI, *New Lights, 195. See also Scots Magazine 1789, the year of Mr. Callender's death. See also Kay, ii,51, and o.& n.e. ii. 162, for some notes anent the family.*

CALTON ROAD

New name given to the North Back of the Canongate in the belief that change of label improves wine. Early 20th century.

CAMBRIDGE STREET

Built 1850. *Roy. Geog. Map 1919.* First intended to be called Watson St. feued 1849. From Watson's Hospital, which receives half the income, *Grindlay.* Cambridge St. formerly Watson's St. *Reg. 12/11/1862.*

CAMERON BANK

Cambrune, *Baird 16.* On the lands of Cameron, owned by Prestons of Craigmillar, through which flows the Cameron burn, with Cameron Bridge spanning it. Cameron House *Ord. Surv. 1852.* The common or Cameron Myre, *m.t.c. 12/6/1816.*

CAMERON CRESCENT
PARK
TERRACE

From same.

See also Cameron House Avenue—Part II.

CAMPBELL AVENUE ROAD

Sir Archibald Campbell of Succoth, superior.

CAMPBELL'S CLOSE

Ainslie, Kirkwood, Kerr. Rae's Close, *Can. Chart. 4/10/1773.*

From Mr. George Campbell, bailie of the Canongate, meal merchant, who owned a tenement on the north side of the Canongate, at Rae's Close, *Prot. J.H. Canong. 9/11/1682; Can. Chart. 10/9/1774.* He owned Campbell's land, east of Reid's Close, and had two sons, William, merchant in the Canongate, and George, 'Lator', *Prot.J.H. Canong. 9/11/1682; Can. Chart. 10/9/1774.*

Campbell's land was occupied later by Arthur Ross, Archbishop of St. Andrews: Col. George Douglas, later 13th Earl of Morton *died 1738:* James 14th Earl of Morton **died 1768:** and Archibald Hope, writer *Can. Chart. 15/5/1801.* By a curious slip Campbell's land is called 'Campbell's London, west of Wadell's London', *Can. Chart. 19/6/1793.*

The former name of the Close was Rae's Close, *Can. Chart. 4/10/1773,* but the origin is unknown.

CANAAN LANE

The ground to the north of the Jordan Burn, q.v., acquired its name in the days of the Covenanters, *o.e.c. x. 179.* Property for sale, *11/1/1775, eec.j.s. D.1827.* Lands of Cannaan, *m.t.c. 30/7/1788.* Lands of Canaan, part of the Common Muir, *m.t.c. 12/6/1816.* Lands commonly called Canaan, *Prot. 28/9/1734. G.I.2.* James Russell, tenant in Canaan, *m.t.c. 27/10/1680, 16/11/1671.* Aikers of Wester common muir, commonlie called Canaan, *m.t.c. 28/8/1761.* Twelve aikers of land with houses & grass of Canaan Set in tack to Jas. Russell in Canaan. Teind land of Braid on s., with a little strand: lands of Mr. Wm. Livingston, sometime possest by heirs of John Tweedie, on w., common back muir on n, lands of wester Grange on e., *m.t.c. 27/11/1667.* Tack to Jas. Russell in Cannan of four aikers of land besyd Simmion Rollog's chapel in the back muir, *m.t.c.30/11/1677.*

CANDLEMAKER ROW

Prot. G.H. 10 24/1/1735. From the Hall of the corporation of Candlemakers. In the first stair-tower, west side, as one descends, coat of arms over the door, *o.& n.e. ii. 267.* Street now so called, made 1612, *Maitland 58.* See Loaning under Appx. Incorporation of Candlemakers intended to make structural alterations, *m.t.c. 3/5/1826.* Adjustment of feus, mention of ruinous candleshop, north of east entry to Greyfriars, *m.t.c. 26/6/1838.*

Lands of "societas Candelariorum" there. Alias Society Wynd *Prot. G.H.8, 7/10/1728, 29/4/1724.* Ruinous candleshops near the Society Port, below entry to Greyfriar's Churchyard, *Prot A.W.6, 17/8/1721.* "Candlemakerrow Street", *Reg. 31/12/1857.* Candlemaker row on west side of "societatis venellae opposite societati; " on south side of entry to Greyfriar's Churchyard. Bounded by said yard on West: by Society Wynd on east. Tent. of Wm. Wilson, candlemaker on south of (blank) Alexander candlemaker, on north. A whole lot of candlemakers all round, *Prot. G.H.4, 11/9/1711.* Candlemaker row seems to have been, at first, the row of candlemaking workshops on the west side of the Society Wynd, *Prot. G.H.8, 7/10/1728.* Vennel called C.maker row, *Prot.G.H.8, 7/10/1728.*

CANNING STREET LANE

Map Stark 1825. From Geo. Canning. Foreign Secretary 1807. Fought a duel with Lord Castlereagh 1810. Premier Feb. 1827, died 8 Aug. 1827. "That man Canning will be the salvation of the cuntra" *Notes Ambrosianae March 1825, Apr. 1827.* Not in any Directory up to and including 1855/6. Seems to be first shown on Knox map 33a 1821.

CANONGATE **CANONMILLS** **CANON STREET**	From the Augustinian Canons of Holyrood, permitted by David I, to build on each side of the gait, and who owned the mills, Canongate St. M. Canon St. Canon Mills, *Littlejohn App. 20.* The burgh finally absorbed by Edinburgh 1856, *m.h.c. 22.* "The Canongate of the Monastery of The Holy Rood near Edinburgh", *c.c.819 6/7/1514.*
	A proposal was made by Sir Andrew Ramsay, Lord Provost, for incorporating the Canongate with Edinburgh, to the Town Council, promising to back it up in the next Parliament. The Council thanked him, and promised to consider it seriously, *m.t.c. 10/10/1669.*
CARGIL TERRACE	From the property, Cargilfield, *d.1827.* Owned by Mr. Kinnear, *Kirkwood, m.t.c. 19/6/1811.*
CARLTON STREET	*D.1827.* Probably from residence of George IV, in memory of his visit in 1822. He occupied Carlton House when Prince Regent.
CARLTON TERRACE	As Carlton St. Compare Royal Terrace and Regent Terrace. Old name Carlton Place, *m.t.c. 3/11/1830. Reg. 25/12/1858.*
CARLYLE PLACE	After Thomas Carlyle, author and philosopher.
CARPET LANE	From Factory there, *j.r.*
CARRINGTON ROAD	From Lord Carrington, Governor of New Zealand, 1885-1890. Carrington House (Fettes Trust). From part of Armiston Estate, of Sir Robert Dundas, one of the Trustees and afterwards a governor. *See also Carrington Crescent—Part II.*
CARRUBBER'S CLOSE	*Edgar. Ainslie. Kirkwood. Kerr.*
	Grant *o.& n.e. ii. 241* derives the name from William de Carabris, bailie in 1454, but gives no authority. Bruce Home repeats this, adding that the bailie was probably of foreign extraction. The name of the close occurs in John Foular's protocols before 1513.
	James Hay of Carruber owned coalyards at the foot of Penston's Close, *Prot. A.W.4, 27/8/1713; J.W.3, 21/7/1755.* There was a tenement called Carrubber's land beside North Gray's Close, *Reg. 24/11/1743,* to which we may attribute the name, without identifying the man, for there were various persons styled of Carrubber—spelling it as each chose—e.g. Monteith of Caruber appears in the Burgess Register of 15th and 29th July 1674; Robert son of late John Mirrie of Carribber is mentioned, *Prot. A.W.7, 27/8/1723.* Wm. Blair of Avontoun and Curriber bank owned property affected by the making of the Union Canal in 1817.
	The close just west of North Gray's Close appears in one entry *Prot. G.H.5, 4/1/1716* as Carrutherber's Close; Maitland gives both Carruther's and Carrubber's, *M.216.*
CASSELS LANE	Cassels Place, foot of Leith Walk, to let: apply to Andrew Cassels, *8/1/1811, eec.j.s. D.1827.* Andrew Cassells' property, Shore, Leith. Andrew Cassels of Cassels Pl. near Leith, *m.t.c. 4/9/1822. D.1810/11.* For Trustees of Andrew Cassels of Cassels Pl., near Leith, tent. built by him in Bernard St. near Weigh-house, *m.t.c. 4/9/1822.* *Cassels Place now part of Leith Walk.*
CASTLE HILL **STREET** **TERRACE**	From the Castle of Edinburgh, being either near to it, or looking towards it. Castle Bank, the slope at the back, or south side of the Castle, *D.1827.* Original name "Fortress of the hill of Agnes". Later "Castrum Puellarum" where resided the daughters of the Pictish Kings till married, *Anderson, 4.*
CASTLE WYND	*D.1827.* Leading up to the Castlehill and Castle, *Edgar 1742/1765. Ainslie 1780/1804. Ord Surv. Prot. 11/10/1710, A.W.3.*

CASTLE ROAD EAST WEST	From Merchiston Castle, behind which they lie.
CAUSEYSIDE	The main road, causey, or chaussée, toward the south. The calsey leidand fra the Societie port to the wind mylne, *m.t.c. 27/7/1735.* *Now Causewayside.*
CHALMERS BUILDINGS	**Beside the church there.** Built 1855 and named after Rev. Thos. Chalmers, D.D. who did so much for church extension. Died 1847.
CHALMERS CRESCENT	Beside the Chalmers' Memorial United Free Church in memory of Rev. Thomas Chalmers, D.D., one of the leaders at the Disruption of Church from State, 1843. He is buried in the South or Grange Cemetery, opposite the church. He died May 1847 in the house which he had built, in Churchill, marked by a tablet.
CHALMERS CLOSE	Shown as Chambers' Close, *D.1799,* Dunsyre's, *G.I.3, 29/11/1739,* and its variants, Deasyre's *Prot. J.W.4, 30/6/1758* and Densquer's **Close** *Reg. 16/10/1860.* Boyd's Close, *Reg. 19/12/1861. Edgar. Ainslie. Kirkwood. Kerr.*

The name is derived from Patrick Chalmers, belt maker, owner of a tenement in the close, which was inherited by his son William, *Prot. W.F.2, 30/6/1747.* Patrick Chalmers was Captain in the Trained Bands, 4th December 1682, probably of 'the Green and Reid' in 1685, *t.b.29, 40, 122.* Many members of the family are mentioned in the protocols, e.g. Roderick, heraldic painter, *Prot.A.W.7, 9/11/1723;* Agnes and Elizabeth, daughters of George Chalmers, W.S., proprietors, *Prot. W.F.2, 30/6/1747;* Laurence, printer, *p.w.1780;* James, S.S.C., *D.1827;* Miss Janet, *m.t.c. 21/10/1829;* Mrs. Janet, relict of Robert Henderson of Kinghorn; and Mrs. Helen, wife of James White in Canada, who owned a tenement between Chalmers' and Monteith's Close, *Reg. 11/12/1760*—all connected with the close.

The name Dunsyre's Close is derived from the tenement owned by Wm. Dunsyre, *Dunsiare, or de Dunsyre,* which stood on the west of the great mansion of Andrew, Bishop of Moray, on the north side of the High Street, *C.C.600, 26/10/1495; Prot.A.W.3, 10/2/1711.*

Thomas de Dunsyre, burgess, with consent of his wife Elen, alienated to the Prior and Convent of Blackfriars, lands on the north side of the High Street bounded on the north and south by those of Wm. de Dunsyre, *C.C. 505, 6/5/1483.*

Boyd's Close, alias Chalmers', *Reg. 19/12/1861,* takes its name from Boyd's land, *alias the Blew or Blue Land, probably from a slated roof. Prot. A.W.8, 1/9/1726, 25/3/1728,* at the head of Chalmers' Close, *Prot. A.W.7, 9/11/1723,* acquired by Hugh Boyd, merchant, from George Smith, merchant in Stockholm, *Prot. W.F.2, 30/6/1747,* and standing between Chalmers' and Sandilands' Closes, *Reg. 1/6/1858.*

CHALMERS STREET	From the Chalmers Hospital at the top of the street, endowed by Geo. Chalmers, plumber, who died 1836. Hospital built 1861, *o.& n.e. ii. 363.*
CHAMBERLAIN ROAD	"From an official of the city named Fairholme who is buried" in the tomb of John Livingstone and his wife Elizabeth Rig, who acquired the lands of Greenhill in 1636, *o.& n.e. iii. 4.* It is named Banner Place in Johnston's map of 1851; from the banner erected on the **Bore** Stone, q.v. Not shewn in Ord. Surv. 1852. Chamberlain Road, *D.M.1852.* Properly Chamberlain's Road, *as Littlejohn map.* Founded on error, *m.t.c. 11/9/1700.* The town council recognising the drawback of frequent change of treasurer, pass an act for the institution of a chamberlain. Thos. Fisher elected first chamberlain 11 Sept. 1700.

He was in active office 6 Oct. 1710. Mentioned as "Late chamber-lane", *m.t.c. 29/11/1710*. He died 26/11/1711.

CHAMBERS STREET From Provost Wm. Chambers, under whom so many "improvements" were effected, including the making of this street, *circa 1870*.

CHANCELOT CRESCENT On the grounds of "Chance Lott", *D.1827*. "Chance Lot", *Kirkwood.*
TERRACE *3/4/1806, eec.j.s.* Chancelot, house and garden, *Ord.Surv. 1852*. "Thos. Davidson, shoemaker. Chance Inn", *m.t.c.16/12/1801*. Lands of Chancelot, *e.e.c. 5/10/1820*.

CHAPEL LANE From old Episcopal Chapel, demolished before 1884, *o.& n.e. iii. 231*. *Irons, ii.b.* Built 1590 *w.o.l.211. D.1800, 70. D.1827*. Chapel's Wynd South Leith. Lees quarter, *m.t.c. 24/6/1812. S.S.L. Map, J.R.S.L. 391.*

CHAPEL STREET From the adjoining Chapel of Ease, of the West Kirk. The name is given to West Nicolson St. in Ainslie 1780, *D.1799, 88*. Altered in 1804, Chapel named "Hope Park Chapel" *St.C. 174*. "West Chappel St.", *m.t.c. 26/11/1794*. Opened for service Jan. 1756, *St.C. 129*.

CHARLES STREET See Chambers' Domestic Annals of Scotland Vol III, p.371—1712.
LANE

CHARLOTTE LANE From Queen Charlotte wife of George III, *Ainslie*, Charlotte Sq.
SQUARE planned, not built, is St. George Sq. 1780. In 1804 Charlotte Sq.
STREETS NORTH "St. George Square to be called Charlotte Sq." *m.t.c. 20/7/1785*.
& SOUTH Evidently to prevent confusion with the existing George Square, *m.t.c. 19/7/1786* by approval of Lord Alva, part proprietor.

CHARTERHALL ROAD On the estate of the Trotters of Mortonhall, owners also of Charterhall in Berwickshire.
See also Charterhall Grove—Part II.

CHESSEL'S COURT *Ainslie. Kirkwood. Kerr.* Chesel Building, *Edgar 1765*.

The court was built by Archibald Chessel on lands acquired from David, son to Alexander Pirie, merchant, and also from David Milne, mason, *Reg. 26/2/1856. See also Pirie's Close and Milne's Close.* Chessel, a wright to trade, had a seat in the Tron Kirk in 1745, *Tron Kirk, 177*. A house was advertised in 1767, *e.e.c. 18/2/1767*, to let, in Chessel's Building, enquire of Mr. Chessels, the proprietor in the court adjoining. His widow applied in 1779 for a water-pipe from the fountain well to the Excise Office, *m.t.c. 18/8/1779, 10/9/1779*, which was the scene of Deacon Wm. Brodie's last and fatal exploit as housebreaker.

CHESSER AVENUE From Councillor—treasurer—Lord Provost, 1919-1921. John Wm. Chesser.
See also Chesser Crescent etc—Part II.

CHEYNE STREET Capt. Alexr. Cheyne, R.E. 15 Cheyne St. *D.1827. D.1831/2.*

CHURCH HILL From Morningside Parish Church closeby. Original name Napier
CHURCHILL PLACE Terrace (from the neighbouring property of Merchiston, formerly owned by the Napier family). *D.M.1852. Johnston 1851. Churchill Ord. Surv. 1852.*

CIRCUS LANE From adjacent Royal Circus.
NORTH WEST
NORTH EAST
& SOUTH EAST
PLACES

CITADEL From the citadel built by General Monk in 1656 on the site of the
CITADEL STREET demolished St. Nicholas Church, *Citadel, p.w. 1780/81—106.* "Citydale", *m.t.c. 1/9/1773.*

CLAREBANK CRESCENT
CLAREMONT ROAD

Suggested by the name of Claremont House, which formerly stood on the ground, *j.r.*

CLAREMONT CRESCENT
  GARDENS
  PARK
  ROAD
  STREETS
  EAST & WEST

On the grounds of Claremount Park, feued by Heriot Trust, *15/10/1825 eec.j.s. Clermont D.1827, 29. Lothians Map 1825, Claremont St. m.t.c. 11/10/1826.*
   See also Claremont Bank, Grove—Part II.

CLARENCE STREET

Ord. Surv. 1852. Letter to the Duke of Clarence (anent monument to his late brother, the Duke of York), who hopes to visit Edinburgh soon, *m.t.c. 14/3/1827.*

CLARENDON CRESCENT

1850 Gilbert. Complete Ord. Surv. 1852. Original name Victoria Cresc., *Forbes 64. Wilson's map issued about 1853.* Geo. Wm. Fred. 4th Earl of Clarendon, born 1800, died 1870. Politician. Named Victoria Cresc. in Thomas C. Jack's map, Claud Shaw, Civil Engineer. Geo. Bartholomew. No date.

CLARK AVENUE
  ROAD

On property of Mr. Clerk, *Ainslie 1804,* or from Sir Thos. Clark, Convener of finance Committee of Heriot's Trust. Sir John Clerk, his son, was chairman of the Heriot Trust, owners of the property, *j.r.*

CLERK STREET

Lothian Map 1825. m.t.c. 27/8/1817. Clark St. *Kirkwood. D.1827.*

From John Clerk, Lord Eldin (conjectured). *See o.& n.e ii. 186. See Eldin St. in Appx.* "The great road formed through St. Patrick Sq", *m.t.c. 6/1/1813.* Footpath from St. Patrick's Sq. to the corner of Salisbury Road, *m.t.c. 16/11/1814.* Charter to Wm. Clerk. Clerk to the Signet, of part of Goose Dub and various grounds belonging to late John Gibson, writer, & Thos. Grinton Smithfield, *m.t.c. 26/6/1816.*

CLIFTON TERRACE

On property of Alexr. Chas. Maitland (see Maitland St) of Cliftonhall.

CLINTON ROAD

From superior, Lord Clinton, son-in-laws to Sir John Stuart Forbes of Pitsligo, (Grindlay Trust).

CLOCKMILL LANE

From the old Mansion of Clockmill House, or "Clokisrwne Mylne", 1569. Name of locality existed before the house. The name is corrupt Gaelic, and has no connection with a "Clock", *o.& n.e. ii, 41.* Robert Donaldson's part of the lands of Clockmill, called the Tennis Court, *v.r.46.* "Clackmill" from the house (Bailie D.W. Kemp). From the mill in the poultry farm, or Clockenmill of the Abbey of Holyrood. Clockenmill burn & bridge, *j.r.*

Clockmylne House, or Cloicksholm (from the Gaelic word cloich—a stone). Latterly Bellevue, *Mackay 154.* Clack-mill House, *M.143.* Land in Cloakmylne disponed by Robt. Ker to Andrew Davidson, tailor in Canongate and his wife Janet Haistie, *m.t.c. 14/6/1648.* Calsey between Wattergait and Clokmilne to be repaired, *m.t.c. 3/12/1669.*

CLUNY AVENUE
  PLACE
  TERRACE
  DRIVE
  GARDENS

From Gordon of Cluny who acquired the Braid Estate before 1800, *o.& n.e. iii. 41.* In 1771 St. Matthews 33. From the Browns.

CLYDE STREET
  ST. LANE

D.1827. Compliment to the river, *m.t.c. 10/9/1806.* "Meuse Lane, now called Clyde St." *m.t.c. 5/1/1841.* There seem to be two Clyde Streets, north & south, *m.t.c. 29/5/1811.*

COALHILL

Descriptive, already so named 1606, *St.C.12. o.& n.e. iii. 247.* Coals were unloaded there. Coalhill, Kirkgate, Leith, *p.w.1773, 64.* So named in 18th century, *j.r.s.l. 176.*

COATES CRESCENT GARDENS PLACE	*D.1827.* From the Manor house of Easter Coates, beside St. Mary's Episcopal Church, Palmerston Pl., belonging to the family of Byres, who gave name of Byre's Close. Probably named from sheep cotes, ovilia, *Reek. 35.* "*Coittis" BB.57.* Coates Cresc. planned, *Kirkwood.* The Crescent on the property of Wm. Walker of Coats, *m.t.c. 18/11/1812.* "The Crescent on the lands of Coats", *m.t.c. 13/1/1813.* Coats Crescent, *m.t.c. 17/7/1816.* Acquired, with superiority by Jas. Walker, *w.s. 7/6/1790, m.t.c. 3/1/1827.*
COATFIELD LANE	From the ancient property of coatfield, owned in 1470 by Patrick Logan, of the Restalrig family, *o.& n.e. iii. 220.* Name originally Coitfield, and referred to a piece of ground set apart for quoit-playing, *t.t.l. 160.* Johne Logan of Coitfield 1561, *7/9/1580, 20/8/1574.* *Irons 1.392.427.ii.43. s.s.l. 78* seems to intimate that it was from a sheep cote in the field, *j.r.l.s. 28.* Robert Logane of Coitfield, *Prot. 18/10/1528.* "Logan of Cotfield", *St. Giles 321, No. 85. Laings Charters 116.* Coat-fold, *s.s.l. map.* Two neutrals to be chosen to arbitrate between the town and Lord Balmerinoch about his encroachments on the lands of Coitfield, *m.t.c. 7/5/1669.*
COBDEN CRESCENT ROAD TERRACE	From Richard Cobden, M.P., founder of the Anti Cornlaw League 1838.
COBURG LANE STREET	From Prince Albert, of Saxe-Coburg and Gotha, husband of Queen Victoria. Married 10 Feb. 1840.
COCKBURN STREET	Properly "Lord Cockburns St" *Reg. 6/2/1861. Imp. Map 1866* who vainly strove to preserve the beauty and interest of Old Edinburgh, leaving his name to the Cockburn Society. He died 1854. The street made 1859. Author of "Circuit Journeys". His bust at north entrance to street, *o.& n.e. 1.282.* A Company formed by Act of Parliament. "The Edinburgh Railway Station Access Coy" in 1853, which bought up, bit by bit, the necessary lands in the closes, which were demolished, and the street made, *Reg.* Made after Ord. Surv. 1852, *76 Reg. 7/9/1860.*
COLINTON ROAD	Leading from Morningside to Colinton, or Collingtown, the ancient name whereof was Hailes, as in Kirk Session records; then Hailes, alias Colintoun, *o.e.c. iv. 32.* *See also Colinton Grove—Part II.*
COLLEGE STREET SOUTH NORTH	On the south side of the College. On the north side of the College. Demolished, *circa 1870,* and place taken by Chambers St.
COLLEGE STREET WEST	From Horse Wynd to Potterrow, *D.1827,* now the lane between the College and the Royal Scottish Museum.
COLLEGE WYND	*Edgar. Ainslie. Kirkwood.* Vicus Academiae, (Gordon). Kirkfield Wynd, *Reg. 24/11/1743.* Wynd of the Blessed Virgin Mary in-the-Field, *Wilson, ii. 140.* Kirk of Field Wynd, *Prot. J.W.6, 15/12/1761.* School Chieff Wynd, *Prot. W.F.4, 9/4/1751.* School House Wynd, *Prot. A.W.4, 9/5/1711.* Its oldest name, Wynd of the Blessed Virgin Mary in the Field, is derived from its being the direct approach to the 'Kirk of Field', the scene of the murder of Darnley, on 9th February 1567. The designation 'in the Field' is due to the fact that, prior to the building of the Flodden Wall in 1513, the site of this church was outside the Town Wall. In 1506 a property in the wynd is described as having the High School ('summa scola grammaticalis') on the north, *Soc.Ant.S.v.147,* from which it took its later name. The College of King James, opened

1583, having been established on the site of the church buildings, the wynd was known thereafter as the College Wynd, *see Gordon's map, and that of the Flodden Wall and area enclosed by it, o.e.c. vol.ii, p.61.*

COLTBRIDGE AVENUE
TERRACE
GARDENS

From the Coltbridge, on the Water of Leith, whence the dragoons bolted in their "Coltbridge Canter" in the '45. Name (fancifully) derived from the colt, which wrought the ferry, before the bridge was built, *w.o.l. 125.* Probably corrupted from Coatesbridge, or Coatbridge, alluding to neighbouring estate of Wester Coates. Andrew Dalrympell at Coltbridge, *Prentice roll 10/1/1683.*

Wm. Toftis admitted miller in Coltsmylne *m.t.c. 22/9/1650.* No indication of locality. A committee, with workmen to visit Coltbridge & report, *m.t.c. 23/8/1637.* Grants were made by the Town towards repairing the Coltbridge & Crawmond bridge, *m.t.c. 16/9/1647.* The committee having visited the cross ways on the lands of the Laird of Coitts, report that the north most way coming from the Coittbridge to Edinburgh may be taken away and no one prejudiced until they come the length of Wester Whythouse, providing that the gait betwix the S. way and this N. gait there be a calsey made, and a hie way settled either on e. or on w.s. of yard & houses of Wester Whythouse, which way is a leading way to the way that goeth to Leith. Agreed: the n. road being useless and a great damage to lands of Coitts, *m.t.c. 3/4/1661. See anon. map 1730.*
See also Coltbridge Vale—Part II.

COLVILLE PLACE

From builder, *e.c.b.c.ld.*

COMELY BANK AVENUE
GROVE
PLACE
MEWS
ROW
ROAD
TERRACE
STREET

From the residence of Sir Wm. Fettes. Comely Bank House to let for summer, *4/5/1774. eec.j.s. Comely Bank mentioned v.r. 43.*

COMELY GREEN
CRESCENT
PLACE

Old House, *Kirkwood. Ord Surv. 1852.* "Beautiful villa owned by George Murray, shopkeeper, High Street. *17/9/1808, eec.j.s. Lothian Map 1825.*

COMISTON DRIVE
GARDENS
PLACE
ROAD
TERRACE

From the adjacent estate of Comiston, at the top whereof stands the Camus Stone, *o.& n.e. iii. 326.* Formerly "Colmanstoun", *o.e.c.iv.72.* Alias Thirsten, *Prot. 4/9/1729. G.1. i.*
See also Comiston Grove etc.—Part II.

COMMERCIAL STREET

"New street of North Leith, now called Commercial Place", *m.t.c. 25/1/1832.*

CONNAUGHT PLACE

Compliment to the Duke of Connaught.

CONSTITUTION PLACE
STREET

Built before 1822, *o.& n.e. iii. 243.* Constitution Road in Robertson's map of Leith Fortifications, 1850, *Irons 1.297.* Constitution Hill, *p.w. 1780/81—110.* C. Lane, *Kirkwood, also Court.* Proposed new street, nameless, on west side of Leith Links, *m.t.c. 29/1/1806.* Constitution Hill seems to have derived its name from the excitement for the preservation of the "British Constitution" when the Movement for Catholic emancipation stirred up the Gordon Riots. See Barnaby Rudge, 1778, *j.r.s.l. 158.*

CONVENING COURT

At Deanpath. Meeting place where the trades were convened.

CORNHILL TERRACE

After corn, fancy, *e.c.b.c.ld.*

CORNWALL STREET	Intended to be Erskine St., *Grindlay 9*. Compliment to the King's eldest son.
CORNWALLIS PLACE	After Lord Cornwallis, who capitulated to the Americans at York Town, Oct. 1781, whereby American Independence was secured.
CORENNIE DRIVE GARDENS	From Aberdeenshire property of Gordons of Cluny, superiors.
CORSTORPHINE ROAD	From the village, originally the Cross of Torphin, *Geo. Chalmers*. Other derivations false—and barely amusing. *See also Corstorphine—Part II.*
CORUNNA PLACE	From the battle in Spain where Sir John Moore fell in 1809. Built and owned by Peter McCraw, Tax Collector in Leith, who as a sergeant in the army, lost an arm in the battle. He is satirised by Robt. Gilfillan in a poem entitled "Peter", *j.r. D.1827.*
COUPER STREET	On property of Mr. Couper, W.S. (Map of Regality of Canongate and North Leith, 1813). *e.e.c. 1810.* Sewer to be made, apply to Mr. Couper, W.S., 4 Duke St. 1810. *eec.j.s. D.1827.* Peter Coupar, shipmaster, Leith, offered passage through his ground to the new dock, *m.t.c. 11/12/1799.* Lands of Rt. C. N. Leith, *m.t.c. 14/10/1812.*
COWAN'S CLOSE	East Crosscausey, *D.1800-84.* James Cowan, shoemaker. East crosscausey, *D.1827.*
COWAN ROAD	From Sir John Cowan, D.L. chairman of Redpath Brown & Co., master 1891/2 of the Mercant Coy. on whose ground it is built.
COWGATE	The name is found at least as early as 1428, *Charters of St. Giles, p.51.* Maitland *M.173* gives Cowgate, the South Street of Edinburgh, and Wellgate as names in use in 1480. Chepman and Millar's books, printed in 1508, appear as printed in the 'Southgaitt' of Edinburgh. Anderson *p.599* declares that the original name was South Street, its later name being Wellgate, from the town wells there. This is clearly borrowed from Maitland. There is no proof that these were names—they were probably descriptive titles. Gordon's 'Vicus vaccarum' is readily intelligible. Robert Chambers has achieved the wildest flight, perhaps, when he states that 'Cowgate is a corruption of Sou'gate—that is, South Street!' *Ancient Domestic Architecture of Edinburgh, p.2.*
CRAIGHALL AVENUE GARDENS BANK CRESCENT ROAD	On property of the Burn-Murdochs, owners of Craighall in Perthshire, *j.r.*
CRAIGHOUSE AVENUE GARDENS ROAD TERRACE	From Craighouse, which takes its name from the Craig, Craiglockhart Hill.
CRAIGLEA DRIVE PLACE	From the Craig of Craiglockhart.
CRAIGLEITH ROAD	From the now exhausted Craigleith quarry, out of which the New Town was built. Original name Barnton Terrace, as being on the road thither. *See also Craigleith Avenue etc.—Part II.*
CRAIGLOCKHART TERRACE	From Craiglockhart Hill (Crig-loch-ard, referring to the ancient Corstorphine Loch, *o.& n.e. III. 42.* Occupied by Alexr. Lockhart of

Covington, *p.w. 1780/81.* Named on request of Merchant Coy., March 1897.

See also Craiglockhart Avenue etc.—Part II.

CRAIGMILLAR PARK

On the property of Major Robert Gordon Gordon Gilmour of Liberton and Craigmillar.

CRAIG'S CLOSE

Known as Cant's Close, Alexr. Dennistoun's or Dennistoun's Close, Birnie's Close, Carmichael's Close, Haliburton's Close, Joysies, Joussie's, or Josiah's Close.

Craig's Close, north side of the High Street, a little below the Cross, took its name from John Craig, wright, burgess, third husband of Ann Hamilton, *her first husband, Gavin Stanehouse, baxter: her second, James Borland, writer,* who acquired property there from the late David Callen, which he left to his widow, *Prot.W.F.8, 11/5/1758.*

It seems almost impossible to disentangle this Craig's Close from that which is also called Warriston's Close; the entries in the protocols are most difficult to follow, and the aliases play bewilderingly one into another.

Cant's Close, called from the tenement of Alexr. Cant, east of Leitche's Close, *Prot.W.F.1, 14/1/1747,* of Henry Cant of Over Libbertoun, *Reg. 11/7/1741,* and also of Patrick Cant, lying to the east of Symone Doweill's land, *c.c. 744, 16/10/1509.* The alias is clearly stated. Elizabeth, daughter to (blank) Cant, owned property in Craig's, formerly Cant's Close, *Prot. J.W.5, 9/5/1759*

Alexr. Denniston's *Prot. J.W.1, 20/5/1748,* or Denniston's Close, *M.216; Prot. G.H.5, 18/3/1718,* now Craig's Close, from tenement of Alexr. Dennistoun, merchant, owner, *Reg. 29/3/1743,* who was 4th bailie, 1634. He is named Danielstoun elsewhere, *Prot. W.F.1, 14/1/1747.* The alias is distinct—Alexr. Dennistoun's Close, now Craig's Close, *Prot. J.W.4, 23/3/1758.*

Alexander Dennistoun, burgess, had a son David, who had a tenement in Leitche's Close *Prot. A.W.3, 12/8/1708* and is also called Dunniston, *Prot. J.W.2, 29/7/1749.* The north fragment of the close still exists between Cockburn and Market Streets.

Birnie's Close, alias Craig's Close, *Prot. A.W.7, 13/7/1725,* containing a tenement bounded by the lands of John Foullar on the east: of Alexr. Cant on the west: of Edward Little on the north: and by the High Street on the south, occupied lately by Richard Birnie, indweller in Edinburgh, *Reg. 3/3/1744. In Prot W.F.11, 21/6/1762, is mentioned a dwelling-house formerly owned by Robert Bruce of Binning: thereafter by the late Mr. Thos. Craig, advocate: thereafter by the late Sir Ludovic Craig his son, one of the Senators of the College of Justice, in the close called Birnie's now Craig's Close. This tallies exactly with Craig's, alias Warriston's Close, and creates uncertainty.*

Carmichael's Close. This close, alias Halyburton's Close, seems to have run east and west, forming the *north* boundary in Craig's Close of a tenement on the street front, *Prot. G.H.5, 25/2/1719; G.H.7, 18/1/1725; Reg. 12/12/1859.* It took its name from Wm. Carmichael, merchant and bailie, *3rd bailie 1673-4,* resident in Little's (or Old Post Office) Close, *Prot. G.H.5, 25/2/1719; G.H.7, 18/1/1725; Reg. 12/12/1859,* just east of Craig's Close.

Its alias, Haliburton's Close, *There were at least four closes of the name,* is derived from the houses acquired by John Haliburton of Garvock, in Craig's, formerly Cant's Close, from Robert Haliburton, and disponed by him to his son Robert—they were on the east side of

31

Craig's Close, *Prot. J.W.4, 23/3/1758; J.W.5, 9/5/1759.* Apparently the close ran from Haliburton's house, east side of Craig's Close, to Carmichael's house on the west side of Little's Close. It is not clearly shown on any map.

Joysies, Joussie's, or Josiah's Close. Birrel's Diary *Walks in Edinr, p. 86,* of 10th July 1598 speaks of the juggler's rope stretcher between the top of St. Geill's Kirk steeple and a stair beneath the Cross, called Josiah's Closeheid. Robert Joussie or Joysie, son and heir of James Joysie, rebuilt in Craig's Close a burned tenement, owned after him in succession by Alexr. Cant: Gilbert Primrose, chief surgeon to His Majesty: his nephew Gilbert Gourlay and his wife Janet Primrose: Alexr. Dennistoun: Thos. Fairholme: and John Bailie, apothecary, who rebuilt the street front, *Prot. G.I.1, 28/12/1728; G.L.2, 18/6/1766; Reg. 12/12/1859.* The heirs of Andrew Jossie owned land, apparently on east of Allan's Close, as also James Jossie and his son Robert, *Prot. W.F.1, 14/1/1747.* Elizabeth Cant, wife of Alexr. Jousie, owned a tenement on the north side of the High Street, a little below the Cross, *Prot. G.I.3, 30/9/1739.* This seems fairly conclusive.

CREWE COTTAGES ROAD	From Crewe house or farm shewn by Kirkwood 1817. "Crue", 2½ miles from Edinburgh, *Denovan 267.* *See also Crewe Bank etc.—Part II.*
CRICHTON STREET	From an architect of the time, *o.& n.e. ii. 329. Ainslie 1780.* James Crichton, mason, **Crichton St.**, *p.w.1780/81.*
CRIGHTON PLACE	From Councillor Jas. Crighton, 16 Dean Terrace, who represented St. Bernard's Ward, 1884, and was convener of Trinity Hospital Committee, on whose ground it was built, *j.r.*
CROALL PLACE	From the coach building Works of John Croall & Sons.
CROFT-AN-RIGH	(Croft of the King, being close to Holyrood). Croftangry, *p.w. 1780/81, 24.* Also "Chronicles of the Canongate". The ancient house said to have been built by Regent Moray. *Alias Grovesend, Maitland 143.* The house and lane, unnamed, *Gordon 1647.* Croft-an-righ Wynd. *D.1827, 123.* Croft Angry, *Ainslie 1804.*
CROMWELL STREET	*D.1827.* From vicinity of citadel built under Oliver Cromwell by General Monk. Old Buildings named "Cromwell's Barracks", *o.& n.e. iii. 257.*
CROSSCAUSEY	*Ainslie 1780 & 1804.* Crossing to St. Leonards or from leading to the Cross House at St. Leonards. (Umphraville's Cross). "Street commonly called Crosscauseway", *m.t.c. 9/9/1801.* *Now Crosscauseway.*
CROWN PLACE STREET	Crown Place formerly Whitefield Lane, so called from Whitefield House, residence of Mrs. Whitefield. Name changed about 1895. Crown St. *D.1827* possibly from discovery of regalia, Edinburgh Castle 1818, *j.r.*
CROWN SQUARE	In the Castle, from the room where are kept the Crown and other regalia.
CUDDY LANE	From a park near Gayfield Square, called the Ass or Cuddy Park— evidently from its habitues.
CUMIN PLACE	From Charlotte, daughter of George Cumin, of Relugas, who married 1808 Sir Thomas Dick Lauder, of the Grange estate, on which it is built. She is called also "Charles", *St.G. 308. 379.*
CUNNINGHAM PLACE	From Peter Cunningham, builder of firm of James Cunningham & Sons, builders and house carpenters, Leith, *j.r.*

D

DAISY TERRACE	Fancy, after the flower, *e.c.b.c.ld*.
DALGETY AVENUE ROAD STREET	On property of the Earl of Moray, priorietor of Dalgety near Doni-bristle. The lands of Restalrig, forfeited by Lord Balmerino, for his share in the '45 were bought in by his nephew, the Earl of Moray, 1755, *j.r.*
DALHOUSIE TERRACE	Sheer fancy, *g.l.b.*
DALKEITH ROAD	Leading to Dalkeith. The old, from St. Leonards by Cameron Bank, Petty France, and into the centre of the town. The new, from Minto St. by Liberton, Gilmerton and Eskbank.
DALKEITH STREET	The daughter of the first duke of Abercorn, married the Earl of Dal-keith, later Duke of Buccleuch. On Abercorn ground.
DALMENY ROAD	After the seat of the Earl of Rosebery, statesman and author.
DALMENY STREET	As preceding. Former name Colston St., q.v.
DALRY ROAD	From Dalry Lane, *D.1827,* leading to Dalry Manor House, the resi-dence of the family of Chieslie, who acquired the property in the 16th century, the most famous of them being John Chieslie, who assassina-ted Sir George Lockhart, Lord President in 1689, and suffered death after torture. *See o.& n.e. ii. 216 and i. 116.* Dalry, gaelic, the King's Vale or Meadow. Dalry House, *D.1827.* Barony of Dalry, *Prot. 26/10/1530.* Dalry Lane, *Littlejohn Map.* Wm. de Touris, Lord of Dalry, *c.c. 23/2/1470-1.*
DALRYMPLE CRESCENT	From Lady Anne Dalrymple, second daughter of the 9th Earl of Stair, alive in 1898, was mother of Sir Thomas Dick Lauder, Bart., also then alive, superior of the Grange estate, *St. G. 360.*
DAMSIDE	Shown as Dean, from its position beside the mill dam or cauld.
DARNAWAY STREET	From Darnoway Castle, near Forres, seat of the Earl of Moray on whose ground the street is built, *D.1827.* Tarnoway Castle, Elginshire, *Edr. Almc. 1812, p.69.*
DARNELL ROAD	From the Rev. Mr. Darnell, founder of Cargilfield Boys' School—now removed to Barnton. *Rev. Daniel Chas., West Darnell House and Schoolhouse in Trinity Road. v.r. 1884.*
DAVIE STREET	*D.1827.* John Davie, brewer in the Pleasance in 1699, *o.e.c. i. 34.* Chemical works founded by the late Mr. Davie in 1700, for sale, *21/3/1811, eec.j.s.* House for sale, *20/1/1812, eec.j.s.* Feu duties on the estate of the late Mr. Davie in Nicolson, Richmond and Davie Streets, for sale, *23/4/1814, eec.j.s.,* from Mr. Davie, chemist, on whose ground it was built, *St. L. 48.* John Davie Esq., Nicolson's St. *p.w. 1780/81, 25.* John Davie Esq. of Gavie Side, 25 Nicolson's St. East side, *D.1800, 122.* Davie's Ground, West Richmond St., *m.t.c. 2/7/1817 Note 2.* For John Davie (cousin and heir of Joseph Davie) brewer in Plisance, south croft of land at back of Crackling house, q.v. lying in the Plis-ance, and Deir enough, having lands of Earl of Roxburgh on the north: common road leading from the Back Row to the Crackling House, on the west. Vennel of St. Leonard's on east, *J.H. Canong. Prot. 29/12/1701.* John Davie and his wife Katherine Kilpatrick, land of North Croft. Pleasance: Duke of Roxburgh superior, *16/6/1773. Can. Chart.* Said John D. indweller in Bristo, *Can. Chart. 6/4/1801.* John D., brewer, Pleasants, *m.t.c. 20/9/1710* as heir to deceased Joseph D., wright in Pleasance, his cussine germane, croft of land at back of Crackling house, *m.t.c. 10/12/1701, 27/9/1710.* Precept of

Clare Constat Johne Davie, brewer in Pleasants, a tenement there. Feuduty 4/- Scots. Entry 24/- Scots, *m.t.c. 21/9/1694.*

Joseph Davie, wright in Pleasance invested as heir to his fr. in a south croft of land at back of Crackton House in the Pleasance or Deiraneuch. Land of Joseph Daves in Pleasants, 1748, *i.w.o.h. vol. ii. p.677, No.268.* John Davie in Bristo, invest in houses and croft of land in Pleasance, disponed to him by using Mr. Robert Ker of Brownlandis, *m.t.c. 17/1/1649.* Wm. Davie indweller in Pleasance and his wife. Isobell Mitchell, invest in thack house and yard, West end of Pleasance, disponed to them by A.W. Malloch, *m.t.c. 28/4/1665.* Wm. Davie in Pleasance and wife Issobel Mitchell, invest in half of barn and yard, *m.t.c. 21/7/1667.*

DEAN LANE PATH STREET TERRACE	From the Den, deans, or narrow valley of the Water of Leith. The haugh is the low lying flat ground by the river side. Common Mills of Dene, 1478. *St. Giles 322, No. 91. Laing's Charters. Appx. lxix.*
DEAN BANK LANE TERRACE	
DEANHAUGH STREET	
DEAN PARK MEWS STREET	
DEAN VILLAGE	
DELHAIG	From old house of the name and estate. *See also further note—Part II.*
DENHAM GREEN AVENUE PLACE TERRACE	Denholm, *D.1827.* House mentioned in Cal. Merc. 31/3/183 . *j.s. Kirkwood, 1817.*
DEWAR PLACE	James Dewar, grocer and mason. Tobago St., *D.1800,* "near Edinburgh", *m.t.c. 2/1/1828.*
DICK PLACE	On the estate of Sir Thomas Dick Lauder, of the Grange of St. Giles.
DICKSON STREET	Dickson's Nursery Garden, *Kirkwood. D.1827-48.* Dickson and Fair, their nursery, Leith Walk. *m.t.c. 3/2/1790. See. D.1810.*
DISTILLERY LANE	Evident.
DOCKGATES DOCK PLACE STREET	From the Docks.
DOUGLAS TERRACE	After Bailie Robert Douglas, formerly head of James Gray and son, ironmongers, George St.
DOUNE TERRACE	On the grounds of the Earl of Moray, whose heir enjoys the title of Lord Doune, from Doune Castle. *See Waverley,Chap. 38-39.* Also the Ballad of the "Bonny Earl o' Moray". Downe Terrace, *D.1800, 30.*
DOWNFIELD PLACE	Patrick Rigg of Downfield is mentioned, *m.t.c. 24/11/1790, 27/11/1822.* Jas. Home Rigg of Downfield, owner of property in Dalry, *c.h.i. 466.*
DRUM TERRACE	From the old mansion of Drum, *o.& n.e. iii. 128. Ord. Surv. 1852. Littlejohn map.*
DRUMDRYAN STREET	The "Yeards of Drumdryan" occurs in feu charter of 1687, *o.e.c. x.241.* Also in Charter of Sept. 1458. "Lands of Dyndryan", *K.50.* Dundryan in charter by Charles II, *r.c.g.9.* House owned by late Mrs. Home Rigg, for sale, *10/2/1794, eec.j.s.* Drumdryan Lane, *D.1827.*

Offered for sale, as newly built, *6/4/1774, eec.j.s.* Apply to Dr. Spens, proprietor, Niddry's Wynd. Lands thereof owned by Chas. McDowall, *m.t.c. 10/11/1790, 11/5/1808.* "Brewarie at Drumdryan" for sale EA 4/2/1766. Lands of Drumdryan, *m.t.c. 27/10/1835.* Dr. Nathaniel Spence, original vassel for Drumdryan Brewery, (site of King's Theatre), *r.o.s. 2/9/1801.*

Arthur Straiton, piriwig maker infested in lands of Drumdryan, *m.t.c. 9/2/1709.* Robt. Gray, maltman, entered in aikers of Drumdryan and house thereof, purchased from Mr. John Watson: also house and yard, purchased from Thos. Gray, lying in Portsburgh, *m.t.c. 23/5/1655.* John Hamilton infest in half of the houses of Drumdryan apprysit from Wm. Miller as son & heir to umq. Wm. M. or as lawfully charged to enter heir to his umq. mother, Issobel Thomson, or umq. gude sire Robert Thomsone, *m.t.c. 20/2/1650.* Charter of confirmation to Thos. Calderwood of annual rent of 220 mks. granted by Mr. John Watson and his wife Sara Logan, from eleven acres of Drumdryan, redeemable for 3600 mks., *m.t.c. 21/12/1653.* John Scott to cause mend the calseyis betwix the end of the West Port and Drumdryan or Wrights house, the gentlemen adjacent thereto furnishing stone & sand, *m.t.c. 10/6/1664.* Jas. Gray s. & h. to Jas. Gray, mt. infest in lands of Drumdryan, High Riggs & Litelflatt, & tent. in Portsburgh, *m.t.c. 20/10/1671.* Clare Constat to Margaret, Elizabeth and Marion Grayes, daughters to umq. Walter Gray, mt. B., for rent upliftable from umq. Robt. Gray, mt. in Edinburgh, his lands in Hie rigs and Drumdryan, *m.t.c. 30/12/1696.*

DRUMMOND PLACE

From Provost George Drummond, whose house stood near the centre, where stood later Bellevue House, afterwards Excise Office. He was six times Provost, first in 1740. Born 1687, died 1766, *m.t.c. 20/6/1804.*

The place was projected 4/2/1808, *eec.j.s.* Given in *D.1827. Ainslie 1804.*

DRUMMOND STREET

From above Provost George Drummond, (behind the Royal Infirmary, his enterprise). Projected 27.11.1790. *D.1827.* Drummond St. and East Drummond St. Old name Back Wall. *Ainslie 1780. Ainslie 1804.* Drummond Street Court entered from Drummond St. *Ord. Surv. 1852. Ainslie 1808. Unnamed. Lothian Map 1825. Do.*

DRUMSHEUGH GARDENS PLACE

From Drumsheugh House (from Meldrumsheugh estate. So named from owner). East of Queensferry Road. The house, occupied by the Earl of Murray, *D.1800,* stood in the middle of Randolph Crescent, beside the rookery; it was demolished 1822, *Stewart Chambers, Ainslie 1804.* The road it marked Drumsheugh—(the house, Lord Moray). As also in Lothians Map 1825. In 1827 Sir Patrick Walker, advocate, is residing in Drumsheugh, as also Mrs. Walker of Coates. In Lothian map an unnamed house, (Lord Colvilles, now W. Walker, Esq.) *Ainslie 1804,* appears, which in Ord. Surv. 1852 is named Drumsheuch House. After the death of Miss Walker in 1877 the ground was feued. House demolished 1877, *o.& n.e. 1.237.* It had been bought and occupied at one time by Charles Erskine, or Areskine, Lord Justice Clerk Tinwald, otherwise Alva, *Trad. 1.231.* The Hon. Andrew Erskine Drumsheugh, *p.w. 1780/81, 31.*

The lands of Meldrumsheugh, or Drumsheugh, owned by the Earl of Moray 1814, *v.r.46.* In Brown's "Epitaphs and Monumental Inscriptions in Greyfriars Churchyard 1867", p.80, the first of the Walkers of Coates, and Drumsheuch *sic semper* was Rev. Geo. Walker, Episcopal minister of Old Meldrum, who died Dec. 1784.

John Scott of Drumsheugh, *m.t.c. 8/10/1680.* Arable land on southside of Water of Leith, opposite Dean Bank, at present posest by Adam Forsyth, tenant in Drumsheugh, *m.t.c. 21/2/1711.* Piece of waste land on east side of calsay leading to the common milns, 16½ elns wide from the dyke x 25½ elns long, and other ground up to the north side of the lang gaitt, feued by town to John Scott of Drumsheugh, *m.t.c. 28/5/1630.* He disponed to Mr. John Achesone, *m.t.c. 30/5/1682.*

Robert Vaus, his corn miln and wauk miln and lying in Drumsheuch in Barony of Bruchton, *vol. 1, p.603, 13/8/1506.* Michael Allan of Drumsheugh, late Dean of Gild 1691-2, *m.t.c. 17/5/1700.* Lands of Drumsheugh, feu form granted to the College by Charles I, *i.w.c.h., vol.3, p.375, 30/9/1641.*

DRYDEN STREET	Intended to be called Reynold St., but Mr. John Balfour of Pilrig suggested Dryden, from the adjacent Rosslyn Crest. "Dryden's groves of oak". Lay of the Last Minstrel. *Canto vi, xxiii, j.r.* *See also Dryden Gardens, Terrace—Part II.*
DUBLIN STREET LANE NEWS	Compliment to Ireland, *Arnot 1816 map. Kirkwood 1817.* Hibernia St. *Ainslie 1804. m.t.c. 9/11/1803, 10/8/1803.* Compare London and Scotland St. The original name that of the country; that fixed later, of the metropolis. Dublin St, *m.t.c. 7/9/1803.* Or Hibernia St., *m.t.c. 24/11/1819.*
DUDDINGSTON CRESCENT PARK ROAD	From the neighbouring village of Duddingston, which derives its name not from the gaelic "sunny side of a hill", but from the family of Dodin, settled there in 11th century, *Baird 5.* *See also **Duddingston Avenue** etc.—Part II.*
DUKE STREET	*D.1827.* Probably from Duke of Buccleuch, and the Golf House there, he being much interested, *j.r.* He had a house here, *j.r.*
DUMBIEDYKES ROAD	"Dumbiedykes, selected as descriptive of the taciturn character of the imaginary owner is really the name of a house bordering on the King's Park, so called because the late Mr. Braidwood, an instructor of the deaf and dumb, resided there with his pupils. The situation of the real house is different from that assigned to the ideal mansion". *Note on Chap. VII of 'The Heart of Midlothian'. Published 1818.* The house shewn by Kirkwood, also Lothian map 1825, who marks the road Dumbie Dykes. "The dumbie dykes", *m.t.c. 29/5/1822.* "Small field known by name of Dumbie Dykes", owned by Fletcher of Saltoun, *m.t.c. 28/3/1832.* "T. Braidwood, teacher of dumb people, Leonard's hill", *p.w.1880.* House shewn on plan of (south) regality of Canongait of 1813, *Register House Hist. Dept, "Potts".* Dumbie House shown in Knox' map 1824. Also in Kirkwood 1817. Also Hamilton 1827
DUNBAR'S CLOSE	*Ainslie. Kirkwood. Kerr.* From the tenements lying on both sides of Dunbar's Close, belonging to David Dunbar, writer in Edinburgh, and his wife Agnes Hutchison, having the lands of the Earl of Panmuir on the east, *Can. Chart. 8/12/1773.*
DUNCAN STREET	After Admiral Duncan, 1731-1804, Victor of Camperdown, 1797. Occupied No. 5 George Sq., *D.1800, 130,* was a patient of Dr.

Benjamin Bell, on whose ground the street is built. His sailors, who believed that he owed his life to Dr. Bell, shewed their gratitude when he arrived at Harwich, 1798, on tour, taking out the horses and dragging the carriage, *B.Bell.* He was publicly entertained in Edinburgh, *m.t.c. 17/1/1797.* Street given in D.1827.

DUNDAS STREET	*Ainslie 1804.* From Rt. Hon. Henry Dundas, Viscount Melville, 1742-1811. M.P. for Midlothian 1774. Lord Advocate 1775. 1791 Home Secretary. As treasurer for the Navy he was accused in 1805 of malversation—acquitted, to the great and uproarious satisfaction of his friends, in particular Sir Walter Scott. Commemorated by Melville St. and Monument, *m.t.c. 3/9/1806. 25/3/1807.*
DUNDEE PLACE STREET TERRACE	Compliment to the city of Dundee.
DUNDONALD STREET	Formerly Duncan St. after Admiral Duncan, victor at Camperdown, 1797. *Ainslie 1804.* Name changed towards the end of the 19th century to prevent confusion with Duncan St., Newington, and the name given of Thomas Cochrane, Earl of Dundonald, 1775-1860. Rear-admiral, "equal of the old Elizabethan adventurers". There are not far distant, Nelson St., Howe St., Rodney St., St. Vincent St.
DUNEDIN STREET	Compliment to the City of Edinburgh, the gaelic form of the name being Dun-Edin, the fort of Edwin.
DUNLOP'S COURT	Grassmarket. *No. 46. D.1827.* From Wm. Dunlop & Co., wine & spirit merchants, 44 Grassmarket, *D.1827.*
DUNROBIN PLACE	Fancy. From the castle of the Duke of Sutherland, *e.c.b.c.ld.*

E

EARL GREY STREET	Named from Lord Grey, as champion of the Reform Bill of 1832. The original name is part of Lothian Road, *Ainslie 1804,* then *Lothian Map 1825* Wellington St. in honour of the Duke of Wellington; who, however strongly opposed the Reform Bill. In 1834 Lord Grey was entertained at a banquet to celebrate the passing of the Bill. During the night "Wellington" was effaced, and "Earl Grey" substituted—and remained there. Houses for sale in Wellington St. now Earl Grey St., *7/7/1834 eec.j.s.* Dinner to be given to Lord Grey, in temporary building at east end of new High School. He was made B and G by Act of Council of 26/9/1834. The Lord Provost took the address to him at Howick Hall (on account of Reform Bill), *m.t.c. 1/9/1834.*
EARL HAIG GARDENS	From Earl Haig so distinguished in the Great War, 1914-1918.
EASTER ROAD	Leading from Holyrood, at the East end of the Canongate, by the East end of the Calton Hill, to Leith. East road to Leith, *D.1827.* There were two western roads, one by Leith Wynd and Leith Walk, the other from Broughton Toll by Pilrig to Leith. Both shewn in anon. map circa 1830, as also East road, as above.
EASTFIELD	From its position. *See also Eastfield Gardens—Part II.*
EDEN TERRACE LANE	From the Biblical neighbourhood of Jordan, Egypt, Canaan, etc. Doubtless an earthly paradise. Eden Grove and Hermitage, *Ord. Surv. 1852.*
EDINA PLACE STREET	From the fanciful name used by Burns for Edinburgh. Built about 1884.

EDINBURGH DOCK	Opened suitably by the Duke of Edinburgh, July 1881, who named it, *o.& n.e. iii. 288. Gilbert 158.*
EGLINTON CRESCENT STREET	One of a local outbreak of titles of nobility like Glencairn, Grosvenor, Lansdowne, Palmerston, Rosebery. It is said that the builder of Eglinton and Glencairn Crescent was an Ayrshire man, who, knowing the ancient rivalry of the two families, set them opposite, as a standing memorial thereof. See Glencairn Cresc. For instances of feud, see Chambers' Domestic Annals of Scotland vol. 1, p. 394. Feued from Heriot's Hospital Nov. 1877.
EILDON STREET	Probably from the Eildon Hills, Melrose. On the lands of the Duke of Buccleuch. From the owner of Warriston, Alexr. Henderson of Eildon Hall, St. Boswells, *j.r.*
	See also Eildon Ter.—Part II.
ELBE STREET	Trade connection.
ELDER STREET	*Ainslie 1804.* From Thomas Elder of Forneth, Lord Provost thrice between 1788 and 1798, *o.& n.e. ii. 176. Stranger's Guide 79.* He died 1799, *Denavan, m.t.c. 13/2/1799, 7/4/1799. For account of him see Kay i, 358.*
ELGIN STREET SOUTH	Elgin Street long before the Terrace and gave it its name, *j.r.*
NORTH TERRACE	Elgin St. proposed name for Coates Gardens, *map D.1872-3.*
ELLERSLEY ROAD	So named by Sir George Campbell, superior, in honour of the birthplace of Sir Wm. Wallace.
ELM PLACE	From trees once there, near Lady Fife's house, *j.r.*
ELM ROW	From trees once there, *o.& n.e. iii. 154. D.1827.* The elms in a fine double row, standing in a line with Baxter's Pl., forming boundary of Mr. Allan's property on the north and extending 600 feet down Leith Walk, *Stranger's Guide 265.* A long report by Mr. Stark.
ELMWOOD TERRACE	Fancy. After the tree, *e.c.b.c.ld.*
ELPHINSTONE COURT	Cowgate. From Sir James Elphinstone of Logie who built it in 1679 (date on lintel), *o.& n.e. 1.271.* At foot of South Gray's, or Mint Close, on the east side, *Prot. j.w. 4. 13/4/1758.*
ERSKINE PLACE	*D.1827.* From family name of Lord Alva, from whom the town acquired the feu in 1820, *r.c.g. 26.* Shewn unnamed Lothian Map 1825.
ESPLANADE	What it is. Portobello—Joppa.
ESSLEMONT ROAD	On the lands of Major Robert G. Gordon Gilmour, elder son to Henry Wolrige Gordon of Hallhead and Esslemont, Aberdeenshire.
ETTRICK ROAD	From Baron of Ettrick and Napier, alluding to Napiers of Merchiston.
	See also Ettrick Court, Grove—Part II.
EYRE PLACE CRESCENT TERRACE	On property of Mr. Eyre, brewer, *Kirkwood.* Feuing proposed 23 June 1823, *eec.j.s. D.1827.* Planned, no name, *Lothian map 1825.* See James Eyre, brewer, Canon mills, *D.1800-134,* also late brewer, Canonmills house, *D.1827, 58.* In P.W.1780/81, p.6 is James Ayre, brewer, opposite the back stairs, (Cowgate), but no Eyre. *See also m.t.c. 5/9/1781.* He seems to have left the Cowgate and gone to Canonmills. Mr. Eyre's Brewerie, near Canonmilns, *m.t.c. 20/6/1810.* Mr. James Eyre, brewer, Canonmills, *m.t.c. 14/1/1818.* Eyre House, *Littlejohn map.*

F

FALCON AVENUE
GARDENS
ROAD

From Falcon Hall, built by Mr. Falconer early in the 19th century, *o.& n.e. iii. 39. D.1827.* Demolished early 20th century. Occupied for a time by Dr. G. Bartholomew, chartographer. Gate pillars, with falcons re-erected at Zoological Gardens. Alexr. Falconer of Falconhall, bought ground in new enclosure in Greyfriars, tomb 51, *m.t.c. 7/9/1814.* Falcon Hall owned formerly by Bailie, later Provost Wm. Coulter, hosier.
See also Falcon Court—Part II.

FERRY ROAD

From Leith to Queensferry.
See also Ferry Road Avenue etc.—Part II.

FETTES AVENUE
ROW

From Fettes College, which was named from Sir. Wm. Fettes, *D.1827. m.t.c. 20/6/1810. Shewn named Ainslie 1804.* West part only built *Lothian map 1825.* "A street called Fettes Row", *m.t.c. 17/7/1816.*
See also Fettes Rise—Part II

FILLYSIDE

Seafield, Leith. Old House *Kirkwood. Phillieside, o.& n.e. iii. 198. Maitland 178.c.2.* Part of the lands of Coatfield *14/1/1796, eec.j.s.* Belonging to Trinity Hospital to West of Seafield Toll *25/1/1796. eec.j.s.* Mentioned 1596, *i.w.c.h. vol. 4, p.193.* Greenbank called Fillyside bank, *i.w.c.h. 5, p.297. 3/6/1597.* March stones needed there for bounds of lands of Trinity Hosp, *m.t.c. 20/5/1674.* Phillyside brae, between Black Rocks and Leith, riding the marches, *m.t.c. 9/4/1718.*
See also Fillyside Ave. etc.—Part II.

FINDHORN PLACE

From the river Findhorn, in the Morayshire estates of the Dick Lauder Family of St. Giles Grange, superiors of the property.

FINGAL PLACE

Shown as Argyle Place q.v. The district is Campbell of Argyllshire, and the Celtic hero, Fingal, figures largely in local tradition, *D.1827.*

FINGZIES PLACE

From builder, *j.r.,* Wm. Fingzies, builder, 1866-1880.

FISHER'S CLOSE

Edgar. Ainslie. Kirkwood. Kerr. Shown as Hamilton's Close (probable), *Prot. A.W.3, 21/8/1707.*

It was named from Fisher's land in the close, *Reg. 9/3/1743.* Thomas Fisher, merchant, built a great tenement on the south side of the Lawnmarket, *Prot. W.F.5, 5/12/1752,* apparently rebuilding a tenement owned formerly by Thos. Cant, of Sanct Geillie Grange, *Prot. A.W.7, 20/10/1725.* He was probably the Thos. Fisher who was sent by the Royal Burghs in 1595 on a fiscal mission to the French Court, *o.e.c. iii. 197.*

Fisher's Close seems to have been called Hamilton's Close, which contained Cant's land, at the foot of the close, on the west side, on the south side of the Landmarket, bounded on the north by Fisher's land, *Reg. 3/5/1861,* and to have been so named from Hamilton's alias Hopeton's land, on the north side of the Cowgatehead, at the foot of the Old Bank Close, opposite the Magdalen Chapel, and owned sometime by Mr. James Hamilton, *Reg. 3/5/1861.* It is described as a property on the west of Baillie's Close, owned at one time by Thomas Hope of Craighall, who rebuilt the house, and by the heirs of John Hamilton, minister in Edinburgh, *Prot. G.H.4, 4/8/1714.*

Kerr shows Fisher's Close as a thoroughfare to the Cowgate—the whole seems to have been called Hamilton's Close also.

There was property on the west side of Baillie's Close, owned in succession by heirs of John Wardlaw: Wm. Little: Thos. Hope of Craighall, who rebuilt the house: and the heirs of John Hamilton, minister in Edinburgh, *Prot. G.H.4, 4/8/1714.* Hamilton's alias Hopeton's land was at the foot of the Old Bank Close, opposite the Magdalen Chapel, owned sometime by Mr. Jas. Hamilton, *Reg. 3 and 21/5/1861.*

FISHWIVES' CAUSEY

The road followed by the fishwives from Musselburgh to Edinburgh, an old Roman road, *o.& n.e. iii. 165.* Torn up by the N.B. Railway *circa 1891, Irons 7,* who had tried to close it, March 1845, but had to preserve the right of way in a new road, *Baird 377.*

FLESHMARKET CLOSE

Edgar. Ainslie. Kirkwood. Kerr. Shown as Provost's Close, *o.& n.e. ii. 277.*

There were three closes leading down to the Fleshmarket. The west-most seems always to have been known as the Fleshmarket Close, but Lawson's Gazetteer, *quoted in o.& n.e. ii. 277,* speaks of it as formerly the Provost's Close, from the official residence of the provost. This lacks confirmation.

FORBES ROAD

On the ground of Sir John Stuart Forbes of Pitsligo, owner of the Greenhill estate, *o.e.c. x. 197.* Acquired by Sir Wm. Forbes, Bt., *m.t.c. 30/8/1809.* Acquired 1806, *o.e.c. x. 197.*

FORRES STREET

On the grounds of the Earl of Moray, one of whose seats is Darnaway Castle, near Forres, *D.1827, Lothian map 1825.*

FORREST ROAD
HILL

From Sir James Forrest of Comiston, Lord Provost, who was asleep when Queen Victoria first visited Edinburgh in 1842. Began during his provostship

FORSYTH CLOSE

Ainslie. Kirkwood. Strachan's Close, D.1809 map. p.w. 1780, p.91, and M.216 may refer to this close. Derivation unknown.

The name is derived from Alexander Forsyth, coachmaker, burgess of Edinburgh, who acquired land there, 12th May 1719, which was inherited by his son Alexander, coachmaker in London, *Can. Chart. 8/6/1744, 5/5/1813.* The tenement and lands were bounded by land of Gilbert Duncan, mason, on the west, and of the Earl of Winton on the east, *Can. Chart. 30/10/1838.* They were on the east side of Callender's Entry, *Can. Chart. 21/9/1768.* Agnes, sister of Alexander Forsyth, junior, married John Brodie, baker in London, and had a daughter Mary, who married Edward Meadows of Bishopsteignton, Devonshire, *Can. Chart. 16/4/1817.*

FORT PLACE
STREET

Back of Fort, *D.1827.* From vicinity to the Fort, which began to be built after 16/8/1780. Caled. Merc. *J.S./m.t.c. 19/10/1803.*

FORTH STREET

Compliment to the river. Built after 1801. *eec.j.s. 5/9/1801. Ainslie 1804.* South side seems only planned, Hart St. is marked North Forth St., *m.t.c. 6/11/1805.*

FOUNTAIN CLOSE

Edgar. Ainslie. Kirkwood. Kerr. Shown as Moubray's Close, *Prot. J.W.3, 16/1/1756,* Stevenson's, *Prot. W.F.4, 11/5/1750,* or David Stevenson's Close, *C.C.2141, 18/2/1568-9.* Bassendean's Close, *Prot. W.F.9, 17/5/1759,* Fullarton's Close, *Wilson, ii. 69,* John Barton's Close, *Reg. 4/2/1744.*

The name is derived from the fountain or street well, which apparently stood opposite to the close, until removed farther up to where the street is wider, above the 'John Knox' house. There was a tenement known as the Fountain a little above the Netherbow on the south side of the High Street, *Wilson, ii, 68: Prot. A.W.8, 30/5/1725.* The fountain well is mentioned in 1736, *t.b.76.* The Town Council gave instructions, 16th June 1813, that the well be moved farther up the street.

The close was also known as Moubray's Close, *formerly Moubray's, now the Fountain Close: Prot. A.W.7, 15/4/1723; J.W.3, 16/1/1756,* from the property of that Robert Moubray who gave his name to the adjacent Moubray's or Foulis' Close. Mr. Wm. Moubray is mentioned in connection with Moubray's Close near the Netherbow, *Prot.G.I.1, 10/9/1729.*

Yet another name was Stevenson's *Bassendean's, thereafter Stevenson's Close; Prot. W.F.4, 11/5/1750* or David Stevinson's Close, *C.C.2141, 18/2/1568-9; 2573, 17/11/1780,* or (South) Bassendean's Close, *Bassendean's, thereafter Stevenson's Close; Prot. W.F.4, 11/5/1750.* A tenement stood on the south side of the King's Street above the Netherbow, having David Stevinson's Close on the west, *C.C.2141, 18/2/1568-9; 2573, 17/11/1780.* James Bassendean owned a tenement at the Netherbow, afterwards the property of David Stevinson, *C.C. 2141, 18/2/1568-9; 2573, 17/11/1780.* There were three entrances to the front of the great building owned by John, Marquis of Tweeddale, namely (first) one by the close sometime of Alexr. Young, thereafter of James Brown, (second) by Sweit's Close, and a third by Bassendean's, thereafter Stevenson's Close, *W.F.4, 11/5/1750.*

The tenement mentioned above, called the Fountain, which sometime belonged to Nicol and Alexander, sons to Michael Bassendean, lay in Bassendean's Close, *Wilson, ii. 68.* The distinct alias is given, 'Bassenden's, now Fountain Close', *Reg. 25/7/1856.* There was also a property owned by Ronald and James Bassenden, just east of South Foulis' Close, *Prot. A.W.8, 8/5/1727.*

A close called Fullartoun's Close seems to be the same as the Fountain Close. It was on the south side of the High Street, a little above the Netherbow, and contained the tenement sometime owned by James Bassendean, *Prot. A.W.2, 4/4/1706.* Adam Fullartoun, bailie in 1561, built or rebuilt a house on the east side of Fountain Close in 1573, *see Wilson, ii. 69, for particulars of the house and Adam Fullartoun.*

And a final, but untraced name seems to belong to the close, John Barton's Close, which was immediately west of Mr. John Laing's, *i.e. Entrance to Tweeddale Court,* Close, *Reg. 4/2/1744.* Only once is it mentioned.

FOUNTAIN PLACE (WEST)

From the fountain which gave name to Fountainbridge.

FOUNTAINBRIDGE

Thomas Hodge, portioner in Portsburgh, feuar & brewer in Fountainbridge, died April 1715. His wife Isobel Paterson, died Feb. 1713. Buried West Kirkyard, near DeQuinay's tomb. East Fountainbridge marked "Glasgow Road", *Ainslie 1780.* Both East and West marked "Fountainbridge", *Ainslie 1804.* The Bridge was over the Dalry Burn, flowing from the Borough Loch by Lochrin to Coltbridge—not over the Canal which was made about 1816. Fountain House, now at Greig's Engineering Works, 28/30 Dundee St, for sale, built a few years ago, between Fountainbridge and Dalry. That fountain from which the street Fountainbridge obtains its name, a famous perennial one, is near, *eec.j.s. 12/3/1774.* Whence also Fountain Close, 113 Fountainbridge, *D.1827.* Fountainbridge, *Prot. 6/9/1758.* Bailie Alexr. Gray had houses and Brewery on land feued by Sir Alexr. Brand, in the Barony of Dalry, beside the ditch conveying the water from the Burrow Loch to the bridge at Bailie Gray's commonly called Lochrin bridge. The Town gave instructions for clearing the channel, *m.t.c. 1/8/1722 & 7/8/1722.*

FOUNTAIN COURT

D.1827. Ord. Surv. 1852. South side of Fountainbridge, *anon. map 1730.* The water supply in Edinburgh up to 1672, when the Comiston water supply was undertaken, was from draw (or pump) wells. The fountains shewn by Gordon were thus really wells. In the later editions of Gordon's map, the "wells", or fountains, are inserted.

FOUNTAINHALL ROAD

From the Estate of the Lauders of Fountainhall and Grange of St. Giles, on which it is built, *o.& n.e. iii. 49-54. See also St. G. 310 et al.*

FREDERICK STREET

D.1827. From Frederick, son of George II and father of George III. Built 1790.

G

GABRIEL'S ROAD

Shown as W. Register St., *D.1827.* Ran from where Register House now stands in a long slant N.W. to the Water of Leith, behind where is now Saxe Coburg Pl. Shewn unnamed, save at south east end, close to Register House, *Kirkwood composite map.* N.W. end named in large scale map, *p.w.1773. 15, 1780. 81 57.* N.W. end marked "Foot Road", *Ainslie, 1804,* its general course evident, also at Register House. It is still represented in the right of way past the Royal Bank, St. Andrew Sq., which is not always recognised.

The name has been wrongly derived from that of the murderer, given as Gabriel in "Peter's letters to his Kinsfolk", but really Robert Irvine. He was a probationer of the Church of Scotland, and employed as tutor to two little boys in a gentleman's family. Having fallen in love with a maid there, he was observed one day by his pupils to give her a kiss—which they mentioned innocently to their parents. Fearful of loss of reputation and failure in the ministry, he brooded over this, until he became mad with revenge. One Sabbath while strolling with his pupils on or near Gabriel's road, he cut their throats with a pocket knife. He was seized, red handed, condemned and executed. Gabriel was a former proprietor of Inverleith, *Walks in Edin. 179.* In the road was a tavern called Gabriels, *b.b.60.* Best known from Ambrose Tavern, scene of the "Noctes Ambrosianae", *m.t.c. 26/7/1780.* "Gabriel's Street", *m.t.c. 11/6/1788, 16/12/1812.* South east end, just west of Register office, named Gabriel Road, in Kincaid's map of 1784. Given in list D.1826-7, also previously up to present date.

GALLOWAY'S ENTRY

Kirkwood, D.1827, o.s. Shown as Galloway's Close, *Ainslie.*

John Galloway owned land on the north side of the Canongate, *Prot. J.H. Canong. 24/1/1683,* but the name seems more directly derived from Alexr. Galloway, stabler, who occupied the land of Wm. Ramsay there, *m.t.c. 10/10/1804.*

GARDNER'S CRESCENT

At Tobago St. *D.1825.* Gardner's Hall, *Ainslie 1804.* Crescent half built, *Lothian map 1825.* Begun 1824. Gardiners Hall mentioned 9/4/1792, *eec.j.s.* In P.W. 1780/81, *p.2.* Francis Garden of Gardenstone, fountainbridge, *D.180, 141.* Alexr. Gardner of Exchequer, west end, Fountainbridge. The Society of Gardeners, their part of Dalry, *v.r. 44.* Field on north side and next to high road leading from West Port to Coltbridge, opposite to Gardener's hall, immediately west of poorshouse lately erected, *e.a. 26/10/1764.*

GARSCUBE TERRACE

From west country estate of Campbell of Succoth, on whose ground it is built at Murrayfield, Nos. 2, 4, 6, 8. *D.1885.*

GAYFIELD SQUARE
PLACE
STREET

From Gayfield House, N.W. of the square, *D.1827.* House built circa 1763, for sale 22/2/1775, *eec.j.s.* Gayfield Sq., first named place, built circa 1800. *o.& n.e. iii. 161.* House still standing 1921, *Ainslie 1804.* Gayfield Sq., *m.t.c. 8/5/1811;* Gayfield Pl., *m.t.c. 26/8/1807.*

GEDDES CLOSE

Ainslie. Kerr. Kirkwood. Formerly Hutcheson's Close. Richardson's Close.

Named after the tenement of Robert Geddes of Scotstoun, surgeon, at the head of the almost adjoining Anchor Close, *Reg. 11/12/1740; Prot. W.F.9, 7/9/1759.*

Its former name, Hutcheson's Close, is given by Edgar, and Kirkwood gives Geddes', formerly Hutcheson's Close. Nothing seems to be known of Hutcheston. *From the fact that Cleghorn's Close, south side of the Grassmarket, was also known as Geddes' or Hutcheson's Close, taking the latter name from Wm. Hutcheson, Dean of Guild, 1712-13, and his son William, merchant, one is tempted to infer a connection between the Geddes and Hutcheson families, and an identity of ownership in the two closes.*

Geddes' Close, now Richardson's Close, *Prot. G.L.1, 10/9/1763,* owes the latter name to Richardson's land, *Prot. G.L.1, 23/11/1763,* within tenement of land of old owned by Wm. Fowler, thereafter by his son John, in Richardson's Close, *Prot. W.F.10, 10/5/1762.* Robert Richardson, W.S., built a tenement on land on the north side of the High Street, a little below the Cross, bought from John Lauder of Fountainhall, merchant. It was disponed by his son Robert to Wm. Livingstone, husband of his sister Margaret, glover, deacon convener of the skinners 1702, 1710-20, *Prot. W.F.6, 9/1/1754; A.W.8, 18/11/1726.* Richardson's land was between Swan's Close (shut up) and Geddes Close, *Reg. 23/10/1860.*

GEORGE IV BRIDGE

Begun 1827, finished 1836. "King George IV Bridge", *Imp. map 1866.* In honour of George IV, who visited Edinburgh 1822. The name was fixed by the Town Council as pleasing to the King, *eec.j.s. 1/10/1827.*

GEORGE SQUARE
SQUARE LANE

In 1761 James Brown, architect, bought 26 acres of ground, which had been refused by the Town Council for £1200. The Town offered him £2000—he refused less than £20,000, which beat them. Feuing began 1766—feuing plan 1769. Built on Ross Park, *Reek 325,* Brown, who built also Brown Sq. and Brown St., named the Square after his elder brother George Brown, Laird of Lindsay lands and Elliston. The family were sib to George Brown, Lord Coalstoun, of Coalston's Close, *o.& n.e. ii. 339. Kay 1.75.*

GEORGE STREET

Craig 1767. Ainslie 1780. Compliment to George III.

GIBB'S ENTRY

78 Nicolson St., *D.1827.* Entrance to the manse of the Rev. Adam Gibb, which stood in the lane, the lane being in front of the church. "For sale, Gib's entry, house which belonged to late Mr. Adam Gib, no. 169 East side of Nicolson St. 7/1/1792, *eec.j.s.* House possessed by Mr. Gib in South end of Nicolson St. for sale. *Edin. Advert. 29/12/1769.* Gib's entry to Simon Square, *D.1800, 218.* "Gibb's Kirk", *Denovan, 271.* Church on West side of road, *Ainslie 1780-1804.*

Adam Gibb, minister, Nicolson's St., *p.w.1780/81, 36, 1773, p.30.* Fraser St. (q.v.), *Reg. 25/2/1859,* now Gibb's Entry, *Reg. 14/2/1787.*

GIBSON TERRACE

From Thomas Gibson, iron fence maker, whose works were here.
Stayed in Bainfield House here.

GIBSON STREET

From Mr. Gibson of Messrs. Gibson & Walker, corn & flour merchants, 200 Bonnington Road, *j.r.*

GIFFORD PARK

On Mr. Gifford's property, *Kirkwood,* 72 Hope Park End, *D.1827. Ainslie 1780-1804.* Gifford Place, *Lothian Map 1825. p.w.1780/81, 76.*

GILES STREET

D.1827. "No doubt" name derived from property owned at one time in Leith by St. Giles Kirk, Edinburgh, *t.t.l. 208.* Hand credendum. On property owned by a family of Giles. Houses etc. to be sold, lying in Dubrow, owned by heirs of late John Giles, brewer: to be shewn by Alexr. Giles, brewer, *eec.j.s. 3/11/1774.* Wm. Giles Brewer, St. Giles St. (sic) *D.1800.* Mrs. Giles & Son, brewers. Lees quarter, *p.w. 1780/81, 107.* Mistakenly St. Giles St., *D.1800. D.1820, 57.* Wm. Giles, Brewer, Leith, *v.r. 33.* Mr. Giles, the brewer, *t.t.l. 152, m.t.c. 9/9/1829.*

GILLESPIE CRESCENT PLACE

From the "Carpenter Gothic". Gillespies Hospital, built on the site of the picturesque ancient mansion of Wrighthouses, demolished to make room for it by the Trustees of James Gillespie, snuff maker. Built 1806. Used as soldiers quarters during the War. New school acquired from School Board at Viewpark.

GILLESPIE STREET

On the ground of the Gillespie Trust.
See also Gillespie Road—Part II.

GILLSLAND ROAD ROAD SOUTH

On ground feued by Merchant Coy. Mr. John Clapperton, master of the coy. named his house there Gillsland, for personal reasons, and the name was extended to the road, and carried over to South Gillsland road by request of the Merchant Coy., March 1897.

GILMORE PLACE LANE PARK TERRACE

On property of Samuel Gilmore, ropemaker, *a.o.e.89. Ainslie 1804.* Gilmore Street. *Arnot 1816 map.* House and some ground owned by Mr. Gilmore for sale 20/11/1811, *eec.j.s.* Gilmore Place, *m.t.c. 13/9/1820.* Samuel Gilmore, ropemaker, Grassmarket. John Gilmore, West Bow, *p.w. 1780/81, 37.* Samuel Gilmore, ropemaker, Grassmarket house park house by Drumdryan, *D.1800. D.1827.* Gives Samuel Gilmore, ropemaker, 100 Grassmarket, and two others. Ainslie 1780 shows projected road, and Gilmour Sq., *Lothian Map 1825.* Gilmour Pl. and rope walk. Gilmore Pl., *m.t.c. 13/8/1823.* Arnot 1816 gives Gilmore St. instead of Place. So map 38.

GILMORE'S CLOSE

101 Grassmarket, *D.1827.* From Gilmore and Gibson, ropemakers, 103 Grassmarket. Old name seems to be Pringle's Cl. Samuel Gilmour, Ropemaker, junr. gave his name to the close, south side of Grassmarket, back of Meuse or Moses Well, *Reg. 1/4/1856.*

GILMOUR ROAD

On the property of Major Robert Gordon Gordon Gilmour of Liberton and Craigmillar.

GILMOUR STREET

Shown as Simon Sq., *D.1827.* Probably from Wm. Gilmour, Currier, etc., 106 Pleasance, *D.1827. Ainslie 1804.* Wm. G, Currier & Oliver G., tanner, tan yard at foot of Pleasance, *m.t.c. 8/11/1842.* Wm. G., currier, and Oliver G., tanner, sons of Wm. G. Senior, lately shoemaker in Fisherrow. Property in Pleasance, *Can. Chart. 8/11/1842.*

GLADSTONE COURT

Shown as Bowling Green Close. Magdalene Entry.

This seems to be a very modern name, appearing for the first time in the Postal Director for 1867-8, just after Gladstone Terrace, Meadows, made its appearance. The inference is inevitable, that it was so named in honour of the Rt. Hon W.E. Gladstone, M.P.

The old name was Entry to Bowling Green, *p.w. list 1779,* or Bowling Green Close, *Ainslie.* Edgar and Kerr show the bowling green, but without naming the close.

Its later name, Magdalene Entry, *D.1827,* or Entrance to Magdalene Asylum, *Kirkwood; o.s.,* is taken from the Magadalene Asylum, which was built on the bowling green. It is mentioned as the Asylum at the foot of the Shoemakers' Close, *m.t.c. 10/9/1800.* Before 1865 it was removed to Dalry.

GLADSTONE PLACE	In honour of Sir Jn. Gladstone of Fasque, *o.& n.e. iii. 251,* father of the Rt. Hon. Ewart Gladstone, statesman.
GLADSTONE TERRACE	From Wm. Ewart Gladstone.
GLEN STREET	From owner of the ground, banker in London, *McK.* Nisbet Glen Capt. R.N. part of lands of High Riggs called Crichens Gardens, q.v., *m.t.c. 28/2/1840.*
GLENCAIRN CRESCENT	See also Eglinton Crescent. West Coates was feued to the Countess of Glencairn in 1792. She died there 1801. (Lady Glencairn. Coats. *p.w.1780/81, 37.* She is mentioned as in Coats or Easter Whitehouse, *v.r.42.* Feued from Heriot's Hospital, April 1877.
GLENDEVON PLACE	After the birth place of the second chairman of the e.c.b.c. ld. who built it. *See also Glendevon Avenue etc.—Part II.*
GLENFINLAS STREET	From one of the estates of the Earl of Moray, on whose ground it is built.
GLENGYLE TERRACE	*D.M. 1869.* Built by W. & O. Macgregor, and named from the Land of the Macgregors, as also Gleneagle Lodge, Bruntsfield Place, the residence of one of them, *w.c. g.l.b.* Lands of Leven Lodge & Valleyfield, owned by Wm. & Duncan McGregor, on which Glengyle Ter. & Leven Ter. are to be built, *c.h.i. 100 Dec. 1867.*
GLENOGLE ROAD	Fancy, from the glen above Lochearnhead, *e.c.b.c.ld.*
GLENORCHY PLACE	From Lady Glenorchy's Chapel, built 1772, demolished and new church built in Roxburgh Pl. 1845. Her body, buried under the old church, transferred. United Free Lady Glenorchy's Church in Greenside, *Littlejohn App. 24.*
GLENORCHY TERRACE	On the lands of Duncan McLaren, Lord Provost, and M.P. for Edinburgh, whose family came from Glenorchy. (His biography by J.B. Mackie).
GLOUCESTER PLACE	*D.1827. Lothian Map 1825. Ainslie 1804.* A different plan as completed, but evidently only planned, "Gloster Place", *m.t.c. 11/8/1824.* *See also Gloucester Lane etc.—Part II.*
GLOVER STREET	Belonging to late Wm. Glover, wright in Leith, 16/1/1813, *eec.j.s. D.1827.*
GOLDENACRE TERRACE	From the lands of Goldenacres or riggs 1685, *o.& n.e. iii. 310.* Goldenriggs, 16 July 1658. *Antiq. 1906/7, 371.* From their fertility compared with Wardie Moss.
GORDON STREET	On property of Mr. Gordon of Halmyre, near West Linton, *j.r.*
GORGIE CRESCENT COTTAGES ROAD	Gorgie, near Edinburgh, *Prot. 9/1/1764.* Mentioned under Robert the Bruce and James IV, *j.r.*
GRANGE COURT LOAN ROAD TERRACE	From the Grange (or granary belonging to a religious house) of St. Giles, which had been granted to St. Giles Kirk before 1151. Acquired by Wm. Dick 1631, now owned by family of Dick Lauder, *St. G.*
GRANTON COTTAGES ROAD SQUARE HARBOUR	From the district. Grantaine Cragge, landing place of English party 1544, *o.& n.e. iii. 169.* Attempt by town to hinder the Duke of Buccleuch from making a harbour at Granton, *m.t.c. 6 & 13/9/1836.* *See also Granton Crescent etc.—Part II.*
GRANVILLE TERRACE	Probably from George 2nd Earl of Granville, Colonial Secretary 1868/76. Foreign Secretary 1880.

GRASSMARKET	Shown as Grasse-mercat 1681, *o.e.c. iii. 55.* Grassmarket St., *M.* The King's High St. called the Cowgate or Grassmarket, *Prot. 5/1/1759, W.F.8; 26/8/1747, W.F.2.*
GRAY STREET (SOUTH) **STREET (UPPER)**	John Gray of Gray & Hourson, shawl manufacturers, Nicolson St., resided at Grange Toll, *D.1827.* Probably same as Grayfield.
GREAT KING STREET	After King George III, to distinguish it from the earlier named King St. (now Little King St.), *Ainslie 1804. Lothian Map 1825.* Little King St., *Ord. Surv. 1852.* Both King St., *Ainslie 1804.* (Gt. King Street, *Lothian Map 1825*). King St., *m.t.c. 16/5/1810.* Great King St., *m.t.c. 19/4/1815.*
GREAT STUART STREET	From James Stuart, Earl of Moray, the Good Regent, half-brother to Queen Mary. Built on the Moray Estate after 1822. Stuart St., *Stark 1825-91.*
GREAT JUNCTION STREET	See Junction St., Great.
GREENBANK PLACE **CRESCENT** **TERRACE** **AVENUE**	From the lands of Greenbank, part of the general estate of Blackford. Alias Over Plewlands, *St. G. 385. o.e.c. x. 224.* Farm at Greenbank, *m.t.c. 7/9/1814.* *See also Greenbank Drive etc.*
GREENHILL GARDENS **PARK** **PLACE** **TERRACE**	From the Estate of Greenhill, *Kirkwood.* Lands for sale, 4/7/1785, *eec.j.s.* "Apply to Mr. Fairholm, George's Sq." Lands and village of Greenhill, *m.t.c. 9/5/1810.* Superiority of the Lands sold to Sir Wm. Forbes, *m.t.c. 30/11/1814.* John Gillespie of Greenhill, *Prot. 7/11/1750. Prot. G.H.6, 21/12/1750* for Adam Fairholme of Greenbank, villas and lands of Greenbank.
GREENSIDE **END** **LANE** **PLACE** **ROW**	Old name of the locality. James II granted Greenside in 1456 for tournaments etc., *i.w.c.h. vol.1, p.833, 13/8/1456, Anderson 10,* at one of which Queen Mary first saw the reckless Bothwell, *Wilson, i. 134.* Named from "the verdant and turfy slope that overhung the path to Leith. *o.& n.e. ii. 101.* A Carmelite Monastery and Leper Hospital stood there. The roode of Greenside, 27 Aug. 1534, *Wilson, ii. 266.* Greenside Well, *Kirkwood.* Greenside House stood in the Lover's Loan, *o.& n.e. iii. 159.* To be let Caled. Merc. 18/7/1785. Apply to Jas. Marshall, Shewn as Marshall's house, *Ainslie 1804. Shewn Ord. Surv. 1852.* Greenside Burn, nearly parallel to Leith Walk, East side, *Ainslie 1804. o.& n.e. iii. 205.* "The lands anciently called the Greenside", *Maitland 246, r.c.g. 11.* Name seems to occur 13/8/1456, *r.c.g. 20.* Lepers still in the Hospital Charter of Charles I, 23/10/1636, *r.c.g. 11.* Originally the name of a piece of the Town's "playground" (for tournaments, sports etc. in the hollow), granted to certain friars Carmelites. Name transferred to leper house, and extended to yards thereof, *m.t.c. 3/1/1827.* Greenside Row, *m.t.c. 9/2/1841.* G. burn, 11/10/1842. Temple lands, wester end of Greinsyde, *Prot. 13/10/1528.* The Boog and piece of arable ground called Greensyde lying between Calton Crags on the east, and the highway leading from Caldtoun to Leith on the west, *m.t.c. 17/10/1707.* Nov. 1633, Mr. John Hairt, M.D. infested in half of tenement of land beside the Greenside holden of the good Town as patrons of the Hospital founded at Leith Wynd foot gratis, as heir to umq. Issobell Cutlate his guid dame; and 6 Nov. 1633 in the other half as oye to umq. John Hairt in Canongate, *m.t.c.*
GREYFRIARS PLACE	Beside Greyfriars church and Churchyard. Monastery founded by James I, 1430, *Anderson 8.*
GRINDLAY STREET	On property bequeathed by Mr. Grindlay, being the Orchardfield Estate, in trust, under the Merchant Coy. "Mr. Grinlay's property", *Ainslie 1804.*

GROVE STREET	From the Grove, property of Mr. Bonar, *Ainslie 1804*. Property
PLACE	formerly Brandfield, q.v. Villa called The Grove, 10/9/1796, *eec.j.s.*
TERRACE	*D.1800, 96*. Thomas Bonar, mcht. Grove St. and house, *D.1827.*
	Lothian Map 1825. Half of North Grove St. (now Grove St.) built,
	Grove Square and South Grove St. planned, never executed.

GULLAN'S CLOSE

Shown as Gillon's Close, *o.s.; Kerr*. Goolen's Close, *p.w. list 1779*. Goolan's Close, *Ainslie*. Gullan's Close, *Kirkwood*. Gillilan's Close, *Brown and Watson's map, 1793*. Haliburton's Close, *Reg. 11/7/1856*. Cant's Close, *Prot. A.W.2, 19/6/1705*.

A stable in Haliburton's Close, on the south side of the Canongatehead, was occupied by James Gollen, stabler, on the west of Robert Gibb's land, *Prot G.L.1, 17/10/1763*. James Dempster, weaver in Haliburton's Close, south side of Canongatehead, owned a tannery, etc., in the close, which he disponed to Robert Walker, tanner, 10th May 1740: he in turn to Archibald Chessils, wright. The stable, etc., were occupied by James Guilland, *Prot. W.F.7, 5/4/1756; G.L.1, 17/10/1763*. James Gillion was in Haliburton's Close, Canongatehead, *Prot. G.I.1, 10/9/1731*. This seems to indicate that Dempster's Close was another name for Gullan's Close. Haliburton's is given as a clear alias, 'now Gullan's Close, Canongatehead', *Reg. 11/7/1856*. It is very difficult to follow the references to Haliburton's Close, but we find that Andrew, son to Andrew Haliburton, owned property on the east side of St. Mary's Wynd; *Prot. A.W.2, 18/5/1705;* that Haliburton's or Cant's Close was on the south side of the High Street below the Netherbow, *Prot. A.W.2, 19/6/1705. It must be remembered that the south side of the Canongate, down to St. John's Street, was reckoned as under the burgh of Edinburgh, and all transfers of property are recorded in the Edinburgh protocols, not in those of the Canongate,* but a tenement stood between Cant's Close on the west and Haliburton's on the east, *Prot. A.W.6, 22/5/1722*, making them clearly distinct. A tenement on the east side of Haliburton's Close was bounded on the east by lands of Robert Gibb, *Prot. W.F.1, 14/12/1744*, from whom Gibb's Close takes its name: Gibb's yard being at the foot of Haliburton's Close, *Prot. W.F.5, 15/12/1752*. There was a bend, or break, in the middle of the close, *Prot. J.W.4, 5/10/1757*.

A tenement stood on the south of the Canongate, near the head thereof, built by Robert Haliburton and owned by Sir John, his brother, *Prot. G.L.1, 22/3/1764*. James Boyd, stabler, or inn-keeper, Canongatehead, owned property on the West side of Haliburton's Close, sometime occupied by James Gullan, stabler, *Reg. 7/12/1767*. These notes prove the identity of the closes and origin of the names. Cant's Close, as an alias, has been mentioned above, and occurs elsewhere, *Prot. G.H.6, 11/5/1722*. The tenement of J. Monteith in St. Mary's Wynd was bounded on the east by Cant's Close, but no indication given of any special Cant, *there seems to be at least five Cant's Closes, and three Haliburton's!* Evidently two closes shared one bewildering name.

GUTHRIE STREET

To honour Rev. Thomas Guthrie, D.D. Disruption leader and philanthropist, who died 24 Feb. 1875, *o.& n.e. ii. 258*. Built where Chambers St. was made by "Improvement" Scheme.

H

HADDINGTON PLACE

D.1827. Beside the "proposed new road to Haddington", *Ainslie 1804*. The London Road was first named Haddington Road, hence Haddington Pl., *j.r.*

HADDINGTON'S ENTRY	See Reid's Close.
HADDON'S COURT	70 Nicolson St., *D.1827.* Haddow's Ct., *Littlejohn App. 46.* Haddon's Court, 112 Nicolson St., *D.1832.*
HAILES STREET	On property of the Gillespie Trust, the founder whereof worked the Spylaw snuff mill on the estate of Hailes, or Colintoun. Hailes alias Colingtoun, *Reg. 10/1/1747.*
HALLHEAD ROAD	On the lands of Major Robt. G. Gordon Gilmour, eldest son of Henry Wolrige Gordon of Hallhead and Esslemont, Aberdeenshire.
HALMYRE STREET	On the property of Mr. Gordon of Halmyre, near West Linton, *j.r.* See Gordon St.
HAMMERMEN'S CLOSE	*Ainslie. Kirkwood, D.1827.*
	Just east of the Magdalen Chapel, *Reg. 3/7/1858.* So called from the Guild of the Hammermen, owners and occupiers of the Magdalen Chapel. The Hammermen's Court behind, *Reg. 19/5/1863.* The close *p.w. 1773, p.39; 1780, p.17* and the Hammermen's land *p.w. 1780, p.54* are mentioned by Peter Williamson, *see o.e.c. vol. viii. for full account of the Hammermen and the Chapel.*
HAMILTON CRESCENT STREET	From builder, *j.r.*, in Great Junction St., Leith. *See also Hamilton Wynd—Part II.*
HAMILTON PLACE	*D.1827.* Mrs. Dr. Hamilton. Hamilton Pl, *D.1800, 80.* Two self-contained houses were the first built there; one was occupied by Mrs. Hamilton. Both were used for the Hamilton Place Academy. *Testa.* Thomas Ross, 14 Saxe Coburg Pl., daughter of the headmaster, Dr.
HAMILTON TERRACE	After the Marquis of Abercorn, superior. *See also Hamilton Drive etc.—Part II.*
HAMPTON PLACE TERRACE	After Hampton Court, royal residence, with Osborne Ter., Kew Ter., adjacent streets.
HANOVER STREET	*Circa 1786.* From the house of Hanover, who came to the British throne in George I. After the War, it was foolishly proposed to change so German a name—but vainly, although "Handover" St. was suggested as improvement, *McK.* Corner House of Hanover St. now built, *m.t.c. 17/10/1781.*
HARDWELL CLOSE	*p.w.1779, p.94.* From the nature of the water, *McK.* Possibly corruption of "Yard well", which occurs in protocols anent breweries etc. *e.g. Prot. W.F.7, 19/4/1756.* Hard-well Close, *p.w.1779, p.94.*
HARRISON ROAD LANE	From Sir George Harrison, Lord Provost 1882-1885, M.P. 1885, *D.M. 1884.* To whom also a memorial arch erected at entrance to Blackford Hill Sept. 1888. *See also Harrison Gardens, Place.*
HARTINGTON GARDENS PLACE	From Lord Hartington, later Duke of Devonshire, a prominent Liberal statesman, when the streets were built. Left the party on Gladstone's Home Rule Bill, *Irish.*
HASTIE'S CLOSE	*Edgar. Ainslie. Kirkwood. Kerr.* Libberton's or Knowis' Close, *Reg. 11/1/1860.*
	Now ending in a court, formerly a thoroughfare. It is mentioned in protocol of 1725, *Prot. A.W.7, 17/7/1725.* Several persons of the name are mentioned in the protocols, as connected with the close: William Hastie, writer, possessed two houses there, *Prot. J.W.7, 3/9/1765.* William Hastie, 'Gemmarius', was on the east side of the College Wynd, *Prot. W.F.2, 3/11/1747.* Robert Hastie, merchant in Glasgow, thereafter in Virginia, disponed property in Hastie's Close

to his son, Robert, millwright in Manchester, formerly in Glasgow, on 1st August 1793, *Reg. 11/1/1860.* Hastie's Brewery stood east of College Wynd, *Reg. 21/11/1863.*

The name Libberton's or Knowis Close, belongs to the close immediately west of Happerlaw's *(sic)* Close, *Reg. 11/1/1860.* There were lands on the south side of the Kowgait, bounded by lands of Nowie Brusse on the east: of John Knowis and Rapperlaw's Wynd on the west: the transe of the Kirk of Field on the south: the highway (the Cowgate) on the north, *c.c. 3011, 24/5/1589.* John Knowis was a baxter, *c.c. 3031, 10/11/1589.* In Libberton's or Knowis Close were land of umquhyle Jas. Libberton and John Knowis. Elizabeth Knows was wife to Thomas Inglis, junior.

HATTON PLACE	From Hatton or Haltoun, property owned by family of Lawdre or Lauder owners of lands of Bruntsfield till 1603, *o.e.c. iii. 201. o.e.c. x. 20.*
HAUGH STREET	From Deanhaugh q.v. *D.1827.*
HAWKHILL AVENUE	Shewn on anon. map, circa 1730. "Halkhill", Birrel's Diary 1593, *Wilson 229.* "A little Knoll, called the Halke-Hill", *Irons 1.277.* Evidently connected with Hawkfield, Restalrig Road, *v.r.31.*
HAWTHORN TERRACE	One tree still there 1920. Probably same as following.
HAWTHORN BANK BUILDINGS	Near Belford Road. From the tree where the Covenanters set up the standard. Still standing 1904. *Stewart Chambers, o.e.b. i. 114.*
HAWTHORNVALE	Hawthornville, Whale Brae, Newhaven, *D.1827. m.t.c. 16/6/1819.*
HAYMARKET **TERRACE**	Formerly Hayweights, *o.e.c. ii. 143.* No name, *Lothian Map 1825,* but in D.1827, Haymarket opposite South Coats, *m.t.c. 17/7/1816.* Hay Weights at west end of Maitland St., *m.t.c. 14/1/1834.*
HAZELBANK TERRACE	Fancy. After the tree, *e.c.b.c.ld.*
HENDERLAND ROAD	From Alexr. Murray of Murrayfield. Lord Henderland. Died 1796, *o.& n.e. ii. 255. iii. 104.* Superior.
HENDERSON GARDENS **STREET**	From Dr. Henderson, who initiated the "improvement" scheme in Leith, *e.s.s. 261. Provost 1875 & 1884.*
HENDERSON ROW **PLACE**	From Alexr. Henderson of Press. Lord Provost 1823/4, *o.& n.e. iii.83.* Founder of National Bank of Scotland and Union Insurance Coy. *Anderson 377.* Chambers inscribes his "Walks in Edinburgh" to him, *p.266.* Died 1827. "Banker. Warriston House", *D.1827.*
HENRY PLACE **STREET**	Shown as Hendry St., *D.1827.* Not in Lothian Map, *Ord. Surv. 1852. In Lothian's map 1829.* Henry Watson, property owned in St. Leonards Vennal, *m.t.c. 30/6/1824*
HERIOT BRIDGE **MOUNT** **PLACE** **ROW** **HERIOT HILL TERRACE**	Original approach to Heriot's Hospital by a long slope, extending out into the Grassmarket, *so in Edgar 1742 & 1765.* Heriot's Work Bridge. Heriot buildings and place from vicinity to Heriot's Hospital which is named from George Heriot, goldsmith to Anne of Denmark. Queen of James VI, who left funds in trust for its erection and endowment. See "Fortunes of Nigel". Heriot's Works, *p.w. 1780/81, 12.* Hospital built 1628-1650. Heriot Mount (St. Leonards), Heriot Row (New Town). Heriothill Terrace (Bellevue) all on property of the Heriot Trust. Heriot Row, *m.t.c. 10/8/1803.*
HERMAND CRESCENT **STREET** **TERRACE**	Built of stone from the Hermand quarries, Hermand Estate, near West Calder, *Terrace, D.1891/92.*

**HERMITAGE DRIVE
GARDENS
TERRACE**

From the Hermitage of Braid so called from its sequestered position, built circa 1780. Owned by Gordon of Cluny, *o.& n.e. iii. 41.* Maitland derives it from a hermit's cell originally at that place, *St. Matthews 33.*

**HERMITAGE PARK
PLACE**

From the old house of that name. "A square to be called Hermitage Sq.", 4/1/1808, *eec.j.s. D.1827.* For sale Mansion house etc. of Hermitage, near Leith, *e.a. 8/4/1765.* Lady Fyfe resident there 1800-20.

HERMITAGE PLACE

From the traditional hermit's cave occupied by St. Bernard in the dean, *o.& n.e. iii. p.75-79.*
Renamed Raeburn Street—See Part II.

HERON'S COURT

Kerr. o.s. D.1827.

Maitland gives Heron's Close, but this must refer to some unidentified close elsewhere, judging by dates. It is shown, unnamed, by Edgar and Ainslie. It takes its name from Patrick Heron, of the family of Heron of Heron, formerly host of the Black Bull Inn, Glasgow, who in 1787 bought the Museum Hall from the Society of Antiquaries of Scotland. It had been built by Alexr. Lockhart, Lord Covington, about 1741, and occupied by him till he sold it in 1766 to Col. Charles Campbell, H.E.I.C.S., of Banbreck, who in turn sold it in 1784 to the Rt. Hon. David Steuart Erskine, Earl of Buchan, to be the Hall of the recently formed Society of Antiquaries of Scotland. Three years later, in 1787, financial straits compelled them to dispose of it to Patrick Heron, who altered it, making it suitable for use as the British Inn. He died, probably there or thereabouts, 1803. The house seems to have been demolished about 1830. It was known as 'Lockhart's House' from its first owner, *Patrick Heron's will,* or the Museum, *p.w. list 1783; Kincaid's map 1784,* or the 'Antiquarian Society's Hall', *see Soc. Ant. S. vol. xiv., 13th February 1911.*

Deacon Brodie was employed for wright's work by Patrick Heron, *see Soc. Ant. S. vol. xiv., 13th February 1911.*

HIGH RIGGS

The old house of the Lawsons on the property demolished 1877, *o.& n.e. ii. 223.* Cultivated land, lying high, Heriot's Hospital built on part. "Lands of Highriggs or Headriggs", *m.t.c. 6/5/1818, 2/6/1824.* Lands of Hieriggs, *Prot. 17/6/1528.* From its position. A charter of 1387 granted the lands of Dalry called Heyriggs to Sir John Towrs Kt. *Charter House Inventory vol. 5, p.432.*

**HIGH SCHOOL WYND
YARDS**

From the Old High School, built 1578, rebuilt 1778. Deserted 1829. Then Surgical Hospital—Fever Hospital—Engineering Laboratory for the University, later, geographical class rooms. Wynd, *M.,* High School Wynd, *Prot. 24/10/1711. a.w.4.* High School Yards named Surgeon St. as leading to Surgeon Square, *Knox map 1824.*

HIGH STREET

Anciently "Regia via", or "Vicus regius", *trad.* Allan Ramsay calls it "the street", *Maitland, p.7.* "Market St" and p.215 "King's St."

**HILL PLACE
SQUARE**

From Peter Hill, (bookseller, south side of High St. opposite the Cross, *D.1800)* who owned the property, *Stark 1825, 249.* To feu, apply to Mr. Hill, bookseller, 5/3/1808, *eec.j.s.* Peter Hill petitions for water pipe to serve his feuars in Hill Place, *m.t.c. 14/6/1809.* Partner of Wm. Creech, Burns' publisher.

HILL STREET

Ainslie 1804. Unnamed in unbuilt plan of 1780. Queen's Mews and George's Mews, *Craig 1767.* James Hill, mason, had a feu in Queen St. west of Castle St., *m.t.c. 12/5/1790.* Called part of Thistle St. *m.t.c. 15/8/1792.* Hill's St., *D.1800, 153.* Originally Thistle St. ran the whole length, but James Hill, mason, having feued part of the section between Frederick and Castle Streets, for a house for Robert

Belshes of Green Yeards Jan. 1788, the street took his name—"now called Hill St.", *m.t.c. 2/1/1799.*

HILLEND PLACE

Descriptive.

HILLSIDE CRESCENT
STREET

On slope of Calton Hill. Old Hillside House, *Kirkwood.* "Hillside, Leith Walk", *p.w. 1780/81, 83.* House to let. Caled. Merc. 7/3/1785, *j.s. D.1827.* Planned. *Lothian Map 1825.* Hillside owned by Mr. Alexr. Allen, *m.t.c. 17/12/1806.* Harts Knows or Hillside, *m.t.c. 3/1/1827, 11/10/1842.*

HOLLYBANK TERRACE

Fancy. From the Holly tree, *e.c.b.c.ld.*

HOLYROOD ABBEY
HOUSE
PALACE
ROAD

From the Monastery of the Holyrood or cross, of the crag—"Monasterium sanctae crucis de Crag", *Wilson, i. 4.* Named from St. Margaret's Black Rood by her son David I, founder of the Abbey 1128, *Wilson, i. 4.5.* (m.b.x. doubts this—the Black Rood probably kept in the Castle). Other attribute it to the rood which saved David I from the Stag.

Holyrood Road was the new name given to the south back of the Canongate in the belief that change of label improves wine. Early 20th century.

HOME STREET

D.1827. Kirkwood shews ground owned by J. Horne Rigg. *Lothian Map 1825.* Hume Rigg of Morton, *a.o.e. 64.* "James Home Rigg of Drumdryan and part of Crichen's gardens" 1814, *v.r. 45.* Home St. on lands of Jas. Home Rigg, of Downfield & Morton, *Reg. 12/11/1857.*

HOPE STREET

m.t.c. 12/10/1803. Marg. A street near Charlotte Square, named Hope St. A letter was read from Mr. Andrew MacWhinnie, writer to James Jackson, South Bridge, city treasurer, telling of a letter from Mrs. Maxwell, senior, of Carriden, who was living in a nameless street running from west end of Princes St. to west row of Charlotte Square, and found it very awkward in many ways that the street lacked a name. The magistrates and Council agreed that the street be named Hope St. probably from Charles Hope of Granton, Lord Advocate and Lord President, M.P. for the city 4/1/1804.

HOPE'S COURT

Ainslie, Kirkwood, and Kerr give Close. Shown as Dr. Hope's Close, Netherbow, *D.1800, 133.*

The Honble. Mr. (John) Baron Maul, one of the Barons of the Court of Exchequer in Scotland, acquired property beside Trunk's Close from Archibald Hope, *Prot. J.W.7, 2/7/1766. Various members of the Hope family are mentioned, but no Dr. Hope.* Mrs. Hope occupied the house in Bryson's Close acquired by John Johnston from Andrew Bryson, *Reg. 20/8/1767.*

HOPE TERRACE

Near to Whitehouse Loan. The trustees of Mrs. Ann Oliphant (relict of Francis Grant of Kilgraston), owner of lands of Whitehouse, disponed the whole (1867) to Lt. Genl. Sir Jas. Hope Grant, etc., *o.e.c. x. 52.*

HOPE PARK CRESCENT
SQUARE
TERRACE

The Meadows were known as Hope Park, *anon. map circa 1730. Ainslie 1780 & 1804. Lothian Map 1825,* as having been leased in 1722 to Thomas Hope of Rankeillor, for the purpose of being drained, *o.e.c. x. 258.* The Chapel of Ease giving its name to Chapel St. is called "Hope Park Chapel", *St. C. 174.* Hope Park, name of the mansion about 1770, *St. G. 83.* Hope's Feu, part of St. Leonards, whereon are built Clerk St., Rankeillor St. and Montague St, *St. L. 45.* Sir Thomas Hope, 8th Baronet, son to Sir Alexr. Hope of Rankeillour, (who was second son to Sir John, 2nd Baronet) was a great agricultural improver, who drained and laid out the Meadows—Hope

Park. He married Margaret, daughter of Ninian Lowis of Merchiston, and died 1771. The Hopes of Rankeillour, those of Luffness, and the Earl of Hopetoun (family name Hope) are descended from John de Hope, see Edward Hope's Close. In Valuation Roll 1872/3, Capt. Henry W. Hope of Rankeillour, address Luffness, Dunbar, *see Burke.* Sir Archibald Hope of Rankeillour, senator of College of Justice, father of Thomas H., advocate, by Lady Margaret, daughter of Mr. James Lowis of Merchiston, *Prot. 17/8/1705, a.w.2.*

The tack of the Burrowloch nearly expiring, the Town Council considered 16 Aug. 1721 how best to set it in tack or feu. On 13 June, 1722 a committee was appointed, with powers to set in tack. On 1 Aug 1722 they instructed the ditch conveying the water from the loch to Bailie Grays, comonly called Lochrin bridge, to be cleared out. On 7 Sept. 1722 a tack was granted to Thos. Hope for 57 years,(to Janet Hewison, relict of John Carmichael, brewer and Andrew, son to deceased Andrew Gardner, brewer). The bounds of the Burrowloch or Meadow were divided (in the paroch of St. Cuthbert's) the King's High St. (Buccleuch St. and Causeyside) on the E. Bruntsfield Links on the S. Lands of Pat. Makdowgall of Crichan, the yards called Lauriston yards and the arable land of George Heriot's Hosp.

HOPES OF RANKEILOR

22/6/1681. Mr. Archd. Hop of Rankeilor, advocate, made burgess and guild brother by right of his umq. fr. Sir John Hope of Craighall, burgess and guild brother, gratis. He was 2nd son of Sir John, 2nd Bart (S. of Sir Thos. 1st Bart by Elizb. daughter of John Bonnet of Wallyford, E. Lothian. Advocate 30/6/1664. Lord Rankeillour (Ld. of Session) at Revolution 1689. Knighted by Wm. III. Born 9/9/1639. Died 10/10/1706. His 2nd son Thomas, succeeded to the baronetcy 5/6/1766, as 8th Bart. Born 5/7/1701, died 17/4/1776. Drained the Meadows. His brother Chas. had son, John, Prof. of Botany. Married Juliana Stevenson.

HOPETOUN COURT

Fountainbridge, from Port Hopetoun. Union Canal.
Port Hopetoun now occupied by Lothian House.

HORSE WYND

J.H. Canong. Prot. 16/2/1705. From Royal Stables, which were there at the time of Darnley's murder, *o.& n.e. ii. 27.* From proximity to Royal Stables, *o.e.c. i. 18, Ainslie 1780, 1804.* King's Stables formerly there, *M.154, c.i.*

HOWE STREET

From Lord Howe, victor at Ushant. June 1794, *D.1827.* How St., *Ainslie 1804, m.t.c. 12/9/1804, 10/2/1808.*

HUGH MILLER PLACE

From the celebrated geologist, author and Disruption leader, *e.c.b.c.ld.*

HUNTER SQUARE

From Sir James Hunter Blair, M.P. 1781. Lord Provost 1784. His own name Hunter, he married and took the name of Miss Blair of Dunskey. He carried out the scheme of the South Bridge, whence Hunter Sq. and Blair St. commemorate him. He died 1787, *Anderson 264.* Ainslie 1780 shows Blair St., Ainslie 1804 shows Hunter's Sq.

HUNTER'S CLOSE

131 Grassmarket. *D.1827 now 79.* At the entrance of which Porteous was hanged in 1736, *Wilson 1.145. ii. 167. o.& n.e. ii. 232. D.1800-200.* Alias Campbell's Close, *trad. 1.151.* Alexr. Hunter, physician in York, owned land there at one time, *Reg. 9/4/1856.*

HYNDFORD'S CLOSE

Edgar. Ainslie. Kirkwood. Kerr. Shown as Collingtoun's Close, *Prot. G.H.12, 7/6/1737;* Charteris' Close, *G.I.1, 27/2/1731.*

Named from the mansion of the Earl of Hyndford which stood in the close, *Wilson, ii. 65; o.& n.e. i. 275.* He acquired part of the ground from the daughters of Andrew Ainslie, *Prot. J.W.4, 23/5/1758.* James, Earl of Hyndford, acquired also land on the south side of the High

Street, on the east side of Gray's Close, *Prot. G.H.4, 20/12/1710.*

Its older name, Collingtoun's Close, now Hyndford's Close, *Prot. G.I.2, 5/2/1733; J.W.5, 9/5/1759,* was derived from the yard owned by Sir James Foulis of Colinton, and later by the Earl of Hyndford, which lay in the close, immediately north of Elphinson Court, *Prot. J.W.6, 28/10/1763.* This close was not a thoroughfare. It bore the name also of Charteris' Close, which is described, *Prot. G.I.2, 27/2/1731; W.F.11, 28/10/1762,* as the first close west of Purvis' or Foulis' Close, from the tenement therein, owned of old by John Charteris, Burgess of Edinburgh, *Prot. W.F.10, 21/4/1762; A.W.3, 22/7/1710.*

I

INCHVIEW TERRACE	From possessing a view of Inch Keith.
INDIA BUILDINGS	Part of Victoria St., built at the date of Queen Victoria becoming Empress of India.
INDIA STREET **PLACE**	*D.1827.* Planned, as if built, *Ainslie 1804. Unfinished Kirkwood 1817.* India Pl. first named Athole St. (Stockbridge 9). India St., *m.t.c. 2/9/1818.*

See India Buildings, no doubt derived from same source.

INDUSTRIAL ROAD	From the Industrial Building Coy., which built all the terraces here, *j.r.*
INFIRMARY STREET	From the Old Infirmary, achieved by Provost Drummond, opened 1741, *Ainslie 1804,* but Jamaica St. 1780. Unnamed in Edgar. *D.1800 189.* "Now called Infirmary Street", *m.t.c. 18/11/1807.*
INGLIS COURT	West Port No. 15, *D.1827.* From Hugh Inglis, printer, West Port, *D.1799 and D.1806.* John Inglis, son to Thos. Inglis, pewtherer, infested as his heir in tent. of land, brewery, yard, etc., in Pocketsleive, *m.t.c. 21/11/1731.* Hugh I. Barber, Portsburgh, *D.1780-81.*
INVERLEITH AVENUE **GARDENS** **PLACE** **ROW** **TERRACE**	The original name of the Water of Leith, was Leith, which gave the name of Inverleith to the port and lands at its mouth. The port became "Leith", the river the Water of Leith, but the lands retain the old name.
	Name Inverleith Terraced fixed 6/3/1800, *eec.j.s.*
IONA STREET	Formerly Falshaw St. From the neighbouring Lorne St., and the connection of Iona with the Argyll family.
IVY TERRACE	Fancy, from the plant, *e.c.b.c.ld.*

J

JACK'S CLOSES **LITTLE** **BIG**	Known as Little Jack's Close. Jack's Court, *Ainslie. Kirkwood.* Jack's Close, *Kerr.*
	This close was known formerly as Mausie Smith's Close, *m.t.c. 28/7/1784.* Massia or Mausey Smith was wife of Patrick Heart, and they owned another tenement, on the south side of the Canongate, a little above the 'Canon Cross'. The subjects on the east side of New Street, sold by Dr. Thomas Young to Henry Home, Lord Kaims, were bounded on the east by subjects belonging to the heirs of John Jack and the close called Mausey Smith's Close or Jack's Close *Can. Chart. 4, 28/7/1784,* (i.e. Little Jack's Close; the 'Big' and 'Little' refer to the width of the entrances).
	Mausie Smith seems to have owned the property in her own right.

The two closes take their names from Jack's land, which lies between them; it was built by Robert Jack, slater, and finsihed after his death by his brother John, also a slater. Robert had acquired part of the property from John Riddle, M.D., and his wife Jean Livingstone, on 10th May 1738, *Can. Chart. 16/12/1818,* and partly from Robert Tod, senior, merchant in Edinburgh, *Can. Chart. 2/1/1799.* John Jack was a captain, presumably of the Trained Bands, but I have failed to trace this, a slater by trade, *Prot. W.F.10, 5/12/1761,* a bailie of the Canongate, with property there and also in Edinburgh; he died before 27th July 1753, leaving two sisters, namely Christian, wife of Wm. Horsburgh of Athlone by whom she had a son William, and Isobel, wife of James Gibson, and mother of James Gibson, younger, surgeon, *Prot. W.F.6, 27/7/1753.*

Elizabeth Home, wife of John Jack, daughter of Wm. Home of Sharplaw, and sister of Robert Home, *Can. Chart. 11/6/1774,* survived her husband, being life-rented in part of the property, but they seem to have had no family, for his two nephews mentioned above were his ultimate heirs, *Prot. G.L.1, 17/10/1763.* Jack's land was occupied by David Hume from 1753 to 1762, *trad. 56.*

There are frequent references in the protocols to John Jack, tiler or sclater, and his scattered properties. He—Bailie John Jack—had a half-seat in the Tron Kirk in 1745, *Tron Kirk, 175.* The only derivation hitherto hazarded of the name of the closes seems to be that of Grant—that it came 'doubtless from some forgotten citizen or speculative builder', *o.& n.e. ii. 19.* From this oblivion he is now rescued.

Big Jack's Close was known also as Jack's Close *Ainslie,* or East Jack's Close, *D.1799.*

JACKSON'S CLOSE

John Jackson owned property in the close, *Prot. J.W.2, 3/8/1751.* Robert Jackson of Loch-houses owned property close by, between the two Fleshmarket gates, *Prot. W.F.8, 30/10/1758.* John Jackson acquired a tenement in Jackson's Close from Edward Dougal, which was inherited by his son John, and later by his grandson, also John, who acquired additional property there, *Prot. W.F.7, 3/7/1755.* A tenement on the west side of the close, owned formerly by John Jackson, was owned later by his children, Mr. John, Rachel, Jannet, Hellen, and Elizabeth, *Prot. W.F.1, 13/8/1746,* and a family of Jacksons, two sisters and a brother, sold some property at the head of the close to the town in 1893.

JACOB'S LAND

53 North Back of Canongate. Probably from Jacob's ladder, the steep paths connecting the Regent Road and the N.B. Canongate; a frequent name for such paths, *Gen. xxviii, 12.*
Jacob's Land not a street. North back of Canongate now Calton Road.

JAMAICA STREET

D.1827. Ainslie 1804, m.t.c. 1/5/1810.

There was also a Jamaica St., Tobago St., *D.1827. Lothian Map 1825,* and in Ainslie 1780 the name is applied to North College and Infirmary Streets.

JAMES BAYNE'S CLOSE

A little close on the east side of Blackfriars' Wynd, behind Bayne's or Bain's land, *Prot. W.F.2, 3/4/1747,* owned by James Bayne, wright, *Prot. J.W.1, 11/3/1747.* Edgar and Ainslie show a recess, or opening about the middle of Blackfriars' Wynd, which may be this close.

JAMES' COURT

Also known as Brownhill's Court.

This court was built, 1725-27, by James Brownhill, wright, from whom it took its name, *Chambers, i. 219; o.e.c. iii. 247.* He also built and owned Brownhill's Land, about the middle of Blackfriars' Wynd,

Prot. J.W.7, 22/3/1765. He died before 23rd January 1729, leaving his affairs in disorder, and trustees on his estate had to be appointed in the interest of his creditors, *Prot. G.I.1, 23/1/1729.* The court was known also as Brownhill's Court, *Prot. J.W.1, 17/1/1745; W.F.10, 4/12/1761.*

He left two sisters, his heirs-general, namely, Janet who married **Bryan Betty**, Collector of Excise as Inverness, and Issobell who married **Robert Finlay**, pewterer in Leith; their son James was tenant in Coats, *Prot. W.F.9, 16/5/1760.* Provision was made in James Brownhill's will for his relict Janet Drummond, of a liferent of his estate, *Prot. G.I.1, 23/1/1729, Edgar. Ainslie. Kirkwood. Kerr.*
For details of various entrances to James Court and other closes here see o.e.c. vol.xii, p.11.

JAMES STREET	From John James Hamilton, Marquis of Abercorn, superior. His own naming 1824, *Baird 360.*
JAMESON PLACE	From the celebrated Dr. Jameson, whose "Raid" resulted in the South African War.
JANE STREET	It bore the name in 1869, when George Sinclair's works were in Great Junction St. It was named from the wife of James Galloway, nephew and succeeder of Peter McCraw, superior of the ground, *D.1869.*
JEFFREY STREET	A poor tribute to Francis Jeffrey, *o.& n.e. 1.290. m.h.c. 111.* Lord Jeffrey, one of the leaders of the Whig party, Lord Advocate 1830. M.P. for Edinburgh 1832. Judge of Session 1834. Died 1850.
JESSFIELD TERRACE	Shown as Jessfield. Whale brae, *D.1827.* Jessefield or Jessiefield, near Newhaven, *m.t.c. 9/2/1814.* On site of old Jessfield House, *j.r.*
JOCK'S LODGE	*D.1827.* Said to be from a beggar who built him a hut there. The name first appears in 1650, *o.& n.e. iii. 142.* "Jokis Lodge" *Nicoll's Diary, p.12. Wilson i, 123.* Andrew Spence, Lorimer, Jockslodge, Burgess Register, 27/1/1692.
JOHN STREET	From John James Hamilton, Marquis of Abercorn, superior. His own naming, *Baird 360.*
JOHN'S LANE PLACE	*D.1827.* West Side Links to Charlotte St. From Church of St. John, *j.r. 1779.*
JOHNSTON'S CLOSE	*Ainslie. Kirkwood. Kerr.*

The first close east of the West Bow, extant, but unnamed. It is clearly shown in a map of the district (specially of the closes demolished for the New College) in a portfolio of Sir Daniel Wilson's, in the Library of the Museum of Antiquities, where the house between the close and the West Bow is marked as that of Sir Patrick Johnston (Lord Provost and knight, 1700, and representative for the city in Parliament, 1709-10), *see p.73.* Johnston's land stood on the west of Riddell's land, *Prot. W.F.10, 4/3/1761.* *(Blank)* Johnston, glover, owned a tenement there, *Prot. J.W.7, 1/3/1764.* The tenement of the late Edward Johnston, junior, is mentioned as being on the south side of the High Street in the Overbow, *Prot. J.W.6, 9/1/1764,* and part of the city wall of 1450 could be seen at the foot of the close, *M.138,c.2.*

See also Burnet's Close.

JOHNSTON TERRACE	Planned, *Lothian Map 1825.* Part of the "Wester Approach" (1825-1836). Named, *Ord. Surv. 1852.* From Sir Wm. Johnston. Lord Provost 1848-1851. Old name "Castle Place", *Reg. 25/6/1861.*
JOLLIE'S CLOSE	A tenement at the top of the close was owned by Patrick Jollie, and later by Alexander Jollie, writer, *Reg. 9/5/1859.* Evidently the family

gave their name to the close. James Jollie was a trustee on the estate of the late Thomas Tod, of the adjacent Tod's Close, *m.t.c. 9/3/1831.* Esther Jollie married George Cunningham, *Reg. 9/5/1859.*

Ainslie. Kirkwood. Shown, unnamed, by Kerr.

JOPPA GARDENS
TERRACE
PARK
ROAD

From Joppa pans, for making salt. Map of 1770, *Baird 302.* Name Joppa goes far back. It was originally a colliers' and miners' row of cottages, and supposed to have taken its name from being near the sea; like Joppa in Palestine, *w.b.*
See also Joppa Grove—Part II.

JORDAN BURN
BANK
LANE

The burn received its name from the adjoining area known as (Little) Egypt, q.v. Its own name the Powburn, q.v., *o.e.c. x. 179.*

JUNCTION STREET
GREAT
NORTH

D.1827. Making a junction between Leith Walk and the Ferry Road. "Proposed new road", *Ainslie 1804. o.& n.e. iii. 206.* "Joining foot of Leith Walk and Wet Docks", *m.t.c. 21/7/1824.*
See also Junction Place—Part II.

K

KEIR STREET

On the land of Mr. Kier, *Ainslie 1804.* Mr. Keir proprietor 23/3/1799, *eec.j.s.* Adam Keir, Lauriston, *D.1800, 170.* Adam & Wm. Keir, bakers, opposite the Exchange, *p.w. 1780/81.* Adam Keir, baker—and heirs of same, *v.r.47.* Late Adam Keir, owner of house at Laurieston, *m.t.c. 7/3/1810.* Robert Keir, brewer, Lauriston Pl., *m.t.c. 21/8/1811.*

KEMP PLACE

After one of the directors of the e.c.b.c.ld. (See authorities quoted).

KEW TERRACE

From Kew Palace, of a piece with Hampton and Osborne Terrace. (Kew Ter. in Littlejohn's map).

KILGRASTON ROAD

On the lands of Whitehouse, acquired in 1819 by Grant of Kilgraston, *D.M.1864. o.e.c. x. 32.*

KILLIEBRAE

26 West Port, *D.1919/20.* Foot of West Port, *D.1827.* Killybrae, *m.t.c. 31/1/1843. Littlejohn, App. 40.* John Kello infest in lands in Portsburgh, owned successively by Adam Purves; Geothodden; his son James John Kello, *m.t.c. 4/9/1667.*
Not a street name.

KILMAURS ROAD
TERRACE

From a place connected with the family of Cunyngham in Ayrshire. On property of Sir Wm. Dick-Cunyngham.

KINELLAN ROAD

From the house of Dr. Cumming at one time tutor in the family of the Duke of Argyll, and named by him from a place in Argyllshire.

KING STREET

p.w.1780/81, 105. Yard yeads to Shirra Brae, *D.1827.* Probably from George III, *m.t.c. 18/1/1792.* The street now called Kings Street, at head of Sheriff Brae. At bottom of road from Bonnington to Leith, facing intended new harbour, *e.e.c. 11/10/1792.*

KINGHORN PLACE

From Hugh Kinghorn, *m.t.c. 25/7/1832,* of H. & W. Kinghorn, builders, Leith, *D.1800. j.r. D.1827,* who inhabited Bonnington Villa.

KINGSBURGH ROAD

After Rt. Hon. Sir John Hay Athole Macdonald, Lord Kingsburgh, Lord Justice Clerk of Scotland, born 1836. Early enthusiast for motor cars; the name was on the feuing plan when the ground was acquired by the Murrayfield Real Estate Co. from the late Mr. Lockhart Thomson.

KING'S PLACE
ROAD

From the route followed by George IV to the Review on Portobello Sands, *e.s.s. 232. Baird 336.*

KING'S STABLES ROAD	From the Royal Mews there, in ancient days below, and not far from the Castle. (King's Stables, at West Port, *D.1800, 234*). "King's Stables, back of Castle", *D.1827*. King's Stables, *m.t.c. 27/3/1728, 1/8/1792*.

Queen's Stables, lying under the Castle wall, at the West Port, between the common highways on the south, east and north, and the place of tourney, otherwise called the "barres", on the west, *c.c.1320, 29/6/1543*. In charter of 3 Oct, 1477 James III forbids the sale of "qwyck Bestis, Ky. Oxon in the Town, bot under the wall, fer (for) West at our Stable", *m.8.c.2*. King's Stables, *m.t.c. 8/10/1697*. Superiority of King's Stables to be purchased from James Boirlands, *m.t.c. 21/3/1655*. Jas. Kyll, couper in Potterrow, infest in piece of land on King's Stables, disponed by Wm. Thomson, *m.t.c. 23/12/1670*. |
KING'S BRIDGE ROAD	Compliment to George IV, 1825-1836. The name originally included present Johnston Terrace, *eec.j.s. 1/10/1827*. Name fixed then.
KINNEAR ROAD	On property of Mr. Kinnear, owner of Cargilfeild, *Kirkwood*. After Lord Kinnear, Trustee and Governor of Fettes Trust. Fettes College close by.
KIRK STREET	From Kirk's Land, Cassels Place. From Robert Kirk, shipowner, resident, *D.1827, 224*, also *D.1827, 210*. At head of Tolbooth Wynd, *m.t.c. 5/3/1823*.
KIRKGATE	The road running by St. Mary's Kirk (South Leith Parish), *D.1827*. *Kirkgate, Liberton—see Part II.*
KITCHEN'S COURT	Cowgate, *D.1827*. Same as Caitcheon's Land, Cowgate, *p.w.1780/81, 48*, which takes its name from John Caitcheon, carver, foot of the horse Wynd, *p.w. 1780/81, 16*. Old name Simpson's Cl., *Ainslie, 1780, 1804. Kirkwood*. A ruinous tenement in Cowgate, called Kitchen's Land, *m.t.c. 8/11/1820*. For John Caitchen, carver son of late John Kaitchen, portioner in Peebles, by Margaret Hunter, daughter of John Hunter, portioner, Abbeyhill: tenement of land south side of Cowgate, opposite Fishmarket Cl. near the New Well, *3 Reg. 27/7/1768*. Tenement of John Caitcheon, south side of Cowgate, just east of Close or Court belonging to umq. Alexr. Kincaid, H.M. printer for Scotland, in "Mr. Kincaid's Cl.", *Reg. 24/5/1862*. Alias Fleming's Close, q.v.

L

LADESIDE	Beside the mill lade or lead, from the Dean Village to Canonmills.
LADY ROAD	From Mayfield to Sharpdale, made early 19th century, formed by the orders of Mrs. Gilmour, the last Laird's mother, hence the name. *"Liberton" by George Good, 1893, p.64*.
LADY LAWSON STREET	As taking the place of the former Lady Lawson's Wynd, q.v., *D.1827*. "Lauriston and West Port" and giving a new entrance to Spittal St. Before the "Improvement scheme" was carried out, the Wynd ran from Lauriston, East of and parallel to Lauriston St. past the Cattle Market, now occupied by the Fire Station and College of Art, and into the West Port—access was gained to Spittal St. by a narrow wynd, *Imp. Map.*, at the west side of Free St. Cuthbert's Church, now the Victoria Tuberculosis Dispensary. This wynd was closed, and a new roadway formed ont he east side of the church, the north portion of Lady Lawson St., *Imp. Maps*. Lady Lawson, wife of Mr. Richard Lawson, Justiciary Clerk of the King James IV 1493, *St. L.A.* of the High Riggs, *o.& n.e.* Sir Richard Lawson of Boghall, *trad. 1.305*,

Late Robt. Lawson of Hieriggs, *Prot. 7/5/1532.*

LADY MENZIES PLACE

Probably from Hon. Grace C.C., eldest daughter of Hon. Fletcher Norton, 2nd wife of Sir Neil Menzies, married 1816. Died 1877. The Menzies of Castle Menzies lived in Abbeyhill House for many years, and the name came from Lady Menzies.

LADY STAIR'S CLOSE

Shown as Stair's Close. Lady Gray's Close.

The older name, Lady Gray's Close, *t.b. 40; Wilson, i. 213,* was derived from Egidia or Geida, wife of Sir Wm. Gray, of Pittendrum, and sister of Sir John Smith of Grothill, Provost of Edinburgh in 1643. Sir Wm. Gray seems to have built the house, which gave its name to the close, in 1622, on land acquired from Mr. Thomas Aikenheid, one of the Commissioners of Edinburgh, *Prot. A.W.5, 24/4/1717,* and owned formerly by Catherine Livingstoun; the initials of Sir William and his wife are carved on the lintel of the entrance. He died in 1648, and his widow survived him for several years, giving her name to the close. After some changes of ownership the house was disponed on 7th April 1719 to Elizabeth, Countess Dowager of Stair, widow of John, 1st Earl of Stair, and daughter of Sir John Dundas of Newliston, by Agnes, eldest daughter of Sir Wm. and Lady Gray, *after the death of Sir John Dundas, his widow Agnes married Sir Archibald Primrose of Carrington, and their son Archibald was 1st Earl of Rosebery.*

It is from this Dowager Lady Stair, who died in 1731, that the house and close are named.

Her son John, 2nd Earl of Stair, who died in 1747, married Eleanor, widow of 1st Viscount Primrose; she survived him twelve years. She may have visited her mother-in-law's house, but to derive the name from her is quite erroneous, although from Robert Chambers downward this false derivation has been given.

For all full account of the house and the families of Gray, Stair, and Primrose, see the Old Edinburgh Club, Vol. iii. p.243.

The short form 'Stair's Close' is also found, *m.t.c. 5/8/1789.*

Edgar. Ainslie. Kirkwood. Kerr.

LADY WYND

West Port, *1617, D.1827. o.& n.e. ii. 224.* From the neighbouring chapel of Our Lady.

LADYSMITH ROAD

From the town in South Africa, famed for its heroic defence in the Boer War.

LAING TERRACE

From David Laing, LL.D. 1792-1878. Bookseller, and antiquarian, occupant of East Villa—now demolished. "The Laing Charters". It is built on the site of his villa, and gardens, *w.b.*

LAMB'S CLOSE

84 Crosscausey, *D.1827.* From Andrew Lamb, Wilson's Close, crosscausey, *D.1800, 178, D.1827, 101.* John Lamb Smith. Lands of old of Patrick Lamb, thereafter of heirs of Sir Simeon Blyth, Pleasance district, *Can. Chart. 9/3/1763.*

LANSDOWNE CRESCENT

From the Marquis of Lansdowne, born 1845. Statesman etc.

LAUDER ROAD

From Sir Thomas Dick Lauder, superior. On the Grange Estate.

LAUDERDALE STREET

On the Warrender Estate. Sir John Warrender, 5th Bart., married as his first wife 1823 Lady Julia, *Maitland,* daughter to James 8th Earl of Lauderdale. Lauderdale, not the dale of the river Leader, but named from Robertus de Lavedre, or Lauder, after 1058, who had aided Malcolm Canmore against Macbeth, and received large grants of land. Known as Lawedre of that ilk, *St. G., 153.*

LAUREL TERRACE

Fancy. After the laurel tree, *e.c.b.c.ld.*

LAURIE STREET	*D.1827.* From owner of ground, *j.r.*
LAURISTON GARDENS **LANE** **PARK** **PLACE** **STREET** **TERRACE**	*D.1827.* From the property of Mr. Lawrie, two houses are shewn in Ainslie 1804 under **his** name. Laurieston appears in Armstrong's map 1773. Wm. Lauder, writer, Laurieston, *p.w. 1780/81, 52.* Robert Laurie, clerk of Excise do. do. Robert Laurie, surveyor of Excise, Laurieston, *D.1800, 1711.* Lowriston, *Maitland 507.* John Lawson of Hie-riggs, feued land in the Portsburgh, south side, to John Lowrie 12/4/1566, *trad. 1.305.* Lauriston Lodge, now St. Catherine's Convent of Mercy, *Ord. Surv. 1852.* Lauriston St. is simply Lauriston, *Ainslie 1804.* In *Ainslie,* 1880, in *Edgar,* Laurieston. Lauriston place is Louriestion. Road west from Teviot Row widened, cutting off a little from George Watson's Hospital ground, *m.t.c. 16/8/1786.* There are various individuals of the name in the district given in Directories & m.t.c. Back Lane, *Stark 1806, map.* Lauriston Lane, *m.t.c. 8/6/1808.* Lauriston, near Edinburgh, *m.t.c. 14/9/1814.* Road from Wester House in Lauriston to Lady Lawson's Wynd, *m.t.c. 20/5/1713.* John Lowrie, son to the deceased Francis Lawrie late bailie in Portsburgh infested in houses and aikers of land in 1713. Wm. Laurie, maltman, infested in half of the lands of umq. Jas. Lermont in Portsburg, *m.t.c. 2/5/1655.* Francis L., *m.t.c. 9/11/1600.*
LAVEROCKBANK AVENUE **ROAD** **TERRACE**	From Laverock bank House; house and grounds to let, *Caled. Merc. 20/9/1780, j.s.* Probably originally from the proprietor. The name Laverock occurs in Leith, *p.w. 1780/81, 109* and Edinburgh, *v.r., p.52, m.t.c. 21/1/1824.*
LAWNMARKET	Land Market, *Maitland, 15.141. 180. 181. Prot. G.H.3, 30/6/1704.* In this last passage he "says" On the southern side of the Land-market street, corruptly called the Lawn-market, on Wednesdays is held a Market for Linnen and Woolen Cloth. Edgar 1742 and 1765 gives Land. Where the produce of the land, as distinct from the town, was sold. *Anon. Map 1767.* Lawn, *Ainslie 1780-1804. Lothian Map 1825. Ord. Surv. 1852. o.& n.e. 1.94,* from the sale of lawn, cloth. Shepherd p.33 and view, fills the street with bales and webs! but corrects the error, p.33. Landmarket St. M. Landmarket, *m.t.c. 24/10/1781.* "Cloath" market mentioned separately. Also m.t.c. 30/10/1782. Land market, *m.t.c. 6/10/1802.* Butter, cheese, land, cloth, and flesh markets, *m.t.c. 11/10/1820.* Land mercate, *Prot. 6/4/1732, 14/5/1714.* Land flesh market (old Fleshmarket Cl.,) *m.t.c. 23/3/1681.* Landmarket, *m.t.c. marg. 28/7/1620.* The Landis Market, *m.t.c. 9/4/1560.*
LEARMONTH GARDENS **GROVE** **TERRACE** **PLACE**	From John Learmonth, provost in 1832, owner of the Dean Estate, who paid most of the cost of the Dean Bridge, in order to open up his land for feuing, *o.& n.e. iii. 70. Gilbert 97.* *See also Learmonth Avenue—Part II.*
LEE CRESCENT	The ground, on which it is built, was feued by Mr. J.B.W. Lee, S.S.C., Edinburgh, who named the crescent after himself.
LEGGATT'S LAND	Dean Village. Formerly Braid's Place, *o.& n.e. iii. 75.* Braid's Row, *D.1827.* From the family of Leggatt who have been there for centuries as tanners. Now part of Deanhaugh St., Stockbridge 9. In D.1827 are three Leggats in the district, Robert, grocer in Legget's Land, Stockbridge.
LEITH STREET **WALK**	*D.1827.* On the road to Leith. Leith Walk, formerly Leith Loan, is on the line of the entrenchment thrown up against Cromwell, 1650, *o.& n.e. iii. 150.* Leith Walk is called the "Walk to Leith", *trav. comp.*

123. Originally the gravel path on the top of the parapet or mound, extending from the Calton Hill to Leith in 1650. It became a carriage way after the North Bridge was opened in 1772, *Wilson, ii. 183*. It is named "Cathrine St", in Ainslie 1780, and, with variations to Ord. Surv. 1852. "Walk of Leith", *m.t.c. 8/2/181* . Leith St., or Cathrine St. *Reg. 4/3/1863*. Leith Walk to be made the "Wester Road to Leith", *m.t.c. 17/4/1776*. Contract given to Joseph Hedley, *m.t.c. 2/8/1776*.

LENNEL AVENUE From a property of the Campbells of Succoth, superiors.
See also Lennel Avenue—Part II.

LEOPOLD PLACE *D.1827. Lothian Map 1825.* In 1817, Provost Kincaid Mackenzie entertained in his house, 5 Gayfield Square, Prince Leopold, afterwards King of the Belgians. Two years later, Prince Leopold, in 1819, opened the Regent Bridge, *o.& n.e. ii. 104. Anderson. e.o.t. viii. p.41.* Near Edinburgh, *m.t.c. 21/1/1824, 21/4/1824.*

LESLIE PLACE From Count Leslie, who occupied Deanhaugh House, where Leslie Place now stands, in the middle of the 18th century, *o.& n.e. iii. 76.* His widow, Anne, married Sir Henry Raeburn, painter.

LEVEN STREET
   TERRACE From Leven Lodge, mansion of the Earl of Leven, opposite the entrance of Gilmore Place, *o.& n.e. iii. 30. Ainslie 1804. Lothian Map 1825.* "Leven Cottage", *Ord. Surv. 1852.* Leven Lodge for sale, 2/10/1806., *eec.j.s.* Lady Leven's property, *Kirkwood. m.t.c. 11/5/1808.* Leven St. "near Edinburgh", *m.t.c. 2/9/1818.* Drumdryan. Leven Lodge. Earl of Leven, 30/8/1749, *r.o.s.*

LEWIS TERRACE From Bailie David Lewis, author of "Edinburgh Water Supply" 1908. A strong radical and temperance worker, he by these characteristics so roused the aversion of the father of Robert Louis Stevenson, that he caused his son's middle name to be spelled Louis, instead of the original Lewis, for fear the two families should be thought in any way connected. "Robert Louis Stevenson's Edinburgh Days", by E. Blantyre Simpson, p.16. Quoted in "Edinburgh Water Supply", p.376.

LILY TERRACE After the flower. Fancy, *e.c.b.c.ld.*

LINDSAY ROAD From Wm. Lindsay, S.S.C. Provost of Leith 1860, who affected various improvements, removing the "man trap" (q.v. appx) beside Leith Fort, and making this new road, which bear his name. Projector of the "Lindsay Act". The General Police and Improvement (Scotland) Act, 1862 and reviser thereof and died 1884, *Irons, ii. 531. t.t.l. 372.*
See also Lindsay Street—Part II.

LINKS PLACE Beside Leith Links.
See also Links Gardens—Part II.

LITTLE KING STREET Originally King St., *Ainslie 1804. D.1827. Lothian Map 1825.* Little was added to distinguish it from its Great rival, *Ord. Surv. 1852.* Perhaps from George III: perhaps a veiled reference to James VIII, by a surviving Jacobite—the name being preserved in St. James Square, *Ainslie 1780. o.e.c. ii. 172.*

LIVINGSTONE PLACE After David Livingstone. African missionary and explorer. Honorary Burgess 1857.

LIXMOUNT AVENUE
   GARDENS From house of that name, Trinity, *D.1827. Ainslie 1800.*

LOCHEND CLOSE *Ainslie. Kirkwood.* Shown as Little Lochend Close, *o.s. Kerr.* East Lochend's Close, *Ainslie. Kirkwood.* Lochend Close, *o.s. Kerr.* Nether Lochend's Close, *Can. Chart. 15/5/1801.*

The name is derived from the yard and house at the foot of the close, formerly owned by William Ferguson in Lochend of Restalrig, and lately by John Ferguson, tanner, burgess of Edinburgh, *Prot.J.H. Canong. 28/12/1703.* Mention is also found of the lands of umquhyle James Fergusson of Lochend, on the north side of the Canongate, *Prot.J.H. Canong. 21 and 24/8/1700.*

Maitland *M.502, c.1.,* mentions the Loch of Restalrig, 'vulgarly Lochend'. It is that end of Restalrig next the loch, Easter Restalrig: the other end, the Craigend next the Calton Craigs, being Wester Restalrig, *o.e.c. iv. 157, 186.*

Another and more amusing derivation of the name of the loch may be quoted: 'The Logans ruled Restalrig ... and Lochend is a corruption of their name!' *e.s.s. 222.*
Redevelopment in 1960's has altered position of original closes.

LOCHEND ROAD	Road leading to Lochend. Lochend is the end of Restalrig next the loch, i.e. the East end: the west end, towards the Calton Craig is the Craigend, *o.e.c. iv. 157,186.* *See also Lochend Avenue—Part II.*
LOCHRIN BUILDINGS **PLACE** **TERRACE**	From Lochrin, *p.w.1780/81. 28,* theryn or run from the south or Boroughloch, which flowed to the water of Leith (under the Fountain bridge) at Coltbridge, *D.1827.* "Delty Burn", *Ainslie 1804.* An unnamed morsel shewn Lothian Map 1825. The Meadows were drained till about 1812 when a new drain was made eastward into the King's Park, *m.t.c. 6/1/1813.* "Lochrin or Newbigging", *e.a. 13/1/1764 and 6/7/1764.* Lochrin turn, *Littlejohn 87. Reg. 10/2/1863.* Lochrin or Newbigging, *e.a. 13/1/1764 and 6/7/1764.* Owing to scarcity of water, the Council resolve to close in the "ryn of the southe loche", and fill up the loch with water, *m.t.c. 24/11/1619.*
LOCKHARTON CRESCENT **GARDENS**	From neighbouring Craiglockhart.
LOGIE GREEN ROAD	Old property name. Logie Green house, *w.o.l. 172.* Logie Green Villa 31/3/1803, *eec.j.s.* Logie Lodge, *b.b.119. Ainslie 1804. Lothian Map 1825.* Logie Green, near Edinburgh, *m.t.c. 14/12/1831.*
LOMOND ROAD	From view of the Fifeshire Lomonds, *j.r.* *Not correct derivation—See Part II.*
LONDON ROAD	Leading to London. "Great London road" head of Leith Walk, *D.1827.*
LONDON STREET	Complimentary to the English metropolis, *D.1827.* In Ainslie 1804 it is Anglia St., but Lothian Map 1825, London St. the metropolis for the country, so also Dublin St. formerly Hibernia St. London St., on the lands of Bellevue, *m.t.c. 19/2/1806.*
LORD RUSSELL PLACE	From Lord John Russell, statesman, prime minister 1846. Leader of the "Reform Bill" passed in 1832. Born 1792. Died 1878. Honorary Burgess 1845, *Ord. Surv. 1852. Gilbert 115.*
LORNE PLACE **SOUTH** **STREET**	From the Marquis of Lorne, later Duke of Argyll, who married the Princess Louise, 24th March 1871.
LOTHIAN ROAD	*Ainslie 1780, 1804,* includes from Princes St. to Tollcross, Princes St. to Bread St., *Lothian Map 1825.* For legend (rather than tradition) of its construction in a single day for a wager, see Walks in Edinr. 195. "New road, called Lothian Road", Caled. Merc. 8/1/1785, *j.s.* "A new road lately cut from Lochrin ... to Princes St.", *Kincaid 106.* The groundless story of the making of the road in one day is given in Kay II, 34. There is no hint or trace of the "one day" legend in the

Minutes of the Town Council.

14 May 1783 a proposal was laid before the Town Council for making a road to the city, leaving the Linton road, *see Ainslie 1804*, a little way to the south of the entry of the road that leads to Lauriston, to be carried northward across the Glasgow road, (now Fountainbridge), Linlithgow road (now Morison St) and Queensferry road (now King's Stables road. For all these see map in Arnot's History of Edinburgh, 1778, and to join Princes St. a little eastward of the Tollbar at the West Kirkbraehead. To be paid for from these four districts of roads. Permission must be got from local owners—the city being owner of the last 300 feet, on the Bearford Lands, after crossing the Queensferry road. No tolls to be exacted, *m.t.c. 14/5/1783*.

On 26 Nov. 1783, the Council voted £5 compensation for loss of glebe, through making of the new road, to each of the ministers of the West Kirk.

On 11 Feb. 1784, the Council resolved that the new road be maintained from the funds of the Middle district. It is mentioned, 31 March 1784, as "the new road to the Extended Royalty at Kirkbraehead".

On 23 June 1784, the estimated cost of the new road is given at £825.15/- of which £675.15/- had been subscribed, the Town having contributed £30.

On 16 Feb. 1785, mention is made of Mrs. Stewart's property "near the Lothian Road". (In Ainslie's map of 1780 the north part of the road is shewn, and named "Lothian Road").

On 15 June 1785, the Council voted 8 guineas as proportion for finishing the Lothian Road, and making up damages occasioned by said road.

On 3 Aug. 1785, a further grant was made for the Lothian Road, which was not quite finished.

12 Jan. 1791, it is spoken of as "the transverse great Road, called the Lothian Road".

LOTHIAN STREET　Shewn Lothian Road, *Scots. Mag. 1801, 297*, from the Lothian farm and steading, at N.W. corner of what is now Lothian St. and Bristo Place, *a.o.e. 122*. Opened 7/1/1796, *eec.j.s.* Shewn Ainslie 1804, named. The farm may have owed its name to the connection between its neighbour, Lord Ross, and the Marquis of Lothian, *m.t.c. 9/6/1802*. "The new street called Lothian St." *m.t.c. 26/2/1806*.

LOVERS' LOAN　Descriptively sentimental. Lovers' Lone, *Littlejohn Map.*

LUSSIELAW ROAD　*D.1936.* Old local name, "Lowsie Law".
> Moor of rising ground just south of the Blind Asylum known as Lussie Law. Here battle took place.

LUTTON PLACE　Sir Robert Preston of Valleyfield and Lutton had charter of 9 acres of lands of St. Leonards, *Can. Chart. 2/5/1843*, formerly possessed by George Lindsay depute Clerk of Edinburgh. His sister Agnes married John Preston of Gorton: his other sister, Jean, married Mr. Hislop and had a son William, *m.t.c. 2/5/1843. c.h.i. 306.* "Preston & Hyslop's property", *Ainslie 1804. See Preston St.*

LYGON ROAD　From Lady Susan Lygon, second daughter of the 6th Earl of Beauchamp and wife (1889) of Major Robt. Gordon Gordon Gilmour, superior of the Land.

LYNEDOCH PLACE	*D.1827.* From Lord Lyndoch, general in the Peninsular War, and "Hero of Barossa", *o.& n.e. ii. 209.* He received the freedom of the city 1815, *o.& n.e. ii. 283. Kirkwood 1821.* "Lyndoc Pl." *m.t.c. 9/6/1819.* Thomas Graham, son of the laird of Balgowan, Perthshire. Born 1748. Died 1843. Distinguished in Peninsular War, chiefly by his victory at Barossa, near Cadiz, 1811. Created Baron Lynedoch of Balgowan 1814.
LYON'S CLOSE	Shown as Old Lyon's Close, *Chambers, ii. 45; e.a. 5/2/1765, etc.* Stalker's Close, *Prot. W.F.7, 19/4/1756; Reg. 10/10/1858.* *Edgar. Ainslie. Kirkwood. Kerr.* The alias is clearly given, but no derivation for either name.

M

MADEIRA STREET	Wine trade connection, *D.1827.* Madeira House, *s.s.l.* Mrs. Paterson, subscriber.
MAGDALA CRESCENT	From the capital of Abyssinia, captured by the British 1868. Feued from Heriot's Hospital, Nov. 1869.
MAGDALEN BRIDGE	From an ancient chapel to the Saint, in the grounds of New Hailes, *o.& n.e. 149. 366.* Named Maitland Water and Pans in Map of 1763, *Baird 50,* the land belonging to the family of Maitland of Lauderdale. Wm. Paton, salt grieve to the Earl of Dysart at the Magdalen Pans, made Burgess and gild brother of Edinburgh 27/6/1699. *See M, p.96.* *See also Magdalene Avenue etc.—Part II.*
MAIN POINT	*D.1827.* Shewn unnamed, *Ainslie, 1780.* "Twopenny Custom", *Ainslie 1804.* Main point, *Lothian Map 1825.* The meeting point of several main streets, Bread St., High Riggs, West Port, Lauriston St.
MAIN STREET	Newhaven. Evident, unless built by John Main, who built part of the South Row there, *m.t.c. 26/4/1809.* Property of Joanna Mayne, Newhaven. Indweller in North Leith. Feu granted in West Newhaven to John Main, indweller in North Leith, *m.t.c. 1/8/1656.* Jean, daughter to umq. John Main indweller in Leith infest in dwelling houses and waste in Newhaven, *m.t.c. 21/11/1677.*
MAITLAND STREET	*D.1827.* East part complete, west begun, *Lothian Map 1825.* South side from Princes St. to end of Morrison St., Shandwick Place north side of east part, *Ord. Surv. 1852.* Maitland St., Torphichen St., and West Maitland St., farther to Haymarket. No Shandwick Pl. Built by Alexr. Chas. Maitland of Cliftonhall, before 27/7/1805, when he wrote to the Town Council anent removing little old houses, which blocked the way to Charlotte Square & Princes St. "New western road called Maitland St", *m.t.c. 12/8/1807.* Built on Mr. Cunningham's property, *m.t.c. 10/8/1808.* The name applied to both north and south sides of the street, *m.t.c. 24/10/1810.* See the tomb in Greyfriars of Maitland Gibson for some of the family. What is now the south side of Shandwick Place was formerly East Maitland Street. The name was changed between 1899 and 1900. *Now Shandwick Place.*
MALTA TERRACE	From old house, "Malta House", *Stockbridge 20. D.1827. Ord. Surv. 1825. m.t.c. 6/1/1835.*
MANDERSTON STREET	John Manderston was elected Lord Provost, 5/10/1819. Died 11/11/1831, *j.r.*

MANOR PLACE	From the Manor house of Easter Coates, Walker Estate, *m.t.c.* 29/4/1807, 29/7/1807, 6/5/1818.
MANSFIELD PLACE	D.1827. Shewn unnamed, *Ainslie 1804*. Named, *Lothian Map 1825*. From the earl of Mansfield, Wm. Murray, who was related to General Scott of Balcornie, owner of the Bellevue property, on which it is built. He was counsel for the city in the Porteous Cause, 1737, *see "The Heart of Midlothian"*, and spoke on the Douglas case 1769, *The Fife Pitcairns, p. 71. o.& n.e. ii. 143. 1705-1793.* His sisters, Miss Nicky being the Lady Directress of all public assemblies in Edinburgh, lived in Smith's Land at the head of Bailie Fyfe's Close, *trad. ii. 27.*
MANSIONHOUSE ROAD	From the mansion house of the Grange of St. Giles, on the estate whereof the road is built.
MARCHHALL CRESCENT **PLACE** **ROAD**	From old house, *Kirkwood*. Land commonly called Rosehall or Marchall, north of Rosebank, nearly opposite to Newington House, on East of Dalkeith Road, 11/12/1813, *eec.j.s.* Rosehall, *Ord. Surv. 1852.*
MARCHMONT CRESCENT **ROAD** **STREET**	The wife of Sir George Warrender, 6th Bart., was daughter to Hume Campbell of Marchmont. These are built on the Warrender property; feuing begun 1878.
MARIONVILLE ROAD	From old House, Marionville, built by the Misses Ramsay, milliners, and therefore known as "Lappet Ha' ". Probably named from one of them. It was owned in 1789 by Capt. James Macrae, "The fortunate dwellist", *o.& n.e. iii. 138. trad. ii. 45. m.t.c. 14/1/1834.* **See also Marionville Avenue—Part II.**
MARKET STREET	(Flesh market to Mound, *D.1827*) *Imp. map. 1866.* For markets see Edgar, Ainslie and Lothian map 1825, which last names the street "Road leading from Bell house at Castlehill to New Port", *Prot. 7/3/1766. j.w.8.* Common high Lane College Kirk to Castlehill, *Prot. 7/3/1766.* Market St. (including Ramsay Lane). **New road** now making, leading from Reservoir & Bell house (q.v.) towards the North Loch. Council to make gutter, raise walls etc. *m.t.c. 16/9/1732.* Committee on public works to visit the road on the north side of the town, leading from the Bell house to the foot of Halkerston's Wynd, *m.t.c. 2/4/1734.* Report, much spoiled by rubbish lately laid down, so that bestiall cannot be driven from the West Port to the Flesh Market booths and many accidents occur thro' driving cattle & bestiall thro' the town and Cowgate, and up vennels and closes. The rubbish and hills of rubbish east of Mr. Dins stables, must be thrown into great pit and fill it up. To fence up the rubbish in a line from the west nuik of Brownhill's yard to the dyke opposite the foot of the close at Milns Square, at the Bowhead, a stone dyke must be built some fathoms westward, *m.t.c. 24/4/1734.* Thos. Lamb, gardener, was paid £22.6/- Scots. for work done at Bellhouse brae *m.t.c. 4/9/1734.* Called the Slaughter road, *m.t.c. 1/9/1736.* Bell house brae, (now Ramsay Lane).
MARSHALL PLACE	Possibly from Mr. Marshall, Greenside House, *Ainslie 1804.*
MARSHALL STREET	John Marshall shoe maker, and Helen Mann his spouse, owned property in Potterrow, *m.t.c. 2/9/1789.* John Marshall, surgeon in Beddington and his daughters Jane, Margaret and Elizabeth, received charter of large new tenement of land in Potterrow, built by Colin Alison. His late wife Margaret Alison. Margaret Alison, grand-daughter of George A. married John Marshall, *Reg. 4/12/1857.* Wm. Marshall, coach-builder, 58 Bristo St., *D.1832/3, do do. D.1846/7.* Also in General's entry, 56 Bristo St., *do. do. D.1851/2. D.1855/6.* General's entry

etc. were cleared away about 1866, and Marshall St. formed.

MARSHALL'S COURT

Greenside. Probably on property owned by Marshall, occupant of Greenside House. *Ainslie 1804. Littlejohn App. 24. o.& n.e. iii. 159.* But see Andw. M. coachwright, feuar of ground, Greenside, *m.t.c. 11/3/1807 & D.*

MARTIN'S COURT

18 Bernard St., Leith, *Ord. Surv. 1852.* From Wm. Martin, general merchant, who was owner, and had his place of business there, *j.r.*

MARYFIELD
PLACE

D.1827. From Maryfield House, *Ord. Surv. 1852.* Top end of Easter Road, *Lothian Map 1825, 19/1/1789, eec.j.s.* Mrs. Veitch, Maryfield Farm, *D.1827, 192.*

MARYFIELD
PORTOBELLO

From wife of Mr. Wilson of Wilson Park, q.v. About 1804, *Baird 317.*

MARY KING'S CLOSE

Also known as Alexander King's, or King's Close, Touris Close, Brown's Close.

Evidently named from the chief owner or occupant. Mary seems to have been the daughter of Mr. Alexr. King, who gives his name to the close. It is also known as King's Close, *Prot. A.W.6, 11/11/1720; King's Close, now Alexr. King's Close.* Alexander King was alive in 1601. He may be Mr. Alexr. King of Dredden or Dreden, whose brother Mr. Adam King of Dreden, one of the Commissioners of Edinburgh, was served heir to him, *Inquisitiones Generales, 397, 17/3/1618.*

Edgar 1742. Kerr.

The old name was Towris' or Towrs' Close, *Prot. A.W.6, 24/10/1722,* from the property of George Towris, on the east side of the close, *Prot. J.W.1, 10/6/1748.* The ancient family of Touris of Inverleith owned much property in and about the town. The close was gradually swallowed up by the Royal Exchange; it was represented for a time by the Royal Exchange Coffee-house stairs; now there is but a fragment of the north end—steps leading up from Cockburn Street to a door just above the back entrance to the City Chambers.

By a slip, probably, Kay calls it 'Lady Mary King's Close', *Kay, i. 292 n. For notes on Alexr. King and Mary, probably his daughter, see m.b. 113.*

Its old name, Brown's Close, *Brown's, later Alexr. King's, now Mary King's Close: Prot. G.H.10, 10/4/1735,* has no known derivation. The neighbourhood was full of Brown's closes; three are given above, and there was another in the Luckenbooths, facing Mary King's Close, which took its name from Alexr. Brown of Brown's land, merchant, Luckenbooths. There may be a connection.

There was a John Towris or Livingstoun's Close, on the north side of the High Street, containing a house owned by Isabella, wife of Thomas Wycht, and her sister Katherine, daughters of the late Henry Levingstoun, *c.c. 1530 a, 12/10/1543.* This seems to be the same as the above-mentioned Towris Close.

MAYBURY ROAD

New road, west of Corstorphine, leading to Barnton. Opened 21/4/1927 by Sir Henry Maybury, Director General of Roads, Ministry of Transport.
See also Maybury Drive—Part II.

MAYFIELD GARDENS
TERRACE
ROAD

From later name of Newlands, q.v. grounds. Mayfield seems to occur first in 1704, *o.e.c. x. 219.* Mayfield Loan known in 16th and 17th centuries as "Cant's Loaning" from the ancient owners of the grounds of the Grange of St. Giles, *St. G., chap. iii. See Cant's Close.* Mayfield

Loan, Grangetoll to Dalkeith Road, *D.1827.* Mayfield Loan, *m.t.c. 20/8/1788.* Mayfield alias Newlands, *m.t.c. 29/7/1801, 12/6/1816.*

MAYVILLE GARDENS

From old villa of Mayville, which formerly stood there. The original name was a fanciful one, like Woodville, another old villa, a little farthur up Laverock bank Road, on the opposite side, *j.r.*

MEADOW LANE
**   PLACE**

D.1827. Beside the Meadows, the bottom of the ancient South or Borough Loch, *o.e.c. x.* Meadow Pl., *m.t.c. 26/8/1807.*

MEADOWBANK AVENUE
**   CRESCENT**
**   PLACE**
**   TERRACE**

Parson's Green from Meadowbank Tower, *Kirkwood. D.1827.* Doubtless originally from situation.

24/11/1736 The Town Council proposed to make an avenue from the City (North, Middle & Meadow Walk) to the middle walk in Hope Park, *26/1/1737, m.t.c.* Estimate for making avenue thro' Heriot's Crofts to the Meadow, *E62-0/6. m.t.c. 21/2/1739.*

Above paragraph would appear to refer to Meadow Lane, Place.

MEADOWFIELD

Cluny Place. A matter of fact reference to situation.

MELVILLE STREET LANE

After Henry Dundas, 1st Viscount Melville. Lord Advocate 1775. M.P. for Midlothian. First Lord of the Admiralty under Pitt. The street was named by the Marquis of Abercorn, who planned when Lord Melville was M.P., *Baird 321.* His trial in 1805 for malversation in office and acquital caused vast excitement. Sir Walter Scott writing a triumphant poem. He died at Dunira 1811. Melville House, Portobello, *c.h.i. 478.*

Melville St. renamed Bellfield St.—See Part II.

MELVILLE PLACE
**   CRESCENT**
**   STREET**
**   ST. LANE**

After preceding Viscount Melville, *D.1827.* Monument in St. Andrew Square erected 1821 by officers and seamen of the Navy. Melville St. *m.t.c. 16/10/1808.*

MELVILLE DRIVE
**   TERRACE**

From Sir John Melville, Provost 1854-1859. He died 1860, *o.& n.e. ii. 348. St. L. 53.* Melville Drive opened 1859, *Gilbert.* Born 1802. Passed W.S. 1827. Burried Newington burying-ground. Married Jane Marshall. Proposed road from Lothian Road, through the Meadows to Duddingston (carried out later), *m.t.c. 12/8/1834.*

MENTONE AVENUE

A gracious reference to an even more famous watering place, by Portobello. Compare Brighton Place and Bath St., *w.b.*

MERCHANT STREET

D.1827. On ground formerly owned by the Merchant Coy., where their Hall stood, originally the Mansion of "Tam o' the Cowgate". Bought by them 1691. Demolished for George IV Bridge, circa 1829. Merchant's Court formerly there, *D.1799, 222.* Chambers "Edinburgh Merchants etc." 23. *Wilson ii. 147. eec.j.s. 25/6/1774. Ainslie 1780, 1804.* "Marchant's Hall, now Excise office", *t.b. 77, 1736. m.t.c. 13/10/1736.* Merchant St. & Court, *m.t.c. 5/9/1810.* 50 ft. broad and to remain so, *Prot. 14/9/1810.* Patk. Carfrae got feu of waste piece of ground in Candlemaker-row opposite Merchants' Yard, 9 elnes long x 5 elns, with tail, 5 elns braod at top x 1 eln at end. He to built on first part, preventing easing drop from falling on tomb adjacent, *m.t.c. 11/7/1694.* To feu large area owned by Merchant Coy. between lodging, formerly Excise Office on north lodgings in Brown's Sq. on south reached from Candlemaker Row by street 60 ft. wide, and footpath from Cowgate to another street 30 ft wide, *e.c.c. 25/6/1774.*

MERCHISTON AVENUE CRESCENT GARDENS PARK PLACE MEWS GROVE	All from Merchiston Castle and grounds, *D.1827,* **formerly** seat of the Napier family, the most famous being John, born there 1550, inventor of logarithms, published 1614. Also fanciful interpreter of the Apocalypse, treasure seeker with divining rod, and reputed wizard. He died 1617. Monument, St. Giles. Archd. Napier of Meryenistoun, *Prot. 25/10/1532.* The villa of Merchiston bank, for sale, 100 yards from the old Castle 13/2/1806, *eec.j.s. Ord. Surv. 1852.*
BANK AVENUE	Mansion house of North Merchiston, past which goes now the Union Canal, 1817, apparently same as Merchiston House, west by Fountain-bridge, *D.1827.* Merchiston Gardens so named on request of Merchant Co. March 1897.
MERTOUN PLACE	From the former family seat of the Earl of Polwarth. *Mertoun House Close to R. Tweed, left bank, 2 miles east of St. Boswalls.*
MEUSE LANE	Shown as Mews Lane, So. St. Andrew St., *D.1827.* In which were the Mews or stables etc., belonging to the dwelling houses. There were others, behind Rose St., Thistle St., George Square, etc. etc. Mews originally where hawks were kept while mewing, or moulting, and from the stables being near, the name was extended to them. See Craig's plan 1767 for mews provided for New Town. Muse Lane, *p.w. 1780/81, 46.*
MIDCOMMON CLOSE	*Ainslie. Kirkwood.* Shown as Common Close, *the mid common close.* Middle Common Close, *Kerr.* This close seems to have been known as Vietche's Close, *M.216,* from John Veitch, burgess of Edinburgh, who built a tenement on the north side of the Canongate, owned later by Thomas Veitch, surgeon in the Canongate, *m.t.c. 7/11/1827 and 1/9/1830,* Wm. Veatch, burgess of Edinburgh, had sasine of a tenement on the north side of the Canongate formerly owned by John Oliphant, *Sasines Canong. 5/2/1671.* Thomas Veitch, advocate, owned lands on the east side of Rae's Close, *Can. Chart. 22/11/1815,* and Logan's Close lay on the east of Veitch's land, *Can. Chart. 24/3/1863.* No definite alias has been found, and Maitland alone seems to mention the close.
MIDDLEBY STREET	*D.1827.* From the churchyard where were buried the grandparents of Benjamin Bell, surgeon, on whose property the street is built, *B. Bell, 81.*
MIDDLEFIELD	Middlefield, George's Place, and "Middlefield house", *D.1827.* Old name of locality, *Arnot 1816 map. Ainslie 1804.* "Country quarters, Leith Walk, to let part of new built house called Middlefield, apply to Mr. McMillan, Milne Square", *eec.j.s. 27/5/1793.* Robert McMillan, paper stainer, owner 1796, *p.w. 1780/81, 61.*
MIDDLE BAXTER'S CLOSE	Now Wardrop's Court, *Reg. 20/8/1743.* The close originally bearing this name was immediately east of the Uppermost Baxters' Close. John Wardrop owned a house in Mid-Baxters' Close, formerly the property of Mr. Wm. Adamson, nephew and heir of Wm. Adamson: thereafter of Adam Newtoun, baxter: thereafter of Patrick Forbes, merchant, and his wife Elizabeth Newtoun: thereafter of Alexr. Hume, merchant: thereafter of his son and heir Thomas Hume: thereafter of his brother David: thereafter of Alexr. Inglis, who rebuilt it after it had been burned: thereafter of his daughter Isabella: thereafter of the Incorporation of Baxters of Edinburgh: thereafter of Charles, son to John Fleming, baxter, burgess: thereafter of John Campbell: and finally of John Wardrop, mason, *Prot. A.W.4, 4/4/1712,* who had an only son James, *Prot. G.H.11, 10/11/1736.*

John Wardrop built a tenement in the close, known henceforth as Wardrop's Court, and the old name, Middle Baxters' Close, now displaced, attached itself to the close below Paterson's Court, given by Edgar as Middle Baxters' Court, and by Ainslie (1780) as Middle Baxters' Close, the most westerly of the three closes cleared away for Bank Street.

It was known, as narrated, as Wardrop's Court, being built by the said John Wardrop and John Henderson, wrights, burgesses of Edinburgh, *m.t.c. 1/9/1790,* the entry being known as Henderson's, or Wardrop's Close, *Reg. 31/8/1856.* The succession of owners has been given above.

MIDMAR AVENUE **DRIVE** **GARDENS**	From Aberdeenshire property belonging to Gordon of Cluny, owner of the ground, which is on the Braid Estate.
MILL LANE	Leith, *D.1827.* Evident, *j.r.s.l.62.*
MILL LANE	Dean. Evident.
MILLAR CRESCENT **PLACE** **LANE**	Morningside. From builder, *w.c.*
MILLER ROW	Dean. From the corn millers there resident.
MILLERFIELD PLACE	From the property of Mr. Millar, *Ainslie 1804,* father of Wm. Miller the celebrated engraver. Site of the house now occupied by Board School, *Wilson, ii. 123.* Wm. Miller, engraver, 4 Hope Park, *m.t.c. 16/10/1833.*
MILTON ROAD	Lord Milton sold the lands of Figgate to Baron Mure 1762, *Gilbert 45, Baird 290. w.b.* See also Milton Drive—Part II.
MILTON STREET	Up to 1885, James Milne & Son, gasfitters and engineers occupied Milton House and grounds, in the Canongate. In that year they removed beyond the Croft-an-Righ, calling the new works "Milton House Works", and the street leading thereto, Milton St. They sold the old premises, the house to the School Board, who built the Milton House School: the ground on the South to Younger's Brewery ("to such base uses etc") Milton House was built by Andrew Fletcher, Lord Milton, between 1742 and 1765, *Edgar's Map,* on site occupied by Duke of Roxburgh, *Edgar 1742. Can. Chart. 29/8/1803.*
MINTO STREET	*D.1827. Kirkwood. m.t.c. 17/7/1816.* From Lord Minto, governor of Bengal 1806-1814. Born Edin. 1751, died June 1814. Sir Robt. Keith Dick was judge under him in Silket, when he returned to inherit Prestonfield and Corstorphine, *Baird 131.* Letter from Lord Minto to Town Council anent straightening the road from Jedburgh to Boroughbridge approved, *m.t.c. 24/3/1819.*
MITCHELL STREET	*D.1827.* On property of Mr. Mitchell 29/11/1780. Caled. Merc., *j.s.* James Mitchell, merchant, Leith, who owing land on Constitution hill, and applied for small gushet of land on north side thereof, *m.t.c. 29/11/1778.* Acquired part of Leith Links, 11/11/1778, *m.t.c. 4/7/1832.*
MOIRA TERRACE	The Earl of Moira occupied Duddingston House, the property of the Marquis of Abercorn, in 1805, as Commander of the Forces in Scotland, *Baird 89, w.b.*
MONCRIEFF TERRACE	After James, Lord Moncrieff, 1811. Lord Advocate 1851. M.P. for Leith 1852-1859, Edinburgh 1859-1868.

MONMOUTH TERRACE	Duke of Buccleugh's ground, descended from James Crofts, Duke of Monmouth, son of Charles II, and claimant of the crown. Executed by his Uncle, James VII, 1685, *Kirkwood*.
MONTAGU TERRACE	Duke of Buccleuch's ground, Henry 3rd Duke of B. married 1767 Lady Eliz. Montagu, only daughter of George, 4th Earl of Cardigan, afterwards Duke of Montagu. Her second son, Henry, succeeded his said grandfather. Died 1845, title expired, *Kirkwood*.
MONTAGU STREET	*D.1827.* Not shewn at all in Kirkwood. In Lothian map, north side built. From Duke of Montague, made honorary burgess & guild brother, along with Duke of Buccleuch, *m.t.c. 6/6/1770.* Duke of B. married 1767 Lady Elizabeth, daughter of late Duke of M.
MONTEITH'S CLOSE	*Edgar. Ainslie. Kirkwood. Kerr.* Also known as Fleming's Close.
	From the booth, *Prot. G.H.6, 11/5/1722,* or tenement in Monteith's, formerly Fleming's Close, *Prot. W.F.5, 12/4/1753; G.I. 1/9/1731,* which older name was derived from Patrick Fleeming, who owned land on the north side of the High Street above the Netherbow, *Prot. A.W. 7, 16/9/1723,* and a 'Tinnice Court' west of Bryson's (Trunk's) Close, *Prot. G.H.10, 28/1/1734.*
	The court at the foot of the close was called Ironside Court, *D.1827; o.s.* No derivation has been found.
MONTGOMERIE STREET	Elm Row to Windsor St., *D.1827.* Ground at corner of Leith St. which belonged to heirs of Wm. Montgomerie, *mentioned m.t.c. 29/6/1825.*
MONTPELIER MONTPELIER PARK TERRACE	House Montpelier Park, *Ord. Surv. 1852.* Montpelier Lodge to let 27./4/1833,*eec.j.s.* Montpelier Cottage, Bruntsfield Links, *D.1827,107.* "Morningside, the Montpelier of Midlothian", *Stranger's Guide 191.* "The Montpelier of Scotland" from its mild sulubrious air", *o.& n.e. iii. 38.* The district so nicknamed from its being a popular summer resort. *New pict. Edin. 1820, 37.* Montpelier was the birthplace of St. Roque, whose chapel was on the Burgh Muir, but any connection must be fanciful.
	The name was descriptively applied to Brunstane House, *Baird 83.* "Mount Pillore Lodge, Bruntsfield Links, west side", *D.1832.* But Montpelier Cottage, p.111. 7 acres of ground to feu for villas, head of Bruntsfield Links, just west of house of Lord Provost, by physicians called the Montpelier of Scotland, *e.e.c. 26/1/1811.*
	"Montpelier", from its place, Inveresk was so called anciently, *Stat. account 1845, Vol. 1, p.24.*
MORAY PLACE	*D.1827.* On the estate of the Earl of Moray. Feuing plan by James Gillespie, *eec.j.s. 11/7/22.* All the streets etc. on the Estate, refer to the Moray family. "Great Moray Place" (feuing plan), *m.t.c. 12/6/1822.*
MORRISON STREET	From name of owner at west end, *Ainslie 1804. D.M.1840. D.1800-83.* Mr. Morison of Rosemount, writer, *D.1800, 202.* Morrison's Park lying at west end of Maitland St. next the Haymarket, with one front of 299 feet to Maitland St. and another of 770 feet to Castlebarns Road, and another of 656 feet to a new street called St. Cuthberts St. running from Morrison St. to Lothian Road, *eec.j.s. 15/1/1825.* Clearly shewn in Lothian Map 1825. The name was at first applied only to the Western part of the line of road.
	Ground at Rosemount, N.S. road from Tobago St. to Whitehouse Toll bar, opp. Gardners Hall. Apply to Mr. Morrison, writing chambers, West End, Princest St., *e.e.c. 9/4/1792.* Wm. Morrison, writer Edin-

burgh, acquired the ground on which part of M. St. West Maitland St. Torphichen St. and Dewar Pl. were built, partly from the Heriot Trust, partly from Nathaniel Donaldson, of the Island of Tobago, 1788-1790. It was acquired in 1807 by Capt. Hugh Morrison, 3rd Lincolnshire Militia, who dwelt in Tobago St. He built some houses in W. Maitland St. and the whole ground was then known as "Morrison's Park". About 1825, the ground was purchased from his heir at Lawbert M. by the Trustees of Thomas M, builder & architect, Edin., who feued it out. He was born in Parish of Muthill, but lived in Edin., died in Duke St. 1820. Buried in St. Cuthbert's Churchyard. He built Abercromby Pl. etc. He left residue of estate to found Morrison's Academy, Crieff. *Murray, Beith & Murray., w.s. 29/3/23.*

MORRISON'S CLOSE

Edgar. Ainslie. Kirkwood. Kerr. Shown as Callender's Close.

Property in this close was owned by John Morrison, merchant, *Reg. 6/12/1857.* On the east side was the great house, owned of old by John Moriesone, and, after him, by John Moriesone of Dairsey, the town wall lying to the north of the close, *Prot. W.F.3, 14/2/1750.* It also appears as John Morison's Close, *Prot. A.W.5, 6/11/1716.* The close next to Gray's Close, and apparently on the east, was called Callender's Close, *Prot. G.H.8, 14/5/1729; G.I.3, 25/6/1740.* John Callender, later of Craigforth, *see Callender's Entry, Canongate,* owned land on the north side of the High Street, having land of Wm. Lindsay on the west, *Prot. A.W.7, 25/1/1725.* This would identify Callender's and Morrison's Closes.

MORTON STREET

From Mr. Morton, who, after being clerk to Mr. Jameson, leased from him the Pipe St. works very early in the 19th century, *Baird 294.* Morton Cottage, Portobello, *m.t.c. 14/1/1836.*

MORTONHALL ROAD

From the old house of Mortonhall, property of the Trotters. Owned by Alexr. Eleis before 1645, *St. G. 290.*
For Mortonhall Park—See Part II.

MOSTON TERRACE

From a little property in Cheshire, owned by John Bright, M.P., which he bequeathed to his three daughters, his sister, Priscilla married Duncan McLaren, M.P., owner of the ground on which it was built (about 1878). See Glenorchy Terrace.

MOUND
MOUND PLACE

From the "Earthen Mound" formed by the earth dug from the foundations and basements of Princes St. and the New Town. "Geordie Boyds Mud Brig". Begun 1779, *Gilbert 16.* Resolved 30/10/1782 by Town Council, that Mound be formed. "North Mound", *m.t.c. 8/3/1786.* "The embankment between Hanover St. and James Court Garden", *m.t.c. 3/10/1787.* George Welsh was employed by the Town, *m.t.c. 14/6/1786,* to cart earth from ground belonging to the Trustees for the Register Office to the Mound at not more than ½d per cubic yard. Mound Pl., *m.t.c. 22/11/1809.* House called Mound Pl., *m.t.c. 2/4/1817, 30/10/1787.*

MULBERRY PLACE

From the Mulberry trees, which the silk-working refugees from France attempted, unsuccessfully, to cultivate for their silkworms, as also on the slopes of Multer's hill, *b.b. 57.* See Picardie Place. Many bleaching mills here in 17th and 18th centuries, *j.r.*

MURIESTON CRESCENT
LANE
PLACE
ROAD
TERRACE

From property in Midlothian, belonging to late Sir James Steel, builder and Lord Provost.

MURRAYFIELD AVENUE DRIVE GARDENS PLACE ROAD	From Archibald Murray, proprietor of the ground early 18th century. He bought it in 1734 from the Nisbets of the Dean, from whom it took its old name of Nisbet Parks. Murrayhall, apparently near Coltbridge, *m.t.c. 17/7/1816.*
MYRESIDE	Name of a farm, on the Merchiston estate: suggestive "myre side, Boroughmuirhead", *D.1827.* Shewn, *Ord. Surv. 1852.* Demolished early 20th Century for South Gilsland Road. *See Myreside Road—Part II.*
MYRTLE TERRACE	Fancy. From the myrtle shrub, *c.c.b.c.ld.*
McCONNOCHIE'S CLOSE	44 Cowgate. *D.1827.* "Head of Cowgate", *D.1800, 158.* Machonochie's Cl., *Ord. Surv. 1852,* or Robertson's Cl., *c.h.i. 516.* From Wm. McConochie, who had wright's shop & yard there, *Prot. J.W.6., 30/3/1763.* He retained right to entry 8′0″ wide when adjoining property was sold, *Reg. 22/1/1861.*
McDONALD ROAD	From Sir Andrew McDonald, clothier, Provost 1894-1897 under whom the Talla water scheme was practically started, Sept. 1895. *See also McDonald Place, Street—Part II.*
MACDOWALL ROAD	On the lands of Major Rt. Gordon Gordon Gilmour, descended from Walter Little Gilmour, of Liberton and Craigmillar, who married in 1805, James Anne Macdowall, heiress of Canonmills, from whose family was named McDowall St., foot of Leith Wynd.
MACKENZIE PLACE	*D.1827.* McKenzie's Place. Shewn on map 39b. In *D.1834/5, p.139,* No. 9 is occupied by Samuel Mackenzie, artist, his name is among the Mackenzies. Portrait Painter, *D.1833/4, p.57, c.1.* In 1830/1 he is in 19 Main St. In 1832/3 in McKenzie Pl., No. 7.
McLAREN ROAD	On ground belonging to Duncan McLaren, M.P. for Edinburgh, 1865-1881. Died 1886. Brother in law to John Bright, M.P.
McLAREN TERRACE	After Duncan McLaren, M.P. brother in law of John Bright, M.P.
McLEOD STREET	From builder.

N

NAPIER ROAD	From John Napier of Merchiston q.v., built on the Merchiston estate. Shewn, but not named, *Littlejohn Map.* (The inventor of Logarithms).
NELSON STREET PLACE	After Horatio Nelson, R.N. "Centre of Abercromby Place", *D.1827.* Off the centre, *Ainslie 1804.* One of the streets commemorative of naval heroes—Howe St., Rodney St., Duncan Street, St. Vincent St., *m.t.c. 22/4/1807.*
NEW ASSEMBLY CLOSE	(Unnamed in o.s.) *Edgar. Ainslie. Kerr.* Commercial Bank Close, formerly New Assembly Close, *Kirkwood.* Back of Bell's Wynd, *Prot. W.F.11, 20/10/1762;* Fairlie's Entry from Cowgate (q.v.); Murray's Close, *Prot. W.F.3, 7/12/1749;* Snawdoun's Close, *Prot. W.F.10, 3/2/1761.* The name was taken from the New Assembly Rooms, which occupied the great house there from 1766 to 1784, *New Lights, 185. o.& n.c. i. 245, mentions the Assembly Room in Bell's Wynd, to which rank and fashion came in 1758. But Edgar 1742 and Maitland 1753 gives the New Assembly Close, showing that it already bore the name.* The name does not occur in the protocols. From its position it was also called the Back of Bell's Wynd, *Prot. W.F.11, 20/10/1762.*

But it was also named Snadoun's Close, *'Snadoun's Close, now back of Bell's Wynd', Prot. G.H.11, 5/2/1737;* *'Snadown's Close, commonly called Back of Bell's Wynd', Prot. W.F.7, 17/2/1756,* under many varieties of spelling: Snaddoun's, *New Lights, 182,* Snadonis, *Prot. 26/6/1533,* Snawdounis, *c.c. 972, 11/10/1525.* The name seems to have leapt from the north side of the Cowgate to the south, and to have been applied to either Peter's Close, or immediately east of it. Stables on the east side of Snawdoun's Close, built by Alexr. Peter, wright, south side of the Cowgate, *Prot. W.F.8, 23/8/1756,* seem to imply this.

The derivation of the name is unknown.

Another name, Murray's Close, was derived from the residence of John Murray of Blackbarony, father of the first Lord Elibank, who in 1580 occupied the great mansion at the top of the close formerly owned by the Bishop of Dunkeld, *New Lights, 183.*

Kirkwood gives 'Commercial Bank Close, formerly New Assembly Close', which is confirmed by the Directory for 1827. The name was due to the occupation by the Commercial Bank, from 1814 to 1847, of the 'New' Assembly Rooms, occupied in succession as the King's Arms Tavern; by the Highland Society; and finally, after various changes, as the Children's Shelter, *New Lights, 185.*

Gordon shows no distinct close between Bell's Wynd and Stevenlaw's Close; Edgar and Ainslie two short blind closes, *in one line,* one on the south side of the High Street, the other on the north side of the Cowgate, giving the impression that formerly there had been some kind of thoroughfare, under one name, but that the middle part had been built up and the ends left. It was after this separation that the lower end became Fairlie's Entry.

NEW LANE	Annfield to Williamfield, *D.1827.* Was so once. **Redeveloped but name retained 1965.**
NEWHAVEN ROAD	So called to distinguish it from the old haven of Blackness, *Irons ii. 457.* Built by James IV, and presented to or bought by the City of Edinburgh 1510, *o.& n.e. iii. 297.* It was known in the 15th century as "Our Lady's Port of Grace", from the chapel there. Newhaven Road formerly Bonnington Road, *Littlejohn Map.* **See also Newhaven Main Street—Part II.**
NEW STREET	Dr. Young's (House). *Edgar. Ainslie. Kirkwood. Kerr.*

It was a new street about 1760, and was at first called Young Street, *o.& n.e. ii. 18; Kincaid 107,* from the house of Dr. Thomas Young, which appears as one of the additions made to Edgar's map in 1765.

The street was a private one, with posts and chains, till declared a public one in 1786, *m.t.c. 19/4/1786,* but it remained private in effect till 1819, when power was reserved by the late Dr. Thomas Young's representatives to make New Street a public access from the High Street of the Canongate to the road at the foot of the Calton Hill, or not, 'as they please', *Can. Chart. 5/5/1819.*

The two names appear combined, 'Dr. Young's new street in Cannongate', *m.t.c. 25/1/1826.* His name appears in 1773, *p.w. 1773,* and later as in New Street. He was married to Barbara Gibson, *Can. Chart. 28/7/1782,* but seems to have had no family, his heir being Robert Powley, watchmaker in Appleby, only brother of Thos. Powley, doctor of medicine in Edinburgh, *Can. Chart. 26/7/1775.* Dr. Young owned property on both sides of the street.

NEWBATTLE TERRACE	In Johnston's map 1851, "Napier Terrace". Newbattle Terrace, *Ord. Surv. 1852.* "Newbattle House, Pitsligo Road", *St. Matthews 37.* On the estate of Sir Wm. Forbes whose heir married a daughter of the Marquis of Lothian. Marriage commemorated in Newbattle Ter. *Anon. note.*
NEWINGTON PLACE ROAD	*D.1827.* "Clunie's brewery on land of Mr. Scott at Newington", 11/2/1794, *eec.j.s.* "Robt. Clunie, brewer, foot of Scienns", *D.1800, 115.* Lands of Newington for sale, holding feu of City of Edinburgh, 23/11/1772, *eec.j.s.* Newington. Causeyside, *D.1800, 220.* Lands of Newington, part of the Old and New Burrowmuir, *v.r. 39.* Newington St., *M.216.* Charter for lands of Newington granted to Benjamin Bell of Hunthill, surgeon, *m.t.c. 24/7/1805.* Acquired from Alexr. Wood, surgeon, *2/6/1803.* Lands of Newington, *Prot. 10/6/1713.* Newington—"Farm house of Newington"—*e.a. 15/5/1764.* Newington, *M.172, c.2.* Mr. Alex. Elleis of Newington, *Prot. 25/8/1740.*
NEW MARKET ROAD	From the new markets for hides, skin and tallow. Slateford Road. Early 20th century.
NEW MART ROAD	From new cattle mart. Slateford Road. Early 20th century.
NEWPORT STREET	Castlebarns, *D.1827.* From the new basin shewn Lothian Map 1825. *Littlejohn, App. 42.* On Union Canal.
NICOLL PLACE	From George Nicol, market gardener, circa 1840, *j.r. (Following derivation given by someone other than Boog Watson.)* Feu charter dated 1892. (In Wm. Robertsone, factors, Atholl Cresc.) Feu contract between Duncan McLaren and David and Albert Nicoll, Dairymen, Bathfield Dairy, North Leith. Minutes of Leith Town Council, 5th Mar. 1900-1, p.189: "that name should be given".
NICOLSON STREET SQUARE	Built between 1765 and 1780. *Edgar and Ainslie.* On the lands of Lady Nicolson, Edgar 1765 shews "New Road" as projected, *Ainslie 1780,* her house demolished and the memorial pillar to her husband, and the street partly built. She removed to a house farther west, "now part of the premise of Andrew Usher & Co., *Gilbert,* West face with pear tree trained on it. Looks toward the Chapel of Ease. *Walks in Edinburgh 248.* West Nicolson St. is named Chapel St. in Ainslie 1780, from St. Cuthbert's Chapel of Ease Nicolson House to let, 26/8/1772, *eec.j.s.* "Sir James Nicolson of that ilk", *m.t.c. 22/1/1823.* "Nicholson's Park, hard by this city", *c.a. 18/6/1765.* Lady N's park, *c.a. 5/7/1765.* Wm. Nycholsoune owned land and house south of St. Leonards, *c.c. 850 4/6/1517.* The Barony of Nicolsone, (now Roseberrie) owned by Sir John & Sir Wm. N., acquired by Archibald, viscount of Roseberrie, *m.t.c. 17/2/1701.*
	Sir James N. of that Ilk, having purchased some acres lying to the S. of the Potterrow (whereon he has built a new house, which he now possesses) bounded by the highway or causeyway leading from Poterow port to the Sheins, with a piece of waste ground between, which he wishes the town to grant him, he having had trouble with the J.P.'s of Midlothian. Granted, feuduty one merk; Sir James to use the ground only for planting trees to be a decorement to the town. The measurements given, *m.t.c. 17/2/1727.* Charter granted in his favour, of waist ground lying opposite the Wind milne, *m.t.c. 28/7/1727.* Sir John Nicolson, as one of the creditors of Sir Wm. Dick was approached by the town, 27/5/1674, for liberty to bring the water pipes through the lands of Braid. £1000 Scots granted to Sir John Nicolson of that Ilk, in acknowledgement of his allowing the water

pipes to be brought through the estate of Braid, which sum he will use in laying lead pipes from a spring to his own house of Nicolson for the use of the family, *m.t.c. 29/9/1675.*

That part of the parish of Temple which was anciently called Clarkington, and formed a separate parish under that name, was in 1695 in the possession of Sir John Nicolson, and formed a barony named Nicolson. In that year it was sold to Archibald Primrose of Dalmeny (2nd son to Sir Archd. P. of Carrington), Bart. Lord Register and Justice Genl. of Scotland, who got a charter under the Great Seal, whereby this and contiguous lands were formed into a new barony of Rosebery, which he assumed as his title when created Viscount in 1700. The first Earl sold it in 1712 to the Marquis of Lothian who named it New Ancrum, but the family disponed it about 1749 to Mr. Hepburne, who gave its old name of Clarkington. It was bought again in 1821 from his descendants by Archibald 4th Earl of Rosebery, who restored the name of Rosebery: created Peer of the United Kingdom 1828. Hepburn began to demolish the old Mansion house 1805; it was finally rased 1812, and a small new house built. *From New Statistical Account of Scotland 1845.* (i.e. Eldest son of his second marriage with Agnes, daughter of Sir Wm. Gray of Pittendrum: anent whom see Lady Stairs Close). It seems that the lands of Nicolsone, pertaining to the deceased Sir John and Sir Wm. Nicolson of that Ilk, came into the hands of the town as part of the bankrupt estate. These lands and barony were acquired by Archd. Primrose of Dalmeny at the public roup, 7th July 1694. On 15th May 1696, said Ar. P. of D. paid the Town £131,350 as the price, also amount due as rent since purchase, which was equivalent to interest on price during the time till it was paid, *m.t.c. 15/5/1696.* Sir John Nicolson of that Ilk made B. & G. gratis, by right of his umq. fr. Sir John N. of Poltoun, B.& G. 4/2/1676.

NIDDRIE ROAD

Leading to the village of Niddrie.
See also Niddrie—Part II.

NIDDRY STREET

Vicus Needrisij, *Gordon.* Nidrie's Wynd, *Edgar.* Niddry's Wynd, *Ainslie 1780.* Niddery Street, *Ainslie 1804.* Niddrie Wynd, *Kerr.*

Now represented by Niddry Street, which is, however, a good deal further east than the old wynd, due to the changes made in building the South Bridge, *St. C.H. 21.*

It is mentioned in a charter of 3rd October 1477, *M.8., c.2.* as 'Nudreis Wynd'. The name 'is doubtless connected with Robert Niddry, magistrate in 1437,' *o.& n.e. ii. 241.* The Rev. Dr. Butler states that the Wauchopes of Niddry had their town mansion in the wynd, *Tron Kirk 48,* but no authority is quoted for either statement. Niddry Street stretched itself across the Cowgate, and captured Aitkin's Close, giving it the name of South Niddry Street, *m.t.c. 9/12/1818.*

The name varies a little in form—Nidery's, *M.216,* Nidrie's, *Edgar,* Nithrie's, *Prot. J.W.3, 29/12/1752,* and Nethery's, *Prot. A.W.7, 25/1/1725,* but nothing has been found to give the true derivation.

SOUTH NIDDRY STREET

Aitken's Close, *Ainslie.*

Considered as a continuation of Niddry Street, formerly Niddry's Wynd. (It is given as Adams' Court in Brown and Watson's map of 1793).

The old name, Aitken's Close, is derived from the property of George Aitken, smith, lying opposite Niddry's Wynd, which he bought from

Marion and Barbara, daughters of the late John Scott, wright, by Helen McGill, *Prot. W.F.8, 25/2/1758.* He purchased also land from the heirs of John Jack, slater, *m.t.c. 6/12/1820,* and built thereon on the west side of Robertson's, or Robison's, Close, at the foot thereof, *Prot. J.W.4, 31/8/1757; W.F.8, 23/2/1758; m.t.c. 17/5/1815.*

NILE GROVE	From the neighbouring district of Egypt, q.v.
NOBLE PLACE	From Grace Noble, wife of Wm. Fingzies, who built the houses there, *j.r.*

NORTH BRIDGE

On the north of the Town. Originally suggested by James, Duke of York, *o.& n.e. i. 336.* Also by Sir Wm. Bruce of Kinross, architect to Chas. II. Do. do. Begun 1763—foundation laid—begun in earnest 1765. Finished 1769. South arch fell Aug. 1769, five passengers killed. Re-opened 1772. Wm. Mylne, builder, widened, 1873. New iron bridge begun 1896. Opened Sept. 1897.

NORTH FOULIS' CLOSE

Fowler's Close, *Edgar. Kirkwood.* Foulis's, *Ainslie.* Fowlis', *Kerr.*

North has been added to distinguish it from *South* Foulis' Close; there is no connection in derivation. It has been suggested that the name is derived from the house, demolished in 1902, occupied by Lady Munro of Fowlis, *o.e.c. i. 8,* but it seems, however, to come from John Foulis, apothecary, owner of a tenement in the close, *Prot. J.W.1, 5/7/1746; W.F.10, 28/4/1761; G.L.1, 10/9/1763.*

NORTH GRAY'S CLOSE

p.w. list 1779. Kerr. Gray's Close, *Edgar. Ainslie. Kirkwood.*

This close has no connection with South Gray's Close—'north' and 'south' being added merely to prevent confusion. The name may be derived from the property owned by Robert, son and heir of the late Alexr. Gray, which lay beside the yard of the College of Holy Trinity, *Prot. 5/8/1528.*

NORTH JUNCTION STREET	See Junction St.
NORTH PARK TERRACE	From position beside Inverleith Park, on the north side of the Town.

NORTHCOTE STREET

From Sir Stafford Northcote, First Lord Iddesleigh, leader of the Conservative party, Lord Rector of Edinburgh University Nov. 1883. Addressed a meeting in the Corn Exchange, Grassmarket. Sept. 1884, *Gilbert 161-163.*

NORTHUMBERLAND STREET PLACE

Built by 1804, *Ainslie.* Mentioned 9/1/1808, *eec.j.s. m.t.c. 17/7/1805.* From the county, which formerly was a part of Scotland. The east part built first and called "East Northumberland St.", *m.t.c. 1/3/1809.*

NORTON PARK
PLACE EAST
PLACE WEST

On the ground of the Hon. Fletcher Norton, Baron of the Scottish Exchequer 1776. Died 1820, *o.& n.e. iii. 28. D.1827.* Property shewn *Ainslie 1804.* His address "new town", *p.w. 1780/81, 2.* Miss Julia Fletcher, residing Norton Place, *m.t.c. 4/4/1832.* Four fields at Abbeyhill to let: apply at Hon. Baron Norton's House, Abbeyhill, *e.e.c. 2/10/1906.* Baron Norton's House, near Norton Place, *Map 83.*

NOTTINGHAM PLACE

Arnot 1816 map. Lothian Map 1825. Site named Mud Island, *Ainslie 1804 q.v.*

Built by Samuel Wordsworth, for his stables, *see D.1800. m.t.c. 22/7/1807.* He probably came from Nottingham, or had some connection with that town. He certainly came from England, *m.t.c. 9/10/1808.* He was boxmaster of the incorporated trades of the Calton, *m.t.c. 11/8/1813.* He was horse dealer & vintner, foot of Nottingham Ter., *D.1800,* and seems to have retired to 9 St. John St.

D.1827. He made petition 1/2/1815 to the Town Council for £30 to meet his expenses in planning a race course at the Meadows, as suggested by the Magistrates, Jan. 1812, and in visiting race courses in England. Refused, but £30 granted him 13/9/1815.

O

OAKFIELD TERRACE	From the oak tree, *e.c.b.c.ld.*
OBSERVATORY ROAD	From the City Observatory, erected on Blackford Hill, opened 1896, after four years' building, *Gilbert 176.*
OGILVIE TERRACE	On George Watson's Hospital ground; named from Dr. G. Ogilvie, headmaster of George Watson's College, *w.c.*
OLD ASSEMBLY CLOSE	*Ainslie. Kirkwood. Kerr.* Assembly Close, *Edgar.* Little's Close, *New Lights, 94,* Durie's Close, *New Lights 89,* Steil's Close, *St. C.H. 259,* Patrick Shiell's, *Prot. J.W.8, 25/6/1767,* or Stiel's Close, *Reg. 4/8/1744,* Gillespie's Close, *Prot. J.W.7, 22/3/1765,* Barnes' Close, *Prot. J.W.5, 13/2/1759,* Zair's Close, *Prot. A.W.6, 3/2/1720.*

From the Assembly (Dancing) Rooms, formerly in the West Bow, but transferred about 1720, *Wilson, ii. 32,* and finally burned out in the great fire of 1824. The Old Assembly Hall was a great hall or room in the great stone tenement built by Wm. Smellie, Henry Wilson, and James Mack, on the east side of Borthwick's Close, entered from both Borthwick's and Steele's Closes, *Prot. J.W.4, 23/5/1758. One of the confusing cases of the same name applied to two adjacent closes bounding the name-giving tenement.*

It 'has had a new name with almost every century of its existence. In the middle of the sixteenth century it was known as Little's, after Mr. Clement Little, advocate (founder of the University Library), who, along with his brother the Provost, lived there. Another change of name took place in the seventeenth century in honour of ... Sir Alexr. Gibson, better known as Lord Durie, whose mansion stood on the site of the Old Assembly Rooms', *New Lights, 89; Wilson, ii. 32,* occupied later, 1835, by one of the Heriot schools.

The name Little's Close has not been found amongst the protocols examined, but Walter Little of Libberton owned a tenement on the east side of the top of the Old Assembly Close, *Prot. J.W.4, 3/1/1758.* A protocol for Gabriel Little or Rankine of Over Libbertoun is recorded, dealing with property in the close commonly called Clement Little's Close, south side of the High Street, *Prot. A.W.6, 28/8/1718.*

Durie's or Durrie's *Prot. A.W.2, 29/11/1704* Close occurs frequently, *e.g. formerly Durie's or Patrick Shiell's, now Old Assembly Close: Prot. J.W.8, 25/6/1767,* named from Lord Durie above; but there is a hint of another derivation in John Durie, 'faber muriarius', resident in Zair's alias Durie's alias Patrick Steill's Close, *Prot. A.W.6, 3/2/1720.*

Zair's Close is clearly the same as Yaris, which was on the south side of the High Street, in part running east and west, and containing the lands of David Gillespy, deceist, *c.c.1400, 30/3/1547,* also Hair's Close, containing a tenement of Katherine Gillespie, on south side of the High Street next to Borthwick's Close, *quoted from charter of Michael Macquhan and his spouse, Janet Rhind: for founding of the Magdalen Chapel.*

Its alias, Patrick Stiell's *Patrick Steill's, now Old Assembly Close: Reg. 4/8/1744,* or Patrick Shiel's *Prot. J.W.8, 25/6/1767,* or Stiel's *St. C.H. 259* Close, is derived from the lodging or tavern, The Cross Keys, sometime belonging to Patrick Steil, in Patrick Steil's or Durie's Close, *Prot. W.F.10, 21/8/1761*. This house seems to have been owned by Archibald, portioner of Inverask, only son and heir of Archibald Shiels, merchant, Edinburgh: its builder being the late John Hamilton, and its position between Durie's Close on the west and Covenant Close on the east, *Prot. W.F.10, 14/8/1761. See also St. Monan's Wynd and Conn's Close.*

The close seems also, wholly or in part, to have been named Gillespy's Close, but the distinct alias has not been found. The name is derived from the lands of David Gillespy close to Borthwick's Close, *Prot. J.W.7, 22/3/1765,* or of Wm. Gillespie whose lands were on the north side of the Cowgate, having the tenement of Lord Borthwick on the west, *Prot. A.W.7, 24/5/1725.* Katherine Gillespie's tenement in Hair's Close is mentioned above, *quoted from charter of Michael Macquhan and his spouse, Janet Rhind: for founding of the Magdalen Chapel.* David Gillespie, baxter, owned a tenement on the north side of the Cowgate, with lands to the west and south and the transe of Suittie's, now Fishmarket Close, on the west, *Reg. 4/6/1741.* The close was on the south side of the High Street, *Prot. G.H.5, 9/7/1718.*

Yet another name seems to belong to this close, Barnes' Close. There was a tenement on the south side of the High Street in Conn's Close, bounded by the transe of the close called Barnes' Close on the west, *Prot. J.W.5, 13/2/1759.* This is the one mention of the name, and no hint is given of its derivation.

OLD FISHMARKET CLOSE

Vicus Fori Pisactorii, *Gordon.* Shown as Fishmarket Close, *Edgar, D.1800.* Old Fishmarket Close, *Ainslie. Kirkwood marks it as now shut up.* Swift's Close. Suittie's Close. Carmichael's Close. Gourlay's Close.

It owed its name to the Old Fishmarket, shown by Gordon and Edgar: later the Poultry Market (as in Ainslie 1780), or Poultry and fish, *Ainslie 1804.* The reduced area of the Market was occupied later by the Union Bank.

An alias of the sixteenth century was Swift's Wynd or Close, *New Lights, 57, n.* It is spoken of as the Fishmercate Close, of old, Swyft's Close, *Prot. W.F.10, 7/6/1762,* the name being derived from the owners of property therein. Alexr. Swift owned a cellar at the head of the close, *Prot. A.W.6, 6/8/1719;* John Swift, a tenement at the south side of the Cross, *Prot. A.W.3, 29/7/1709,* and on the east of Barrie's, now Fishmercat Close, *Prot. G.H.6, 22/7/1724.* There was a tenement, with the land of the Laird of Borthwick on the east, and of the late Thomas Swift on the west, *Prot. 16/7/1528 and 21/12/1530.*

It appears also as Suittie's, now Fishmarket Close, *Reg. 4/6/1741,* or Suttie's Wynd, now Fishmercate Close, *Prot. J.W.8, 23/12/1765,* but no derivation has been found, unless the conjecture that Suttie's is a corruption of Swift's. This may be Toddis Close described above; the identification is not clear.

The lower end of the close, named Humph's Close *Prot. W.F.8, 24/8/1757* in the Ordnance Survey, may be still traced in the open space above the Free Breakfast Building, where it yet exists, 3 feet 6 inches wide, in the building occupied by Messrs. Geo. Duncan & Son. The lower end, on the Cowgate, is closed with a sheet-iron gate.

The name seems to occur as Home's Close. A tenement on the east side of Fishmercat Close (Probably the Back of Fishmarket Close) near the end of the close, and opposite the Fishmarket, had Home's Close on the east, *Prot. A.W.3, 31/1/1707,* but no derivation has been found. Edgar names it simply 'Back of Borthwick's Close'. Ainslie indicates the whole as Old Fishmarket Close.

It seems also to have been known as Carmichael's Close, which was immediately west of Borthwick's Close, *Prot. J.W.4, 23/2/1757,* and immediately east of the Fishmarket Close, *Prot. A.W.6, 22/10/1722.* A great stone tenement stood at the back of the Mercat Cross, on the south side of the High Street, now possessed by Mr. Wm. Carmichael, advocate, *Prot. A.W.4, 28/12/1711,* and a tenement is mentioned as being in Borthwick's Close, having the close formerly called Carmichael's Close, now part of the Old Fishmarket Close, on the west, *Reg. 12/10/1860.*

Carmichael's or Gourlay's Close was just west of Borthwick's Close, *Prot. J.W.3, 2/7/1756; J.W.4, 23/2/1757,* but no hint as to Gourlay's identity has been found.

OLD PLAYHOUSE CLOSE

Kerr. Upr. Playhouse Close, *Ainslie.* Upper Playhouse Close, *Kirkwood.* Old Playhouse Close, *D.1827, as shown by comparing the street numbers with Kirkwood.* Dallas' Close, *Prot. J.W.4, 31/8/1757 and J.W.8, 5/12/1767, where the alias is distinctly given.*

It was named from the Playhouse, fitted up in 1747, *Wilson, ii. 86,* between the two closes to which it gave its name.

It was also known as Dallas' Close, *Reg. 1/5/1741,* from the tenement sometime owned by the late James Inglis, now by Wm. Hunter, and other houses owned by *(blank)* Dallas, now by Wm. Hunter, the 'Ingurium Calmentarium, lie, *Lie= 'which being interpreted is',* Mason's Lodge,' owned now by Richard Coopar, being on the east, *REG 1/5/1741*

The other Playhouse Close, Downmost, *p.w. list 1779; Ainslie 1780,* Undr., *Ainslie 1804,* Old Playhouse, *o.s.; Kerr,* takes its name from its position, being lower down the street.

It was called also Inglis Close, from the property of James Inglis mentioned above, and of Wm. Inglis, W.S., *'Inglis Close or Playhouse Close', the lower, or eastmost close, property of Wm. Inglis, W.S.: Can. Chart. 15/5/1875.*

OLD STAMP OFFICE CLOSE

Shown as Newbank Close, *Edgar.* Ship Close, *Ainslie.* Old Bank or Ship Close, *p.w. list 1779.* Formerly New Bank Close, *Kirkwood.* Fortune's Close.

In Williamson's Directory for 1779 we find George Thomson, Stamp Office, Old Ship Close, *D.1799, p.6.* Stamp Office, Old Ship Close. The Stamp Office remained in this close till 1821, when it was transferred to Waterloo Place.

Edgar calls it the Newbank Close, as containing the New, or Royal Bank, constituted in 1727, whose office was in the close till 1753. It is mentioned under the same name in the Council Minutes of 19th June 1805. In Peter Williamson's list of 1779 he calls it the Old Bank (or Ship) Close, which name properly belongs to the close on the south side of the Lawnmarket, now removed **for** Melbourne Place, where the Bank of Scotland was opened in 1695. It owed its alias of Ship Close, *Ainslie,* Old Ship Close, *p.w. 1780, p.34; D.1799, p.6,* or Ship Tavern Close, *Prot. J.W.1, 29/8/1745,* to the 'Ship' tavern built by Thomas Wilson, *Prot. A.W.5, 19/9/1716.*

It took its name of Fortune's Close, *p.w. 1773, p.69; m.t.c. 5/8/1795;M,* from John Fortune of the famous tavern, opposite the Guard, *p.w. 1773*, or in the Old Ship Close, *p.w.1780*. The house itself was owned by the Earl of Eglinton, *m.t.c. 2/5/1770*.

ORCHARD BRAE

Road leading to orchard of Dean House.
See also Orchard Bank etc.—Part II.

ORMELIE TERRACE

Lord Ormelie, title of the eldest son of the Marquis of Breadalbane.

ORMIDALE TERRACE

Compliment to George L. Macfarlane, Hon. Lord Ormidale, senator of College of Justice in Scotland 1910. The name was on the plan when the property was acquired by the Murrayfield Real Estate Coy. from the late Mr. Lockhart Thomson (Jas. Stewart). Died at Ormidale, Argyllshire 6/7/1804. Alexr. Campbell of Ormidale Esq., *Scots Magazine 1804*.

ORWELL PLACE
TERRACE

Appears first in D. 1876/7. Orwell is a parish, with ancient chapel in Kinross-shire, adjoining Loch Leven.
1887 v.r. Dalry House was on Episcopal Training College. Orwell Place was constructed to give Dalry House a frontage. College may well have had an influence in choice of name, namely from a religious source, the ancient chapel of Orwell.

OSBORNE TERRACE

From Royal residence as its neighbours, Hampton and Kew Terraces.

P

PAISLEY'S CLOSE

Shown as Smith's Close, *Edgar*. East Bailie Fyfe's Close, *Ainslie*. East Bailie Fife's Close, formerly Smith's, *Kirkwood*.

Both the closes leading into the court were known as Bailie Fyfe's Close, *'The two closes called Bailie Fyfe's'. Reg. 14/1/1859.*

Its present name, Paisley's Close, is derived from Henry Paislie, who acquired lands there sometime owned by George Henderson of Fordell, *Prot. A.W.4, 25/10/1711; A.W.5, 25/6/1716.*

Its older name, Smith's Close, is derived from the great Smith's Land, built by Mr. James Smith of Whitehill, *Prot. J.W.4, 6/2/1758; J.W.7, 21/11/1764; J.W.8, 18/12/1765*, from whom it was inherited by his son Gilbert, mason, who disponed it to Andrew Barclay, writer, *Prot. W.F.9, 23/8/1759.*

A modern shield, inscribed Smith's Land, may be seen carved on the wall, just east of Bailie Fyfe's Close. Smith's land occurs frequently in the protocols.

PALMERSTON PLACE

From Lord Palmerston (Punch's favourite "Pam"). Foreign secretary 1830, premier 1855. Lord Rector Glasgow University April 1863. Made Burgess of Edinburgh and banqueted (1863). Feued from Heriot's Hospital April 1877.

PALMERSTON ROAD

From same source as Palmerston Place.

PANMURE CLOSE

Ainslie. Kirkwood. Kerr. M'Kell's Close, *Can. Chart. 3/7/1838; m.t.c. 3/7/1838.*

So called from its giving access to Panmure House, the town residence of the Earl of Panmure, occupied later by the Countess of Aberdeen, and in 1778 by Adam Smith till his death in 1790, *Wilson, ii. 109; o.& n.e. ii. 20.*

It seems to have had an earlier name, M'Kell's Close, derived from Jean and Catherine M'Kell, who owned property in M'Kell's Close, which they disponed to William, Earl of Panmure, *Can. Chart. 3/7/1838.* They are mentioned as former owners in the Minutes of the Town Council, *m.t.c. 15/2/1797, 3/7/1838.* The alias is not definite, but seems sufficiently indicated.

PANMURE PLACE	From Earl of Panmure, minister for war at the time of the Indian Mutiny.
PAPE'S COTTAGES	Roseburn. Almshouses under philanthropic bequest of Mr. Geo. Pape, specially for behoof of dwellers in village of Coltbridge.
PARK AVENUE	From Parkhouse, originally Portobello Park, a small farm, *Baird 297.*
PARK ROAD PLACE	Newhaven. From situation. *Park Crescent etc.—Liberton—See Part II.*
PARKSIDE STREET TERRACE	From vicinity to the King's Park, which gave its name to Parkside House. East side of Pleasance, a little within the turnpike (toll) on the Dalkeith road (i.e. the Gibbet toll) to let, *eec.j.s. 12/2/1772.* Parkside buildings Parkside St. St. Leonards, *D.1827.* Parkside, near the Gibbet, east side of road leading to Dalkeith, *m.t.c. 12/9/1810, 5/6/1822.*
PARKVALE PLACE	Fanciful, beside Leith Links, *j.r.*
PARLIAMENT SQUARE	*D.1827.* Formerly Parliament Close, *D.1800, 126.* from the neighbouring Parliament Hall, finished 1639.
PARLIAMENT STREET	Also ancient Parliament Court. (Parliament Close, St. Leonard's Lane and St. Andrew St., *D.1827.* Parliament Square, *D.1800.* Probably because the Earl of Lennox and the Earl of Mar held their councils there from 1571, *o.& n.e. iii. 247.* Parliament Close, *Kirkwood, j.r.s.l. 292.*
PARSON'S GREEN TERRACE	Near Piershill, *D.1827.* Pearsons Green end Duke's Walk, *D.1800, 234.* Not from an English family resident there 250 years ago, as stated in Edinburgh Evening News. In days of James VI known as Parson's Knowes , owned by Logan of Parsons Knowes, *i.w.c.h. col. 4, p.193, 1596,* before the Reformation it was church land, belonging to the Parson of Restalrig, *j.r.* Occupied, *Kirkwood and D.1827,* by Wm. Mitchel of Royal Bank. Pearson's Knows, and Parson's Knows both occur, *v.r. 31.* "Personis Knowis", 1593, *s.s.l. 78.*
PATRIOT HALL	Stockbridge, *D.1827.* House and grounds to let or sell, apply to Mr. Le Pique, Shennen Close, 18/2/1775, *eec.j.s. m.t.c. 11/4/1827.* Patriothall buildings, built 1861.
PATTISON STREET	47 Elbe St., *D.1827.* Patison's row. Elbe St., *D.1827, 240.* From John Pattison, town clerk, Links of Leith, *p.w. 1780/81, 112.* Do.do. Charlotte St. Links, *D.1800, 71.* Wm. Patison, merchant Elbe St., house, Links, *D.1827, 231.* An old Leith family. John Pattison appointed Town Clerk of Leith, *m.t.c. 31/8/1774.* Burgess of Edinburgh, 14/2/1776. An old Leith family. The tombstone of John Pattison, Town Clerk of Leith showing beautiful carved symbolism is on south side South Leith Churchyard, *j.r.*
PEACOCK COURT	Main St., Newhaven. Probably from family of Thomas Peacock, who acquired subjects on Newhaven, *m.t.c. 20/5/1778.* Thos. Peacock, vintner, Newhaven, *m.t.c. 4/9/1793.* Thomas Peacock got feu at east end of Newhaven 5/8/1767, *m.t.c. 26/7/1809.* Peacock Inn, Newhaven, 1779, *s.s.l. 115.* Thos. Peacock of Stenhouse, *m.t.c. 5/4/1842.*
PEEL TERRACE	From Sir Robert Peel, *Littlejohn, App. 50.* P.M. at the time.
PENTLAND TERRACE	Looking over to the Pentland Hills. (Properly Benland Hills, that is the hilly or mountainous country. Sir Robert Sibbald, quoted by Maitland 506, c.2.) *See also Pentland Avenue etc.—Part II.*
PICARDY PLACE	"Little Picardy", *M.215.c.2.* From the Protestant refugees, who fled from Picardie after the revocation of the Edict of Nantes in 1685, *o.& n.e. ii. 186. Maitland 215.c.2.* "To the North West of

Greenside is a large Edifice, denominated Little Picardy, erected by the Edinburghers from the Habitation of a Number of French Families, who carry on a Cambrick Manufactory therein", *Anon. map, circa 1730, "Pickardy". do. do. circa 1767. Ainslie 1780 "Picardie".* House gone and now Picardy Place, *Ainslie 1804.* One of the streets on the ground sold by the governors of Heriots Hospital in 1730 for behoof of refugees fleeing after the revocation of the Edict of Nantes. Street named 1809, *b.b.57.* Feu Charter from Heriot's Hospital dated 7 Dec. 1730 .... five acres feued by the City to the predecessors of the Board of Manufactures, for the encouragement of the silk-weavers, French refugees, *r.c.g. 27/28.* A body of weavers brought over by the British Linen Coy. *Walks in Edin. 217,* quoted by Wilson II, 213. There was a silk weavers' factory west of the Calton Hill, *m.t.c. 2/10/1771.* Board of Trustees offered to sell Picardy to the Town, *m.t.c. 11/6/1800.* 5 Acres at Broughton, called Picardy, *m.t.c. 6/5/1801.* Also mention is made of Picardy Street.— *m.t.c. 23/3/1807, 22/4/1807.* Picardy Pl., *m.t.c. 20/5/1807.* Mention is made in m.t.c. 29/8/1832 of Nicolas Dassauville, weaver in Picardy evidently French.

| PIER PLACE | At Newhaven. Evident. |

| PIERSFIELD GREEN
PLACE
TERRACE | From Captain Piers of Piershill.
Possibly not correct derivation—see Piershill—Part II. |

| PIERSHILL PLACE
TERRACE | From Piershill house, residence of Col. Piers, in the middle of the 18th century. Apparently so named by his successor, Ronald Crawford, *o.& n.e. iii. 142.* Thomas Stark, master at Leith mills got sasine of 10 acres of land called Piershill & three steps, in Dec. 1676. In Mr. D. Robertson's South Leith Records the said Thomas Stark was cited for his mills going on the Sabbath morning.
Possibly not correct derivation—See Piershill—Part II. |

| PILRIG PLACE
STREET | From Pilrig house, owned in 1584 by Patrick Monypenny. In 18th century by James Balfour, with whose family R. Stevenson was connected. Named from the ridge whereon in the 15th century the Peel tower stood, *e.s.s. 256.* It was owned by 1506 by Monypenny family. Later new house built by Gilbert Kirkwood, goldsmith, 1638. It is said to have been the country house of Mary of Gueldres, *Irons II, 71.* Peilryge ... lying in the Barony of Brochton, 12th Oct. 1458. *Antiq. 1906/7, 314.* "Lands of Peilrig" 1448, *St. Giles, 318, No. 61. Laing's Charters p.81. j.r.s.l. freq.* Bought by James Balfour 1719.
See also Pilrig Gardens—Part II. |

| PIPE STREET
LANE | From the large pipes bringing water from the Figget burn to the end of the cross lane, between Pipe St. and Bridge St., then known as Tobago St. where was a large trough or tank, *Baird 296.* |

| PIRIE'S CLOSE | D.1827. *o.s. Kerr.* Shown as Perrie's Close, *p.w. list 1779.* Perry's Close, *Ainslie 1780.* Pierry's Close, *Ainslie 1804.* Pierie's Close, *Kirkwood.* Foord's or Fuird's Close, *Prot. G.I.1, 23/12/1731,* Kinnaird's Close, *M.216; Prot. A.W.7, 11/6/1723.*

From a tenement beyond the Netherbow, bounded on the west by Gibb's Close, belonging to the heirs of *(blank)* Peirie, *Prot. J.W.1, 26/1/1748.* The lands of Elizabeth Murray and her husband Alexr. Pirie were here, *Prot. A.W.5, 13/7/1714.* They were acquired by Archibald Chessils by purchase and excambion from Elizabeth Dundas, relict of Wm. Cerser, master of the pin manufactory in Leith, former relict of Thomas Pierie, writer in Edinburgh, son to the late Wm. |

Pierie, and brother to the late Gripheth Pierie, sailor in Leith. David Pierie appears as an owner, being son to Alexander Pierie, master of the pin factory. The last owner seems to have been Mrs. Shaw Pirie or Skeen; the first, Wm. Pirie, *Prot. J.W.7, 4/4/1765*. The property was bounded on the west by Robert Gibb's Close, and by Pirie's Close on the east. James Pirie, late staymaker at the Canongatehead, thereafter soldier in General Beauclerk's Regiment of Foot, disponed part of the property, *Prot. W.F.8, 23/5/1757*. His wife was Isobel McEan, McEuan, or McEwan, *Prot. W.F.6, 9/1/1754*. There was a brewery in Pirie's, formerly Foord's Close, built by the father of the late Thomas Pirie, *W.F.3, 14/2/1750*. The relationships are not easily traced.

Its other name, Foord's, Fuird's, *Prot. G.I.1, 23/12/1731*, or Ford's Close, *Reg. 23/5/1862*, has been mentioned above. It is derived from Alexander Foord, who had land, barn, kiln, etc., there, *Prot. G.L.2, 4/4/1764; J.W.7, 4/4/1765*. The property was owned at one time by John Alexander Fuird, *Reg. 18/2/1744*, and later by the heirs of Alexander, *Prot. A.W.7, 11/6/1723*, John being his son and heir, *Prot. A.W.2, 23/8/1705*. The alias is given clearly, 'Foord's now Pirie's Close', *Prot. G.I.1, 23/12/1731*.

This close may be Kinnaird's Close, given in Maitland's alphabetical list. Malcolm Kinnaird owned a tenement on the south side of the High Street beyond the Netherbow, owned thereafter by the heirs of the late Alexr. Foord, *Prot. A.W.7, 11/6/1723*.

PIRNIEFIELD PLACE	From Pirniefield House, *Ainslie 1804. Kirkwood 1817.* *See Pirniefield Bank etc.—Part II*
PIRRIE STREET	From David Pirie, wright, 34 Yardheads, *D.1827. L.L.L. 152*, speaks of Mr. Pirrie's property, in the neighbourhood. Builder, and house agent, Duke St., Leith, 1877. *j.r.*
PITSLIGO ROAD	From Sir Wm. Forbes of Pitsligo, banker, who bought the village and lands of Greenhill in 1805, (See Forbes Road), and from Sir John Stuart, also of Pitsligo, his descendant, *o.e.c. x. 197, 251.*
PITT STREET	From William Pitt, P.M. in 1783, son of the Earl of Chatham, died 1805.
PLEASANCE	From St. Mary of Placentia, whose convent stood just south of the Cowgate Port, *Bruce Home, Maitland 176.c.2.*, who derives St. Mary's Wynd, from the same. Pleasance, St. Mary Wynd to St. Leonards, *D.1827.* Pleasance Court, just south of and on the same side as Arthur St., *Ord. Surv. 1852.* Bought from the Earl of Roxburgh by the Edinburgh Magistrates 1636, *Arnot 328.* Maitland states that the Priory of Nuns stood sixty yards from the south-east angle of the wall, p.176. Sometimes named the Pleasants. Pleasants St. Pleasance, *l.c. 734, 10/4/1562.* Evidently some writers derive the name from a mistaken idea connected with the King's Pleasance, or pleasure ground. "Street called St. Leonards or Pleasance", *m.t.c. 17/1/1797.* Ralph Richardson, p.3 of "Coutts & Co., bankers, Edinburgh & London derives it from the French "plaisance" a place, "poury allor prendre L'air quelquefois".
PLEWLANDS GARDENS AVENUE TERRACE	From old Plewlands farm. Over Plewlands, alias Greenbank, *St. G. 385.* Owned by John Sievewright, 1705. History of the Merchant Coy. 76. Plewlands Farm, *m.t.c. 11/9/1833.* Lands of Plewlands, *Prot. 10/1/1531.*
PONTON STREET	*D.1800, 88, D.1827. Ainslie 1804.* Property at or near Haig's Distillery, Lochrin, owned in 1814 by Mr. Ponton and Mr. Haig, *v.r.43,*

Scots. Mag. 1802, p.273. Thomas Ponton was builder of tenement in Wharton Pl. and elsewhere, Lauriston, *m.t.c. 29/5/1816.* Thos. Bishop, meal maker, resided in Ponton's St. His son Robert entered apprentice *5/12/1782.* For sale building area, e.s. Ponton St. Apply Gray & Ponton, solicitors, *e.e.c. 2/11/1805.*

POPLAR LANE
D.1827. From trees there, shewn *Ord. Surv. 1852, j.r.*

PORTERFIELD ROAD
Old house of the name.

PORTLAND PLACE
TERRACE
Regent St. to Albany St., *D.1827. m.t.c. 20/11/1822.* The Duke of Portland, Prime Minister 1807.

See Portland St.—Part II.

PORTSBURGH SQUARE
In the Portsburgh, *Edgar 1742, 1765, Ainslie 1780, 1804,* which takes its name from the West Port. Wester Portsburgh, Easter Portsburgh, being outside the Potterrow Port. Portsburgh belonged originally to the barony of Inverleith, owned by the family of Touris, but was disjoined from it in 1649, and formed into a barony with High Riggs, West Port, Crofts of Bristo, etc. King's Stables added 1663, *St. C. 14.* Portsburgh St., *M.*

POTTERROW
From the industry of the residents. From neighbouring pottery, *Stark 1806, 96.* Called "a village", *o.e.c. ii. 70.* Potter-row port. Port shewn, *Edgar 1742, 1765.* Potterrow St., *M.* "Alias Easter Portsburgh," *m.t.c. 5/4/1786.* Alias Bristo, *l.c. 1859, 4/4/1621.* Potterrow Know, see Goose dub. Charles Hogg, potter in the Potterrow, *20/4/1610, i.w.c.h., vol. 1, p.746.*

PRESTON STREET EAST
WEST
On property of Mr. Preston, *Ainslie 1804, D.1827.* "Formerly Gibbet Loan" *27/11/1820, eec.j.s. Ainslie 1804.* Property of Hislop and Preston at Hope Park end, *m.t.c. 9/12/1812.* Captain Preston, owner of about nine acres in St. Leonard's. Hislop and Preston were heirs to Geo. Lindsay, Town Clerk 1757, in lands of St. Leonard's, *m.t.c. 3/6/1831.*

George Lindsay, one of the city clerks of Edinburgh, had two sisters: of these Agnes married John Preston of Gorton, and survived him; he died before 1793.

The other, Jean, married John Hislop, merchant, Dalkeith, their eldest son, William, married and had a daughter Margaret: she died before 1822. A charter was granted, *Can. Chart. 11/9/1822,* to said Margaret of lands of said George Lindsay, bounded by the Gibbet Loan on the south: by the lands of *(blank)* Spittal, now of *(blank)* Irvine, on the east: of *(blank)* Gifford on the north, and of Robt. MacLellan on the west. Apparently Margaret Hislop had just come of age. George Lindsay married Christian Tytler, who survived him.

PRIESTFIELD ROAD
On the lands of Priestfield, which are mentioned in a charter by Robert II, 16 June 1376. Also called Prestonfield, *o.e.c. x.* Name changed from Priestfield to Prestonfield 1689 by Sir James Dick, *Baird 121.* Conferred with other lands upon the Abbey of Holme—Cultram, *St. G.2.* David Prestonne, *11/10/1609,* is made burgess of Edinburgh by right of his father, George Prestonne, in Camrunne. Burgess Register James Murray of Priestfield, disponed two aikers of land called Common Myre, to his Uncle Sir Robt. Murray of Camrone, *m.t.c. 3/4/1663.* The lands of Priestfield, purchased by Sir Jas. Dick Provost of Edin., near end of reign of Chas. II, were named Prestonfield along with lands purchased from the Prestons of Craigmiller. Catalogue of Lords of Session 1794, p.29, note.

See also Priestfield Avenue etc—Part II.

PRIMROSE STREET	*D.1827. Lothian Map 1825.* On the grounds of Miss Primrose, *Ainslie 1804.* The Hermitage on her ground.
PRIMROSE BANK ROAD	Sentimental. *Old house, Primrose Bank, Ord. Surv. 1895.*
PRIMROSE TERRACE	After the flower, *e.c.b.c.ld.*
PRINCE REGENT STREET	*D.1827.* To honour George IV, Prince Regent 1810-1820.
PRINCES' STREET	Prince's St., *Ainslie 1780, Arnot 1788, D.1827, Craig 1767, Ainslie 1804.* Princes St., *Lothian Map 1825, Ord. Surv. 1852, Kincaid 1787.* Should be Princes', plural. The intention was to call it St. Giles St. after the patron saint of the city, but when this was told to George III, his narrow stupidity hindered his imagining aught beyond a London slum, and he would have none of it. The name was therefore changed so as to refer to the Royal Princes, the Duke of Rothesay, afterwards George IV, and the Duke of York, *o.& n.e. ii. 117.* Marked "South Street", Craig's plan, City Museum.
PROMENADE TERRACE (WEST)	Evident.
PROSPECT BANK ROAD	At Restalrig Road, *D.1827.* From the outlook, *j.r.* *See also Prospect Bank Crescent etc.—Part II.*

Q

QUARRY CLOSE	26 Crosscausey, *D.1827.* From an ancient quarry probably the "Quarry holes" of the Fortunes of Nigel, chap. 2 in connection with the Guse Dub. q.v. The quarry in the Town's loaning at the Windmylne, *m.t.c. 7/12/1655.*
QUEEN STREET	*Craig 1767, Ainslie 1780.* From Charlotte of Mecklenburg—Strelilz, Queen of George III. Married 1761. Originally included south side of York Place, *m.t.c. 10/8/1794 & 9/9/1795.*
QUEEN'S BAY CRESCENT	Fanciful, there being no such bay. From Queen Victoria.
QUEEN'S CRESCENT	From Queen Victoria.
QUEEN'S PARK AVENUE	From neighbouring Royal Park, known as the Queen's Park during the reign of Queen Victoria 1837-1901.
QUEENSFERRY STREET GARDENS TERRACE ROAD STREET LANE	On the way to Queensferry, named from St. Margaret, Queen of Malcolm Canmore, who landed near North Queensferry, at St. Margaret's Hope, in 1068, after two years wanderings as exile, after the English defeat at Hastings. It was the great ferry for Fife and the north, *m.t.c. 7/12/1808. Lothian Map 1825.* "Ferry St.", *m.t.c. 21/6/1809, 20/11/1809. As now Kirkwood.*

R

RAEBURN PLACE	On the ground of the famous Sir Henry Raeburn (1756-1823), who was born in the neighbourhood. He occupied 16 York Pl., *D.1800,* 19 St. Bernard's Crescent, *D.1827.* Raeburn Pl., *m.t.c. 17/7/1816;* Raeburn Feus, *m.t.c. 4/9/1833.* *See also Raeburn Street—Part II.*
RAMSAY LANE GARDEN	The name is almost certainly derived from Ramsay Garden, lying to the west of the lane, and acquired bit by bit by Allan Ramsay, who began as a wigmaker, developed into a bookseller with a circulating library, and ended as a poet, his best-known piece being 'The Gentle Shepherd'. His first shop was a little above 'John Knox House'; he left it in 1722 for a larger one at the east end of the Luckenbooths,

afterwards occupied by Provost Wm. Creech, Burns's Edinburgh publisher. About 1740 he built Ramsay Lodge, which, from its shape, was known among the wags of the town as the 'Guse Pie'. On his complaining to Lord Elibank of this levity, he received but little comfort from the reply, 'Indeed, Allan, when I see you in it, I think the wags are not far wrong!'

He died in 1758, and was buried in Greyfriars; his monument stands in the west Princes Street Gardens, in sight of his old dwelling. His son and namesake (1713-84), a well-known artist, settled in London, and became portrait-painter to George III and Queen Charlotte. He acquired the estate of Kinkell, by which he is generally known, to distinguish him from his father.

By some, however, the name is derived from Ramsay's land, the town house of the Ramsays of Cockpen, one of whom, Sir Andrew, forcibly held the Provost's Chair for some fifteen years in the days of Charles II. This house stood at the east side of the top of the lane, where Dr. Guthrie's Ragged School flourished later, *Wilson, i.187.* Marked 'Cockpen' by Kerr.

(This Ramsay Lodge must not be confused with another built by James Ramsay, accomptant of Excise, which stood on the site occupied later by the old Cattle Market, Lauriston, *Ainslie 1804,* and now by the College of Art. David Laing, LL.D., librarian of the Signet Library, succeeded his father as resident here *D.1832* till he removed to Portobello.)
Kerr.

RANDOLPH CLIFF **CRESCENT** **PLACE**	Crescent, *D.1827.* From Randolph, Earl of Moray. Thomas Randolph nephew of Robert the Bruce, for a time follower of Edward Longshanks, became one of Bruce's most loyal supporters, and was created Earl of Moray. He surprised and captured Edinburgh Castle, March 1312-13. After his line had died out Queen Mary revived the title, and conferred it, 1562, on her half-brother, James Stewart, "the Good Regent".
RANKEILLOR STREET	From Thomas Hope of Rankeillor, Fifeshire, who took over the Borough Loch in 1722, in order to drain it, and bring it under cultivation. (See Hope Park etc.), *e.o.c. x. 258.* In p.w. 1780/81 Mrs. Hope of Rankeillor is in Jack's land, Canongate. In 1827 Rankeillor was the property of David Maitland Makgill, *D.1827.* The street is shewn planned, not built, in Kirkwood. In Lothian Map, north side complete, south side half built, *m.t.c. 2/9/1818.*
RAVELSTON DYKES **PARK** **PLACE** **TERRACE**	From Ravelston House, a favourite haunt of Sir Walter Scott when a boy. The name occurs in 1511, in a lease of the quarry. Raylistoun 1363, *St. Giles 7.* *See also Ravelston House Grove etc.—Part II.*
REDBRAES	From Redbraes mansion house, occupied in 1688 by Sir Patrick Hume of Polwarth, father of the heroic Grizel, *o.& n.e. iii. 89.* Denied by w.o.l. 173. See. Appx. Edinburgh Vauxhall. Owned and occupied by Sir Hew Crawfurd, *p.w. 1780/81. eec.j.s. 21/1/1789. Ainslie 1804, D.1827.* *See also Redbraes Grove, Place—Part II.*
REGENT BRIDGE **TERRACE** **LANE** **ROAD**	Compliment to future George IV, regent. Bridge begun 1815, opened 1817. Lord Cockburn speaks of it as the "Waterloo Bridge", *o.& n.e. ii. 107.* Seems to have been first suggested, *m.t.c. 25/7/1787.* Definitely proposed, *m.t.c. 2/3/1814.* Regent Bridge, *m.t.c. 18/3/1818* "Regent's Terrace", *m.t.c. 15/6/1825.*

REGENT PLACE	Probably from neighbouring Regent Road, but as it is on or near the Earl of Moray's property, *o.& n.e. III, 158*, it may be fancy, refer to the "Good Regent".
REGENT STREET STREET LANE	Compliment to George IV while Regent.
REGISTER PLACE STREET (WEST)	From proximity to Register House, which was founded 1774, paid for partly from estates forfeited after the '45, *D.1827*. Register Office, *Ainslie 1780*. Register St., *Ainslie 1804*.
REID TERRACE	After Professor Reid, *e.c.b.c.ld. Littlejohn App. 22*, Glenogle Road.
REID'S CLOSE	*Ainslie. Kirkwood.* Bailie Reid's Close, *p.w. list 1779*.

From Andrew Reid, bailie of the Canongate, who owned malt barns, etc., recently built by George Hog, brewer in the Canongate, being bounded by the property of the Duke of Queensberry on the east, and on the west by other property of the said Andrew purchased from the creditors of Robert Reid, *Can. Chart. 22/9/1770*. The property is described as bounded by the Duke of Queensberry's garden on the east, and by the property of the late Andrew Reid, brewer, on the west, *m.t.c. and Can. Chart. 22/1/1794*. Andrew Reid's name appears on the Roll of Superiorities, 22nd September 1770. The weavers of the Canongate acquired property from the late Andrew Reid on the east of Strathie's Close, *Can. Chart. 1/3/1830*. Robert Reid, presumably Andrew's brother, figures as brewer, near Milton's Lodging, in 1773, *p.w. 1773*.

Reid's Close and Haddington's Entry, *Reid's Close, 80 Canongate; Haddington's Entry, 80 Canongate: D.1827*, have a common entry from the Canongate, but divide and open independently into the South Back Canongate, Haddington's Court being on the South Back Canongate, *o.e.c. i, 14, 18*. It contains the town house of the Earl of Haddington, built in the late seventeenth or early eighteenth century, *o.e.c. i, 14, 18*. The Town granted a charter to the Earl of Haddington on yard and gardens, sometime owned by Wm. Wilson of Soonhope, writer, *m.t.c. 11/9/1782. See Wilson's Court, p.118*. It is spoken of as Haddington's Close, *Can. Chart. 22/12/1876*. Haddington House is shown in the O.S.

REID'S COURT	*Kirkwood. o.s. Kerr.* Reid's Yard, *Ainslie*. Reid' Coach Yard, *p.w. list 1779*. Reid' Close, *Can. Chart. 31/1/1833*. Blyth's Close, *Prot. J.H. Canong. 21 and 24/8/1700*.

James Reid was a coachmaker 'opposite Milton's Lodging', *p.w. 1773*. A new stone tenement stood at the head of Lochend's Close, with the lands of James Reid, coachmaker, on the east, *Can. Chart. 15/5/1801*. The site seems to have been long owned by the family. John Reid, smith, owned land east of that of James Fergusson of Lochend before 1682, *Prot. J.H. Canong. 9/11/1682, 21 and 24/8/1700*. James Reid acquired land in the Tolbooth Wynd, 26th January 1757, from Wm. Lawder, coachmaker, probably father or brother of Agnes Lauder, spouse of the said James Reid, and mother of his son James Reid, writer in the College Wynd, *Can. Chart. 10/2/1780; p.w. 1780*. Mention is made of George Reid, cutler, probably a son of John, *Prot. J.H.Canong. 9/11/1682*.

The entry to the court seems to have been known as Blyth's Close, which is described *Prot. J.H. Canong. 9/11/1682, 21 and 24/8/1700* as lying to the west of Rae's (now Campbell's) Close, but this seems to be the only mention of it, and no derivation is even suggested.

REIKIES COURT	65 Nicolson St., *D.1827.* Reikies Land, *D.1800, 127.* Reikies Court, *D.1800.*
RELUGAS ROAD	On Grange estate. From seat of Sir Thomas Dick Lauder of Grange. See Cumin Place. *See also Relugas Gardens etc.—Part II.*
RESTALRIG AVENUE GARDENS ROAD TERRACE	Old form Lestalrig. From the ancient village of Restalrig—or Lochsterrock, *o.& n.e. iii. 130.* Lastalric between 1178 & 1188, *c.c.* *See also Restalrig Circus etc.—Part II.*
RICHMOND LANE PEND PLACE	*Armstrong's map 1773. Ainslie 1780.* Shows only Richmond St. running N.E. and S.W. South Richmond St. nearly completed 8/2/1794, *eec.j.s. Ainslie 1804,* N. and S. Richmond Streets, and Richmond St. running E. & W. Richmond Lane shewn as Back Row. James Richmond land surveyor, made plan of lands in Pleasance, touching property of Wm. Gilmour, tanner, and Oliver Gilmour, currier, 25 Dec, 1769, on west side of road made by Nicolas Dick, spouse of Wm. Hall, merchant, through their park in Pleasance, *Reg. 12/7/1858,* as Richmond, land surveyor, Grassmarket, *p.w. 1773-4 1780-1.*
RIDDLE'S CLOSE	Sir John Smith's Close, Royston's Close, Shaw's Close, McMorran's or John McMorran's Close. Giving entrance to Riddle's double court, *Edgar. Ainslie.* 'Court' *Kirkwood. Kerr.*

Takes its name from 'Riddal's land', built by George Riddell, wright, burgess, *Prot. G.I.2, 7/6/1733.* Fisher's land and close lay on the east; the tenement of David Home of Grange on the south; the area and tenement of *(blank)* Johnston, glover, on the west, *Prot. G.L.2, 22/8/1764.* George Riddell had a large family—George, Andrew, James, John and Robert, also Katherine and Barbara. James seems to have inherited the property, in which his sisters continued to reside, while he emigrated to England, being known later as Riddell of Caisters, Norfolkshire, *Prot. W.F.10, 17/12/1760; Wilson, i. 217.* He enjoyed a servitude over the house of the notorious Major Weir, or Wear, formerly owned by his father, George Riddell, *Prot. J.W.7, 28/1/1764; W.F.6, 6/12/1753.*

James Riddle, son of the occupant of Riddle's Court, succeeded Patrick Maule, one of the Panmure family, as a soap boiler in Leith, giving his name to Riddle's Close, 50 Tolbooth Wynd, now misnamed Market Street, *j.r.s.l. 321, 347.*

It was also called Sir John Smith's, now Royston's Close, *Prot. G.H.8, 18/2/1730,* from the property there of Sir John Smith of Grothan, or Gortham, owned formerly by George McMorran, merchant, burgess, and his son George: thereafter by David Home of Grange, *Reg. 8/7/1743.*

Royston's Close, *p.w. 1773, p.4,* formerly Sir John Smith's, and now Riddle's Close, *Reg. 23/5/1857,* took its name from Sir James Mackenzie of Royston, senator of the College of Justice, who died 1744, having owned two dwelling houses in the close, *Prot. W.F.3, 30/3/1749, 25/5/1749.* It was also called Shaw's Close, *trad. 74,* but no derivation suggested.

The name M'Morran's *Rom. Edinr.69* or John M'Morran's *Prot.G.H.3, 6/12/1708* Close, comes from John M'Morran, to whom the property there was disponed by his brother, Ninian M'Morran of Newhall. This John seems to be Bailie John M'Morran, City Treasurer 1589-91, 2nd bailie 1594, and shot in 1595 by Wm. Sinclair at a barring-out of the High School, *o.& n.e. i. 110.* In his house, yet extant, James VI, his queen, Anne of Denmark, and her brother, the Duke of Holstein, were entertained, March 1593, *o.& n.e. i. 110.*

The protocols are a little confused as to the relationships of John M'Morran, senior, John, junior, Ninian, George, and perhaps William, who was 1st bailie 1607. They were probably father and four sons.

There was a throughway from Riddell's or M'Morran's Court by Alison's, alias Wardlaw's, Close to the Cowgate. Jas. Wardlaw's property lay to the east, *Prot. G.H.3, 19/11/1706,* and we find mention of Wardlaw's Close, south side of the Lawnmarket, *Reg. 28/7/1767,* which arrangement is most clearly shown by Kerr.

Another entrance was from the West Bow, through Major Weir's Close, *Wilson, ii. 162,* into Johnston's Close, and to the back of Riddell's Court, *See Edgar, Ainslie, Kerr.*

RIEGO STREET

D.1827. Laid out, not built 1817, *Kirkwood.* On property of Major Weir, *Ainslie 1804.* Complete, *Lothian Map 1825.* See notes at end of volume, pp. 8 & 10. Riego is a Spanish and Portuguese surname, (meaning literally, irrigation). Elizabeth Barrett Browning has two poems, one "on a picture of Riego's widow, placed in an Exhibition", the other on "the death bed of Luisa del Riego" showing Britain's feeling towards the general, her unfortunate husband. Riego St. is built on ground once owned by Major Weir, while the site of Lynedoch Place, q.v., was owned by Captain Weir, both given in Ainslie's map of 1804. Both the streets are shewn in Lothian Map 1825, and in the Postal Directory for 1826/1827. Mrs. Major Weir occupies 6 Lynedoch Pl. An inference, plausible if not correct, may be drawn that Major and Captain Weir are the same, and that he had fought in the Peninsular Wars, where he had known Lord Lynedoch and the Spanish general Riego, of whom an engraving has been seen in Edinburgh, *j.s.,* whose names he thus perpetuated in the city. The fact that the former name of Earl Grey St., (q.v.) was Wellington St. seems to support this theory. Major James Weir of Tollcross, *m.t.c. 22/1/1812.* His property cut in two by Lothian Road, *m.t.c. 20/5/1812, 6/5/1812, 18/11/1812.* Major Jas. Weir of Drumsheugh, *m.t.c. 17/2/1819.* House possessed by Jas. Weir, beyond Twopenny Custom, *c.a. 31/1/1766.*

RIDDLE'S LAND
(See Riddle's Close)

Lately built by Geo. Riddell, wright, burgess, on south side of Lawnmarket, with Fisher's land and its close on the east: tenement of David Home of Grange on the south: area and tenement of *(blank)* Johnston, glover, on the west: and the High St. on the north *Prot. G.L.2. 22/8/1764, 7/6/1733, Reg. 6/12/1859.* Occupied by Katherine and Barbara, sisters of Jas. Riddell of Caister, *Prot. 17/12/1760, W.F.10.* George's sons George, Andrew, James, John & Robert. He owned Major Wear's (sic) house, *Prot. W.F.6 6/12/1753.* See Sir John Smith's, now Roystoun Cl. also.

RILLBANK CRESCENT TERRACE

From house there, *Ainslie 1804,* which stood on the bank of the rill, running into the Burgh Loch, the line of the Lovers' Loan.

RINTOUL PLACE

After one of the directors of the e.c.b.c.ld., *Littlejohn App. 22.*

ROBERTSON AVENUE

From W.W. Robertson, Master of the Merchant Coy., 1895/6, on whose ground it is built. He was one of the Trustees of Sir George Campbell's superiors, *Stewart.*

Thomas Robertson had the tack of the Society as a brewery, before it was let to Magnus Prime in 1677, and there was much ado over the 'working plant taken over', *m.t.c.*

ROBERTSON'S CLOSE

Vicus Robertsoni, *Gordon. Ainslie. Kirkwood.* Wynd, *Kerr.* Dickson's Close, *Prot. G.H.4, 24/9/1714.* Melrose Close, *m.t.c. 6/12/1820.*

The close owes its name to the tenement of Mr. Alexander Robertson, brewer, which was on the south side of the Cowgate, on the east side of the close of old called Dickson's, now Robertson's Close, which tenement was owned later by John Foular, wright, Prestonpans, *Prot. G.I.2, 2/6/1735.* This seems to be the Mr. Alexr. Robertson whose children and apparent heirs disponed, 9th November 1673, property on the east side of the close to Joanna Alexander, wife of Adam Cleghorn, *he was 4th bailie 1704, and died in office: Prot. A.W.3, 20/7/1710.*

On 3rd April 1652, Thomas Robertson acquired from John Denholm, merchant, a brewery in Bailie Robertson's Close. His son, Thomas Robertson of Lochbank, *known also as Halkerston's Croft in Bareford's Parks: v.r. 43,* by Mary Cleghorn, *suggesting kinship with Adam Cleghorn above,* succeeded him. This, the second Thomas, was Treasurer of the Good Town 1671, 2nd bailie 1681, and 1st bailie, 1684, *see under Campbell's alias Balie Robertson's Close, 109 Cowgate.* He was succeeded in Robertson's Close by John Robertson, presumably his son, who seems to have disponed the property to John Steill, *Prot. W.F.3, 24/2/1749.* Mention is made of land which belonged to the late Alexander Robertson, pertaining of old to the Blackfriars, on the south side of the Cowgate, *e.a. 8/2/1765.* In 1780 David Robertson, smith, was in the close, who may be of the family, but this is the less likely in that he was before that, opposite the Magdalen Chapel, *p.w. 1773.*

The old name, Melrose Close, is clearly identified and accounted for: Melrose or Robertson's Wynd, leading to the church built by 'Domina de Yester', on the property formerly of the Abbot and Convent of the Monastery of Melrose, *Prot. A.W.3, 7/6/1710; A.W.5, 9/3/1715. But the closes are named elsewhere as distinct—Tenement in Melrois Close bounded on the east by Robertson's Close, south side of Cowgate: Prot. A.W.3, 13/4/1709.*

William Mellros, wright, and after him his son David, owned property in Dickson's or Robertson's Close, which was owned next by James Anderson, writer, and thereafter by Alexr. Robertson, merchant, brewer, and burgess, on the south side of the Cowgate, *Prot. A.W.3, 20/7/1710; G.H.12, 6/7/1737.* The name of the close may be connected with William and David Mellrois.

The name Dickson's Close, *Prot. G.H.4, 24/9/1714; J.W.3, 31/7/1752; G.I.2, 2/6/1735,* is derived from the family who owned the tenement on the south side of the Cowgate, especially Elizabeth and Janet, sisters and heirs of James Dickson, burgess, bounded on the east by the lands of umquhyle Thomas Cant: on the west by those of the sometime Bishop of Dunkeld; and on the south by the way or transe to the Kirk of Field, *clearly shown by Gordon; Prot. W.F.8, 14/6/1757*—Dickson's, now Robertson's Close, on the south side of the Cowgate, *Prot. G.H.7, 29/7/1726; Reg. 24/6/1743.*

The mention of Thomas Cant shows that his family owned lands on both sides of the Cowgate.

It is not clear whether the Dicksons, who gave their name to the close on the north side of the Cowgate, are the same as those on the south side.

ROBERTSON'S COURT	This court—or at least this name—seems to occur first about 1827, *D.1827.* In it was Robertson's land, named from the owner, Wm. Robertson, cowfeeder at Croftangry, or foot of Canongate, who acquired, 24th March 1797, bake- and dwelling-houses in the close or area on the north side of St. Thomas' Chapel. These he left in life-rent to his widow Janet Baxter, and in fee to his children by her, viz. Christian, George, Margaret, and Agnes. His widow married Thomas Wilson, also a cowfeeder. Margaret, his heiress, married Thomas Thomson, baker, *Can. Chart. 20/6/1818. 23/6/1858.*
	The close, or its former representative, seems to be the 'Clausura Sancti Andree et Sti. *(sic)* Catherine', leading to the hospital built, 1541, by George Creighton, Bishop of Dunkeld, at the Watergate, foot of the Canongate, *Prot. J.H. Canong. 12/4/1678.* The charter and rules of this so-called Hospital of St. Thomas are given fully by Maitland, *M.154, c.2,* in which charter the trustees are specified as 'chaplains celebrating Divine Service at the altars of St. Andrew and St. Katherine within the monastical church of Holyrood house'. The position is clearly shown by Kerr, and the close, unnamed, by Edgar. *Redeveloped but name retained 1971, now off Calton Road.*
RODNEY STREET	From Admiral Rodney who bombarded Le Havre 1759. Victor at St. Vincent 1780. Honorary burgess of Edinburgh 21/3/1781, *New Lights 127.*
RONALDSON'S WHARF	*D.1827. No derivation has been established.*
ROSE STREET **STREET LANES**	Complimentary to the flower of England, the Tudor rose. Unnamed in Craigs Plan 1767. "St. David's Lane", *Ainslie 1780.* Name fixed by Town Council 2/7/1785, *eec.j.s.* Rose and Thistle streets, named so in 1784, intended to be "Meuse Lanes", *o.& n.c. ii. 198.* St. David's Lane, now called Rose St., *m.t.c. 17/11/1835.*
ROSEBANK	Pilrig. From Rosebank House, occupied by George, Lord Reay 1768, *Ainslie 1804.* *Not a street name.*
ROSEBANK LANE	Portobello. From the terraced gardens here, in which the Rose was largely cultivated, *w.b.* *Rosebank Cottage here.*
ROSEBANK COTTAGES	Morrison St. Rosebank, near Whitehouse Toll (near present Haymarket), *D.1800, 226,* beside Rosemount, *Ainslie 1804, Lothian Map 1825.*
ROSEBANK ROAD	From old Mansion, *w.o.l. 172.* *See also Rosebank Gardens, Grove—Part II.*
ROSEBERY CRESCENT **CRESCENT LANE**	After Lord Rosebery, 1860. The estate of Coates, west of the city, was acquired in 1704 from Archd. Earl of Rosebery (for the same price that he had paid John Byres) by Heriot's Hospital.

ROSEBURN AVENUE
  CLIFF
  CRESCENT
  DRIVE
  GARDENS
  PLACE
  STREET
  TERRACE
	From the ancient Roseburn house, as old as 1560, perhaps 1526. Said to have lodged Queen Mary—as later Oliver Cromwell, *o.& n.c. iii. 102.* The name given in Jn. Adair's Map of 1680 is "Dary Mil" (Dalry Mill), *o.e.c. 184.* Name originally from the burn draining Corstorphine loch, George Old, smith, in Roseburn *Prentice Register 26/8/1740.*

ROSEFIELD AVENUE **PLACE**	"To let, House of Rosefield" *e.e.c. 18/6/1814, j.s., Baird 295 map.* *See also Rosefield St.—Part II.*
ROSEMOUNT BUILDINGS	Morrison St. Tobago St., *D.1827.* Rosemount was the property of Wm. Morison, writer, *D.1800, 202.* "Near Whitehouse toll", *D.1800,*

195. Ground at Rosemount, opposite Gardners' Hall, apply to Mr. Morison 9/4/1792, *eec.j.s. Ainslie 1804.* Rosemount house possessed by Lady Belhaven, 15 minutes walk from the cross on the Corstorphine road, 31/3/1803, *eec.j.s.* There was a specially good quarry on the ground. Morison St. named from above. Mr. Wm. Morison . Built 1860.

ROSENEATH PLACE
STREET
TERRACE

From vicinity to Argyle Place. Roseneath, Dunbartonshire is one of the seats of the Duke of Argyll. See "The Heart of Midlothian".

ROSEVALE PLACE

Built through the rose garden of Lady Fife's house, *j.r.*
See also Rosevale Terrace—Part II.

ROSSLYN CRESCENT
TERRACE

So named by James Cowie (Jas. Cowie & Son, builder, still extant) who was very fond of Roslin, although not connected therewith, *j.r.*

ROXBURGH PLACE
STREET
TERRACE

From the Earl of Roxburgh, superior of the lands of the Pleasance, etc., *w.c.* Ground formerly belonging to the Duke of Roxburgh 7/12/1799, *eec.j.s. Prot. 29/12/1701, J.H. Canong.* Roxburgh Park 27/1/1806, *eec.j.s.* The lands of St. Leonard's were acquired by Robert, Earl of Roxburgh 1627, *St. L.* See Arnot 328. Roxburgh St. or Parks, *m.h.c. 101.* The Earl of Roxburgh was superior of the Canongate also, *Walks in Edinr. 130, 15/8/1630 m.h.c. 27.* He sold it, part of Broughton (adjoining the Water of Leith) and the Pleasance to the Magistrates 1636. Confirmed by Charter of Charles I, 11/12/1639. *r.c.g. 23 (2).* Roxburgh St. is shewn in Lothian Map 1825, not in Ainslie 1804, and m.t.c. 21/5/1823 mentions "the road along the town wall of Edinburg, from the Pleasance to Drummond St." John, 1st Duke and 5th Earl of Roxburgh (1741) infested in north croft of land in Pleasance inherited from his brother, Robert, 3rd Earl, died 1696, *m.t.c. 9/9/1698.*

ROXBURGH'S CLOSE

Cant's Close, Newton's Close, Cruik's Close, Henderson's Close.

The name is not derived from the Earl of Roxburgh, as generally conjectured and asserted, *Wilson, ii. 13; o.& n.e. ii. 223; Rom. Edinr.60.* The original name was Cant's Close, *Prot. J.W.3, 18/12/1755,* and is probably derived from the Henry Cant of Over Libbertoun who owned property in the adjoining Advocate's Close. It is called Roxburgh's, formerly Newton's Close, *Prot. W.F.1, 26/9/1746,* but no hint is given of who Newton was.

Another alias was Cruik's, *Prot. J.W.4, 21/7/1758,* Crook's, *Reg. 1/7/1859,* Craick's, *Reg. 1/7/1859,* or, by a slip, 'Orrock's, *Prot. A.W.6, 20/4/1720,* Close, taken from the tenement there of William Crockie, *Prot. A.W.8, 17/2/1726.*

A later name was Henderson's Close, derived from the house therein of Walter Henderson of Grantoun, *Prot. J.W.3, 6/6/1755.* This was at the street front, sometime owned by Walter Henryson of Cranburn (*sic*) on the north side of the High Street, on both sides of the close called Crook's, alias Henry Sands, *phonetic for Henryson's,* Close; having the land disponed by Alexr. (Napier) to the late John Roxburgh on the north, *Reg. 13/4/1741.* John Henderson and his son Alexander are mentioned in connection with the close, *Reg. 9/3/1743,* as also umquhyle Alexr. Henrysone, son and heir to Henry Henrysone, as owning land in Cruik's Close, *Prot. G.H.4, 7/9/1714.*

Its present name is derived from the dwelling-house disponed by the said Walter Henderson to Alexr. Napier, by him to Robert Napier, by him to Wm. Napier of Wrightshouses, and by him to John Roxburgh, cook by profession, husband of Christian Dowgall, *Prot. J.W.3, 6/6/1755; G.L.2, 13/6/1764. In Prot A.W.6, 20/4/1720, Alexr.*

Napier is said to be second son of John Roxburgh, cook, husband of Catherine Sword, and father by her of Joanna Roxburgh, wife of Thos. Noble, and (apparently) mother of Jannet Noble, relict of Archibald Johnston, merchant. The close is called Orrock's Close, alias (sic) Henderson's Close, and the former owner of the house, Walter Howison of Granton! John Roxburgh 'cuik' was made a burgess of Edinburgh, 20th March, 1605.

ROYAL CIRCUS	Circus Royal, *D.1827*. From its shape, and complimentary to Royalty. "Circus", *Ainslie 1804*, who is incorrect in shewing the plan completed "Royal Circus", *Lothian Map 1825*.
	In a plan by Craig, he shews a circus at the intersection of George St. and Frederick St.
ROYAL CRESCENT	*Ainslie 1804*, as if finished, which was not the case. In Lothian map, unbuilt, *Ord. Surv. 1852*, incomplete. Compliment to Royalty after visit of George IV, *m.t.c. 6/8/1823*.
ROYAL TERRACE	Projected under that name, 31/8/1820, *eec.j.s.* "Royal Terrace: Great London Road", *D.1827*. Honouring George IV, Regent, along with Carlton and Regent terraces. Shewn with house built at east end. *Lothian Map 1825*. Still incomplete, *Ord. Surv. 1852*.
ROYAL PARK PLACE	From neighbouring Royal Park, usually known as "King's" or "Queen's", as the monarch may be.
ROYSTON TERRACE	From the old barony of Royston, mentioned in Act of Parliament, 1685. Property came to Henry, 3rd Duke of Buccleuch by inheritance 1794, *o.& n.e. iii. 311*. Granton Castle was formerly known as Royston Castle. On property of Duke of Buccleuch, *o.& n.e iii. 311*. *Kirkwood*.
RUSSELL PLACE	From Mr. James Russell, market gardener there, *j.r. 1842*.
RUSSELL ROAD	Colloquially, from former residents "The Piggeries", from Sir Jas. Alexr. Russell, Lord Provost 1891.
RUTLAND STREET **SQUARE** **PLACE** **COURT**	Map of 1821 projected. Planned, *Lothian Map 1825*. N. and W. sides of square built, nothing more, *Ord. Surv. 1852*. To be feued by James Stuart, designed by Mr. Elliot, *m.t.c. 6/1/1819*. See Kirkwood's perspective map.
RYEHILL AVENUE **GARDENS** **GROVE** **PLACE** **TERRACE**	Fancy, from the grain, *e.c.b.c.ld.*
SAINT ANDREW SQUARE **STREETS** **STREET LANE**	Complimentary to patron saint of Scotland. Original intention to balance it by St. Georges Sq. at the other end of George St., *Ainslie 1780. Craig 1767*.
ST. ANDREW STREET	*D.1827*. "This part of the town anciently called St. Leonard's". *t.t.l. 193, o.& n.e. iii. 226*. Old name Dubb-row, *K.223, w.o.l. 204*.
ST. ANTHONY LANE **PLACE**	From ancient church dedicated to St. Anthony. There was also St. Anthony's port in the wall of the foot erected by D'Esse in 1548, *t.t.l. 6, o.& n.e. iii. 217*. St. Anthony St., *p.w. 1780/81, 107*. Kirkgate, *D.1800, 76, D.1827. Kirkwood. t.t.l. 151*. "St. Anthony's Court", *D.1800, 241*. Hospital of St. Anthony (of Egypt) built by Sir Robert Logan, 1430, first of the Logans of Restalrig through his wife Katherine, daughter and heiress of Sir John de Lestalric, who died 1382, *j.r.s.l. 105*.

ST. BERNARDS CRESCENT PLACE ROW	From legendary but unidentified St. Bernard, who occupied a cave near the mineral well or spring, of which he drank. The statue and temple of Hygeia built by Lord Gardenstone, May 1789. Mineral well discovered by three boys of Heriot's Hospital before 1760, *o.& n.e. iii. 74-75.* Lora Gardenstone died 22/7/1793. St. Bernard's Row, *m.t.c. 6/1/1813.* Villa of St. Bernard's, on bank of Water of Leith, once a mineral well, *e.e.c. 8/2/1796.*
ST. CATHERINE'S PLACE	From the convent of St. Catherine of Siena, founded 1517 by Janet, widow of George, third Lord Seton, slain at Flodden, 1513, destroyed by the English 1544, and the occupants evicted 1567, *o.e.c. x. 54.*
ST. CLAIR TERRACE	Fançy, no connection with anything, *g.l.b.*
ST. COLME STREET	From one of the titles of the Earl of Moray, on whose ground it was built. The Earl of Moray was commendator of Inchcolm in the middle of the 16th century, *o.& n.e ii. 205.*
ST. DAVID'S STREET	Compliment to the national, or patron saint of Wales, *Ainslie 1780.* Not from David Hume, who built his house at the corner of St. Andrew Sq. despite the story that ere the name was painted on the street, *Rev. D. Webster,* or the daughter of Chief Baron Orde, *o.& n.e. ii. 161,* chalked up on the house front, "St. David's St" as a hit at the philosopher's infidelity. When informed of this by his servant lass, he remarked quietly, "Never mind—I am not the first man of sense that has been made a saint of", *Walks in Edinr. 183.* In his Autobiography, *Blackwood & Sons 1860, p.276,* "Jupiter" Carlyle states that David and Miss Nancy Ord got a workman to paint on the cornerstone of the house which he had built in the S.W. corner of St. Andrew Sq., "St. David's St." where it remains to this day, *o.& n.e. ii. 160.* St. Davids St., *m.t.c. 15/4/1772.* Home or Hume died 1/7/1771. Direction by Town Council that names of streets in New Town be painted on corner houses, *m.t.c. 24/5/1780, 17/12/1788.*
ST. DAVID'S PLACE TERRACE	From the parish church. *Office block built on site of Church—1973.*
ST. FILLAN'S TERRACE	Baseless, fancy, *g.l.b.*
ST. GILES STREET	From its proximity to Collegiate Church of St. Giles, dated 1875. Original name proposed for Princes' St. q.v.
ST. JAMES' PLACE	Possibly from James VIII, by fervent but cautious Jacobites, *o.e.c. ii. 172,* who hid the King under the Saint, letting a hint occur in King St., now Little King St., q.v. St. James, *Ainslie 1780, do. 1804, Lothian Map 1825. Ord. Surv. 1852.* "James", *Denovan 271. Scots. Mag. 1814, p.1, map, m.t.c. thrice 28/2/1810.* Areas to feu, with advantages enumerated, apply to Walter Ferguson, writer, the proprietor. Gavenlock's land, head of Lawnmarket, *e.e.c. 3/2/1781.* Complaint in Edinburgh Evening Courant, 6/7/1810, of local confusion— by resident in the square, there are St. James Sq: St. James St: two North St. James Streets: South St. James Street, East St. James St., West St. James St.; also St. James Pl. and St. James Lane. The name suggests "ideas of courtly splendour and royal magnificence", but the confusion is great. *St. James Centre now on this site not including St. James Place.* *See St. James Centre—Part II.*
ST. JOHN'S STREET	Named from St. John's Close so named from the Cross of St. John, in the High Street of the Canongate, which marked one corner of the Temple lands of the Canongate, a triangular enclosure with its apex on St. John's Hill, *o.e.c. i. 16.* The close seems to have been known also as Paterson's Close, although

no alias is given, which is described as just west of St. John's Street and containing the property of the late George Paterson, architect, *Can. Chart. 8/8/1821*. John Paterson, architect, was resident in St. John's Street in 1780; Paterson's Close was separated by a march dyke from the houses on the west side of the top of St. John's Street, *Can. Chart. 9/9/1829*.

ST. LEONARDS BANK **LANE** **HILL** **STREET**	From the ancient chapel of St. Leonard, which stood on what is now Mount Hooly. St. Leonard's hill, *Ainslie 1780*. The present St. Leonard's Hill was originally "Holyrood St", the name is cut on the corner of Carnegie St. "The village of St. Leonard's," *m.t.c. 24/5/1797*. Street called St. Leonard's or Pleasance, *m.t.c. 17/1/1797, 6/11/1822, 28/3/1832*. Village of St. Leonard's, *m.t.c. 16/11/1814*. Streets of St. Leonard and St. Leonard's Vennel, *c.c. 850, 4/6/1517*. Village of St. Leonard's, *Can. Chart. 24/5/1797*.
ST. MARGARET'S ROAD	From its proximity to St. Margaret's Convent, 1834, *o.e.c. x. 31*, in which is enshrined a bit of the backbone of St. Margaret of Scotland, obtained by Bishop Gillies from Madrid, in the early part of the 19th century, *o.e.c. v. 61*. Founded 1832.
ST. MARK'S PLACE	From St. Mark's episcopal church, opened May 1825.
ST. MARY'S STREET	Formerly Wynd, *Edgar. Ainslie. Kerr.*
	It takes its name from a chapel and convent dedicated to the Virgin Mary, which included a hospital, at the head of the wynd, on the west side. These were destroyed, probably about 1572, *o.& n.e. i. 297; Wilson, ii. 125*, and must not be confused with the convent of St. Mary of Placentia, which lay south of the line of the Cowgate and South Back of the Canongate, and to which the Pleasance is supposed to owe its name, *Wilson, ii. 125*. There was a tenement of land of old called the church or chapel of St. Mary, lying beyond the Netherbow on the south side of the King's High Street, in the vennal called St. Mary's Wynd, on the west side, entering from the foot of the World's End Close, *m.t.c. 26/4/1826*. The lands of the Hospital of the Blessed Mary were in St. Mary's Wynd, *Prot. 12/9/1528*. The Hospital of St. Mary was at the top of the Wynd on the west side, *Prot. W.F.5, 7/8/1751*. James Makalyeane, burgess, sold to the matrons or hospitallers of the Hospital of the Blessed Virgin Mary in Sanct Mary Wynd an annual rent of a booth in the Buthraw (Luckenbooths), *c.c.943, 25/2/1522-3*. Butler, *Tron Kirk, 45*, quotes Spottiswoode as authority for the derivation of the name, in 'Religious Houses' 1755, p.283. Maitland, *M.9, c.2*. quotes a charter of 3rd October 1477 in which Sanct Mary Wynde is mentioned. The poverty of the hospital in 1499 is also alluded to by him, *M.10, c.2*.
ST. NINIANS TERRACE	Baseless, fancy, *g.l.b.*
ST. PATRICK'S SQUARE **STREET**	Planned, *Ainslie 1804*. Complete, *Lothian Map 1825*. Partly built before 28/6/1783, *eec.j.s.* Property thereabouts owned by Patrick Tod, 1767. Kirkwood 1817 shews west side planned property of David Wemyss. Formerly the four sides bore the name.
ST. PETER'S BUILDINGS **PLACE**	From St. Peters United Free Church, generally known from its local position, as "Viewforth".
ST. RONAN'S TERRACE	Baseless, fancy, *g.l.b.*
ST. STEPHEN'S PLACE **STREET**	From St. Stephen's Parish Church.
ST. THOMAS ROAD	From Sir Thomas Dick Lauder, superior of the Grange estate.

ST. VINCENT STREET	From the naval victories of Rodney, 1780, and Lord Howe, 1794, *Ainslie 1804, m.t.c. 6/8/1823.*
SALAMANDER STREET	From the fiery glass and chemical works there, suggesting what single type of creature could live there. The first cones or furnaces were erected by the Bottle House Coy. in 1740 on the sands, near Salamander St., *Irons, ii. 143. D.1827.* *See also Salamander Place—Part II.*
SALISBURY PLACE ROAD STREET	*D.1827. Lothian Map 1825.* From the Salisbury Craigs. Arnot derives the name from the Earl of Salisbury, who accompanied Edward III in his invasion of Scotland in 1327 or 1333, *Arnot 309. Anon. Map 1730.* Salisbury St., *New. Pict. Edin. 1820 map,* not in *do. do. 1818.* Salisbury Terrace between Arthur St. and Prospect Pl. facing the Salisbury Craigs. Salisbury Road, *m.t.c. 16/11/1814.* Salisbury Pl., *m.t.c. 24/3/1819.* Lord Hailes derives the name from seles, a wilderness, *Reekiana 38.*
SANDFORD GARDENS	From Bishop Sandford of Edinburgh who inducted the Rev. George M. Drummond as first minister in St. Marks Episcopal Church, *Baird 459.* The Episcopal chapel stood at its west end, where now stands the R.C. church, *w.b.*
SANDPORT STREET	From the old gate opening to the sands, *D.1827.* From the port or gate in the rampart of Monsieur D'Esse leading out to the Short Sands, where the Custom House now is, *j.r.s.l. 271, 1549.* *See also Sandport Place—Part II.*
SAUGHTON AVENUE CRESCENT	From the old mansion of Saughton, suggestive of willows by the Water of Leith, owned and occupied by generations of the Bairds, a branch of the houe of Auchmedden, *o.& n.e. iii. 319.* Saughtonhall, *c.c. 431B, 23/2/1470-1.* *See also Saughton Gardens etc.—Part II.*
SAUGHTONHALL DRIVE	As Saughton. *See also Saughtonhall Avenue etc.—Part II.*
SAUNDERS STREET	*D.1829-30.* Possibly connected with John Saunders who acquired property in Leith from Sir Henry Raeburn, painter, *m.t.c. 14/2/1827.*
SAXE-COBURG PLACE	*D.1827.* Planned and partly built, *Lothian Map 1825.* Almost complete, *Ord. Surv.* Prince Leopold of Saxe Coburg married 1816 Charlotte, only daughter of George IV, then Regent, she died 1817. He visited Edinburgh that year and again in 1819, when he opened the Regent Bridge, (q.v. also Leopold Place). Edward, Duke of Kent married 1818, Victoria, princess of Saxe Coburg; their daughter, Victoria born 1819 succeeded to the throne, 1837 as "Queen Victoria", *e.o.t. lviii. 41. Anderson 333, 339.* *See also Saxe-Coburg Street—Part II.*
SCIENNES GARDENS PLACE ROAD HILL PLACE STREET	From the Convent of St. Catherine of Siena (sometimes confused with St. Catherine of Alexandria). Built 1517. Destroyed 1559. Pronounced SHEENS, *o.e.c. x. 163.* Scienes, *p.w. 1780/81, 10. D.1827.* See St. Catherines Pl., *Ainslie 1804, o.& n.e. iii. 52.* "Shiens", *m.t.c. 14/12/1791.* Sciennes Loan, *m.t.c. 27/3/1799.* Now Sciennes Road. "Locus olim sororum monatium de Sheens", *Prot. 13/2/1734, G.I.2.*
SCOTLAND STREET	Complimentary to our own country, *D.1827.* First name proposed Caledonia St., *Ainslie 1804,* where Dublin St. is Hibernia St. Lothian Map has Scotland and Dublin Streets, 1825, *m.t.c. 13/10/1819.*
SEAFIELD AVENUE PLACE ROAD STREET	From district and house, *D.1827. o.& n.e. iii. 266, map 233.*

SEAVIEW TERRACE

Evident.

See also Seaview Cresc—Part II.

SEMPILL'S CLOSE

Or Semple's Close, (Williamson's Close).

From the old mansion at the foot of the close, bearing the date 1638. It was occupied prior to 1734 by Grissel, Lady Semple, widow of Francis, 8th Lord Semple; and was acquired in 1743 by Hugh, 11th Lord Semple, the original owner being David Brown. In 1755 it was conveyed to Sir John Clerk of Penicuik and others, trustees for the creditors of Lady Semple's brother Archibald, 1st Earl of Rosebery, *Prot. G.H.10, 27/2/1734.* It is now used as kitchen, etc., for the New College.
Ainslie. Kirkwood. Kerr

The close seems to have borne also the name of Williamson's Close, from a small house in 'Williamson's Close', and tenement at the head of Jollie's Close (q.v.) owned by Joseph Williamson, advocate, *Reg. 9/5/1859, 10/9/1860.* There was a dwelling-house on the north side of the High Street, owned and rebuilt by Hugh, Lord Semple, who was succeeded by John, Lord Semple; and he by Sir James Clerk of Penicuik, who disponed it to Mr. Williamson of Foxhall, *Prot. W.F.9, 2/9/1760.* (Foxhall was at the east side of the head of the Mound, *Reg. 9/5/1859*). These Williamsons seem to have been connected with those of Leven Lodge, and Foxton alias Taxton, alias Golfhall, near Wrightshouses.

SEMPLE STREET
    COURT
    CLOSE

Ainslie 1804. Lothian Map 1825. From local proprietor, Kirkwood. Robert Semple, brewer, Castle Barns, *p.w. 1773 and 1780/1.* Mr. Semple's brewery, *eec.j.s. 9/2/1782. D.1827.* Property owned 1726 by Campbell: afterwards by Semple: now by heirs of Robert Semple, *v.r.44.* Robert Semple, late brewer, Castlebarns, *m.t.c. 20/3/1811.* Semple St., *m.t.c. 10/10/1821.* Robt. Sempill, brewer, Castlebarns, *Prot. 21/8/1810.*

SETON PLACE

From maiden name of the grand mother of Sir Thomas Dick Lauder. Sir John Lauder of Fountainhall married in 1696 his cousin, Margaret Seton. Wm. Dick, 3rd Baron of Grange married Anna, third daughter of Sir Alexander Seton of Pitmedden, *St. G.*

SHANDWICK PLACE

m.t.c. 2/5/1810 and 15/3/1809. The north side of Maitland St. Not in Ainslie 1804, where a winding roadway is shewn, but in Lothian Map 1825. To feu, garden ground at end of Princes St. belonging to John Cockburn Ross of Shandwick, north side, from Queensferry Road to be in straight line along the new Glasgow Road, *e.e.c. 4/9/1806.* Not shown by Kirkwood. Plan in Record Office, Register House, of new road from Whitehouse Toll (beyond Haymarket) to Kirkbraehead, Morison's property on S. Mr. Walker's on N. Mr. Ross' on N. Mr. Fraser's between Mr. Ross' on N. and Mrs. Stewart's on S. These all shown on Ainslie's plan of 1804.

What is now the south side of Shandwick Place, was named East Maitland St. till 1899-1900.

SHAWS PLACE
    SQUARE
    TERRACE
    STREET

From James Shaw, house agent, who feued the ground. His office in 1877 in 6 York Pl., *j.r.*

SHERIFF BRAE

Shirra-brae, Coalhill to King St., *D.1827.* So called in 1572, *t.t.l. 219.* "Sheref Bray", 15 Sept. 1574, *Irons 1.393. do. ii. 322.* "Mansion house commonly called Sheriffbrae", *m.t.c. 30/9/1835, 10/9/1823.* "Sherra Brae", *s.s.l. 68.* The Sheriff brae, *e.a. 6/1/1764.*

Jas. Logan infest in S. to umq. John L. of Cowstoun, in lands, viz. mansion called the Shrefbrae in Leith: tent. called the Culles: land called the Hauche: lands etc. called the catchpell: land in vennell called the Hill, *m.t.c. 14/11/1649.*

SHORE	On the shore, or east bank, of the Water of Leith, *D.1827.*
SHORE ROAD	Descriptive.

SHRUB HILL
    PLACE
    LANE
	D.1827. Old name of locality, *o.& n.e. iii. 155.* A "villa", *o.& n.e. iii. 163. D.1800, 257.* Its position, see Ainslie's map 1804 and Lothian Map 1825, suggests a connection with the Physic, or Botanic Gardens. Shrub House, *Ord. Surv. 1852.* Shrub Place, *m.t.c. 9/1/1828.* Shrub hill, Leith Walk, *D.1799.* Wm. Wilson, sherub hill, Leith Walk, *D.1799-1800.*

SILVERMILLS	*D.1827. Ainslie 1804.* From the mills erected for extracting silver from the ore produced at Hilderstone, West Lothian, belonging to Tam O' the Cowgate, the Earl of Haddington 1607. Chambers quoted by *o.& n.e. iii. 83. Wilson, ii. 208,* suggests alchemical projects of James IV or James V. Baird 104 quotes *o.& n.e. iii. 83.* Silvermills St., Stockbridge, *21/4/1827, eec.j.s. D.1827.*
SIMON SQUARE	See Symon Square.
SLATEFORD ROAD	Leads to the village of Slateford.
SLEIGH DRIVE	From Lord Provost, Sir Wm. Sleigh, 1926. *See also Sleigh Gardens—Part II.*
SLOANE STREET	From Bailie Sloane, contractor, *j.r.* *See also South Sloan Street—Part II.*
SMITH'S PLACE	From local proprietor, *Kirkwood.* For sale, apply to James Smith, Leith 16/4/1814, *eec.j.s.* Chas. Smith & Co., grocers there, *D.1827.*
SOLICITORS' BUILDINGS	Cowgate. From the society of Solicitors to the Supreme Courts, who own the buildings, and whose Library etc. occupy the upper part, having access from the Parliament House.
SOUTH BRIDGE	(High St. to Nicolson St., *D.1827*). The bridge over the Cowgate, lying to the South of the High St. Built 1785-1786. Finished 1788. Foundation laid at bottom of fishmarket, between Merlin's Wynd and Niddrie's Wynd, *Caled. Merc. 18/7/1785. j.s. o.& n.e. 1.374.* Named Cowgate Bridge, *Ainslie 1780.* South Bridge St., *Ainslie 1804.* Building proposed, *Scots. Mag. 1775.* Proposed in Town Council 11/10/1775. First suggestion in anonymous pamphlet, *m.t.c. 26/1/1785.* Application made for Parliamentary bill 18/2/1785. Open for traffic 11/7/1788. Took the place of Niddrie's Wynd, Martin's Wynd, Peebles Wynd, and Kennedy's Close, *m.t.c. 21/1/1789.*
SOUTH CLERK STREET	See Clerk Street.
SOUTHFIELD PLACE **VILLAS**	From old house, *Kirkwood, Braid map 89.*
SOUTH FOULIS CLOSE	Fowler's Close, *Edgar;* Foulis Close, *Ainslie 1780, Kerr;* Foules Close, *Kirkwood;* South Foulis' Close, *D.1827;* Purves' Close, *Reg. 19/12/1756;* Power's Close, *error for Purvis: Prot. W.F.7, 12/3/1756;* Mowbray's Close, *Prot. W.F.7, 12/3/1756;* Alexr. Uddart's Close, *Prot. W.F.7, 12/3/1756.*

It took its name from Sir James Foulis of Colinton, whose acquisition of the property therein is thus given: Pro Domino Jacobo Foullis de Collingtown. Tenement formerly of Hugh Tod, merchant, burgess, on the south of the High Street, waste land and yard of umquhyle John Gray and Walter Scott on the south: land, built and waste, now of heirs of umquhyle John Purves and John Charters on the north:

waste land of umquhyle Andrew Mowbray, thereafter of umquhyle Alexr. Udward on the east, on the east side of Gray's Close; Sir James being son to the late Sir James, by his spouse Barbara Ainslie, *Prot. A.W.3, 22/7/1710*, of Dolphinton.

It was also called Purves' Close, *Purves', now Foulis' Close, south side of High Street: Prot. A.W.4, 3/12/1711; W.F. 11, 28/10/1762*, as containing the tenement of John Purves, *Prot. W.F.11, 26/11/1762*, burgess, *Prot. A.W.8, 8/5/1727*. A tenement stood on the south side of the High Street, within the 'Arcus Inferiores', *note the plural form*, having the lands of the late Andrew Purves on the east, *Reg. 4/2/1744*. It is described as Purves' Close above the Netherbow, having Charteris' Close on the west, *Prot. A.W.6, 10/2/1721*. It occurs also as Power's Close, *Prot. W.F.7, 12/3/1756*, and Powrie's Close, *Prot. A.W.4, 8/2/1712*, evidently variants of Purves.

(There was another Purves Close on the north side of the High Street, alias Bryson's or Trunk's.)

It was called also Moubray's Close, from the lands of the late Robert Moubray on the east side of the close, *Moubray's, now Fouls's Close: Prot. W.F.7, 12/3/1756*. Mr. Walter Moubray owned a tenement in the close, *Prot. A.W.2, 19/3/1706*, and Andrew Moubray had lands on the east, *Prot. G.H.4, 20/12/1710*.

Though no distict alias has been found, this close seems to be the same as Alexr. Uddart's or Udwart's Close, which is mentioned, *Prot.W.F.7, 12/3/1756; A.W.8, 24/2/1728*, as if identical with Moubray's now Fouls's Close, which contained lands and yard of Alexr. Uddart at the foot of the close.

SOUTH GRAY'S CLOSE

Vicus Graii, *Gordon;* Gray's or Mint Close, *Edgar;* Gray's Close, *Ainslie 1780;* Mint Close, *Ainslie 1804;* South Gray's Close, *Kirkwood. Kerr;* Skinners' Close, *Prot. W.F.9, 2/7/1759;* Coyne-House Close, *o.& n.e. i. 270;* Coinyie Close, *Prot. W.F.1, 8/1/1747*.

'South' was added to 'Gray's' Close to distinguish it from the other Gray's Close on the north side of the High Street, with which it has no connection.

It is named Gray's Close in a charter of 1512, with mention of umquhyle John Gray as the author of earlier titles, *Wilson, ii. 65*. The late John Gray owned waste land in Gray's Close, *Prot. A.W.3, 22/7/1710; Reg. 20/5/1857*, and there was a tenement in the close occupied by Janet Gray, relict of Robert Hill, *Prot. G.L.1, 6/9/1763*.

John Gray and Walter Scott were former owners of lands acquired by James, Earl of Hyndford, *Prot. G.H.4, 20/12/1710*.

From the fact that the Royal Mint or Cunyie House stood at the foot of the close till its demolition in 1877, the close got the name of the Mint Close, *Edgar; Ainslie 1804*, or 'Coinyie Close,' *Grays, vel Mint, vel Conyie Closs: Prot. W.F.1, 8/1/1747*, or, as it is given in George Heriot's will, 'the venall callit Gray's Clois or Coynehous cloise', *o.& n.e., i. 270*.

SPEY STREET

Pilrig. Originally Moray St., *Kirkwood, D.1826/7, 1832/3*. Moray St. *D.1885/6*. Spey St., *1886/7*.
See also Spey Gardens—Part II.

SPITTAL STREET

From Sir James Spittal, provost 1833-1837. Silk mercer, South Bridge, *D.1827*. Begun about 1835, *Gilbert 215*.

SPITTALFIELD CRESCENT

From the lands of the Hospital attached to the Chapel of St. Leonard, *o.& n.e. i. 383*. Ground to feu 1810, *eec.j.s. Lothian Map 1825*.

SPOTTISWOODE ROAD STREET	On the Warrender property. Sir George Warrender married Helen, daughter to Sir Hugh Hume Campbell, 5th Baronet, of Marchmont, Berwickshire, by his wife Margaret Penelope, married in 1834, daughter to John Spottiswoode of that Ilk.
SPRINGFIELD BUILDINGS STREET	Leith Walk. From an old row of houses of that name, before 1780. Springfield, Leith, *p.w.* *1780/81, 110. D.1800/75, D.1827, 64,* m.t.c. 17/7/1816.
SPRINGVALLEY GARDENS TERRACE	House Spring Villa in Johnston's map, 1851. Also Ord. Surv. 1852.
SPYLAW ROAD	On ground of George Watson's Hospital, under the Gillespie Trust. The brothers James and John Gillespie owned and worked the snuff mill at Spylaw, Colinton, James residing there, and John attending to the shop in the Lawnmarket. John died 1792, and James 1797. *See also Spylaw Avenue—Part II.*
STANLEY STREET	Probably from Henry Morton Stanley, American journalist and African explorer, who "discovered" in 1870, David Livingstone, who had vanished in Africa, *w.b.*
STANWELL STREET	From Stanwell Lodge, Bonnington Road, *D.1827.* Originally Standwell Lodge, *j.r.*
STARBANK ROAD	*D.1827.* Starbank, *m.t.c. 26/3/1823.* From old Starbank House which stood there, *j.r.*
STEAD'S PLACE	To let or sell, house fronting the Leith Walk, by Stead's Card Manufactory, 21/1/1792, *eec.j.s. D.1800, 103 & 240. Ainslie 1804. D.1827, 176.*
STEEL'S PLACE	From the house of Dr. Steel, *Ord. Surv. 1852.* Magnesia Works on Dr. Steel's property, *Kirkwood.* Feued by him from Wm. Mosman of Canaan, 1797, *o.e.c. x. 207.* See Tipperlinn Road.
STEVENLAW'S CLOSE	Vicus Stepani Lawi, *Gordon;* Stanelaw's Close, *Edgar;* Stonelaw's Close, *Ainslie. Kirkwood. Maitland.*

The name is probably that of Stephen Law or Loch, glazier, resident there in 1571, an adherent of Queen Mary, *o.& n.e. ii. 242,* or from Stewin Law, a wealthy flesher of the Queen's party, *New Lights, 190.* His name suffers under many forms, as shown above, or in connection with lands of umquhyle Stephen Law *sive* Stephen Lawder, *Prot. G.H.12, 10/5/1737.*

Stephen Law is mentioned fairly frequently in the protocols. There was a tenement in Peebles Wynd with the lands of the late Stephen Law on the west, *Prot. J.W.2, 24/6/1749; J.W.6, 9/1/1764.* He also owned land at the Vennel of the Kirk of Field, *Prot. 4/5/1529,* and on the south side of the High Street, near the Upper Bow, *c.c.913, 29/10/1521.* Various members of the family appear as owners of lands in the close: Griselda, *Prot. G.I.2, 10/2/1734;* Mariota or Marion, relict of John Stoddart, *Prot. A.W.2, 28/3/1706; A.W.3, 3/11/1709; Reg. 14/1/1859;* Margaret, *Prot. A.W.4, 6/1/1714,* and Robert, *Prot. G.H.13, 28/11/1739.*

It bore formerly the name of Telpher's Close, from the family of Taillyiefer, one of whom, Laurence Telfer, husband of the sister of John Carkettil, cousin to Andrew Halliburton, conservator of the Scots at Middleburg, left the close about the end of the sixteenth century, and settled on the north side of the High Street, in what was later Don's Close, q.v., *New Lights, 190.* Thus we find the lands of umquhyle Laurence Telfer, thereafter of Mr. Patrick Bannatyne in Tailyifiar's Close, with the lands of Stephen Law lying on the south, |

Prot. A.W.3, 22/11/1710; A.W.7, 8/8/1724. Marion Telfer owned property between Kennedy's Close and Peebles Wynd, *Prot. W.F.8, 12/5/1756.*

It was also known as Kennedy's Close, confusing it with the close of that name immediately to the east. Tailyifiar's Close, now Kennedy's Close, containing 'croce' house formerly owned by late Quintain Kennedy, W.S., *Prot. A.W.3, 22/11/1710; A.W.7, 8/8/1724.* One of the closes, possibly both, owned the two names, Telfer's or Kennedy's Close, *Prot. G.H.10, 4/7/1734, 'Telfer's, now Kennedy's Close',* but probably the large, thoroughfare close was the one known as Telfer's, Kennedy's, or Stephen Law's.

STRATHEARN PLACE **ROAD**	On Whitehouse estate, bought in 1819 by Grant of Kilgraston, in Strathearn, *D.M.1860, o.e.c. x. 52.* Strathearn Place not in Littlejohn Map.
STRATHFILLAN ROAD	Suggested by its neighbour, Strathearn Road.
SUCCOTH AVENUE **GARDENS** **PLACE**	From the Dunbartonshire estate of the Campbells of Succoth. Old charters give the forms Strekith, Scekith and Suketh, *Jas. Stewart.* Account of charges of Factors of third Marquis of Montrose, from 13/1/1680. Docqueted 10/6/1684. Among receipts, "Item from Succoth £243". Also "Item from John Campbell of Succoth in name of the Earl of Argyl for a year's annual rent £1160". The factors, who sign are Christian Montrose, widow of said 3rd Marquis James (grandson of the famous Montrose) who died 25/4/1684. She was 2nd daughter of John Duke of Rothes, chancellor of Scotland, She married again May 1687 Sir John Bruce of Kinross: Charles, Earl of Haddington: William Hay of Drumelyier; and Sir Wm. Bruce of Kinross. Signed by all four. Name of counter, or agent, is not given.
SUGARHOUSE CLOSE *See after Young Street*	
SUMMERFIELD **GARDENS**	Old house, *Kirkwood.*
SUMMERHALL **SQUARE**	Hope Park, *D.1827.* From the old name of the district, *o.& n.e. iii. 51.* Lands and well frequented inn on east side of highway leading from Potterrow by the Sciennes to Liberton, owned by late Wm. Hall, teller, Royal Bank, 15/12/1773, *eec.j.s.* Somerhall, foot of Sciennes, *D.1800, 190.* Sommerhall House, *Ord. Surv. 1852.* Summerhall Place, *m.t.c. 17/10/1827.* Jas. Hay, W.S., purchased from the heirs of deceased Geo. Manson, wigmaker, part of the lands of St. Leonard, called Summerhall, with small house. Allowed to enclose parterre, *m.t.c. 12/8/1741.*
SUMMERSIDE PLACE **STREET**	Suggested by the adjacent Summerfield, *j.r.*
SUNBURY MEWS **PLACE** **STREET**	Sunbury distillery, Water of Leith, *D.1827.* The name seems to occur in sasine 1/9/1690, *r.c.g. 19.* Sunbury House, *Ord. Surv. 1852.* Whitewashed old mansion, demolished, *w.o.l. 134.* Lands of Sunberry, *m.t.c. 16/7/1794.* Coates haugh alias Sunbury, *m.t.c. 20/9/1836.*
SURGEON SQUARE	Back of High School, *D.1827.* Infirmary St. immediately behind (to the north of) the old surgeons' hall, *o.& n.e. ii. 302. Shepherd 10, m.t.c. 13/12/1826.*
SYLVAN PLACE	*D.1827.* Stands close to where the rill (which gave name to Rillbank terrace and crescent) ran down to the Burgh Loch, and was doubtless descriptively named. It lies just east of the Cage (a pavilion called the Meadow Cage, *Ainslie 1804.*
SYMON SQUARE	*D.1800, 85.* Simon Square, *D.1827. Ainslie 1804.* Named from the builder.

T

TANFIELD	From Tanyard once there.
TANTALLON PLACE	On the estate of Sir Thomas Dick Lauder, of the Lauders of the Bass. Alan de Lawedre was Keeper of Tantallon Castle, circa 1370, *St. G. 165.*
TARVIT STREET	*Littlejohn, App. 42.* Seems to be Tamiet St., Drumdryan, *D.1855/6.*
TAY STREET	Compliment to the river.
TAYLOR GARDENS	From Wm. Taylor, chairman of Parish Council etc., partner in Messrs. Jas. Miller & Son, Leith. Built on his land, *j.r.*
TEMPLE PARK CRESCENT	From the Temple, whose ruins appear N.W. of Merchiston Castle, among trees, *Kirkwood. Ord. Surv. 1852.*
TENNANT STREET	Tennant Engineer, Bowershall Works. Drowned in the "London", circa 1860, *j.r.,* on his way to Australia, on business.
TEVIOT PLACE / ROW	From Mount Teviot, seat of the Marquis of Lothian, uncle to the last Lord Ross of Ross Park, who died at Mount Teviot, *o.& n.e. ii. 339. p.w. 1780/81, 14, eec.j.s. 30/11/1774.*
TEVIOTDALE PLACE	Fancy, from the Teviot hills, *e.c.b.cld.*
THIRLESTANE LANE / ROAD	On Warrender property. Sir George Warrender's mother was daughter to the Earl of Lauderdale, whose seat is Thirlstane Castle.
THISTLE COURT / STREET / LANE	Complimentary to the Scottish national flower, (compare Rose St.) 1784. The name was fixed, for the whole length of the street, as for Rose St., by act of Town Council 2/7/1785, *eec.j.s.* The east most block named, *Ainslie 1780.* In Ainslie 1804 Hill St. and Young St. appear as now. Thistle Court, consisting of 4 houses, *m.t.c. 25/6/1777.*
THISTLE PLACE	Compliment to the national flower of Scotland.
THOMSON'S COURT	Abbeyhill. Abbey strand, *D.1827.* Gavin Thomson, writer: inter alia Thomson's Cl., *v.r. 33.* Thomson's Cl. within precincts of Abbey of Holyrood House, from Gavin T., surgeon, R.N., *Can. Chart. 26/8/1806.* From Adam T., brewer, bailie of the Canongate, *Can. Chart 16/3/1888.* Two are shewn, Ord. Survey connected by close.
THOMSON'S COURT	66 Grassmarket, *D.1827.* Mrs. Wm. Thomson, merchant. John Thomson, corn merchant, David Thomson, all at 66 Grassmarket, *D.1827.* Evidently from the family. Named Carmichael's Cl., *Ainslie 1780-1804.*
THORNTREE STREET	From the tree which grew at the north end of the row of hinds' cottages, of the form of Lower Quarry holes: farm house still standing 1921, west side of Easter Road, *j.r., Ainslie 1804.* Act anent repairing of the highway leading from the Watergate to the thorn tree south side of Leith Links, *m.t.c. 13/10/1686.* The thorntree near Leith, *m.t.c. 15/4/1718.* Report on highway betwixt the thorne at Leith Links and the Abbeyhill. The saurer to see the laying of Calsay betwixt the Abayhill and the thorne: to consult Sir Wm. Purves who is concerned in a part of the ground, also Sir Wm. Bruce as to how to do it best and save expense to the town, *m.t.c. 2/4/1673.* Dwelling house and ground lately built by Jm. Paterson, mt. tasks man of Leith Links, at S.W. end of said Links at highway leading from Leith to the thorn tree which is at the end of the highway leading to the Abbey of Holyrood house.
THORNVILLE TERRACE	After the thorn tree, fancy, *e.c.b.c.ld.*
THORNYBAUK	*D.1827. Ainslie 1804. o.& n.e. ii. 218.* "A ridge covered with thorns, long unploughed and untouched", *m.t.c. 15/12/1824.* Property

bounded by a Thorn hedge, near Tollcross, *Reg. 23/3/1860*. There was a "briery baulk" at Dishinglfat—evidently descriptive, *Can. Chart. 27/12/1809*. Shown in Knox' map of 1824. Robert Stivenson, tenant in Orchardfield, and Marion Aitkman, relict of Robt. Brown, tenant, in Coatts, got authority to remove fuilyie and dung from the avenues leading from the West End of Portsburgh to the Thornbalk, including all the mid-way and the north way, *m.t.c. 19/3/1718*. North way seems to be the Linlithgow Road, and the mid-way the Glasgow Road, and the other avenue, the Twopenny Custom, as in Ainslie 1804. The Thornybank is shown, unnamed, by Brown and Watson 1793; Semple St. seems to be the northern part of it between Linlithgow Road and Glasgow Road. The Town owned itself responsible for the road from the end of the West Port the length of the Brierie balk near Tolcross, leading to Wright's houses, *m.t.c. 3/1/1750*. Offer of Trustees on Corstorphine road to pay half cost of repairing piece of road leading towards the Coltbridge from Ronalds to the Briery Baulk or east end of Castlebarns, *m.t.c. 23/6/1756*. Thornhedge at Tollcross, *Reg. 75, 23/3/1860*. John Spence, Son of John S., cowfeeder and portioner of Thoneback, (sic) at Fountainbridge near Edinburgh, p. to Wm. Gibson, plumber 18/2/1812. Adam Paterson, son of Adam P.,cowfeeder, Thornybauk, Fountainbridge, p. to John Spence, plumber, born 12/6/1821 as from 1/5/1821. John Spence, plumber, Spence's Pl., *D.1827/8*. Thornybauk, Fountainbridge, *D.1827/8*. Charter to John & George Spence, resident (No. 7) in Thornybauk, of ground in Duncan St. Bought for Port Hopetoun Union Property Co., *m.t.c. 15/12/1824*.

TIMBER BUSH

6 Shore and 41 Bernard St., *D.1827*. "Bush" is the corrupt form of "Bourse". Originally the open piazza in the lower storey of an ancient building adjoining Queen St. Chapel, where the merchants and traders met for business—the Bourse, or Exchange. Later the whole ground was used as a timber market—whence its name. It was known also as the "Timber Howff", *Calderwood, Sept. 1616*, or "Timber Holf", *o.& n.e. iii. 231*. Situate in Paunch Market, now Queen St., *t.t.l. 39*. See Common Closes. The name is used as equivalent to Timber Yard; by order of the Town Council, no Timber Bushes were allowed on any part of Princes' St. or the pleasure grounds there, *m.t.c. 16/8/1780*. "Timber hoof", *m.t.c. 12/2/1794, 1/6/1831*. "Locus lignarius", *Prot. A.W.3, 23/5/1710*. Timber house, *Prot. 24/8/1705, A.W.2*. The councils "timber house in the halfe of Leith", *m.t.c. 23/10/1635. See.Vol. 3, p.24*.

TINTO PLACE

Note written by other than Boog-Watson:— Irrelevant allusion to Tinto Hill.

TIPPERLINN ROAD

From the village of Tipperlinn (well of the Cascade?), which existed before 1586. Tipperlin Loan is mentioned in report on riding the Marches 1701. In 1770 Dr. Thomas Steel of Burghmuirhead, (see Steel's Place) established the Tipperlinn Chemical Works. In 1809, the Edinburg Lunatic Asylum was founded, and in 1853 the site of the Chemical Works was purchased from Isabella Steel, relict of Walter Oliphant, for the extension of the Asylum, *o.e.c. x. 206, 207, 209, 210. a.o.e. 130*. Tipperlinn, Boroughmuirhead, *D.1827*. James Steele, chimist. Burrow-muir-head, *D.1827, 240*. Road between Merchiston Tipperlin, *Prot. 18/10/1727 A.W.8*. Alexr. Napier of Tipperlyne, *m.t.c. 6/1/1569-70*.

TOBAGO STREET

Castlebarns, *D.1827*. Also Tobago Place, *Ainslie 1804. Lothian Map 1825*. Tobago St. so named before 9/4/1792, *eec.j.s. m.t.c. 21/7/1819*. From Nathaniel Donaldson, "of the Island of Tobago", who conveyed property to Wm. Morrison, writer, 1788-90. See Morrison St.

TOLBOOTH WYND 15 Canongate, *D.1827*. Entered through archway or pend at the base of the tower of the Tolbooth, leading to the N.B. Canongate, *Ainslie 1780, 1804. Prot. 31/3/1679.*
See Old Tolbooth Wynd—Part II.

TOLBOOTH WYND Leith. North end of Kirkgate to upperdrawbridge, *D.1827.* From the Tolbooth, built under Queen Mary 1563-1565: demolished 1819, despite the pleadings of Sir Walter Scott and others, *o.& n.e. iii. 228, 230.*

TOLLCROSS Foot of Lauriston, *D.1827. D.1800, 172, 219.* The name is found in Charter of Lands of High Riggs, dated 1458, *w.c.* In the map in Kincaid's History of Edinburgh, 1787, the name is given to the street known later as Cowfeeder Row, and now High Riggs. Lothian map 1825 shews it. The old Toll-cross, in front of Valleyfield House, *o.& n.e. iii. 30.* "Tow-cros" mentioned 1669, *o.& n.e. iii. 42.* "Lands of Tolcross". Charter of Charles II, 4/4/1649, *r.c.g. 9(30).* South parts of Tollcross owned by Major James Weir, 1814, *v.r.42.* "That part of the village of Portsburgh called Tollcross", *m.t.c. 14/6/1836.* Tollcross, near Edinburgh, *Prot. 26/6/1764, G.L.2.* Hierigs and Tollcroce, *m.t.c. 20/10/1697.* Tollcroce, *m.t.c. 20/10/1697.*

TOWER PLACE STREET From the old signal tower at the N.E. corner thereof originally, *Maitland 496 c.2.* a windmill for making rope-oil, *o.& n.e. iii. 245.*

TRAFALGAR LANE STREET From Nelson's last and greatest victory over the French fleet.

TRINITY CRESCENT ROAD South-west of Newhaven, *D.1827.* From the Trinity House, a seamen's Hospital, dedicated to the Holy Trinity, 1555, erected by the shipmasters and mariners, from the "primo gilt" dues, levied on all vessels entering the port. It stood on the Western side of the Kirkgate, where the present Trinity House, built 1817, now stands, *Irons, 1. 303. o.& n.e. iii. 223. e.s.s. 275.* Superior of the lands. The mariners' guilds in sea ports dedicated the Hospital to the Holy Trinity. The Masters and Mariners invested much of their funds in land in Trinity, which takes its name from the Incorporation, *j.r.s.l. 130.*
See also Trinity Court—Part II.

TRON SQUARE From the neighbouring Tron Kirk, (opened 1647—finished 1663).

TRUNK'S CLOSE Bryson's Close, *Reg. 29/10/1860; Prot. A.W.2, 9/1/1705.* Stirling's Close, *Reg. 29/10/1860; Prot. A.W.2, 9/1/1705.* Purvis Close, *Prot. G.H.10, 28/1/1734; 19/2/1734.*
Edgar. Ainslie 1780. Kirkwood. Kerr.

Formerly Touring's, thereafter Bryson's, now Trunk Close, *Prot. W.F.5, 12/4/1753,* owing its name to the Aberdeenshire family of Turing of Foveran, one of whom, James, had his town house in the close, *Prot. 26/6/1529, 6/9/1529.* A tenement on the north side of the High Street, having the tenement of John Aikman on the west and that of Andrew Moubray on the east, opposite the Fountain Well, was owned by Walter Turing, his heirs and successors, *Prot. J.W.7, 11/12/1764.*

Its alias, Stirling's Close, was derived from the tenement acquired from John Forman by Mr. Wm. Stirling, *Prot. A.W.3, 22/8/1710; A.W.4, 24/1/1712.*

Andrew Bryson of Craigtoun rebuilt a tenement in the close; he was son of Wm. Bryson, merchant, burgess, by Christian Orr, and father of Alexander and Christian by Agnes Scott. His sister Mary married Mr. Alexr. Bailie, writer; another sister, Margaret, married ———

Foullis, and had a son, Alexander Foullis of Ratho. Walter Ewing, W.S., married another Mary Bryson. Hence the name of the close, *Reg. 29/10/1860; Prot. A.W.2, 9/1/1705.*

It seems—the alias is not given—to have been called Purvis' Close, which was on the north side of the High Street, above the Netherbow, *Prot. G.H.10, 28/1/1734; 19/2/1734*, and seems to take the name from the tenement in Bryson's Close owned in succession by John Purvis, John Forman, Wm. Stirling, Andrew Handyside, and Mr. Andrew Bryson, *Prot. G.H.10, 28/1/1734; 19/2/1734.*

TWEEDDALE COURT

Kerr. Marquess of Tweeddale's Close, *Edgar. Kirkwood.* Tweedale's Close, *Ainslie.* Alexr. Young's Close, later James Brown's Close, *Prot. W.F.4, 11/5/1750.* John Laing's Close, *Prot. W.F.4, 11/5/1750.*

So called from the town mansion of the family of Hay, Marquis of Tweeddale, *Wilson, ii. 71; o.& n.e. i. 278.* Edgar shows the 'Marquis of Twedale's garden'.

The first of the family who lived there was John, 2nd Earl of Tweeddale, *died 1697*, to whom it was bequeathed by his grandmother, Margaret Ker, the famous Lady Yester, and the last, William Henry, the 4th Marquis, *died 1775.*

An older name was John Laing's Close, *John Laing's Close, now the Marquis of Tweedal's: Prot. W.F.4, 11/5/1750*, derived from Mr. John Laing, Keeper of the Signet, successor to the late Neil Laing, writer, builder of the great tenement acquired later by Sir Wm. Bruce of Balcaskie, architect of Holyrood Palace and first designer of the North Bridge, *o.& n.e. i. 336, ii. 74,* Kt., Clerk of Session, and his wife Dame Mary Halket; and from them by John, Marquis of Tweeddale. A tenement stood on the south side of the High Street, beside the Netherbow, having the land of the late Neil Layng, writer, now of Mr. John Layng, on the east and south, *c.c. 3043, 23/2/1589-90.* Robert Lang or Laing, merchant in Glasgow, owned property at the head of Tweeddale's Close, *Prot. W.F.1, 9/3/1745.*

It was also called Alexr. Young's, *Prot. W.F.4, 11/5/1750,* Close, later James Brown's Close, but of them we know nothing.

TYNECASTLE LANE
PLACE
TERRACE

From ancient toll of that name, *o.& n.e. ii. 218. Kirkwood.* Tynecastle, part of the estate of Merchiston, feued by the late John Alison from governors of George Watson's Hospital, who built house, circa 1793, *eec.j.s. 30 June 1801. Mentioned in v.r. 41.* Tynecastle Toll, *m.t.c. 17/7/1816, 14/1/1834.* Possibly derived by gaelic Tigh-na-caistel, or Tigh-an-chaisteil, meaning the castle near that place.

U

UNION COURT

16 Richmond Place, *Ord. Surv. 1852.*

UNION PLACE
STREET

D.1827. Ainslie 1804. North Union Place, Picardy, 4/12/1805. From the "Union of Ireland with Great Britain" effected 1 Jan. 1801.

UPPER BOW

Lawnmarket, as compared with the Nether bow, at the East End of the High St., *o.& n.e. i. 219.*

V

VALLENCE CLOSE

o.s. Kerr. Vallene's Close, *Ainslie.* Vallen's Close, *D.1800.* Valentine's Entry, *D.1827.*

Named from the lands of Adam Vallange (west of the Duke of Queensberry's lands, *Can. Chart. 26/7/1775*). He was a barber by trade. His lands were bounded on the west by those of the Incorporation of Baxters, the Bakers' lands, *Can. Chart. 31/1/1776, 17/7/1822.* The succession of owners of the property is given in the Canongate Charters.

VALLEYFIELD STREET

From the lands known as Valleyfield, feued by the town to John Marshall, 27 April 1687, *o.e.c. x. 241.* For sale *2/10/1806, eec.j.s.* Valleyfield House stood till Glengyle Terrace was built, about 1809. *o.& n.e. iii. 30.* It bore the date of 1687, and the initials M.C.M., probably for Marshall. It was also know as Villafield, *Kirkwood.* Charter of waste ground commonly called Valleyfield, to Lt. Col. David Williamson, *m.t.c. 4/8/1813.* Lands of Valleyfield, *m.t.c. 12/6/1816, 21/5/1828.* Alexr. Galloway, writer, infested in house and yard acquired from deceased John Marshall, west end of Bruntsfield Links commonly called Valliefield, *m.t.c. 2/3/1705.* James Galloway infested in house & yeard called Villefield, *18/1/1712.*

VANBURG PLACE

D.1827. S.E. of Links (or Vanburgh). After Sir John Vanburgh, architect, 1666-1726, designer of Blenheim Palace, etc., the houses being classical in design, *j.r.*

VEITCH'S SQUARE

Veitch's Court, Stockbridge, *D.1827.* From the builder, "a reputable old baker, *o.& n.e. iii. 75.* Thomas Veitch, baker, Stockbridge, *D.1827.* Veitch's Place, *Ord. Surv. 1852.* Called also Virgin Square, from the washerwomen resident, q.v.

VENNEL

Grassmarket. There were at one time several vennels in Edinburgh, this alone retains the name. The word is French, meaning a steep narrow lane, as may be seen in Morlaix, Brittany. West Port Vennel, *p.w. 1780/81, 81, 35. D.1800, 152. m.t.c. 19/8/1801.*

VERNON COTTAGES

Portobello. From Admiral Vernon, under whom served Hunter, the builder of "Portobello Hut". See Portobello.

VICTORIA STREET
TERRACE

Compliment to Queen Victoria between 1837 & 1852. New Street called Victoria St. leading from George IV Bridge to Grassmarket, *Reg. 10/5/1856.*

VIEWFORTH
GARDENS
SQUARE
TERRACE

From the house, Viewforth, Bruntsfield Links, occupied by Alexr. Smellie, printer to the University, *D.1827.* So named from possessing a view of the Firth of Forth, *m.t.c. 17/7/1816.*

VIOLET TERRACE

Fancy, from the flower, *e.c.b.c.ld:*

W

WADDELL PLACE

From the stables of Andrew Waddel & Son, contractors, *j.r.*

WALKER STREET

From the family of the Walkers of Coates, on whose ground it stands. *D.1827. See Ainslie 1804.* Nearly finished, *Lothian Map 1825.* Sir Pk. Walker, feues, *m.t.c. 4/9/1833, j.r.* Walkers of Dalry & Hanley. Named Murray St. in map 38.

WALKER TERRACE

Note written by other than Boog-Watson:— James Walker & Sons, Engineers, Gibson Ter.

WARDEN'S CLOSE

89 Grassmarket, *Ord. Surv. 1852.* George Warden, stabler, Grassmarket, South side, *p.w. 1780/81. Littlejohn 40.* Alias Burt's Cl.

WARDIE CRESCENT ROAD SQUARE STEPS	Crescent planned 11/3/1822. From the district Weirdie, *o.& n.e. iii. 179.* Wardie Castle mentioned in 1544, at the time of the English invasion, *b.b.16.* Wardie Muir mentioned 1558, *o.& n.e. iii. 306.* Waldie Muir, two miles from Edinburgh Castle, where the ball shot from Mons Meg landed, *t.o.e. 207.* Weirdy brae and Weirdy brow, *Maitland 242 and 245.* Weirdy Brow, 2 Dec. 1573, *Irons I. 389.* Wardie brow or burn, *m.t.c. 15/6/1824.* "Werdibrown apon the sey coste", *28/1/1499–1500, m.m.s II.* *See also Wardie Avenue etc.—Part II.*
WARDLAW PLACE STREET TERRACE	From Genl. Wardlaw, one of the Trustees of Sir George Campbell's superiors, *Stewart.*
WARDROP'S CLOSE COURT	Lawnmarket. See Middle Baxters' Close.
WARRENDER PARK CRESCENT ROAD TERRACE	On the estate of the family of Warrender, held before 1381 from the Crown as the King's Serjeant lands, since then under feu charter by Robert II to Alan de Lawdre. Bruntsfield estate was purchased in 1695 by George Warrender, then bailie, and later Lord Provost, 1713; and 1714 as Sir George. For full particulars, as also of properties feued from the town, *see o.e.c. x. 24 etc.* The mansion house is Bruntsfield House. George Warrender Esq., Bruntsfield Links, *p.w. 1780/81.* Miss Warrender, Warrander's Lodge, No. 1 west from Meadow Cage, *D.1800.* Mr. Warrender's house shewn east of Meadow Cage, *Ainslie 1804,* which shows the property S.W. of the Meadows. They seem to have had a house, 625 Castlehill, *p.w. 1780/81. D.1800 and D.1827.*
WARRISTON'S CLOSE	Bruce's Close, Craig's Close. It takes its name from Wariston's land, the house of Sir Archibald Johnstoun of Wariston, the leading framer of the National Covenant first signed in Greyfriars' Church in 1638, who was betrayed and executed 23rd July 1663. For a masterly and appreciative sketch of him see Dr. Smellie's 'Men of the Covenant', chap. ix. He was uncle of Gilbert Burnet, Bishop of Salisbury, whose references to him in his 'History of My Own Times' show a lamentable inability to recognise his true greatness. He took his title from the estate of Warynston near Currie, some seven miles from Edinburgh, *Grant, o.& n.e. iii. 99, confuses this Warriston with the district north of Canonmills. Edgar. Ainslie. Kirkwood. Kerr.* The house belonged formerly to Sir Thomas Craig of Riccartoun, uncle to Sir Archibald Johnston, and was known as Craig's land, giving to the close the name of Craig's Close, *Craig's, now Warriston's Close: Prot. W.F.4, 31/10/1750.* A yet older name was Bruce's Close, derived from the residence of Robert Bruce of Binnie or Binning, Stirlingshire, who occupied the house in 1566, *John Knox, 82, 109.* The lintel of his dwelling is still on the west side of the close, bearing the inscription Gratia dei Robertus Bruiss. John Knox's manse was directly opposite, on the east side of the close, as marked now by a tablet. The court at the foot of the close was known as White's Court, from Wm. White, smith there, *D.1799, 255; D.1826-7, x.*
WARRISTON CRESCENT PLACE ROAD	From the estate of Warriston, N.E. of Canonmills, owned early in the 16th century by Somervilles, by 1581 by Kincaids, *o.& n.e. iii. 98.* The property of Warriston n. of the city was acquired from Robt. Gray of Warriston by Heriot's Hospital (1706). *See also Warriston Drive etc. Part II.*

WATER OF LEITH	The river was originally the Leith, *Maitland 485.c.1. 496.c.1. 498.c.2.* and the district and village at its mouth. Inverleith, which in time was curtailed to Leith, and the dispossessed river became, and remained the Water of Leith, *o.& n.e. iii. 164,* mentions and contradicts the derivation of the name from the family of Leith, who owned Restalrig etc., in the days of Alexander III. *Not a street name.*
WATER STREET	Old name the Pipes, *D.1827.* From the reservoir at the foot of the Kirkgate, *o.& n.e. iii. 213.* The chief of water supply was from Lochend, *Irons, ii. 168. Maitland 502-3 754* by permission of Earl of Moray, to whom were granted in return pews in South Leith Church, formerly possessed by Lord Balmerino, executed 1746, *j.r.*
WATER LANE	*D.1827.* Anciently Rotten Row, *Kirkwood.* Now Water St. "Rotten row, now called Water Lane", *Kincaid 209.*
WATERLOO PLACE	From Wellington's victory over Napoleon 1815, *D.1827.* The first intention was to name it Wellington Bridge, *o.& n.e. ii. 107., m.t.c. 8/9/1819, 30/10/1822.*
WATSON CRESCENT	From Bailie James Watson.
WAVERLEY BUILDINGS BRIDGE PARK TERRACE PLACE STEPS	From Sir Walter Scott's first novel, which gave so many names to so many objects, from Railway Stations to pen-nibs. Although the hero is an Englishman, the novel is Scottish, and flavours all to which its name is applied. Waverley Buildings, Cowgate, where Waverley Brewery stood.
WELL COURT	Dean. From well there.
WELLINGTON STREET PLACE (LEITH)	After the Iron Duke, The Duke of Wellington, Victor at Waterloo.
WEMYSS PLACE	From the Earl of Wemyss, whose town house was close by: his gardens the westermost division of the Queen St. gardens. In 64 Queen St., *D.1827. trad. i. 52. o.& n.e. ii. 194. Kirkwood. D.1827.* Earl of Wemyss' house, west end of Queen St., *m.t.c. 8/8/1810.*
WEST BOW	From its position at the west end of the town. Name dates from the days of David II, *Gordon. Edgar. Ainslie.* Jamieson gives "Bow, the curve or bending of a street", instancing the West-bow Street as given by Maitland. This, however, would not suit the Netherbow, which is more suggestive of Jamieson's "Bow, an arch, a gateway". This is the derivation given in trad, p.48, viz. the arch or bow forming the gateway in the "West-bow". The port of the West Bow was considered to be a public nuisance whose removal would widen the passage about a yard; it is to be taken down tomorrow morning early, *m.t.c. 11/6/1735.*
WEST COATES	From the Mansion of Wester Coates (or White house) formerly owned by James Finlay of Walliford, and possessed by Lord Covington, *o.& n.e. iii. 116.*
WEST END PLACE	At West end of Dalry.
WEST MILL LANE	Dean. Descriptive of position.
WEST MAITLAND STREET	See Maitland St.
WESTMOST CLOSE	Newhaven. Descriptive.
WEST PORT	Originally the most westerly gate in the Flodden wall, leading out of the Grassmarket, *Gordon. Edgar. Ainslie,* into the (wester) Portsburgh. Also Lothian map 1825. In the Ord. Surv. 1825 the road through the Portsburgh is named West Port, as it is to this day. It is so in *D.1827,* "West Port, Grassmarket, to Main Point".

WEST PROMENADE TERRACE	At the West Promenade by the beach.
WESTER COATES AVENUE GARDENS ROAD TERRACE	From the mansion of Wester Coates, and the district, *Ord. Surv. 1852.* *See West Coates.*
WESTERN TERRACE	From its western position. *See also Western Corner etc.—Part II.*
WHITE PARK	Gorgie. Built by Mr. White, formerly of Royal Hotel, Bathgate, on Merchant Company's ground. *1887 v.r. Owned by David White, Spirit Dealer, 161 High Street.*
WHITEHORSE CLOSE	*Ainslie. Kirkwood. Kerr.* Davidson's Close, *D.1827.* Laurence Ord's Close, *Prot. J.H. Canong. 12/4/1678.*

This close must, of course, be carefully distinguished from the close of the same name but on the south side of the Canongate*head.*

It is not named from the White Horse of Hanover: the name is much older, *o.& n.e. ii. 21.* Tradition, refuted by the date 1603, *Chambers, ii. 295,* or 1623, *Wilson, ii. 114,* cut over one of the windows, affirms that Queen Mary kept a favouite white palfrey here when the Royal Mews occupied the building, *Chambers, ii. 295.* It is more probable that it was the title of an inn. Storer, *Vol. ii,* states that the White Horse Close, now called Davidson's land ... once formed the stable-yard of Queen Mary. The date 1523 now on the building is a modern error.

Its later name, Davidson's Close, comes from Davidson's land, the property of John Davidson, brassfounder, son of umquhyle Robert Davidson, shoemaker, *Can. Chart. 28/6/1842.* Mrs. Davidson was resident in the close in 1799, *D.1799.* Robert Davidson acquired the lands, 10th January 1752, from Patrick Tod, merchant in Edinburgh, *Can. Chart. 3/6/1767.*

Its oldest name was Ord's or Laurence Ord's Close, taking the name from the lands formerly owned by Laurence Ord, merchant, burgess of Edinburgh, *made burgess and guild brother, 18th August 1680, by right of his spouse Marie, daughter to John Young, litster,* and his daughter Christian, *Prot. J.H. Canong. 21/1/1683; m.t.c. 20/3/1838, 30/10/1838,* wife of Walter Graham, goldsmith in the Canongate, who sold them to Mr. John Mitchell of Alderston, 10th December 1695, and he to Mr. Nicol Graham, 21st December 1745. They finally came into the hands of Robert Davidson, 10th January 1752, *Can. Chart. 3/6/1767, where the succession of owners is given.* This tenement, formerly owned by Mr. Niccol Grahame of Gartmore, *entered as advocate. Gartemore in p.w. 1773,* was bounded by Laurence Ord's Close on the east; by the Canongate on the south; by Mr. Nicol Grahame's land on the north; and *(blank)* Close on the west, *Can. Chart. 3/6/1767, where the succession of owners is given.*

Laurence Ord rebuilt the tenement as court, haylofts, and houses, evidently as an inn, facing towards the Canongate on the south, and having a large gate at the entry. He may have named the inn the 'White Horse'.

On 18th February 1680, Laurence Orr, Lieutenant, and his Captain, Wm. Hepburne, of the Cannongait, were imprisoned and fined in 500 and 200 merks respectively for mutinous behaviour against Captain Meinyies, at the embarking of His Royal Highness (Duke of York), at Leith.

Captain Hepburne had quarrelled with Captain Meinyies, and exclaimed, as they attacked his Company—'Charge with ball, and fyr upon the dogs!' *m.t.c. 18/2/1680.* **Redeveloped but name retained, 1960's.**

WHITEHOUSE LOAN
TERRACE

D.1827. On the lands of Whitehouse, originally Hogiston, Hogstoun, or Ogstoun. Name Whitehouse later than 1444, *o.e.c. x. 5.35 etc.* O.& n.e. iii. 45 states that St. Margaret's Convent was engrafted on the old house in 1835. The estate, owned by Mrs. Grant of Kilgraston, to be feued, 2/2/1824, *eec.j.s.* In Lizar's Directory Map 1835 the house is shown where the St. Margaret's Convent now stands; the old bits may still be distinguished. No. 17 now called Whitehouse, and white washed, is in Lizar's maps, 1835 & 1856. Ville, and in O.S. White House Villa. John Davidson, Clerk of Justiciary, was owner, and was allowed by the Town Council to straighten his dike, on the e.s. of the broad loaning leading from Canaan Muir to Bruntsfield Links, *m.t.c. 23/4/1729.*

WILLIAM STREET

On property of William Walker, of Coates, *D.1824, D.1827, Ainslie 1804.*

WILLOWBANK ROW

From old house, *Kirkwood.* From the great willow tree growing there, *j.r.s.l. 240.*

WILLOWBRAE AVENUE
GARDENS
ROAD

Enclosure "Willows", on map of 1783, *Baird 294.*

WILSON'S PARK

Probably from Mr. Wilson, sub-feuar of part of the lands of Figget from Mr. Jameson, 1804, *Baird 316-317.*

WINDMILL LANE

D.1799, D.1827. From the windmill erected by the city for their tenants, "The Fellowship and Society of Ale and Beer Brewers of the Burgh of Edinburgh", as contracted 20 Feb. 1597-8, to pump water from the Burgh, or South, Loch, to the Brewery just inside Bristo Port. The wind mill and circular reservoir stood where is now the desecrated graveyard attached to the Chapel of Ease, Buccleuch Parish Church, *Kincaid 100, o.e.c. x. 227-239.* Property of Windmill Acres, *m.t.c. 6/2/1822.* Site of Windmill now part of Churchyard. Original feuars 6/8/1760. St. Cuthbert's Session, *r.o.s.* The Kirk Session of the West Kirk got a disposition of ground whereon windmill formerly stood, for conversion into burying-ground, *m.t.c. 6/7/1768.*

WINDSOR TERRACE
PLACE

Originally Nicholson St. from the maiden name of wife of Wm. Jameson, industrial maker of Portobello. Name changed in 1822, in commemoration of the visit of George IV to Portobello, *Baird 294.*

WINDSOR STREET

D.1827. Lothian map 1825. In commemoration of the visit of George IV in 1822. On lands of Hillside, *m.t.c. 29/6/1825.*

WOLSELEY CRESCENT
GARDENS
PLACE
TERRACE

From Viscount Sir Garnet Wolsley, in command during the Ashantee War 1873-4, etc. etc. Honorary burgess of Edinburgh 1898.

WOODBINE TERRACE

Fancy, after the flower, *e.c.b.c.ld.*

WOODBURN PLACE
TERRACE

From the old house, shewn Ord. Surv. 1852. Woodburn, Morningside, *D.1827, 160.* Probably name originated in position of the house, in a wood, beside the jordan burn. House shewn in Littlejohn map.

WOODSIDE TERRACE

Locally descriptive.

WOODVILLE TERRACE

After woods generally: fancy, *e.c.b.c.ld.*

WORLD'S END CLOSE

Prot. G.H.7, 18/1/1725. Edgar. Ainslie. Kirkwood. Kerr. Swift's Close.

So named from its position, almost at the very end of the High Street.

It was 'formerly Swift's Close', *Prot. J.W.6, 9/1/1762.* The late John Swift owned a foreland house there in 1595, *New Lights, 57, n. Strangely enough, there was at one time a fishmarket held in this close, and the Old Fishmarket Close, near the Cross, was also known as Swift's Close (q.v.). Were the family in the fish trade?* In 1427 James I granted a tenement on the south side of the King's (High) Street to John Swyft, burgess, *Soc. Ant. S. 14/6/1886.* It may be the same. Sweit's Close, *Prot. W.F.4, 11/5/1750,* is evidently a slip for Swift's.

At one time it was known as Sir James Stanfield's Close, *Wilson, ii. 73,* the tragedy of whose death in 1687, and execution of his son Philip, proved guilty of the murder by the ordeal of blood, is given fully by Grant, *o.& n.e. i. 281.* Sir Wm. Bruce and his wife disponed part of the property *(vide supra)* to James Stanfield, merchant, *Prot. W.F.4, 11/5/1750.*

WRIGHTS HOUSES

And toll. Bruntsfield (sic) Links, *D.1827.* From the picturesque ancient mansion ruthlessly demolished 1800 to give a site to Gillespies paltry Hospital. "Hideous", *o.& n.e. iii. 31,* which bore various dates, the earliest being 1339. It was the property of a branch of the Napier family. Maitland 507 mentions as erroneous the derivation of the name from the wrights who felled and wrought the oak timber on the Burghmuir, giving as the true derivation, from the Laird of Wryte. It gave its name to a small village which grew up on both sides of the road, from (West) Linton, till the road was widened in 1794, when the houses on the west side were swept away, *o.e.c. x. 248, o.& n.e. iii. 33, 36 (view).* House and grounds offered for sale, *Caled. Merc. j.s. 16/7/1785.* Called Barganie House, by Gillespie Trustees, from occupant, *o.& n.e. iii. 34. o.e.c. iv.* In m.t.c. 12/1/1791 it is called Bruntsfield Castle occupied and owned by Mr. Hamilton of Bargeny. Alexr. Napier of Wrightshouses, *Prot. 8/1/1533-4.* A bailie of Edinburgh, *c.c. 1342, 8/3/1543-4.*

WRITERS' COURT

This court was built by Robert Miln of Balfard *(sic)* and Patrick Steel, with entry from Warriston's Close, *Prot. J.W.3, 5/1/1753.* It was acquired by the Society of the Writers to His Majesty's Signet, as a home for their Library in 1699, a board being put up, bearing the name 'Writers' Court', *John Knox, 84.* The 'Wryters' Court' had also an entrance from Mary King's Close, *Prot. G.I.1, 22/1/1731.*
Edgar. Ainslie. Kirkwood. Kerr.

Y

YARDHEADS

St. Anthony's Lane to north end King St., *D.1827.* Originally a few scattered cottages close to the boundary wall of the gardens, or yards, of the Preceptory of St. Anthony, *t.t.l. 182. j.r.s.l. 101.* Soldiers to be quartered there, *m.t.c. 22/12/1675.*

YEAMAN PLACE LANE

From John A. Yeaman, W.S., superior.

YORK BUILDINGS PLACE

From the English title of the King's second son, as Albany St. from his Scottish title, *o.& n.e. ii. 190.* "The continuation of Queen St. now called York Place", *4/3/1797, eec.j.s.* St. Georges Chapel, Queen St. founded 3/7/1792. Opened in York Place, 17/10/1793, *eec.j.s.* Name thus altered between these dates, *D.1827. Ainslie 1804.* York Pl. seems to have been regarded at first as part of Queen St.

"The Episcopal Chappel, Queen St.", *m.t.c. 26/11/1794,* referring to St. George's. York Place on northside, see patched map "Strangers' Guide" 1820, but south side of York Place mentioned, *m.t.c. 29/11/1797.*

YOUNG STREET

Charlotte Sq., *D.1827.* Unnamed in Craig's plan 1767, as also Ainslie 1780. Young St., *Ainslie 1804,* which shows the east part of the west-most division of Queen St. gardens as "Mr. Young's". John Young, wright, feued much in the extended Royalty, his own house in Thistle Court, *p.w. 1780/81, 104.* The division of Thistle St. between Castle St. and Charlotte St. now called Young St.—house there lately bought by Lieut. Col. Wm. Duncan, with extra bit of ground bought in by consent of Robert Young, merchant, Edinburgh, to whom the feu was originally granted, *m.t.c. 18/4/1801. 1/7/1801. 16/6/1802. 28/7/1802.* Ground in Thistle St. originally feued to John Young, wright, 30/5/1787, *m.t.c. 12/2/1806.*

SUGARHOUSE CLOSE

Ainslie. Kirkwood.

So called from the old sugar refinery to which it led. A company was formed, 24th April 1752, who acquired the house formerly of the Earl of Dunkeld, on the south side of the Canongate, having the land of the Earl of Moray on the west and of the Hammermen of the Canongate on the east. A charter of confirmation was granted, 3rd June 1767, *Can. Chart. 3/6/1767,* to the trustees of the Edinburgh Sugar House. The 'Sugar Work House' is inserted in Edgar 1765. It was burned, 8th January 1800, *Scots Magazine,* but is mentioned in the Council Minutes of 20th May 1807; and David Jardine & Co., sugar refiners, Edinburgh Sugar House, 154 Canongate, appear in the Directory for 1824 *P.110,* and later.

PART II

NOTES COMPILED IN THE CITY ENGINEER'S DEPARTMENT

STREET	NAMED	DERIVATION
ABBEYHILL CRESCENT	19.9.68	Corporation development on site of original Holyrood Terrace. Name from the neighbouring Abbey of Holyrood. *Similar to what's shown in Part I. See also Abbeyhill—Part I.*
ABBEY LANE	4.5.66	Formerly Rose Lane named because of duplication. Also from the Abbey of Holyrood.
ABERCORN DRIVE	31.3.32	From John James Hamilton, Marquis of Abercorn, later
GROVE	25.2.32	created Duke of Abercorn. The lands of Duddingston were acquired by the Marquis of Abercorn from the Argyle family in 1745. *See also Abercorn—Part I.*
ACADEMY STREET	1.3.68	Formerly Morton Street renamed because of duplication with Morton Street, Portobello. Thus named because it is adjacent to Leith Academy.
ADELPHI GROVE	4.5.66	Adelphi Grove formerly Livingston Place renamed because
PLACE	—	of duplication with Livingston Place, Sciennes. Possibly an attempt to **imitate** Adelphi Buildings, a noted Work of Robert Adam the famous architect, in Strand, London. Demolished 1772. The name "Adelphi" has on occasions been used in naming buildings etc.
AFTON PLACE	9.9.27	Afton Place: application by Fyfe, Ireland & Co. for street
TERRACE	—	order on the date shown. Named thus because adjacent to Afton Terrace—derivation unknown but possibly fanciful name from River Afton, Ayrshire. "Flow gently sweet Afton".
AFFLECK COURT	14.2.74	Development by T. Boland & Co. Houses contained within an enclosed courtyard and thus the theme chosen was names of Scottish Castles because these names would reflect the nature of the development. Affleck Castle beside Monikie, Angus.
ALLAN BRECK GARDENS	28.2.57	Corporation South Clermiston scheme where all names were selected from Robert Louis Stevenson's novel, "Kidnapped". The appropriate Committee felt this theme was suitable because of Stevenson's connection with Edinburgh and in his novel it was Clermiston Hill that David Balfour crossed before looking down on old Ebenezer's house.
ALEXANDER DRIVE	16.1.36	On this date approval was given to application for order to construct the street. Application was made by Williamson, Watt & Co., on behalf of Mr. Alexander Glass after whom it is presumed the street is named.
ALLAN PARK CRESCENT	23.3.33	Street order application of 23.3.35 by T.L. Rae & Co.
ROAD	23.3.33	for construction of new streets "at Allan's Park".
DRIVE	23.3.33	Application of 18.1.34 by J. Miller, Architect. Probably
GARDENS	23.3.33	Allan was a local proprietor.
LOAN	18.1.34	
ALLERMUIR ROAD	June 1923	Named from Allermuir Hill in the Pentland Hills.

ALLOWAY LOAN	23.1.75	On a suggestion of the chairman of the Highways & Road Safety Committee that streets in a new development be named from the works of Robert Burns, the Kirk Brae development was selected as available. Alloway is the birth place of Robert Burns.
ALMOND BANK COTTAGES	—	Evident—near the bank of the River Almond.
ALMOND GREEN SQUARE	11.10.73 11.10.73	Not named after River Almond. This is part of the Southfield and East Craigs development where ground was allocated to various housing societies to develop. This area was developed by the Almond Housing Society.
ALNWICKHILL ROAD DRIVE GARDENS VIEW TERRACE COURT LOAN GROVE CRESCENT PARK	— 25.1.73 25.1.73 25.1.73 25.1.73 25.1.73 25.1.73 25.1.73 25.1.73 25.1.73	Name from Alnwickhill House situated on this road. Streets named 25.1.73 developed by Scottish Residential Estates (Crudens Ltd.) named thus simply because they were off Alnwickhill Road. Alnwickhill House was at one time the Edinburgh Industrial Home for Fallen Women. It is now divided into 13 self-contained flats. The name probably derives from the fact that the old road to the south passed this way and eventually to Alnwick, Northumberland.
ANDREW WOOD COURT	16.4.70	Situated in Newhaven redevelopment on the line of the original James Street. Duplication with James Street, Portobello, necessitated a new name. Sir Andrew Wood was a famous sea captain and commanded "The Great Michael" during the reign of King James IV. Buried at Largo Church, Fife.. The Great Michael was a famous fighting ship built at Newhaven and was the largest ship in the British Isles at that time.
ANNFIELD STREET	15.7.65	Formerly Ann Street renamed with effect from 1.3.66 because of duplication with Ann Street, Dean. Name from Lady Ann Stewart, widow of John Stewart of Blairhaw, thereafter Annfield.
ANTIGUA STREET	—	Shown on Ainslie's Map of 1804. Referred to in Town Council Minutes 26/8/1807. Compare Jamaica Street. Both islands in the West Indies were of great importance in 1800 and it would therefore not be unusual for these streets to have been named from this source.
ARDSHIEL AVENUE	28.2.57	Corporation South Clermiston scheme. See Alan Breck Gardens.
ARGYLE TERRACE	—	Compare Atholl, Breadalbane, and Richmond. The theme chosen was names of Dukes. In this case the Duke of Argyle.
ARNOTT GARDENS	8.10.36	Named Redhall Gardens at the request of superiors of Redhall Estate. Altered with committee approval to Arnott Gardens. Application for street order dated 26.3.36 was by Arnott & Lawend, Builders, from which firm the street name is derived.
ASHLEY DRIVE GARDENS GROVE	20.10.32 20.10.32 —	A note exists in Part I written other than by Boog Watson "Off Ashley Terrace which is next to Shaftesbury Park and Ashley is the family name of the Earls of Shaftesbury". Boog Watson in Part I however, gives a reference of the secretary of the Edinburgh Co-op Building Company Limited as fanciful from the ash tree which is probably

correct and the Shaftesbury name was introduced later in the mistaken belief that Ashley of Ashley Terrace was named from the Earls of Shaftesbury. No connection can be found to associate this earldom with the Merchiston Estate. The earl in 1878 was made a freeman of the city on 13.4.78 however.

ASHLEY PLACE	—	Ordnance Survey Map of 1852 shows ground here as a fruit and vegetable nursery and also shows it as well planted with trees. The name therefore is probably fancy—from the Ash tree.
NEWHAVEN ROAD		
Continued		

ASHTON GROVE	25.5.50	Committee decision taken on this date, after much debate, that all streets in the Corporation's Inch Housing Scheme be named from novels of Sir Walter Scott.

ATHOLL TERRACE	—	Of the 26 dukes in the United Kingdom the names of 19 are used in Edinburgh street names and all the Scottish Dukes' names are used.
CRESCENT	—	These streets are most probably named from the Duke of Atholl.
CRESCENT LANE	—	
PLACE	—	

AUCHINLECK COURT	16.4.70	In the redevelopment of Main Street, Newhaven, this court was built on line of original Auchinleck's Brae named from local proprietor.

See also Auchinleck's Court—Part I.

AVENUE VILLAS	—	A short line of villa houses forming an avenue off Crewe Road South. Formerly known as Black's Entry.

AVON ROAD	15.2.34	Name Avon Road originally suggested by John A.W. Grant, Architect. A check was made to the firm of this name on 12.4.73. Original John Grant deceased and the question of derivation could not be answered. However, the street is near to the River Almond and it is possible that it was named after another river, River Avon.
GROVE	29.6.72	
PLACE	29.6.72	

BABERTON AVENUE	—	The original street, Baberton Avenue, led to the driveway of Baberton House after which the street was named.
COURT	—	
CRESCENT	15.4.37	Baberton Loan was formerly called Station Road, renamed with effect from 1.2.68 because of duplication with Station Road Corstorphine.
LOAN	13.7.67	
SQUARE	—	
PARK	7.6.62	

Baberton House; James IV gave lands to Alexander Brand who became known as Brand of Baberton. Other owners were Cissor, Crawford, Forrester, Wardlaw, Elphistone and Murray. The mansion house was built about 1622. The last mentioned occupier was Sir. James Murray, Master of Works to James VI but it is not certain that he rebuilt or extended the property.

BABERTON MAINS ROAD	—	
DRIVE	4.11.71	
TERRACE	4.11.71	
VIEW	4.11.71	
PLACE	4.11.71	
GROVE	4.11.71	
GARDENS	4.11.71	
AVENUE	28. 6.73	
ROW	28. 6.73	
BANK	28. 6.73	
WYND	28. 6.73	
GREEN	28. 6.73	
LOAN	28. 6.73	
COURT	28. 6.73	
PARK	13.12.73	
CRESCENT	13.12.73	
WOOD	13.12.73	
HILL	13.12.73	
DELL	13.12.73	

Baberton Mains Road was the original road which led to Baberton Mains Farm. All other "Baberton Mains" streets were constructed by Messrs. George Wimpey & Co. The name "Kilbaberton" (an old name for Baberton) considered but "Baberton Mains" name prefered. Baberton Mains road formerly part of Wester Hailes Road (formerly Theives Road).

BACK STATION ROAD —

The road at the back of the road leading to former Craigmillar Station.

BAILIE PLACE	26.11.36	
TERRACE	20. 5.37	
DRIVE	11.10.56	
GROVE	11.10.56	
PATH	11.10.56	

Named after William Bailie, glass and bottle manufactuer who was the first Provost of Portobello in 1833.

BAIRD DRIVE	—	
GARDENS	—	
GROVE	—	
TERRACE	16.10.25	

Baird Drive, Gardens and Grove taken over as public streets on 5.7.28 but date of naming cannot be traced. The Baird family are first mentioned in 14th century. The present Baron is Sir James Richard Gardiner Baird of Saughton Hall, Edinburgh (in title only). He resides at Wareside, Ware, Herts. He is the 10th baron.

See also Baird Avenue — Part 1

BAKER'S PLACE —

This street was in fact named after a **Baker. Built** about 1857 all the houses and shops in the block were owned by Andrew Tait, baker of 33 Rose Street.

BALBIRNIE PLACE —

Balbirnie is an estate with a Mansion erected by General Balfour in Markinch, Fife. Compare Osborne, Hampton, Kew, Carberry, and Borthwick Street nearby. All are noted Mansions and this was obviously the theme naming some of the Streets in this area. Balbirnie Place was built about 1865.

BALCARRES STREET —

Much of the original property in this street when constructed in 1885 was owned by Messrs. Mackenzie and Moncur. Extensive works for garden furniture, glass houses, etc and a large timber yard existed. The other branch of the business was iron foundry in Slateford Road (now demolished) just **west** of Appin Terrace.

Bailie Mackenzie built Appin Terrace named from Appin, Fife where he was born. Although no proof exists it is conceivable that he chose the name Balcarres from Balcarres House also in Fife. Balcarres is in East Fife ¾ mile N.W. of Colinsburgh. The Mansion looks across the Firth of Forth to the Bass Rock, Lammermuirs and Edinburgh.

BALDERSTON GARDENS	25. 5.60	Corporation Inch Housing — See Ashton Grove.
BALFRON LOAN	28. 2.57	Corporation South Clermiston Housing. See Alan Breck Gardens.
BALLANTYNE PLACE	—	Built about 1900 Grieve Ballantyne was the Builder.
ROAD	—	

BALMWELL AVENUE	15. 3.56	It is said that St. Katherine stopped on journey to
GROVE	15. 3.56	Edinburgh and miraculous well appeared. Oil contamination
TERRACE	15. 3.56	was said to be a balm for certain diseases.
PARK	13.11.58	*See also St. Katherine's Gardens*

BALGREEN AVENUE	—	From the old house and property of Balgreen. Balgreen
GARDENS	3. 6.26	House was situated where Balgreen School is now, opposite
PARK	—	Stevenson Road.
		See also Balgreen Road — Part I

BANGHOLM AVENUE	24. 7.24	Named from the Farm of Bangholm.
PARK	24. 7.24	Bangholm consisted of a small community with cottages
PLACE	24. 7.24	and a smithy on the south side of Ferry Road, between
ROAD	24. 7.24	South Trinity Road and Clark Road. Bangholm Farm was
VILLAS	24. 7.24	situated where these streets are today.
GROVE	7. 5.25	*See also Bangholm Terrace — Part I*
LOAN	7. 5.25	
VIEW	7. 5.25	

BANGHOLM BOWER AVENUE	7.10.26	The large Mansion House and extensive grounds of Bangholm Bower were situated on the north side of the present day street. The street was constructed on the original driveway to the house.

BANKHEAD AVENUE	13. 3.47	Although all named on the same date, Bankhead Avenue
BROADWAY	13. 3.47	was the first to be constructed. This street runs parallel
CROSSWAY N	13. 3.47	to the main railway line to the west which lies on a
CROSSWAY S	13. 3.47	considerable bank at this part. It is thought that the name
DRIVE	13. 3.47	is derived from this source.
LOAN	13. 3.47	
MEDWAY	13. 3.47	
PLACE	13. 3.47	
STREET	13. 3.47	
TERRACE	13. 3.47	
WAY	13. 3.47	

BARNSHOT ROAD	—	A corruption of Burnshot Park, a field which was located between Dreghorn Loan and Munro Drive. This was the first street to be constructed off the original road to Woodhall.

BARNTON AVENUE	—	Named from the estate of Barnton owned in 1482 by
AVENUE E	30.10.24	the family of Touris afterwards of Inverleith. It changed
AVENUE S	11.12.58	hands many times, coming last to the Ramsays — near
AVENUE W	18. 9.24	Muttonhole or Davidsons Mains, a barony bought by
BRAE	26.11.36	William Davidson in 1776. Peter Ramsay's famous stables
GARDENS	—	and Inn were at the foot of St. Mary's Wynd, whence he
GROVE	—	withdrew and settled at Barnton.
LOAN	3. 4.24	Barntony or Berntoun — a farm with a barn
PARK	—	

BARNTON PARK AVENUE	16. 7.59	Land commonly known as Barnton Park prior to building
CRESCENT	16. 7.59	of houses there. This was of course the parkland of the
DELL	12. 4.73	former Barnton House. Development by James Miller
DRIVE	16. 7.59	& Partners

Continued

BARNTON PARK GARDENS	16. 7.59	
GROVE	16. 7.59	
PLACE	16. 7.59	
VIEW	16. 7.59	
WOOD	16. 7.59	

BARNTONGATE AVENUE	10.10.68	Southfield Avenue and Drive renamed Bartongate 10.10.68 with effect from 1.1.69; Terrace renamed 13.7.67 with effect from 1.2.68. Formerly Southfield Avenue, Drive and Terrace from the local farm. Renamed because of duplication with the Southfields at Duddingston.
DRIVE	10.10.68	
TERRACE	13. 7.67	

Streets are situated near to one of the main gates to the former Barnton House.

BARNTALLOCH COURT — 14. 2.74

From the castle of that name near Langholme, Dumfriesshire.
See Affleck Court.

BEACH LANE — 26. 1.67

Formerly Ramsay Lane, renamed with effect from 1.8.67 because of duplication with Ramsay Lane (Castlehill). This lane leads to Portobello beach.

BEAUCHAMP ROAD	29. 5.30	The first baron of Liberton and Craigmiller Estate was Major General Robert Gordon Gordon Gilmour, a distinguished officer in the Grenadier Guards and who married on 19.10.1889 Lady Susan Lygon second daughter of Earl of Beauchamp of Madresfield Court, Malvern, Worcester. This street was constructed on the Craigmiller Estate.
GROVE	29. 5.30	

BEDFORD COURT
Stockbridge — 18.11.71

Built on the site of former Bedford Street and Bedford Crescent, probably named as a compliment to the 8th Duke of Bedford 1809–1872.

BEDFORD TERRACE
Portobello — —

The 2nd Marquis who became the first Duke of Abercorn married in 1832 Lady Louisa Jane Russell, second daughter of the sixth Duke of Bedford and this is probably the source of the name.

BEECHMOUNT CRESCENT — 2. 9.71

Although off Saughton Crescent, the developers, Crescent Housing Society did not want name "Saughton" used. Beechmount House stands opposite development on north side of Corstorphine Road.

BELFORD AVENUE	22. 9.32	There must at one time have been a ford giving access to Bell's Mills (Bell Ford). A proposal that these streets be named Blinkbonny Avenue and Road was not approved.
GARDENS	—	

See also Belford – Part I

BELGRAVE CRESCENT	—	No doubt these fine Georgian houses were similar to those in the Georgian Belgravia district of London where Buckingham Palace stands and Buckingham Terrace is adjacent to Belgrave Crescent.
CRESCENT LANE	—	
MEWS	—	
PLACE	—	

Dean

BELGRAVE ROAD	26.11.26	Belgrave Park Nursery was situated to the south of Cairnmuir Road and west of Kaimes Road.
GARDENS	26.11.26	

Corstorphine

BELHAVEN TERRACE — —

Built in 1880. There does not seem to be any connection with the Lords Belhaven of Wishaw. Probably named from Belhaven, a coast village in the parish of Dunbar but no evidence exists to associate the name with this district of Edinburgh.

BELLENDEN GARDENS	25. 5.50	Corporation Inch Housing Scheme— see Ashton Grove.
BELLEVUE GARDENS	23. 3.33	Development by J. Miller, Architect. Name from the
GROVE	15. 3.34	house and grounds of General Scott at Balcornie, Crail. Bellevue House was built on the site of Drummond Lodge, purchased by Provost Drummond 1757. It became later customs and excise office and was demolished in 1846 when the Scotland Street railway tunnel was made.

See also Bellevue — Part I

BELLFIELD LANE	—	Bellfield Street formerly Melville Street, renamed with
STREET	12.10.67	effect from 1.4.68 because of duplication with Melville
TERRACE	—	Street, Edinburgh. Named from the adjacent Bellfield House.
BELMONT AVENUE	11.12.30	Named from Belmont House.
CRESCENT	**3. 6.26**	From Wood's history of Corstorphine Parish (1792) —
GARDENS	6. 2.30	"a pleasant villa belonging to David Smeaton. It was
PARK	6. 2.30	built and grounds laid out by David Campbell, a writer
TERRACE	3. 6.26	who sold it to Captain Pelham Maitland who then disposed
VIEW	6. 2.30	of it to Mr. Smeaton."
Corstorphine		
BELMONT ROAD	—	Name taken from Belmont Dairy Farm formerly about
Juniper Green		midway down Juniper Avenue (formerly Belmont Avenue) on west side.
BELVEDERE PARK	4. 8.71	Present development is on site of original old house, Belvedere House.
BERNARD TERRACE	—	Derivation can not be traced. Constructed as a cul-de-sac in 1868. Formerly it was open ground between Lutton Place and Montague Street. Made a continuous street to St. Leonards in 1929. Possibly from a local proprietor.
BEAUFORT ROAD	—	Built in 1868. Probably named from the 8th Duke of Beaufort 1824—1899. Of the 26 Dukedoms in the United Kingdom the names of 19 have been used in naming streets in the city and at the time of naming Beaufort Road the peerage was held in high esteem.
BIGGAR ROAD	—	Evident. The road to Biggar.
BINGHAM AVENUE	11. 7.46	Original name Bingham Road named because ground
BROADWAY	11. 7.46	belonged to Duke of Abercorn whose wife, the Duchess,
CIRCLE	11. 7.46	prior to her marriage, was Lady Rosaline Bingham, daughter
CRESCENT	11. 7.46	of the Earl of Lucan.
CROSSWAY	11. 7.46	
DRIVE	11. 7.46	
MEDWAY	27. 1.66	
PLACE	11. 7.46	
ROAD	26.11.36	
STREET	11. 7.46	
WAY	27. 1.66	
BIRCH COURT	27. 5.65	Development by Link Housing Society who selected names of shrubs and trees for streets all starting with "B" to facilitate easier filing of tenants records.
BLACKBARONY ROAD	22. 7.37	On the estate of Sir John Gilmour who married four times. His third wife was Margaret, eldest daughter of Sir Alexander Murray Bt. of Blackbarony, Peebles. Sir John Gilmour acquired the lands of Craigmillar in 1660.

BLACKFORD GLEN ROAD	—	Situated in the Glen between Blackford Hill and Braid Hills, at western end of which is "Blackford" where presumably a black ford existed through the Braid Burn.
BLACKFORD HILL RISE	9. 3.61	Development mainly by Albert Thain Limited. Name
GROVE	6. 9.62	evident, from Blackford Hill but see also Blackford Glen
VIEW	6. 9.62	Road.
BLACKTHORN COURT	27. 5.65	Development by Link Housing Society — See Birch Court.
BLAEBERRY GARDENS	27. 5.65	Development by Link Housing Society — See Birch Court.

BLANTYRE TERRACE — This street requires to be considered along with Mardale Crescent and Rochester Terrace. All three streets were constructed after the development of the rest of the Merchiston Estate on the former cricket field of Merchiston Academy (O.S. sheet 1895).

The theme would appear to be antiquity being adjacent to the old former Merchiston Castle built in 15th century. Blantyre, a district in Lanarkshire and noted as David Livingstone's birthplace (see also Mardale Crescent and Rochester Terrace). All three locations are small but extensive Roman remains can be found at each and this is the only connection that can be found to link these names. Blantyre Terrace was built in 1881.

BLINKBONNY AVENUE	3. 6.26	Names were taken from the Farm of Blinkbonny which
CRESCENT	1905	was situated slightly to the south of where the Esso Motor
GROVE	20. 4.28	Motel is, i.e. on the south side of Queensferry Road opposite
ROAD	20. 4.28	Craigleith Road. The streets were constructed on the former
GARDENS	20. 4.28	farmland.
GROVE W	30. 4.36	
TERRACE	3. 6.26	

BOGSMILL ROAD — Called Bog's, Bogg's and Boag's Mill variously — presumably the one time owner.

The first bank notes in Scotland were printed at Bog's Mill.

BONALY AVENUE	11. 6.59	All streets took their name from Bonaly Road which
CRESCENT	11. 6.59	existed as a country road leading to the house known as
DRIVE	11. 6.59	Bonaly Tower, and estate.
GARDENS	13. 4.61	Mr. Gillespie (see Gillespie Road) had once owned Bonaly.
GROVE	17. 4.69	The ground at Bonaly Hills had been leased by the
ROAD	—	Governors of Gillespie Hospital to the Town for water
TERRACE	11. 6.59	supply. Bonaly — gaelic Bonn-aill-the foot of the rocks or
BRAE, RISE, LOAN	3. 4.75	cliff.

BONNINGTON AVENUE 17. 7.30 From the mansion house of Bonnytown, evidently flattering. Mills there known as Bonnytoun Mills.

See also Bonnington — Part I

BORDEAUX PLACE — When Mary Queen of Scots stayed at Criagmillar Castle her French ladies in waiting stayed at the community of Burdiehouse (Bordeaux House).

BORTHWICK PLACE — Borthwick is a parish s.e. of Edinburgh 4¾ miles s.e. of Dalkeith but street is probably named from Borthwick Castle ancient home of the Lord Borthwicks. Compare adjacent streets, Kew, Hampton, Osborne, Carberry, Balbirnie, all distinguished residences.

BOSWALL AVENUE	24.11.21	Only Boswall Road existed prior to 1921. All other streets
LOAN	24.11.21	are in Corporation Housing development.
DRIVE	24.11.21	Boswall Road was constructed on property of Boswall of
QUADRANT	24.11.21	Blackadder one member of the family being Captain
TERRACE	24.11.21	Donaldson Boswall of Wardie.
CRESCENT	24.11.21	
GROVE	24.11.21	*See also Boswall — Part I*
PARKWAY	24.11.21	
GARDENS	24.11.21	
SQUARE	24.11.21	
GREEN	16.10.25	
PLACE	26. 3.31	
BOTHWELL LANE	—	Derivation unknown but could be named from the Earl
STREET	—	of Bothwell a powerful noble and influencial politician
		during the time of Mary Queen of Scots.
		Bothwell is a town in North Lanarkshire 8 miles south east
		of Glasgow containing the norman ruin of Bothwell Castle.
		It was the scene of a battle in 1679 in which the covenanters
		were defeated by the Royal troops under Monmouth.
BRAE PARK	—	These were old roads. Brae Park Road was formerly known
ROAD	—	as Old Cramond Bridge Road.
		There is quite a hill or brae on this road across the Almond.
BRAEFOOT TERRACE	—	At the foot of Liberton Brae.
BRAEHEAD AVENUE	6. 1.27	Name from Braehead House which stands at the head of
BANK	22. 9.60	Brae Park Road.
GROVE	27.10.55	
LOAN	22. 9.60	
PARK	21. 8.67	
ROAD	31. 1.46	
VIEW	22. 9.60	
BRAID MOUNT	18. 1.34	Braid Mount formerly known as Braid Hills Quadrant.
BRAID MOUNT CREST	24. 2.55	Braid Hills Approach formerly known as Braid Hills Access
RISE	24. 2.55	Road.
VIEW	24. 2.55	
BRAID FARM ROAD	—	Evident
BRAID HILLS APPROACH	—	Braid Estate is well known and gave its name to the Braid
AVENUE	23. 4.26	Hills. One of the best known of the early family owners was
CRESCENT	23. 4.26	Sir William Dick of Braid.
DRIVE	—	Braid is of gaelic origin meaning upper part or upland.
ROAD	—	*See also Braid — Part I*
BRAMBLE DRIVE	27. 5.65	Development by Link Housing Society — see Birch Court.
BRAMDEAN GROVE	25. 4.57	The woods in the Bramdean Rise area were named after
PLACE	25. 4.57	Bramdean Lodge, the family home of Mrs. Elaeson Gordon,
RISE	26.11.36	the owner of the estate of Braid, at Bramdean, a small
VIEW	25. 4.57	village near Winchester.
BRAND DRIVE	12.12.57	Alexander Brand, the last Provost of Portobello prior to
GARDENS	12.12.57	amalgamation with Edinburgh — 1896.
BRANDON STREET	—	Built about 1830. This street is named from the secondary
TERRACE	—	title of the Duke of Hamilton. The 10th Duke of
		Hamilton was also the 7th Duke of Brandon 1767—1852.

BREADALBANE STREET	—	Breadalbane is a district measuring 33 miles in length and 31 in breadth bounded on the north by Lochaber and Athole, on the south by Strathearn and Monteith and on the west by Lorn and Lochaber. It gives a title to the Marquis of Breadalbane. At the time these streets were built about 1878 the Earldom was held by Gavin Cambpell, 7th Earl and 1st Marquis of Breadalbane 1851—1922.
Leith		
BREADALBANE TERRACE	—	
Dalry		
BRIDGE ROAD	—	Obviously the bridge spanning Water of Leith at Colinton. Formerly part of Colinton Road.
BRIGHTON STREET	—	Derivation unknown. The street is mentioned in minutes of the town council 4/3/1834 and is first mentioned in the Edinburgh Street Directory in 1827.
BRITWELL CRESCENT	21. 1.32	Application for street order was made by S.R. Christie-Miller and was obviously named after the English estate of Thomas Wakefield Christiemiller of Craigentinny, at Britwell, Bucks.
BROOMBANK TERRACE	28.. 7.38	All names constructed from "Broomhouse" or Broom House, a mansion house and farm which was situated at the junction of Meadowplace Road and Broomhouse Road. This was in fact a house when broom grew.
BROOMBURN GROVE	28. 7.38	
BROOMFIELD CRESCENT	12.12.35	
BROOMHALL AVENUE	12.12.35	
BANK	31. 3.55	
CRESCENT	16. 9.48	
DRIVE	14. 6.56	
GARDENS	31. 3.55	
LOAN	31. 3.55	
PARK	31. 5.56	
PLACE	30.10.52	
ROAD	30.10.52	
TERRACE	31. 3.55	
BROOMHOUSE AVENUE	24. 4.47	
BANK	25.11.65	
COTTAGES	8. 9.66	
COURT	30.11.50	
CRESCENT	24. 4.47	
DRIVE	24. 4.47	
GARDENS	24. 4.47	
GROVE	24. 4.47	
LOAN	24. 4.47	
MEDWAY	30.11.50	
PARK	24. 4.47	
PATH	24. 4.47	
PLACE	27.11.47	
ROAD	—	
ROW	30.11.50	
SQUARE	24. 4.47	
STREET	27.11.47	
TERRACE	30.11.50	
WALK	24. 4.47	
WAY	30.11.50	
WYND	14.12.50	
BRUCE STREET	—	In 1885 when the property was built the former owner of the ground was James Bruce per Kerr Couper and Cook 37 George Street. He owned stables and houses there.

BRUNSTANE BANK	19. 9.35	Named from the old mansion of Brunstane or Gilbertoun.
CRESCENT	19. 9.35	The Barony of Brunstane is of a very ancient date.
DRIVE	11. 4.35	The name "Brunstane" could be associated with the
ROAD N	26. 1.67	local coal seams.
GARDENS	4. 4.74	
MEWS	4. 4.74	Brunstane Road N. formerly Hamilton Street renamed with effect from 1st August 1967 because of duplication.

see also Brunstane — Part I

BRUNTON GARDENS	—	Although many tenements exist in these streets today
PLACE	—	the first name was Brunton Place which started with
TERRACE	—	a small tenement block fronting London Road in 1832.

No derivation has been found but might possibly be named from William Brunton (1777—1851). Born at Dalkeith, engineer and inventor and quite famous in his day. He designed and executed a great many important works. He was member of the Institute of Civil Engineers, and knew Thomas Telford and others. He had a large share in steam navigation, mining machinery and ventilation. He was the last of the celebrated engineers of the time.

BRYCE AVENUE	16. 1.06	Andrew Bryce was farm manager of the Craigentinny Estate.
GROVE	2. 5.29	Later when more and more ground was developed he became factor for the Christiemiller family. He was succeeded by his daughter as factor.

BUCHANAN STREET	—	Built about 1878 and named possibly from James Buchanan town councillor at the time. He sat on the Works and Housing committee, Cleansing committee, and Streets and Buildings committee.

BUCKINGHAM TERRACE	—	Possibly from Buckingham Palace in the Belgravia district of London and Buckingham Terrace is adjacent to Belgrave Crescent. (see also Belgrave Crescent).

BUCKSTANE PARK	11. 9.30	Named from the Buck Stone (or Stane) — a standing
BUCKSTONE AVENUE	31. 5.34	stone where Royal hunting parties traditionally unleashed
BANK	16. 9.65	hounds when hunting deer. This stone can still be seen
CRESCENT	16. 9.65	at the side of Morningside Road.
DELL	24. 1.63	
DRIVE	27.11.30	
GARDENS	31. 5.34	
GREEN	1. 3.73	
GROVE	8. 7.73	
HILL	16. 9.65	
LOAN	4. 8.71	
PLACE	4. 8.71	
ROAD	31. 5.34	
ROW	16. 9.65	
TERRACE	9. 9.27	
VIEW	28.11.35	
WAY	16. 9.65	
WOOD	16. 9.65	
WYND	1. 3.73	
COURT	6. 6.74	
RISE	6. 6.74	

BURDIEHOUSE AVENUE	17. 3.38	Burdiehouse Road formerly Penicuik Road was renamed
CRESCENT	27. 2.47	on 2.10.27 when Howden Hall Road, Nether Liberton and
CROSSWAY	27. 2.47	Straiton Road were also named to give association with
DRIVE	27. 2.47	the district name. From the Village of Burdiehouse which
LOAN	27. 2.47	in turn took its name as a corruption of Bordeaux House

Continued

BURDIEHOUSE MEDWAY	27. 2.47	— see Bordeaux Place.
PLACE	27. 2.47	
ROAD	21.10.27	
SQUARE	27. 1.38	
STREET	19.11.64	
TERRACE	—	

BURLINGTON STREET — Built 1878 and owned at that time by William Stewart, Sawmiller, Bonnington. No doubt named from the Duke of Devonshire the secondary title of which was the Earl of Burlington. The Duke at the time of the naming of this street was Spencer Compton, the 8th Duke of Devonshire who at the time was Secretary of State for India 1880–1882, Secretary of State for War 1882–1885. He also held many other posts in the Government of the time.

BURNBRAE	11.10.73	Names from the Bughtlin Burn which flows through the
BURNSIDE	11.10.73	area.

BURNHEAD CRESCENT	15. 3.56	The small community of Burnhead was located at the
GROVE	15. 3.56	head of the Stenhouse Burn situated just south of the
LOAN	15. 3.56	junction of Ellens Glen Road and Lasswade Road.
PATH E	17. 9.59	
PATH W	17. 9.59	

BURNS PLACE — Derivation unknown. Could be local proprietor.

CADDELL'S ROW — Around 1730 Cramond was a busy community at the height of its prosperity. There were extensive (for that time) iron works here. A Mr. Caddell and Edington owned the ironworks. These cottages were no doubt built for their workers.

CADOGAN ROAD 10.12.26 Sir John Little Gilmour 2nd Baron of Liberton and Craigmillar estate married on 22 July 1922 the Hon. Victoria Laura Cadogan O.B.E. youngest daughter of the late Viscount Chelsea.

CADZOW PLACE — Built 1898 on the grounds of the former Abbeyhill House the last owner of which was the Hon. Fletcher Norton. He occupied the house in 1776 and died there in 1820. He was greatly interested in music and became a patron of Alexander Campbell the author of "Albyn's Anthology" which contained a donation from Sir Walter Scott.

Cadzow is a village and a ruined castle in Lanarkshire near Hamilton and was the scene of Sir. Walter Scott's famous ballad of Cadzow castle. It is no doubt from this source that the street is named.

Comparison requires to be made however with nearby streets Dalziel, Cambusnethan, and Wishaw, built by Sir. James Steel former Lord Provost of Edinburgh who came from Lanarkshire. It could be that he also built Cadzow Place and named it from the place in Lanarkshire.

CAERLAVEROCK COURT	14. 2.74	From the castle of that name on the Solway Firth. See "Affleck Court".
CAIRNMUIR ROAD	5. 7.23	This road's position gives a very fine view of the Pentland Hills. Cairnmuir is a part of the Pentland Hills which is situated between Midcalder and Penicuik.

CAIYSTANE AVENUE 22. 3.34 — Named from the Caiy Stane known as General Kay's
    CRESCENT 22. 3.34 — Monument and also called Kel, Kay, or Camus Stone.
    DRIVE 25.10.56 — This marked the site of an ancient battle and can be
    GARDENS 25.10.56 — seen on east side of Caiystane Drive.
    HILL 25.10.56 — Battle stone means Kel Stone from which derived Kay
    PLACE E 22. 3.34 — Stane, the corruption of which is Caiystane.
    ROAD E and W 22. 3.34
    TERRACE 25.10.56
    VIEW 25.10.56

CALDER COURT 8. 6.67 — Corporation development so named because it is adjacent
    CRESCENT 8. 6.67 — to Calder Road.
    DRIVE 8. 6.67
    GARDENS 8. 6.67
    GROVE 8. 6.67
    PARK 8. 6.67
    PLACE 8. 6.67
    VIEW 8. 6.67

CALDER ROAD	—	Evident. The road to East, West and Midcalder.
CAMBRIDGE AVENUE	—	Built in 1883. One of Queen Victoria's chief officers
GARDENS	—	of state was Field Marshall H.R.H. the Duke of Cambridge, Prince George Frederick William Charles, cousin to the Queen.
CAMBUSNETHAN STREET	—	Said to have been built by Lord Provost Sir James Steel, builder, who had a connection with Cambusnethan, Lanarkshire. He was Lord Provost 1900–1903. Compare Dalziel, Wishaw, also in Lanarkshire and streets which he probably also built.
CAMERON HOUSE AVENUE	19. 2.31	This street was laid on the original driveway to Cameron House. Corporation development. Sir Robert Murray of Camrone obtained land known as Common Myre from James Murray of Priestfield, his nephew. The house was built in 1770 and two wings added in 1930. It was formerly owned by the University and is now divided into flats.

See also Cameron — Part I

CAMERON TOLL GARDENS	2. 3.67	Development by James Miller & Partners. A Toll existed at the junction of Old Dalkeith Road and Peffermill Road on land belonging to Sir Robert Murray of Camrone.

CAMMO BRAE 28. 3.57 — Known also as Cambok and Cambo in 1296. The house was
    CRESCENT — built in 1693 by John Menzies, occupied also by Charles
    GARDENS 22.10.31 — Watson who changed name.
    GROVE — North section of Cammo Road was formerly called
    HILL 28. 3.57 — Saughton Entry North, renamed 19.4.56. The whole of
    PARKWAY 28. 3.57 — Cammo Walk was formerly called Saughton Entry South,
    PLACE 28. 3.57 — renamed 19.4.56.
    ROAD — Cammo House was formerly known as New Saughton
    WALK 19. 4.56 — and the above roads were the original driveways.

CAMPBELL PARK CRESCENT	27. 2.58	Named from Campbell Public Park adjacent. The land was given by Mr. Campbell of Woodhall who also owned and farmed Woodhall farm.
DRIVE	27. 2.58	

CAMUS AVENUE	15. 4.37	From the Camus Stone, a battle memorial. See "Caiystane".
PARK	21.11.68	
PLACE E & W	15. 4.37	
ROAD E & W	15. 4.37	

CANNON WYND	18. 4.63	Corporation development on site of Leith Fort which accounts for name "Cannon". Leith Fort was speedily constructed as a defence against American Admiral John Paul Jones.

CAPELAW ROAD	30.11.23	Name suggested by The Merchant Company who owned the ground. Cape Law is a hill in the Pentland range.

CAPTAIN'S DRIVE	15. 3.56	Captain's Road was formerly part of Kaimes Road. Originally called Captain's Ride, it was the habitual route taken by a French Prisoner during the Napoleonic Wars.
LOAN	15. 3.56	
ROAD	—	

CARBERRY PLACE	—	A mansion at Inveresk near Musselburgh. Carberry Towers, the seat of the Earls of Elphinstone. Compare Kew, Hampton, Osborne, Balbirnie, adjacent streets and all noted residences.

CARFRAE GARDENS	23. 4.31	These streets were constructed by the Civil Engineering firm of Carfrae and Morrison and streets were named after the original partner, George Somervel Carfrae.
GROVE	29. 7.26	
PARK	29. 7.26	
ROAD	29. 7.26	

CARGIL COURT	14. 3.63	Named from Cargil Terrace which in turn derives its name from the property Cargilfield. Cargilfield School, now at Barnton, used to be here.

See also Cargil — Part I

CARNEGIE COURT	8. 7.65	Constructed on site of original Carnegie Street which was named after Thomas Carnegie, owner of the ground and who also owned a house there.

CARNETHY AVENUE	30.11.23	Name suggested by The Merchant Company who owned the ground, Carnethy Hill, in the Pentland range.

CAROLINE PARK GROVE	9.12.71	Off Caroline Park also known as Caroline Park Avenue named from Caroline Park House. The history of the Parish of Cramond states: John Riddell of Grantoun sold estate to John, Duke of Argyle and Greenwick. By this purchase Grantoun became united to Roystoun and they are now included under the general name of Caroline Park. 'Caroline', consort of George II.

CAROLINE TERRACE	5. 5.27	Caroline Forrester was the daughter of the 5th Lord Forrester and became Baroness Forrester of Corstorphine in 1763.

CARRICK KNOWE AVENUE	11.10.28	The only clue to the derivation of this name is in the history of Balerino House, Leith, home for some time of the Earls of Carrick. Built in 1631 by John Stewart, Earl of Carrick. The area near Corstorphine could have been owned by this family as hunting grounds. The "Kingdom" of Carrick is in South Ayrshire and is of ancient origin.
DRIVE	25. 4.35	
GARDENS	25. 4.35	
GROVE	25. 4.35	
HILL	25. 4.35	
LOAN	25. 4.35	
PARKWAY	25. 4.35	Carrick Knowe farm was situated where the golf club house is now. The fields are now Carrick Knowe golf course.
PLACE	25. 4.35	

Continued

CARRICK KNOWE ROAD	25. 4.35	
TERRACE	25. 4.35	

CARRINGTON CRESCENT   13. 7.67

Formerly Moredum Crescent renamed with effect from 1.2.68 because of confusion with "Moredun" district of the city.
Name from Carrington Road which was named after Lord Carrington, Governor of New Zealand 1885—1890 and who was connected with Fettes College.

See also Carrington — Part I

CASSELBANK STREET   14. 4.66

Formerly Hope Street renamed with effect from 1.11.66 because of duplication.
Name Casselbank was a variation from other streets prefixed "Cassel". Andrew Cassel, a former owner of the property here. A member of Trinity House.

See also Cassel — Part I

CASTLE AVENUE   —
Corstorphine

From the ancient Corstorphine Castle the site of which is situated centrally in the rectangle formed by this street, Dovecot Road, Saughton Road, and Broomhouse Road. This was the home of the Forresters of Corstorphine. 14th century, ruins could still be seen in 1870.

CASTLE ROAD EAST	—
WEST	—
Merchiston

Named from Merchiston Castle, built in the 15th century now incorporated within the buildings of Napier College. This was the home of John Napier of Merchiston who invented lorarithims. Also Alexander Napier, former Lord Provost.

CASTLELAW ROAD   29. 5.25

Name suggested by The Merchant Co. who owned the ground. Castle Law, a hill in the Pentland range.

CATHCART PLACE   —

Notes on the lands and Manor House of Dalry (Smith);— Allan Whitefoord in 1716 was the 5th son of Sir Adam Whitefoord,Blairquhan,by Hon. Margaret Cathcart only daughter of Allan 7th Baron Cathcart. He became a Merchant and was admitted a Burgess and Guild brother by the Town Council in 1723. He lived in the vicinity of Fountainbridge on the lands of Dalry. The street was built in 1880.

CATHEDRAL LANE   15.10.67

Formerly Chapel Lane, renamed with effect from 1.4.68 because of duplication with Chapel Lane, Leith. Street is adjacent to St. Mary's R.C. Cathedral.

CATHERINE PLACE, WEST   —

Derivation unknown.

CATTLE ROAD   28. 2.35

Refers to adjacent slaughterhouses.

CHARTERHALL GROVE   10. 3.60

Development by James Miller and Partners named from Charterhall Road, on property of the Trotter family of Mortonhall, owners also of Charterhall, Berwickshire.

see also Charterhall — Part I

CHESSER CRESCENT	2. 3.21
GARDENS	2. 3.21
GROVE	2. 3.21
LOAN	2. 3.21

Motion at committee meeting on 18.2.21 that name 'Delhaig', the estate name, be used but this was not approved. Named from existing Chesser Avenue which derived its name from former Lord Provost John William Chesser (1919—1921).

See also Chesser — Part I

CHESTER STREET	—	Possibly commemorating the visit of George IV to the city in 1822. One of his titles was Earl of Chester.
CHRISTIAN CRESCENT GROVE	12.12.57 12.12.57	A Major Christian was twice provost of Portobello in the 1880's. Adjacent streets, Brand, also named after former provost.
CHRISTIEMILLER AVENUE	17. 9.31	Named from the Christiemiller family of Craigentinny owners of the estate.
CLACKMAE ROAD GROVE	22. 8.56 22. 8.56	Name suggested by James Miller & Partners, the developers. On the estate of Sir John Gilmour who also owns Carolside Estate, near Melrose. Clackmae Farm is situated on this estate.
CLAREMONT BANK GROVE	12. 3.35 12. 3.35	Application made for naming by J. Miller, Architect. Names from adjacent streets built on grounds of Claremont Park, feued by Heriot Trust. *See also Claremont — Part I*
CLARINDA TERRACE	23. 1.75	On a suggestion of the Chairman of the Highways and Road Safety committee that streets in a new development be named from the works of Robert Burns, the Kirkbrae development was chosen as suitable. Clarinda was the Lady friend of Robert Burns in Edinburgh.
CLAVERHOUSE DRIVE	13. 7.67	Formerly Northfield renamed with effect from 1.2.68 because of duplication with the Northfield district of the city. All names of adjacent streets taken from Sir Walter Scott's novels and this name was also taken from that source.
CLEARBURN CRESCENT GARDENS ROAD	30. 9.27 30. 9.27 30. 9.27	The community of Clearburn was situated in the area within the 3 streets Priestfield Avenue, Gardens and Road. In 1880 this was a thriving village celebrated for its breweries. Named from a burn that flowed through here to Duddingston Loch.
CLERMISTON AVENUE CRESCENT DRIVE GARDENS GREEN GROVE HILL TERRACE LOAN MEDWAY PARK PLACE ROAD ROAD N VIEW	11. 2.37 26. 2.53 26. 2.53 26. 2.53 26. 2.53 26. 2.53 26. 2.53 26. 2.53 26. 2.53 26. 2.53 26. 2.53 26. 2.53 — — 26. 2.53	All streets were named from Clermiston Road, a narrow country road before widening and the development of surrounding area. In 1250 the area was known as Clerbandistun. A medieval owner was called Clerebald.
CLERWOOD BANK GARDENS GROVE LOAN PARK PLACE ROW TERRACE	10.10.63 10.10.63 10.10.63 10.10.63 10.10.63 10.10.63 10.10.63 10.10.63	Streets were to be called Clermiston House Bank, etc. but developers, Messrs. George Wimpey, preferred Clerwood as a name. Clerwood House, now a home, stands opposite on the west side of Corstorphine Hill. Name obviously derived from 'Clermiston' and the wooded area in the vicinity of the house.

Continued

CLERWOOD VIEW	10.10.63	
WAY	10.10.63	

CLOVENSTONE DRIVE	4. 9.70	In a former field called Clovenstone Park there stood a
GARDENS	4. 9.70	large upright stone known as the Clovenstone, probably
PARK	4. 9.70	marking the site of a prehistoric grave. The field was
ROAD	4. 9.70	probably where Kingsknowe Golf course is now.

COCHRANE PLACE — First shown in valuation roll in 1878. A Mr. Cochrane
Leith Links owned the house called "The Hermitage", Leith Links ·
(P.O. Directory 1850). The street was constructed on
ground owned by him.

COCHRANE TERRACE — From Cochrane Place now part of East London Street.
London Street Cochrane Place was built about 1873 partly by the
Southern Building Association. The valuation roll of the
time shows several houses owned by Mr. Archibald
Cochrane. He may have had a connection with the
Southern Building Association.

COLLIESDENE AVENUE	25. 6.31	Named from Coillesdene House, but not the block of flats
CRESCENT	22. 2.34	which stand there today. The former Coillesdene House
DRIVE	25. 1.34	stood on this site, which was formerly Joppa Pit — hence
GARDENS	29.11.34	Coilles (coals) Dene (Dean).
GROVE	15.12.55	
LOAN	26. 1.67	
TERRACE	29.11.34	

COLINTON GROVE 22. 9.32 Development by James Miller and Partners named from
Colinton Road which of course leads to Colinton Village.
Ancient name of Colinton was Hailes as in the kirk session
records. Also known as Collingtoun but little information
exists about the source of the name Colinton.

See also Colinton — Part I

COLINTON MAINS CRESCENT	15. 4.37	Colinton Mains Farm was situated at the junction of
DRIVE	15. 4.37	Oxgangs Road North and Firrhill Loan just north of
GARDENS	26. 8.54	Firrhill Loan.
GREEN	15. 4.37	
GROVE	15. 4.37	
LOAN	15. 4.37	
PLACE	15. 4.37	
ROAD	15. 4.37	
TERRACE	15. 4.37	

COLTBRIDGE VALE 14. 3.63 For full derivation of Coltbridge see Coltbridge Avenue
etc — Part 1.

COLUMBA AVENUE	26.11.36	St. Columba Church, adjacent, was in existence prior to
ROAD	29. 7.26	the construction of Columba Road and obviously the
		names are derived from the Church.

COMISTON GROVE	13.11.58	Named from the district and existing streets.
RISE	6.12.23	Comiston is a corruption of Camus Stone; See Camus
VIEW	15.10.34	Avenue and Caiystane.

See also Comiston — Part I

COMISTON SPRINGS AVENUE 29.11.34 These springs were the only source of water for the
Edinburgh citizens prior to the formation of a Water
Co., to introduce water from Crawley. Some of these
springs are still preserved in their ornamental stone
enclosures in the gardens of houses in the area.

CONSIDINE GARDENS	15. 2.34	These names were suggested in a letter to the Corporation from the legal firm of W. & H. Considine, W.S., after whom the streets are named.
TERRACE	15. 2.34	

CORBIEHILL AVENUE	5. 1.28	Said to be a farm name but no farm of this name can be traced on old maps of this area. Names of other streets derived from the original Corbiehill Road. Corbie Hill — Crow Hill.
CRESCENT	3. 9.36	
GARDENS	5. 1.28	
GROVE	5. 1.28	
PARK	12. 3.70	A house called Corby Hall is shown located where the school is on ord. survey map of 1895. See also "House o'Hill".
PLACE	3. 9.36	
ROAD	—	
TERRACE	3. 9.36	

CORSTORPHINE BANK AVENUE	19.12.24	Corstorphinebank Farm was situated just south of Craigmount View where the Rainbow restaurant is today.
DRIVE	19.12 24	
TERRACE	19.12.24	

CORSTORPHINE HIGH STREET	14. 9.67	Formerly High Street renamed with effect from 1.3.68 because of duplication with other High Streets. Derivation of Corstorphine is Cross of Torphine not the Carse of Whitehill. Cors-Carse (there was marshy ground here) Torr — hill, Finn — white.

CORSTORPHINE HILL AVENUE	30. 3.33	All streets developed by J. Miller, Architect, Corstorphinehill Farm was situated at the junction of Old Kirk Road and Corstorphine Hill Road. Corstorphinehill House is now within the zoo grounds.
CRESCENT	22.12.32	
GARDENS	23. 7.31	
ROAD	23. 7.31	

CORSTORPHINE HOUSE AVENUE	18. 6.31	Named from Corstorphine House, now Nos. 13 and 14 Corstorphine House Avenue which street is laid out on former grounds.
TERRACE	17.11.66	Corstorphine House Terrace formerly Whitehouse Terrace renamed with effect from 15.5.67 because of duplication.

CORSTORPHINE PARK GARDENS	26.11.26	This street was constructed on the former Parkland of Corstorphine House.

CRAIGCROOK AVENUE	29. 7.26	Extract from the history of the Parish of Cramond — "To the S.W. of Drylaw in the hollow at the foot of Corstorphine Hill where it makes a turn or crook to the east whence name is derived, stands Craigcrook Castle".
GARDENS	—	
GROVE	29. 7.26	
PARK	29. 7.26	Owners include Adamson family (1500–1650), John Mein, John Hall, Walter Pringle, John Strachen and Lord Jeffrey.
PLACE	—	
ROAD	—	
SQUARE	29. 7.26	These streets were laid out on the former estate.
TERRACE	—	

CRAIGENTINNY AVENUE	17. 9.31	Named from Craigentinny House near the junction of Loaning Road and Restalrig Road South and estate, owned formerly by the Christiemillar family.
AVENUE N	9.11.33	
CRESCENT	18. 2.32	
GROVE	18. 2.32	Craigentinny from the gaelic Rock of (the) fire.
PLACE	23. 9.54	
ROAD	17. 9.31	

CRAIGHILL GARDENS	21.12.23	This name was approved after decision that no action be taken on a query that confusion would result with Craighall Gardens, Trinity. Name is derived from the adjacent Craiglockhart area, and in particular Craiglockhart Hill.

CRAIGIEVAR WYND	14. 2.74	Named from the castle of this name in central Aberdeenshire — see Affleck Court.

CRAIGLEITH AVENUE NORTH	25. 2.37	Streets named after Craigleith Quarry, the stone of which
AVENUE SOUTH	25. 2.37	was used in the building of the New Town. The stone was
BANK	17. 9.31	carted from the quarry to the New Town sites on an old
CRESCENT	3. 6.26	road which became known as Craigleith Road.
DRIVE	20. 4.28	
GARDENS	15. 9.27	*See also Craigleith — Part I*
GROVE	2. 2.28	
HILL	16. 4.64	
VIEW	3. 6.26	

CRAIGLEITH HILL AVENUE	11. 9.30	These streets constructed on the hill adjacent to Craigleith
CRESCENT	17.12.31	Quarry, the hill in fact from which the stone was quarried.
GARDENS	11. 9.30	Development by James Miller & Partners.
GREEN	24.11.32	
GROVE	18. 2.32	
LOAN	11. 9.30	
ROW	24.11.32	

CRAIGLOCKHART AVENUE	—	These names continued from the original and first
BANK	28.12.33	"Craiglockhart" street — Craiglockhart Terrace named
CRESCENT	20. 5.27	1897. Name derives from Craiglockhart Hill. An opinion
DRIVE	15. 2.23	exists that it refers to the ancient Corstorphine Loch —
GARDENS	14.12.23	Craig-loch-art.
GROVE	25. 6.31	
LOAN	14.12.23	*See also Craiglockhart — Part I*
PARK	14.12.23	
PLACE	6.10.32	
QUADRANT	24. 1.30	
ROAD	14.12.23	
ROAD N	17. 3.32	
VIEW	23. 6.32	

CRAIGLOCKHART DELL ROAD	17. 7.47	The part of Colinton Dell adjacent to this street is known as Craiglockhart Dell.

CRAIGMILLAR CASTLE AVENUE		Evident, from the ancient Craigmillar Castle. Name from
	14. 4.38	the gaelic Craig-mail-ard signifying a rock bare and high
GARDENS	14. 4.38	running out on to a plain. The Castle was built prior to
GROVE	14. 4.38	1427 and was the home of the Gilmour family, later the
LOAN	14. 4.38	Prestons.
ROAD	—	
TERRACE	14. 4.38	

CRAIGMOUNT APPROACH	10. 3.66	The name is derived from Craigs Road. Craigmount
AVENUE	21. 9.33	Avenue was the first to be named and this mounts from
AVENUE N.	26. 8.64	Craigs Road.
BANK	29. 5.69	
BANK W.	29. 5.69	
COURT	10. 6.71	
CRESCENT	30. 3.39	
DRIVE	—	
GARDENS	29. 9.33	
GROVE	21. 9.33	
GROVE N.	30. 3.39	
HILL	26. 8.64	
LOAN	24. 4.53	
PARK	21. 9.33	
PLACE	23. 4.53	
TERRACE	22.10.36	
VIEW	30. 3.39	
WAY	11. 6.59	

CRAIGOUR AVENUE	27.11.47	Craigour Farm was situated on the south side of Old
CRESCENT	29. 1.48	Dalkeith Road centrally between Moredunvale Road and
DRIVE	27.11.47	Fernieside Drive.
GARDENS	24. 9.48	Reference here is to the same Craig (hill) on which
GREEN	26. 5.66	Craigmillar Castle stands.
GROVE	28. 4.48	
LOAN	29. 1.48	
PLACE	26. 5.66	
ROAD	27.11.47	
TERRACE	29. 1.48	
CRAIGS AVENUE	8.10.31	Street names derived from Craigs Road formerly called
BANK	21. 4.32	Old Stirling Road.
CRESCENT	8.10.31	Craigs Road leads to the farms and districts of West
GARDENS	17. 3.32	Craigs and East Craigs.
GROVE	8.10.31	
LOAN	8.10.31	
ROAD	—	
CRAMOND AVENUE	28.11.35	In roman times a fort stood at the mouth of the river
BANK	11. 6.64	Almond. The gaelic for fort is Caer and the River Almond
CRESCENT	1931	was in bygone days known as Amon. Thus Caeramon —
GARDENS	30. 1.36	the fort on the river, from which the name "Cramond"
GREEN	7. 7.66	evolved.
GROVE	27. 1.55	
PARK	—	
PLACE	22.10.53	
ROAD N	—	
ROAD S	—	
TERRACE	27. 1.55	
VALE	7. 9.72	
CRAMOND REGIS	30. 5.68	Development by Albert Thain Limited. The street was constructed on ground which was owned by the Kings of Scotland and was not feued to lesser nobles, thus "Regis".
		There was also an old house nearby called Cramond Regis now demolished.
CRAMOND GLEBE ROAD	13. 7.67	Cramond Glebe Gardens was named thus simply because
GLEBE GARDENS	15. 7.71	it was off Cramond Glebe Road.
CLEBE TERRACE	13. 7.67	Cramond Glebe Road formerly Glebe Road and Cramond Glebe Terrace formerly Glebe Terrace renamed with effect from 1.2.68 because of duplication with similar names in Corstorphine. Name refers to the Glebe or church land of Cramond Kirk.
CRARAE AVENUE	29. 5.30	Name suggested by Capt. George Ilay Campbell Younger of Succoth who also owned Crarae House on Loch Fyne, Argyle. He owned the Murrayfield estate in 1930.
CRAWFURD ROAD	—	The derivation has not been established but considering the closeness of Minto Street, named after Lord Minto, the following could be taken as a reasonable assumption.
		John Crawfurd (1783–1868) orientalist, born in Islay studied medicine in Edinburgh until 1803 when he went to India and served in the Army for 5 years. Lord Minto who was then Goveneror of Bengal undertook an expedition which ended in the conquest of Java in 1811

Continued

He was glad to avail himself of Crawfurd's services who had acquiried a great knowledge of the ways and language of the people. He filled some of the most principal civil and political posts of the island.

Crawfurd Road was built in 1875.

CULTINS ROAD	—	This is an old country road which used to be outside city boundary — derivation unknown.
CUMBERLAND STREET	—	Like so many streets in the new town named from George III, the 1st Duke of Cumberland was the 5th son of George III, his other titles being the Duke of Brunswick and the King of Hanover.

CREWE BANK   22. 2.34

CRESCENT	22. 2.34
GROVE	22. 2.34
LOAN	22. 2.34
PATH	24.10.35
PLACE	22. 2.34
ROAD N	1.10.26
ROAD S	1.10.26
ROAD W	24. 2.38
TERRACE	22. 2.34
ROAD GARDENS	24. 2.38

Named from Crewe Toll.
The name Crewe Toll is well know today as the junction of Ferry Road, Crewe Road, and Telford Road. In bygone days however there only existed a community of cottages and a toll house surrounded by open fields and countryside. The origin of the name "Crewe" is not known.

See also Crewe — Part I

CUMLODDEN AVENUE   9. 9.27   Cumlodden is situated in the parish of Inverarey on the N.W. side of Loch Fyne near Crarae House, home of the Campbells of Succoth owners of Murrayfield Estate on which this street was constructed.

CUMNOR CRESCENT   25. 5.50   Named from one of Sir Walter Scott's novels. See Ashton Grove.

DALZIEL PLACE   —   Compare adjacent streets Cambusnethan Street and Wishaw Terrace both in Lanarkshire. Dalziel is a parish in Lanarkshire bounded on the s.e. by Cambusnethan which is now incorporated in the burgh of Wishaw. Former Lord Provost James Steel had a connection with Cambusnethan. He was a builder and built the street Cambusnethan Street and no doubt built Dalziel Place too.

DANUBE STREET   —   This street is adjacent to Carlton Street named from a residence of George IV. Danube Street built at the same time (about 1825) possibly named from the European river because this street is near to a lesser river, the Water of Leith. The european connection of the Kings George II, III and IV may have had an influence.

DAVIDSON GARDENS   26. 6.25   Corporation development which it was proposed be named Muirhouse or Silverknowes Cottages. Decision taken to name Davidson Gardens, from Davidson's Mains. The Davidson family lived in the mansion of Muirhouse.

DAVIDSON PARK	25. 4.35	Application for street order was made by Bannochburn
ROAD	25. 4.35	and Sauchie Estates c/o Wm. C. Davidson of Sauchie Estates Office after whom streets were named. Mr. Davidson was factor for many years for Lady Steele-Maitland the owner.

DECHMONT ROAD — 27.10.36 — Street Order dated 25.1.34 made application for street to be named Alison Road from the Alisons who owned North Gyle Farm. When built the street was called Dechmont Road, most probably from the village of that name in West Lothian.

DELHAIG — — — At present a row of houses fronting to Gorgie Road but formerly a village and estate with Water of Leith to north and fields of Gorgie Farm to south.

DELL ROAD — — — One of the older streets in Colinton Village which leads to Colinton Dell.

DERBY STREET — — — Adjacent to Stanley Road and Stanley is the family name of the Earls of Derby. Shown in valuation roll as being in existence from 1883. The 15th Earl Derby was Edward Henry Stanley, died 1893, and he was secretary of state for colonies 1858 and 1882—85, secretary of state for India 1858—59, secretary of state for foreign affairs 1866—68 and 1874—1878, and was rector of Edinburgh University 1875—1880.

DINMONT DRIVE — 25. 5.50 — Corporation Inch Housing. Names taken from novels of Sir Walter Scott — See Ashton Grove.

DOCHART DRIVE — 28. 2.57 — Corporation South Clermiston housing. Names taken from novel "Kidnapped" by R.L. Stevenson — See Alan Breck Gardens.

DORSET PLACE — — — At the time of building all property was owned by James Mckelvie, coal merchant of 9 Clifton Terrace. He also owned much property in Surray Square, Devon Place, Pembroke Place, and Sutherland Street (West Coats) which are all names of counties and it would appear that he chose this theme for naming streets. It could therefore be assumed that Dorset Place was named from the county of that name.

DOUBLE HEDGES ROAD — — — This road is lined on both sides with hedges.

DOUGLAS CRESCENT — — — Ground feued from Heriots Hospital May 1875. No
GARDENS — — doubt named from the Earls of Douglas. Compare
GARDENS MEWS — — similar type named streets, Grosvenor, Eglinton, Lansdowne etc, all names of Dukes or Earls.

DOVECOT GROVE — 26. 4.34 — Name from the ruined Dovecot of the old castle of the
PARK — 7. 9.28 — Foulis family in the grounds of Merchiston Castle School
LOAN — 1. 2.62 — on the south bank of the Water of Leith.
Lanark Road

DOVECOT ROAD — — — This dovecot is still in a good state of repair and can be
Corstorphine seen in the garden of 2 Dovecot Road. It was the Dovecot or "Pigeon House" of the Forrester family of Corstorphine Castle.

DOWNIE GROVE — 15.12.60 — Off Downie Terrace existing at that time. A note exists
TERRACE — — in Part I written by other than Boog Watson as follows:—
Continued Mrs. Downie lived at 2 Downie Terrace and in the Edinburgh Street Directory of 1919—20, Downie, Nursery Man is

shown. The street Downie Grove was built on the original nursery.

DREGHORN AVENUE	24. 8.66	From Dreghorn castle and estate. The Castle was built
DRIVE	24. 8.66	by Alexander Trotter in about 1800. Name Dreghorn
GARDENS	20. 9.51	however is of Ancient Origin and is mentioned in a
GROVE	24. 8.66	charter of King Robert II of Scotland.
LOAN	—	
PARK	—	
PLACE	—	

DREGHORN MAINS ROAD	24. 8.66	The road leading to Dreghorn Mains or Farm.

DRUM AVENUE	21.12.67	These streets at Gilmerton were named after Drum House
COTTAGES	24. 4.25	the ancient residence of the Somerville family. The Drum
CRESCENT	21.12.67	or Brae, is obviously from Nether Liberton to Gilmerton.
PLACE	21.12.67	
STREET	24. 4.25	

DRUM PARK	—	From the old mansion house of Drum which stood where Drum Terrace is today. The "Drum" is the brae from the foot of Easter Road.

See also Drum Terrace — Part I

DRUM BRAE AVENUE	21. 1.60	All street names originate from the old original Drum
CRESCENT	9. 2.56	Road renamed Drum Brae Road and divided into North
DRIVE	26. 2.53	and South on 24.1.30. Drum is the hill or brae on the
GARDENS	13.11.58	west side of Corstorphine Hill.
GROVE	9. 2.56	
NEUK	15. 4.71	
PARK	21. 1.60	
PARK APPROACH	28. 6.73	
PLACE	22.10.59	
TERRACE	26. 2.53	
WALK	26. 8.64	
NORTH	—	
SOUTH	—	

DRYDEN GARDENS	16. 1.36	Named as adjacent to Dryden Street. John Balfour of
TERRACE	29.11.34	Pilrig suggested this name from the Rosselyn Crest
Pilrig		(Rosselyn Crescent adjacent) ("Dryden's groves of oaks").

DRYDEN PLACE	—	A note existed in Boog Watson original notes written by
Newington		other than Boog Watson "Newington proprietor", a question mark is also shown. Dryden is an estate near Roslin. It is a centre of rural economy for agriculture and allied research based on Bush estate. The estate originally had many fine trees and shrubs and the naming of this street may suggest that an attempt was made to duplicate the environment.

DRYLAW AVENUE	—	Names suggested by W.C. Davidson factor for Lady Steele
CRESCENT	22. 5.25	Maitland, owner of estate at the time.
GARDENS	22.10.26	Named from Drylaw House and estate which still exists
GREEN	19. 7.34	in the centre of the Easter and Wester Drylaw housing
GROVE	22.10.26	area.

DUART CRESCENT	28. 2.57	Corporation South Clermiston Housing. Names taken from novel "Kidnapped" by R.L. Stevenson — See Alan Breck Gardens.

DUDDINGSTON AVENUE	23. 2.33	Named from the village of Duddingston which derives
GARDENS N	23. 2.33	its name not from the gaelic "sunny side of a hill", but
GARDENS S	31. 5.54	from the family of Doden (Dodinston) settled there
GROVE E	19. 8.37	in 11th century.
GROVE W	19. 8.37	Duddingston View formerly Bingham Terrace and
LOAN	8. 9.66	Duddingston Rise formerly Bingham Gardens, renamed
PARK	—	at request of residents.
RISE	1. 7.74	
ROAD	—	
ROAD W	13. 3.58	
SQUARE E	23. 2.33	
SQUARE W	23. 2.33	
VIEW	1. 7.74	

See also Duddingston – Part I

DUDLEY AVENUE	—	Dudley Avenue South formerly called Allan Street renamed
AVENUE SOUTH	—	with effect from 4.5.66 because of duplication. The
BANK	—	derivation of this name has not been found. The book,

Leith andits Antiquities (Irons) states that the Lord High
Admiral of England, Admiral Dudley, bombarded Leith
in the 16th century but it is doubtful whether this would
be a reason for naming these streets thus.

DUFF STREET	—	Derivation unknown. Duff Street was formerly Maxwell
STREET LANE		Street and was renamed thus in 1890. No reason can be

found for the alteration in name.

DUKE PLACE	13. 7.67	Formerly Duncan Street renamed with effect from 1.2.68

because of duplication. Named from Duke Street. For
derivation see Part I.

DUMBRYDEN DRIVE	7. 9.67	First 3 streets named because adjacent to original
GARDENS	7. 9.67	Dumbryden Road, the road leading to Wester Hailes
GROVE	7. 9.67	smallholdings prior to development in 1966 and which
ROAD	17. 6.43	included Dumbryden Cottages, and Dumbryden House.

These were located just west of where the canal
terminates on east side of development.

DUNBAR STREET	—	Derivation unknown. The valuation roll of 1855 shows most

of the property owned by Mrs. Janet Spence 1 Thornybauk.

DUNCAN PLACE	—	See Duncan Street Edinburgh. The following extracts are
Leith		taken from Leith andits Antiquities (Irons) page 128 "In

1797 Spain and Holland united in naval strength against
Britain". Victory of Admiral Duncan over Dutch at
Camperdown. Elevated to peerage as Viscount Duncan of
Camperdown. Page 129 — Trinity House of Leith asked
Admiral Duncan to accept the freedom of the Incorporation
in order to "honour such a noted scottish seaman". Page
131,—He accepts, "I feel myself much flattered". Masters
of Trinity House commissioned a portrait of Duncan
to be painted by Raeburn.
There can be little doubt that this street is named from
this source.

DUNDRENNAN COTTAGES	25. 5.50	Corporation Inch Housing. Names taken from novels

of Sir Walter Scott — See Ashton Grove.

DUNOLLIE COURT	14. 2.74	Name from the castle of that name north of Oban

Argyleshire — See Affleck Court.

DUNSMUIR COURT	12. 7.51	Dunsmure mansion house stood on this site. Used by Auxilary Fire Service during the war and later became used as emergency housing. New street was constructed in grounds in 1951. Dunsmure House was demolished in 1959.
DURAR DRIVE	28. 2.57	Corporation South Clermiston housing. Names taken from novel "Kidnapped" by R.L. Stevenson — See Alan Breck Gardens.
DURHAM AVENUE	18. 6.31	All Streets were named from the original Durham Road. This road was laid out on the estate of the 1st Duke of Abercorn whose daughter married the Earl of Durham.
DRIVE	28. 4.32	
GARDENS N	28. 4.32	
GARDENS S	28. 4.32	
GROVE	28. 4.32	
PLACE E	23. 7.31	
PLACE LANE	23. 3.39	
PLACE W	28. 4.32	
ROAD	—	
ROAD S	28. 4.32	
SQUARE	28. 4.32	
TERRACE	18. 6.31	
DURWARD GROVE	26. 6.52	Corporation Inch Housing. Names taken from novels of Sir Walter Scott. See Ashton Grove.
DUNVEGAN COURT	12.12.74	Development by Bacal Construction Limited on ground and former site of house called "Dunvegan".
EARLSTON PLACE	—	Built by the Edinburgh Co-op Building Company who chose many fanciful names for their streets but also from names of Directors of the Company, or perhaps where they were associated with (see Glendevon for example).
		Earlston no doubt a fanciful name from the border town or it may have had a connection with one of the Directors.
EAST COURT	23. 8.67	A small development on east side of Ravelston House Park.
EASTER BELMONT ROAD	21. 3.35	Originally one of the driveways to Belmont House — see Belmont Avenue etc.
EASTER DRYLAW AVENUE	17. 7.52	East of Drylaw House there was located the farm of Easter Drylaw. The location was just south of the mid point of Easter Drylaw Place. See also "Drylaw".
BANK	17. 7.52	
DRIVE	30. 1.36	
GARDENS	17. 7.72	
GROVE	17. 7.72	
LOAN	17. 7.52	
PLACE	30. 1.36	
VIEW	30. 1.36	
WAY	1. 7.71	
EASTER PARK DRIVE	1. 3.73	Constructed in the grounds of the old house of Easter Park still in existence. The house is located to the east of Barnton Park, thus Easter Park.
EASTFIELD GARDENS	25. 6.31	From the district of Eastfield. Named thus because of its location east of Joppa.

See also Eastfield — Part I

EDMONSTONE ROAD	—	Named from Edmonstone House, the entrance to which is off Old Dalkeith Road opposite Ferniehill Drive. An old family, the Edmonstones lived there for centuries.
EILDON TERRACE	21.12.33	Named from Eildon Street adjacent. For derivation see Eildon Street - Part I
ELCHO TERRACE	—	First shown in Edinburgh street directory in 1915. Elcho is a semi-ruined castle in Perthshire 4 miles upstream from Perth. It is owned by the Earl of Wemyss and gives to him the title of Lord Elcho. The clue to the naming of this street appears to be from the family name, Bingham, of the Earls of Lucan. The 3rd Duke of Abercorn, on whose ground this street is constructed, married in 1894 Lady Bingham the only daughter of the 4th Earl of Lucan. The 9th Earl of Wemyss married in 1817 the second daughter of the Earl of Lucan Lady Louisa Bingham.
ELGIN STREET NORTH	12. 9.67	Formerly East William Street renamed with effect from 1.4.68 because of duplication. For derivation see Elgin Street — Part I.
ELLANGOWAN TERRACE	26. 6.52	Named from one of Sir Walter Scott's novels. In Inch housing scheme — See Ashton Grove.
ELLEN'S GLEN LOAN ROAD	4. 5.66	Ellen's Glen sometime known as Helen's Glen situated between the village of Stenhouse and Hyvot's Bank Farm. Ellen's Glen Road formerly Stenhouse Road renamed 4.5.66 because of duplication.
ELLIOT STREET *Easter Road*	—	The builders when built about 1878 were J. & W. Elliot.
ELLIOT GARDENS PARK PLACE ROAD *Colinton*	7. 2.74 26. 2.31 22. 1.30 28.10.26	Application was made in 1926 for a street order to name Elliot The application was made by Miss Margaret Nina Trotter who was owner at the time of Colinton House and estate. She died unmarried 27.4.38. Her sister was Mary Elliot Trotter who also died unmarried 10.5.29. The streets were obviously named by Miss Margaret Trotter in memory of her sister.
ELTRINGHAM GARDENS GROVE TERRACE	5. 5.27 30. 6.27 18. 1.34	In 1927 Councillor Mrs. Miller, whose husband Adam Miller was also a Councillor, made arrangements on behalf of a number of persons to free the ground for building houses. In appreciation of her work the owners asked for the street name "Eltringham" which was Mrs. Miller's maiden name.
ESSENDEAN PLACE TERRACE	28. 2.57 28. 2.57	Corporation South Clermiston Housing. Names taken from R.L. Stevenson's novel "Kidnapped", see Alan Breck Gardens.
ESSEX BRAE PARK ROAD	23. 6.55 10. 3.60 8. 9.32	The Corporation received a letter from John A.W. Grant, Architect in 1932, asking for approval of this name. A check was made with a firm of this name on 12.4.73. Original J.A.W. Grant deceased and the question of derivation could not be answered.
ETHEL TERRACE	—	A note exists in the Boog Watson Notes written other than by Boog Watson, "After the builders daughter, Ethel Clarke".
ETON TERRACE *Continued*	—	Built about 1850 this street was to have been called Cambridge Street. As there is an Oxford Street adjacent it is most probable that the intention was to perpetuate the respective universities.

Eton would be the famous school whose pupils more often than not attented these universities.

It should, however, be mentioned that the developer of this street was Col. Learmonth of Dean and of _Eaton_ Place, London. There might have been a phonetical error in the use of the name but this is not likely.

ETTRICK COURT	—	The name derives from the Napiers of Merchiston on which estate the streets are constructed. In 1699 the Mistress of Merchiston Castle married Sir William Scott of Thirlestane which is situated on the R. Ettrick. In 1872, following a distinguished service in the diplomatic corps the then Lord Napier was made a Baron and chose the title of Lord Ettrick.
GROVE	19. 1.33	

See also Ettrick Road — Part I

EVA PLACE	—	Built on the Mortonhall Estate owned by the Trotter family. The owner, Major General Sir Henry Trotter of Mortonhall married in 1866 the Hon. Eva Gifford, daughter of the 2nd Baron Gifford.

FAIR-A-FAR	16. 9.71	From the farm of that name which stood where the flats at No. 6 "Fair-A-Far" are today, and from Fair-A-Far Mill on River Almond formerly Niddery's Mill. Reason for this farm name is not known.
FAIR-A-FAR ROW	—	
FAIRFORD GARDENS	25. 5.50	Corporation Inch Housing. Names taken from Sir Walter Scott's novels — see Ashton Grove.
FAIRMILE AVENUE	22. 3.34	Name derived from the junction of Fairmilehead which is located at the "head" of a "fair mile" from Morningside Toll.
FALCON COURT	12.10.61	From Falconhall, built by Mr. Faulkener early in the 19th century. For full derivation see Falcon Avenue etc Part I.
FALKLAND GARDENS	7. 7.66	Development by James Miller & Partners. New houses are on the site of the former Falkland House, possibly named from a finer house, Falkland Palace, Fife
FARRER GROVE	27. 1.66	Information received from the 98 year old present owner (1974) of the Christiemiller Estate, Mr. W. Christiemiller, states that his wife's grandfather was Sir William Farrer and that his godfather was Gaspard Farrer, Merchant Banker in London and that these streets were named after them.
TERRACE	14. 1.37	
FEATHERHALL AVENUE	7. 4.27	Name from Featherhall Farm, very old, and which has long since disappeared. It was situated where these streets are laid out today.
CRESCENT N	7. 4.27	
CRESCENT S	19. 2.31	
GROVE	25. 6.36	
PLACE	2. 5.29	
ROAD	28. 7.27	
TERRACE	28. 7.27	
FERNIEHILL AVENUE	3. 3.66	Named from Ferniehill House and the road leading thereto. The house is now 73 and 75 Fernieside Road. The obvious conclusion is that Ferns grew in the vicinity.
DRIVE	13. 2.47	
GARDENS	3. 3.66	
GROVE	3. 3.66	

Continued

FERNIEHILL PLACE	3. 3.66	*Derivation on previous page*
ROAD	—	
SQUARE	3. 3.66	
STREET	3. 3.66	
TERRACE	3. 3.66	
WAY	3. 3.66	

Moredun

FERNIELAW AVENUE   1924

Colinton

Named from Fernielaw House and farm which is still located on the west side of the street. Fernielaw Avenue was the driveway to these properties. A field existed here called Jamielaw later called Fernielaw.

FERNIESIDE AVENUE	29. 1.48	Fernieside Lodge or House is situated adjacent to 125
CRESCENT	29. 1.48	Moredun Park Road. Probably took name from Fierhiehill
DRIVE	29. 1.48	being at the side of Ferniehill House and grounds.
GARDENS	29. 1.48	
GROVE	29. 1.48	

Moredun

FERRY ROAD AVENUE	28. 7.38	Named from Ferry Road or the road which one would
DRIVE	28. 7.38	take from Leith to the former ferry at South Queensferry.
GARDENS	28. 7.38	*See also Ferry Road — Part I*
GROVE	28. 7.38	
PLACE	28. 7.38	

FETTES RISE   12. 3.70

Named from the surrounding streets but in particular this new street was constructed on a driveway to the house called "Fettes Rise". From Fettes College — Endowment of Sir William Fettes.

See also Fettes — Part I

FIGGATE BANK	21.10.65	Formerly Tower Bank and Tower Street, renamed with
STREET	21.10.65	effect from 4.5.66 because of duplication with Tower Street, Leith. Before any buildings appeared at Portobello the area was known as the Figgate Whins. Portobello was formerly knows as the Village of Figgate. (Figgate — a Saxon word — a common pasture for cattle).

FILLYSIDE AVENUE	18. 5.33	Fillyside House stood off Seafield Road between the
ROAD	20. 7.33	Eastern General Hospital and the Cemetery. Fillyside
TERRACE	18. 5.33	Dairy Farm was located where the Cleansing yard is today.

See also Fillyside — Part I

FINDLAY AVENUE	4. 2.26	The houses in these streets were government sponsored
COTTAGES	4. 2.26	steel constructed, erected by the Second Scottish
GARDENS	4. 2.26	National Housing Co. (Housing Trust) Limited. The
GROVE	4. 2.26	Chairman in 1926 was Sir John R Findlay BT KBE LLD
MEDWAY	4. 2.26	DL (See also Fraser Avenue, etc).

FINLAGGAN COURT   14. 3.74

Named from the Castle of that name on Isle of Islay, Argyleshire — see Affleck Court.

FIRRHILL CRESCENT	26. 8.54	The Southern part of Wester Craiglockhart Hill was known
DRIVE	26. 8.54	as Firrhill where Firrhill House stands. The District name
LOAN	26. 8.54	grew from that source. There are Fir trees on the hill but confusion arises regarding spelling "Firr" unless this was a phonetical error that crept in at some time.

FISHMARKET SQUARE   12.10.67

Formerly St. Andrews Square renamed with effect from 1.4.68 because of duplication.
Newhaven being a fishing port, the derivation is obvious. The square is of course near the market.

FORD'S ROAD	13. 6.35	Part of this road was the driveway to Saughtonhall House. It is thought that there existed a Ford over the Water of Leith here but spelling "Ford's" makes it more likely that road is named after farmer of that name who farmed land at Saughtonhall House, formerly nearby.
FORRESTER PARK AVENUE DRIVE GARDENS GREEN GROVE LOAN	28. 1.65 28.. 1.65 28. 1.65 28. 1.65 28. 1.65 28. 1.65	These streets were to be named Forrester Avenue etc., but owing to likely confusion with existing Forrester Road the name Forrester Park Avenue etc., was introduced For derivation see "Forrester Road".
FORRESTER ROAD	—	Named from the ancient Forrester family of Corstorphine who inhabited Corstorphine Castle — long since disappeared.
FORTHVIEW ROAD TERRACE	12.11.66 2. 4.25	Forthview Road formerly Hillview Road renamed with effect from 15.5.67 because of duplication with similar name in Corstorphine. Open fields existed to the north in 1925 and an open view of the Firth of Forth could be obtained .
FOULIS CRESCENT	29.11.34	From the old Foulis family of Woodhall on whose estate the street is built.
FOWLER TERRACE	—	Built 1880. No information can be found about the derivation of this name. When built by the Scottish Lands and Building Co. in 1880 most was owned by William Rattray of Edinburgh Industrial Brigade General Property Investment Co. The "Fowl" of "Fowler" may be a corruption of "Foull". Through the lands of Dalry flowed the Lochrin Burn which was nothing but an open sewer; it was also known as the Foull burn. Somewhere above Grove Street it was spanned by a bridge called the Foull bridge (from whence Fountainbridge obtained its name).
FOX COVERT AVENUE GROVE	19. 8.59 19. 8.59	Named from an old Mansion house where no doubt foxes did take covert. Entrance was just north of Fox Covert Hotel and Nos. 35 and 37 Rannoch Place occupy the site today.
FOX SPRING CRESCENT RISE	11. 6.59 11. 6.59	Natural springs found at Comiston became the first source of water supply when piped to Castlehill. Each spring was marked with a stone image of either a swan, hare, fox or peewit. These can still be seen in a monumental stone structure in a private garden there.
FRASER AVENUE CRESCENT GARDENS GROVE	22.10.26 22.10.26 22.10.26 22.10.26	The houses in these streets were government sponsored steel constructed built by the Second Scottish National Housing Co. (Housing Trust) Limited. Head office was in Dunfermline and on the Board of directors in 1926 was Provost Fraser of Dunfermline.
FROGSTON AVENUE GARDENS GROVE ROAD E ROAD W TERRACE	29.11.34 29.11.34 8. 4.65 — — 29.11.34	In 1447 Alexander Frog was granted permission by Lady Christian of Straiton to farm the lands of Straiton. Frogston was once a small hamlet on the road between Kaimes Village and Morton House at the foot of the hill, called Frogston Brae. Whole road was later called Frogston Road.

GAMEKEEPER'S LOAN	30. 1.36	Gamekeeper's Road existed prior to 1794. A map of this date shows estates of Cramond Regis and Barnton House surrounded by Gamekeeper's Road, Whitehouse Road, Queensferry Road and Cramond Road South. Gamekeeper of one of these estates most likely had his house in this road or the road was used by Gamekeepers of one of these estates.
ROAD	—	

GARDEN TERRACE	1. 3.73	Part of the Easter Park development where names were chosen from parts of the house and grounds of Easter Park. "Garden" refers quite simply to the garden of the old house.

GARDINER GROVE	17. 9.31	Dr. Gardiner, Minister of Kirknewton Church, was Chairman of Trustees of Craigcrook Mortification for many years prior to the naming of Gardiner Road in 1926. The estate became a trust in 1719.
ROAD	29. 7.26	
TERRACE	21. 1.32	

GILLESPIE ROAD	—	Gillespie Road. Not to be confused with "Gillespie" Streets in the Bruntsfield area although named from the same source. Gillespie Road was outside the city boundary until 1920. Named from the brothers James and John Gillespie who owned and worked the Spylaw Snuff Mill by the Water of Leith. James resided at Spylaw House still in existence in Spylaw Public Park. John attended the snuff shop in the Lawnmarket. They were founders of Gillespie School.

See also Gillespie — Part I

GILMERTON DYKES AVENUE	29. 5.52	The name "Gilmerton" existed in the reign of David l. Reference is made to the "Lands of Gilmerton and Drum". Streets obviously named after the village of Gilmerton which for centuries existed as a separate community.
CRESCENT	30. 1.36	
DRIVE	29. 5.52	
GARDENS	29. 5.52	
GROVE	29. 5.52	
LOAN	29. 5.52	
PLACE	29. 5.52	
ROAD	27. 3.52	
STREET	29. 5.52	
TERRACE	29. 5.52	
VIEW	29. 5.52	

GILMERTON ROAD	—
GILMERTON STATION ROAD	13. 7.67

GLANVILLE PLACE	—	Derivation unknown. This is a very old name which became a side name to Kerr Street Stockbridge. It first appears in the Edinburgh Street Directory in 1827.

GLEBE GARDENS	3. 1.24	The reference here is to the glebe or church land of Corstorphine Old Parish Church dating back to 14th Century.
GROVE	29. 7.26	
ROAD	3. 1.24	
TERRACE	—	

GLENALLAN DRIVE	26. 6.52	Corporation Inch housing. Names are taken from novels of Sir Walter Scott. See "Ashton Grove".

GLENDEVON AVENUE	3. 6.26	Streets named from Glendevon Place which has existed since 1903. Named from the birth place of the second chairman of the Edinburgh Co-operative Building Co, the builders.
GARDENS	15. 8.34	
GROVE	15. 8.34	
PARK	15. 8.34	
ROAD	16. 6.38	
TERRACE	15. 8.34	

See also Glendevon — Part I

GLENDINNING CRESCENT	26. 6.52	Corporation Inch Housing. Names taken from the novels of Sir. Walter Scott — See Ashton Grove.
GLENISLA GARDENS	—	This could simply be a fanciful name because the street descends from Mortonhall Road into a small glen at the Pow burn. Glenisla is in west Angus on the river Isla 9 miles N.W. of Alyth.

GLENISLA GARDENS — This could simply be a fanciful name because the street descends from Mortonhall Road into a small glen at the Pow burn. Glenisla is in west Angus on the river Isla 9 miles N.W. of Alyth.

However, the connection may be that one of the Trotters (on whose estate this street is built) married a descendant of the 3rd Duke of Atholl (Glenisla is only 19 miles from Blair Castle). The Trotter concerned was Richard Trotter who in 1836 married the great-granddaughter of the 3rd Duke of Atholl.

Queen Victoria visited Glenisla on occasions being one of her favourite spots. This may have had an influence on the choice of name. Street built in 1868

GLENLEE AVENUE — Glenlee is a Mansion in Kells parish N.E. Kirkcudbright
GARDENS — near river Ken. The connection here may be stately homes. Comparison should be made with adjacent streets, Lismore (Lismore Castle), Scone (Scone Palace), Kenmure (Kenmure Castle).

Glenlee Mansion was occupied in 1750 by two eminent judges Sir William and Sir Thomas Miller who both had titles of Lord Glenlee. Glenlee, Kenmure, and Lismore were all constructed at the same time, namely 1907.

GLENLOCKHART BANK 7. 9.33 Glenlockhart Road was formerly called City Poorhouse
ROAD 15.12.32 Road (City Poorhouse now Glenlee Old Peoples Home)
VALLEY 6. 6.74 renamed because this name was unsuitable as an address. Glenlockhart Road is situated in the Glen between Easter and Wester Criaglockhart Hills.

GLENURE LOAN 28. 2.57 Corporation South Clermiston Housing. Names taken from R.L. Stevenson's novel "Kidnapped". See Alan Breck Gardens.

GLENVARLOCH CRESCENT 26. 6.52 Corporation Inch Housing. Names taken from the novels of Sir Walter Scott — See Ashton Grove.

GLOUCESTER LANE 14. 4.66 Gloucester Street, Lane, Square formerly Church Street,
STREET 14. 4.66 Lane, and Lane Square respectively. Renamed with effect
SQUARE 14. 4.66 from 1.11.66 because of duplication. Church Lane was an old historic route taken by residents of Stockbridge and the surrounding area to St. Cuthberts Parish Church (at the West end of Princes Street).

The name Gloucester was chosen from Gloucester Place adjacent and no doubt named from a Royal Dukedom namely the Duke of Gloucester similar to the other Royal names in the new town. *See also Gloucester — Part I*

GORDON LOAN 5. 7.23 On Corstorphine Hill Estate which was feued in 1886
ROAD 5. 7.23 by the owner Charles Ferrier Gordon of Halmyre.
Corstorphine

GORDON TERRACE — Named after one of the Gilmour family of Liberton and
Newington Craigmillar Estate, Major Robert Gordon Gordon Gilmour. (Later Brig-gen Sir, 1st Baron).

GOSFORD PLACE — Gosford is in Aberlady Parish near Longniddry and is the seat of the Earl of Wemyss. The Mansion house was built in the latter half of the 18th century by the 6th Earl.
Continued Gosford Place is adjacent to Dalmeny Road and Dalmeny

is the seat of the Earl of Roseberry to the West of Edinburgh and by the Firth of Forth. It would therefore be appropriate for the name Gosford to be introduced here as named from the seat of the Earl of Wemyss to the east of Edinburgh and also by the Firth of Forth.

GRACEMOUNT AVENUE	15. 3.56	From Gracemount House still in existance as part of Gracemount R.C. School. The House and grounds stood on the church lands of St. Catherines. Formerly known as Priest's Hill. Idea of name "Grace Mount" is from "Priest's Hill".
DRIVE	15. 3.56	
PLACE	15. 3.56	
ROAD	20.12.34	
SQUARE	15. 3.56	

GRAHAM STREET —

Built about 1883 the builder was Richard Bishop 8 Gladstone Place Edinburgh. The derivation is not known but from Leith and its Antiquities Vol. 2 page 312 the following is stated "Sir Thomas Graham, Lt. Gen in 1810 the hero of St. Sebastion, afterwards Lord Lynedoch, and proprietor of Balgowan in Perthshire, began life as a Leith Merchant". This extract is taken from a page on noted Leith citizens

GRANBY ROAD —

This street requires to be considered in conjunction with Wilton Road, Suffolk Road, and Gilmour Road all of which were constructed about 1888.

Granby. Granby is situated 10 miles west of Grantham Notts and gives the title of Marquis of Granby to the Duke of Rutland in 1888 Henry John Brinsley Manners was the 8th Duke. He was Parlimentary Private Secretary to the Prime Minister in 1885—1886 and 1886—88, M.P. 1888—95. His seat is at Belvoir Castle, Grantham.

Wilton. The 4th Earl of Wilton born 1839, was Seymour John Grey Egerton, Captain Life Guards. The 5th Earl of Wilton was Arthur George Egerton, Col. Manchester Regiment, born 1863. The seat is at Wilton Castle Co. Hereford.

Suffolk. The 18th Earl of Suffolk, Henry Charles Howard, M.P. for Malmesbury 1859—68. The seat is at Charlton Park, Malmesbury, Wiltshire.

Gilmour. Major General Sir Robert Gordon Gordon Gilmour of Liberton and Craigmillar estate on which all these streets are constructed was created first baron in 1887 and the assumption is that he named adjacent streets after Lords as a celebration of the event of himself being elevated to the peerage.

The other theory that exists is that these streets were named after members of the House of Lords in opposition to streets further north which were named after members of the House of Commons namely McLaren, Bright, Cobden, and Peel.

GRANT AVENUE 1923

Street was constructed on ground belonging to the Merchant Company and Master of the Merchant Company between 1905 and 1907 was William Grant.

GRAY'S LOAN —

This is quite probably connected with Gray's Mill at Longstone and was an old road leading to the Mill from the south.

Following the capture of Edinburgh and after camping at Gray's Mill for two days, Bonnie Prince Charlie proceeded to the City by way of Buckstone and Grange. Such a route would have taken his army from Gray's Mill by way of Gray's Loan.

GRANTON PARK AVENUE	12. 9.67	Formerly Broompark Avenue renamed with effect from 1.4.68 because of duplication of similar type names Broomhouse, Broomhall etc.
GRANTON CRESCENT	1.12.32	Named from the district and Granton Road existing.
GARDENS	12. 9.35	The first mention of this name is recorded as the landing
GROVE	12. 9.35	place of an English Party in 1544 at Grantaine Craggs.
MEDWAY	1936	Granton means "The Farm by the Shore".
PLACE	23.. 6.32	*See also Granton — Part I*
TERRACE	23. 6.32	
VIEW	23. 6.32	
GOFF AVENUE	1906	One of the Christiemiller family, Major Edward Goff Christiemiller of Craigentinny estate on which the street is constructed.
GREAT MICHAEL RISE	12.12.57	The Great Michael was one of the famous Leith Fighting
SQUARE	13. 7.67	ships built at Newhaven. It was the largest ship in either the Scottish or English navies at the time of James IV.
		Great Michael Square formerly Parliament Square renamed with effect from 1.2.68 because of duplication.
GREEN STREET	8. 1.25	Application for naming was made by the Hope Trust owners of the ground. None of the Trustees were called by this name and it can only be presumed that the name derives from the fact that an open green parkland existed in the vicinity in 1925. The derivation may however be from the Gallow Green next to the Gallowlee, a former public hanging place, on the Shrub Hill nearby.
GREENBANK DRIVE	1928	Named from existing streets Greenbank Place, Crescent,
GARDENS	21. 7.32	Terrace and Avenue.
GROVE	21. 7.32	Named from the lands of Greenbank, part of the general
LANE	25. 1.31	estate of Blackford. Another old name for Greenbank
LOAN	26. 2.31	is Over Plewlands. Greenbank Drive was formerly Hospital
PARK	23. 6.32	Road, the road leading to the City Hospital.
RISE	7. 9.33	*See also Greenbank — Part I*
ROAD	26. 2.31	
ROW	23. 6.32	
GREENDYKES AVENUE	13. 3.47	In 1549 Alexander Lord Home was defeated by the Earl
DRIVE	13. 3.47	of Bothwell. The battle was known as the raid of Greenside
GARDENS	13.12.62	or Greendykes. Described as at Niddrie Edge, to the south
LOAN	13.12.62	of Niddrie, where these streets are constructed.
ROAD	13. 3.47	
TERRACE	13. 3.47	
GREENEND DRIVE	9. 6.66	Named from the village of Greenend where Ellens Glen
GARDENS	9. 6.66	Road meets Gilmerton Road today. Approaching the City
GROVE	9. 6.66	this was where the open fields gave way to a more wooded area.
GREENMANTLE LOAN	26. 6.52	Corporation Inch Housing. Names taken from the novels of Sir Walter Scott — See Ashton Grove
GRIERSON AVENUE	7. 5.25	Sir Andrew Grierson was Town Clerk of the City from
CRESCENT	7. 5.25	1918—1934 and although no proof is available it is thought
GARDENS	7. 5.25	streets were named after him.
ROAD	7. 5.25	
SQUARE	7. 5.25	
VILLAS	29. 7.26	

GRIGOR AVENUE	25. 4.35	A Mr. Grigor was factor for the Maitland family, owners of the estate for many years prior to 1920. His full name and the years he was factor are not known.

GROATHILL AVENUE	25. 4.35	Before the construction of Telford Road, Groathill Farm
DRIVE	1. 2.62	was situated at the north end of Groathill Road South.
GARDENS	25. 4.35	The road leading from Queensferry Road was where
TERRACE	1. 2.62	Groathill Road South is today, and the road to the farm from Ferry Road was where Groathill Road North is today. Prior to 1929 both were known as Groathill Road. The name, however, is older, and lands were known as Grotthill incorporated in the estate of Drylaw.

GROVENOR CRESCENT	—	From the Earls of Grovenor the secondary title of the
GARDENS	—	Dukes of Westminster, Grovenor being the family name
STREET	—	of the Duke of Westminster. Compare other streets in the vicinity such as Rosebery, Lansdowne, Glencairn, and Eglinton all names from the peerage.

GYLEMUIR ROAD	—	On the north side of Corstorphine lay a wide and treacherous swamp known as Gyle Muir.

HAILES APPROACH	..	Hailes was the ancient name for Colinton or more precisely
AVENUE	23. 7.36	Colinton or Collingtoun was contained in the Estate of
BANK	24. 1.63	Hailes. Colinton Old Parish Church records refer to "Hailes
CRESCENT	23. 7.36	Kirk". The Church of St. Cuthbert and church lands in
GARDENS	—	the parish of Hailes had been bestowed by Ethelred, Brother
GROVE	23. 7.36	of King David I upon the Monks of Dunfermline.
PARK	28. 4.32	
TERRACE	24. 8.36	

HAILESLAND GARDENS	7. 9.67	This name was introduced in the Wester Hailes housing
GROVE	7. 9.67	scheme as a variation of the name "Hailes" already in
PARK	7. 9.67	use.
PLACE	9.12.71	
ROAD	7. 9.67	

HALL TERRACE	—	Known as part of Saughton Road (later Saughton Road N.) until 1892 when the Public Hall was built in Kirk Loan opposite, whence the name Hall Terrace was used.

HAMILTON DRIVE	11. 4.35	Named from John James Hamilton, Duke of Aberborn in
DRIVE W	11. 4.35	1824 on whose land the streets were constructed.
GARDENS	29.11.56	*See also Hamilton — Part I*
GROVE	11. 4.35	
PARK	11. 4.35	
TERRACE	—	
Duddingston		

HAMILTON WYND	18. 4.63	Named from Hamilton Street and Crescent adjacent
Leith		which were named after the builder.
		See also Hamilton — Part I

HARBOUR ROAD	—	Simply the road leading to Portobello Harbour which has long since disappeared.

HARDEN PLACE	—	This street is off Polwarth Terrace and another title of Lord Polwarth is Baron Harden. Harden is the Hawick seat of Lord Polwarth situated 4 miles west of Hawick on the left bank of the Harden Burn. Compare Mertoun Place nearby. Also a seat of Lord Polwarth.

HARELAW ROAD	6.12.23	From the reservoir of that name and the hill Harelaw due south in the Pentland Hills.
HAREWOOD CRESCENT	27.11.30	Her Royal Highness Princess Mary, who was Countess
DRIVE	27.11.30	of Harewood was given the freedom of the city in 1930.
ROAD	5.12.29	It is presumed that these streets were named from this source

HARRISON GARDENS	15. 7.65	Formerly Bonaly Road and Bonaly Place renamed with
PLACE	15. 7.65	effect from 1.3.66 because of duplication with similar name at Colinton. Named from Harrison Road adjacent named after Sir George Harrison, Lord Provost 1882–1885 and M.P. after 1885.

See also Harrison — Part I

HART STREET	—	Derivation unknown. It is first mentioned in the Edinburgh Street Directory of 1827, and is shown on Ainslie's Map of 1804 as North Forth Street. Obviously the named was changed between 1804 and 1827.

HAUGH PARK	—	Parts renamed Longstone Road and Kingsknowe Road in 1924. Haugh meaning 'Along side of Water' and this is near enough the Water of Leith for the name to be appropriate.

HAWKHEAD CRESCENT	29. 5.30	One suggestion regarding the derivation of this name is
GROVE	29. 5.30	that there is a connection between the Ross family of Hawkhead and the Gilmours of Liberton and Craigmillar on whose estate the street was constructed. Sir Alexander Gilmour was created a baronet in 1678 and he married the Hon. Grisel Ross eldest daughter of George, 11th Lord Ross. The 4th Earl of Glasgow of Hawkhead an estate in Renfrewshire on the White Cart was created Baron Ross of Hawkhead.

HAWTHORNBANK LANE	—	The Anchorfield Burn flowed through the area between
PLACE	—	where these streets are now and the street called
TERRACE	—	Hawthornvale slightly to the north. No doubt hedges of hawthorn were in evidence in the area.

HAY AVENUE	24.11.32	Councillor for Portobello ward 1920–1944, John Hay,
DRIVE	24.11.32	was convenor of Streets and Buildings committee 1923–1926,
PLACE	24.11.32	convenor of Housing Sub-committee of Public Health
ROAD	28. 1.32	Committee 1930–1933, and chairman of the Streets and
TERRACE	24.11.32	Buildings Committee 1936–1939.

HAYFIELD	11.10.73	Name selected by Link Housing Association. Descriptive of the farmland that existed in this area prior to development.

HAZELDEAN TERRACE	26. 6.52	Corporation Inch Housing. Names selected from the novels of Sir Walter Scott — See Ashton Grove.
HAZELWOOD GROVE	25. 5.50	as above
HEADRIGG ROW	25. 5.50	as above
HILLHOUSE ROAD	8. 7.27	Variation of the name House o'Hill — See House o'Hill Avenue etc.

HILLPARK AVENUE	24. 6.37	All streets developed by Mactaggart and Mickel Limited.
CRESCENT	4. 2.65	The "Hill" is of course Corstorphine Hill and as the name
DRIVE	24. 6.37	was already widely used the name "Hillpark" was selected
GARDENS	27. 1.38	as a variation.
GROVE	27. 1.38	
LOAN	15.10.70	
ROAD	24. 6.37	
TERRACE	11. 6.70	
WAY	18. 4.68	

HILLVIEW *Blackhall*	—	A view of Corstorphine Hill could be obtained prior to the further development in the area.
HILLVIEW CRESCENT DRIVE ROAD TERRACE *Corstorphine*	22. 1.31 7. 2.24 — 1925	Most probably the reference is again to Corstorphine Hill but a good view of the Pentland Hills can also be obtained from these streets.
HOLYROOD PARK ROAD	12.10.67	Formerly Park Road renamed with effect from 1.4.68 because of duplication. The road leads to Holyrood Park.
HOPE LANE	—	Hope's Lane is mentioned in the Annals of Portobello and Duddingston (Baird) page 435, which would seem to indicate that Hope was perhaps a local proprietor. Nothing else has been found with regard to the derivation of this name.
HOPEFIELD TERRACE	14. 4.66	Formerly Hope Terrace renamed with effect from 1.11.66 because of duplication. "Hope" made "Hopefield" simply to alter name sufficiently to avoid confusion. Derivation of Hope Street not known, but mention is made in historical records of Leith of a Mr. Hope owning property in Leith.
HOPETOUN CRESCENT STREET	14. 4.66 7. 5.25	Formerly Hope Crescent renamed with effect from 1.11.66 because of duplication. Named thus because it is adjacent to Hopetoun Street named from the Hope family of Hopetoun. In 1792 the 3rd Earl of Hopetoun succeeded to the Annandale estate through his wife, the heiress.
HORNE TERRACE	—	Built about 1855. In investigating the derivation of Horne Terrace off Viewforth, in conjunction with Westhall Avenue, also of Viewforth, there might appear to be a link. Westhall House is located near Oyne, Aberdeenshire. In 1681 the Rev. James Horne, vicar of Elgin, bought the property. His son succeeded and the lands were erected into the barony of Horne. Nothing further has been found with regard to the derivation of Horne Terrace or the reason why the names Westhall and Horne should be appropriate for this area of the city.
HOSEASON GARDENS	28. 2.57	Corporation South Clermiston Housing. Names taken from R.L. Stevenson's novel "Kidnapped". See Alan Breck Gardens.
HOUSE O'HILL AVENUE BRAE CRESCENT GARDENS GREEN GROVE PLACE ROAD ROW TERRACE	1. 4.26 17. 6.37 1. 4.26 1. 4.26 21. 4.32 1. 4.26 22. 6.33 1. 4.26 1. 4.26 —	House o'Hill farm stood on the north side of where the street House o'Hill Brae is today, just off Corbiehill Road. Geographically, looking from Blackhall Village or the Ferry Road side the "House" would in fact be on a hill which may have been the Corby Hill of Corbiehill Road.
HOWARD PLACE STREET	— —	First appears in the Edinburgh Street Directory in 1827. It is quite probable that considering the use of names from the peerage, in naming Edinburgh streets, that Huntly Street, situated opposite Howard Place and Street at Cannonmills and also built about 1827, was named from the Earls of Huntly. The link between the names could be from

cont.

the 4th Marquess of Huntly who became 1st Duke of Gordon in 1684 and in 1676 he had married Lady Elizabeth Howard the 2nd daughter of Henry, Duke of Norfolk.

Considering that both Howard Place and Street and Huntly Street were constructed at the same time this may well be the correct derivation.

HOWDEN HALL COURT	21.12.72	On the west side of the junction of Alnwickhill Road and
CRESCENT	21.12.72	what is now Howden Hall Road stood either a house or a
DRIVE	21.12.72	row of cottages known as Howdenshall or Howden's Hall.
GARDENS	21.1272	
LOAN	21.12.72	
PARK	21.12.72	
ROAD	21.10.27	
WAY	21.12.72	

HOWDEN STREET	—	This street came into existence under the City improvement
HUNTLEY STREET	—	scheme of 1866 when several streets and closes were widened and many old buildings and closes were demolished. At that time councillor Peter Howden was a member of St. Stephens ward 1865–1876, he was a baillie 1870–1876, and was a constant attender to the improvement commission of 1867.

HUNTLY STREET

Probably named from the Earls of Huntley. The 4th Marquess of Huntley was elevated to become the 1st Duke of Gordon in 1684. This was no doubt in appreciation of the prominent part the Earls of Huntley had taken in the affairs of Scotland especially during the reign of Mary Queen of Scots. See also Howard Place and Street.

HUTCHISON AVENUE	20. 4.22	Named after Sir Thomas Hutchison, a former Lord
COTTAGES	—	Provost.
CROSSWAY	20. 4.22	At a meeting of the Committee responsible for naming
GARDENS	20. 4.22	streets on 20.4.22 names prefixed "Saltoun" were
GROVE	20. 4.22	approved. No reason is given in the minutes for the change
LOAN	—	of mind.
MEDWAY	20. 4.22	
PLACE	—	
ROAD	20. 4.22	
TERRACE	20. 4.22	
VIEW	9. 9.37	

HYVOT AVENUE	7. 6.62	Name "Hyvot" derives from Hyvot's bank farm which
COURT	7. 6.62	existed in Hyvot Loan where Gilmerton Dykes Drive
GARDENS	7. 6.62	meets Hyvot Loan today. The farm took the name from
GREEN	7. 6.62	Hyvot's Mill on the Stenhouse burn.
GROVE	4. 2.60	"Hyvot's" is a corruption of "Heavy Oats".
LOAN	27. 3.52	
PARK	7. 6.62	
TERRACE	7. 6.62	
VIEW	7. 6.62	

HYVOT BANK AVENUE	26. 5.38	Named from the above farm

INDUSTRY LANE

In 1883 property in this street was owned by Joseph Taylor, Architect, of Carron Works, Falkirk. Carron Works, still in existence, has been noted for Iron foundry work which could be described as heavy industry.

INGLEWOOD PLACE	26. 6.52	Corporation Inch Housing. Names taken from Sir Walter Scott's Novels — see Ashton Grove.
INGLIS GREEN ROAD	—	Formerly part of Hailes Quarry Road. Inglis-green was an old laundry, bleaching and dye works. It may be connected with John Alexander Inglis, one time owner of estate and house of Redhall. The name is quite old however as an advert in the Edinburgh Advertiser of 1788 read "Mr. MacWhirter of Inglis Green, Bleachfield, bleaches in the best manner at the following prices etc."
INVERALMOND DRIVE GARDENS GROVE	9. 3.72 9. 3.72 9. 3.72	The streets were constructed on the site of house and grounds of Inveralmond former home of Lord Salveson, Shipping Executive. Obviously name is from River Almond adjacent.
IVANHOE CRESCENT	26. 6.52	Corporation Inch Housing. Names taken from Sir Walter Scott's Novels — See Ashton Grove.
JAMES CRAIG WALK	1. 6.72	James Craig was the architect who planned much of the New Town. In making plans for the celebration of the bi-centenary of building of the New Town, the Lord Provost's Committee decided that a street in the St. James Square Redevelopment should be named after James Craig.
JEAN ARMOUR AVENUE	23. 1.75	Corporation Kirk Brae Development where names are selected from associations of Robert Burns. See Alloway Loan. Jean Armour was the wife of Robert Burns.
JEFFREY AVENUE	3. 4.24	Lord Francis Jeffrey, Lord Advocate 1830, M.P. for Edinburgh 1832, Court of Session Judge 1834 occupied Craigcrook Castle until his death in 1850. The street is constructed on the Craigcrook estate.
JOHN KNOX WAY	1. 6.72	A letter from Loyal Orange Institution of Scotland dated 29.11.71 asked that a street be named to commemorate 400th Anniversary of the Death of John Knox. This existing un-named walkway was chosen as suitable.
JOPPA GROVE	5. 1.22	Joppa Gardens, Park, Road, and Terrace existing and giving rise to district name Joppa. The name is very old and was originally a row of miners cottages and said to have taken name from being near to the sea like Joppa in what was known as Palestine. *See also Joppa — Part I*
JUNCTION PLACE	26. 4.29	Formerly 89 Great Junction Street. Named from existing Great Junction Street which makes a junction between Ferry Road and Leith Walk. *See also Junction Street — Part I*
JUNIPER AVENUE GARDENS GROVE TERRACE PARK ROAD	26. 1.67 14.10.71 19.10.67 13. 7.67 12. 8.67	Juniper Avenue formerly Belmont Avenue, renamed with effect from 1.8.67 because of duplication with Belmont Avenue, Corstorphine. Juniper Terrace formerly Pentland Terrace renamed with effect from 1.2.68 because of duplication. Juniper Park Road formerly Park Road renamed with effect from 1.2.68 because of duplication. Name "Juniper" selected

cont.

simply because these streets are contained in the village of Juniper Green.

KAIMES ROAD	6. 3.24	"Kame" or "Ka(i)m(e)s" means a long narrow steep sided mound or ridge, a hill ridge of zig-zag shape. This street mounts the ridge of Corstorphine Hill steeply and obviously this is the source of the name.
KATESMILL ROAD	—	Paper manufacturers and printing house proprietors, Hamilton Balfour & Neill decided in 1783 to add to their mills and rebuilt an old mill further upstream which was called Kate's Mill named after Katherine Cant, wife of John Balfour of the above firm who was connected with the Balfour family of Pilrig House.
KEDSLIE PLACE	22. 8.56	Name suggested by the builders, James Miller & Partners.
ROAD	22. 8.56	Kedslie is a farm near Lauder on the estate of Sir John Gilmour, superior of Liberton and Craigmillar Estate.
KEITH CRESCENT	—	The Keith Family occupied Ravelston House for many
ROW	—	years. One was knighted and became Earl Marischal in
TERRACE	—	1822.
KEKEWICH AVENUE	2. 5.29	Following the death in 1898 of the member of the Christiemiller family who owned the estate of Craigentinny a solicitor, Mr. C.G. Kekewich took over and for a number of years did much work in the running of the estate.
KENILWORTH DRIVE	26. 6.52	Corporation Inch Housing. Names taken from Sir Walter Scott's Novels — See Ashton Grove.
KENMURE AVENUE	—	Possibly from Kenmure Castle, Kirkcudbrightshire the seat of Viscount Kenmure. Compare other streets in the vicinity, also noted residences, Lismore, Scone, and Glenlee all built at the same time (1907). See also Glenlee Avenue.
KERR STREET	—	The buildings in Kerr Street were demolished in 1973 but the carriage-way still exists. In 1843 numbers 2 to 9 existed and numbers 8 and 9 were owned by a Mr. J. Kerr, a local proprietor.
KINGSKNOWE AVENUE	20. 9.34	From the old house and estate of Kingsknowes now a
COURT	8. 7.65	roadhouse called "The Kings Knowe". The "knowes"
CRESCENT	20. 9.34	or hills would be from the hilly landscape of what is now
DRIVE	20. 9.34	Kingsknowe Golf Course.
GARDENS	25.11.27	
GROVE	29. 7.36	
PARK	20. 9.34	
PLACE	8. 7.65	
ROAD N	—	
ROAD S	—	
TERRACE	20. 9.34	
KILCHURN COURT	14. 3.74	Named from the castle of that name at Loch Awe, Argyllshire — See "Affleck Court"

KINGSTON AVENUE	14. 7.38	Formerly called Craigs Road. Named from Kingston Grange (formerly "Craigs"). The owner was at one time a Mr. Hay of Duns Castle who changed the name from Craigs to Kingston Grange in 1780 in memory of his ancestor, Viscount Kingston.

KIRK BRAE —
     PARK 2. 2.61
KIRKGATE —
Liberton

Named from the old Liberton Kirk which stood at the west end of Kirkgate.   Demolished 1815. Not named from the kirk that stands in Kirkgate today as is generally thought.

(Kirkgate, Leith — See Part I)

KIRK LOAN —
Corstorphine

The loan which led to the ancient Parish Church of Corstorphine in existence since 14th century.

KIRK STREET —
Leith

Part of this street formerly Union Street renamed with effect from 15.5.67 because of duplication. For dervivation see Part I

KIRKHILL DRIVE 6. 1.27
    GARDENS 6. 1 27
    ROAD 1909
    TERRACE 3. 5.28

Kirkhill Road (1909), probably a made-up name because it was constructed on a hill and the religious reference (Kirk) may be to the lands of Priestfield on which the street is constructed. These were church lands conferred with other lands upon the Abbey of Holme-cultram.

KISIMUL COURT 14. 3.74

Named from the castle of that name on Isle of Barra, Invernessshire see "Affleck Court".

LADY NAIRNE CRESCENT 11.10.56
    GROVE 11.10.56
    LOAN 11.10.56
    PLACE 11.10.56

Caroline, Baroness Nairne was a famous song writer. She wrote songs such as "The Rowan Tree", "Laird O' Cockpen", "Caller Herrin". She and her husband Lord Nairne came to live in Portobello in 1806 and soon after purchased Caroline Cottage, later called Nairne Lodge in Willowbrae Road now Lady Nairne Hotel.

LADYFIELD PLACE —

An old street off Morrison Street. Derivation is not known.

LADYWELL ROAD 15.12.55
    GARDENS 8.10.64

A spring known as the "Well of our Lady" was discovered in 1745 which brought fame to Corstorphine and turned it into a fashionable Spa. The well was situated at the west end of Corstorphine High Street.

LAMMERMOOR TERRACE 25. 5.50

Corporation Inch Housing. Names taken from Sir Walter Scott's Novels. See "Ashton Grove"

LAMPACRE ROAD 11.10.28

In the gable of the east wall of the chancel of Corstorphine Church is a niche where a lamp was hung to guide travellers along the dangerous swampy tracks from the east. To endow this light the "lamp acre", a piece of ground lying on the left bank of the Water of Leith at Murrayfield, was granted.

LANARK ROAD —

Obvious. The road to Lanark.

LANG LOAN ROAD —

Also known as Lang Loan which is purely descriptive of the distance one would have to walk along this loan to get from Gilmerton to Straiton or vice-versa.

LANGTON ROAD 1938

This street is situated on the estate of the Gilmour Family owners of the Liberton and Criagmillar Estate and is no doubt named from Langton House, in Gavinton Village, 2 miles S.W. of Duns. The present house was built in 1862.
There does not appear to be a connection between the owners of Langton estate and the Gilmours but it is situated only 15 miles from the Gilmour's border estate near Earlston and the two families were no doubt on friendly terms which may have prompted the use of the name.

LAPISIDE PLACE	—	This street was constructed about 1827 to the rear of the former Leith Fort. It is shown in the Edinburgh Street Directory of 1855 as Lapside Place. Lap,— To environ; applied to the surrounding of a place with armed men, in order to beseige. The name could have originated thus because Leith Fort was built to withstand a seige by Admiral John Paul Jones.
LARGO PLACE	—	The Boog Watson notes state that "Perhaps as enjoying a view of Largo in Fife" (J.R.) this may well be the case but in Leith and its Antiquities (Irons 1 page 144) it is stated that there was much local trade with Largo. In addition Sir William Wood, a famous Leith sea captain at the time of the wars with Henry VIII and Elizabeth I and commander of "The Great Michael" was a Largo man and lies buried in Largo Church.
LASSWADE ROAD BANK GROVE	— 6. 2.30 6. 2.30	The road to Lasswade the derivation of which is doubtful. It is said that a lass called Jennie ferried people over the River Esk on her back especially the local laird who once on her back would shout "right Jennie lass, wade."
LAURISTON FARM ROAD	—	Formerly part of Silverknowes Road. Named from Lauriston Castle known in 1593 as Laurenstoun. King David II gave lands to John Tennand in a charter. Lauriston Farm lies adjacent to the castle.
LAVEROCKDALE LOAN CRESCENT PARK	21.12.67 21.12.67 9.10.69	Named from Laverockdale House and the only reference to this name is in the writing of a past minister of Colinton Church about the village of Bonailie (Bonaly). "The distillery has disappeared, the skinnery its name is lost, having given place to the more poetic designation of Laverock Dale." The house would take its name from this source.
LEADERVALE ROAD TERRACE	22. 8.56 31. 1.57	Development by James Miller & Partners. These streets are constructed on the Liberton and Craigmillar estate which is owned by Sir John Gilmour who also owns an estate near Lauder. The streets were named from Leadervale House on this estate and through which the river Leader flows.
LEAMINGTON PLACE ROAD TERRACE	— — —	Possibly named from the English Spa of this name in Warwickshire the idea originating from the adjacent district of Montpelier (see Montpelier — Part I). Montpelier, a city in the south of France and the area at Bruntsfield having been known as "The Montpelier of Scotland - a popular summer resort".
LEARMONTH AVENUE COURT CRESCENT PARK VIEW	26.10.33 29.11.45 16.12.37 26.10.33 4. 4.74	Named from John Learmonth, Lord Provost in 1832, owner of the Dean Estate and who paid most of the cost of the Dean Bridge to open up his land for feuing. *See also Learmonth — Part I*
LENNEL AVENUE	9. 9.27	The present owner of the Murrayfield Estate is Mr. Islay Campbell. His mother, now known as Mrs. Sitwell, owned the estate of Lennel, near Coldstream
LENNOX STREET *Dean*	—	Derivation not known but a good view of the Lennox hills may be obtained from here.

LENNOX ROW *Trinity*	—	Built about 1877 on the estate of Trinity House, in which masters and mariners had invested money. Compare Stirling (Road), Zetland (Place), Lomond (Road). All found to be names of ships with a Leith port of registration at that time. The "Lennox" was built in Glasgow about this time. Mention should be made however of the Earls of Lennox who had much to do with the administration of affairs in Scotland during the 16th century. In "Leith and its Antiquities" (Irons) it is stated that in 1570 Matthew, Earl of Lennox established his headquarters in Leith. He was Regent at that time and his council chamber was known as that of Lennox, Marr, and Morton, at Coalhill.
LIBERTON BRAE DAMS DRIVE GARDENS	10. 9.26 — — 10. 9.26	Argument exists about the correct derivation of "Liberton". One theory is that the name is a corruption of Leper Town, there having been a leper (or liper) hospital in the vicinity. Early manuscripts refer to Lipperton, supposed to mean "a place for lepers". Other sources say that the word "lipper" (Scots for leper) did not appear in the Scots language until much later, and the name is derived from the Old English — hilth beretum "corn farm on a hill slope".
LILYHILL TERRACE	—	A note exists in the Boog Watson notes written by other than Boog Watson "After the builders daughter".
LINDEAN PLACE	17.11.66	Formerly Waverley Place, renamed with effect from 15.5.67 because of duplication. Name fancy and was chosen as a pleasant sounding name by the residents.
LINDSAY STREET	18. 4.63	Part of the Leith Fort redevelopment named thus simply because it was located off Lindsay Road. Named from William Lindsay, Provost of Leith in 1860. *See also Lindsay Road — Part I*
LINKS GARDENS GARDENS LANE GROVE	21.10.65 21.10.65 21.10.65	Formerly James Place, Place Lane, and Lane respectively renamed with effect from 4.5.66 because of duplication. All these streets are adjacent to Leith Links. *See also Links Place — Part I*
LISMORE AVENUE GRESCENT	— —	Built about 1907. Possibly named from Lismore Castle, the seat of the Duke of Devonshire. Compare adjacent streets, Kenmure, Glenlee and Scone, all noted residences. See also Glenlee Avenue.
LITTLE ROAD	16. 7.31	Sir Alex Gilmour's daughter, Helen, married William Little of Over Liberton, nephew of William Little, builder of Liberton House. Name "Little Gilmour" became included in names of future generations of the Gilmour family owners of Liberton and Craigmillar estates. The Little family were a well-known family in Liberton.
LOANHEAD ROAD	—	The road to Loanhead. One of the main streets in the village is called The Loan, which probably accounts for the name.
LOANING CRESCENT ROAD	22.12.32 —	"Loan" means a path between fields. Loaning Road is part of an older road which ran from Restalrig Village, past Craigentinny House, through Craigentinny Meadows (now golf course) to a point on the sea-shore near the junction of the Promenade.

LOCH ROAD	21.12.33	Craigcrook Road was formerly known as Loch Road and this street no doubt took its name from this source. A loch did exist at the junction of Craigcrook Road and March Road which is now no more than marshy ground. The derivation is more likely to be from the following:—

In 1659 Craigcrook was purchased by John Mein. His son, also John Mein, married 1662 Catherine, daughter of James Loch of Drylaw.

LOCHEND AVENUE	22. 5.25	Lochend Road existing prior to 1925. It was divided
CRESCENT	22. 5.25	into Lochend Road and Lochend Road South on
DRIVE	22. 5.25	26.6.25. The derivation is that this is the part of the
GARDENS	22. 5.25	district of Restalrig which is at the loch end or the
GROVE	22. 5.25	part which is near the loch, as opposed to the part
PARK	10.12.26	nearest Calton Hill known as the Craig end.
QUADRANT	—	
SQUARE	—	*See also Lochend — Part I*

LOCKERBY COTTAGES	—	Thomas Lockerby who died unmarried and left an endowment for the building of these almhouses off Lasswade Road.

LOGAN STREET	—	The derivation cannot be definitely established. The street was built about 1909 and at that time all the property was owned by Thomas Anderson, 172 Easter Road. He may have had something to do with the naming of this street and chosen the name of Logan of Leith and Restalrig, see Loganlea.

LOGANLEA AVENUE	28. 4.32	Committee decided on 18.2.32 that name "Loganlea"
DRIVE	28. 4.32	be used for this development as a variation of the name
GARDENS	28.12.33	"Logan" — the old and historic Logan family of
LOAN	28. 4.32	Restalrig, who in the 14th century had possession of
PLACE	28.12.33	the lands of Leith. The first of the Logans was Sir
ROAD	28. 4.32	Robert Logan, baronial Lord of Leith whose castle
TERRACE	28. 4.32	overlooked the loch at Lochend. He was married to Katherine, daughter and heiress of Sir John de Lestalrig (1382) from whom the name Restalrig derived.

LOMOND ROAD	—	Constructed on the estate of Trinity House where some of the streets were named after ships with a Leith Port of Registration. See Lennox Row. Possibly named from Ben Lomond, a ship of the Ben Line.

LONGFORMACUS ROAD	6. 2.30	Application for naming was made by Brig Gen Sir Robert Gordon Gordon Gilmour Bart on whose estate the street is constructed. Sir Alexander Gilmour M.P. for the County of Edinburgh 1698—1731 married Hon. Grizel Ross, daughter of Lord Ross. Their son Sir Charles Gilmour, M.P. in 1737, married in 1733 Jean 2nd daughter of Sir Robert Sinclair of Longformacus Berwickshire.

LONGSTONE AVENUE	30. 5.35	Named from the village of Longstone which was a
CRESCENT	31. 5.23	separate community prior to the development of the
GARDENS	29. 5.52	city around it.
GROVE	13. 2.47	It is said that a long stone existed here spanning the
PARK	9. 4.64	Water of Leith which was used as a bridge.
PLACE	13. 2.47	
ROAD	—	

cont.

LONGSTONE STREET	30. 5.35	*Derivation of previous page*
TERRACE	29. 5.52	
VIEW	16.12.65	

LONSDALE TERRACE — No definite evidence exists about the derivation of this name. Comparing adjacent streets however, Panmure Place (Earl of Panmure) and Brougham Street (Lord Henry Brougham) the street could have been named from the Earl of Lonsdale. However the street was built between 1850 and 1875 and the Earl of Lonsdale at that time was of no particular importance.

Lonsdale Terrace, being close to the Royal Infirmery, could have been named from Henry Lonsdale M.D. a noted Edinburgh Physician (1816—1876). He was admitted to the Royal College of Physicians in Edinburgh in 1841. He was President Royal Medical Society. He made a noted contribution on Diphtheria and introduced in Edinburgh for the first time the use of Cod Liver Oil.

LYNE STREET — No derivation has been found for this street. It could quite simply be a fanciful name from the River Lyne.

MCDONALD PLACE	24. 1.30	Named from McDonald Road, existing, which was named
STREET	24. 1.30	after Sir Andrew McDonald, Lord Provost 1894—1897

See also McDonald Road — Part I

MCNEIL STREET — No derivation has been found for this street. It was built about 1855.

MAGDALENE AVENUE	25.10.56	From the old community of Magdalene Bridge, at one
DRIVE	25.10.56	time also known as Maitland Bridge where dwellers
GARDENS	25.10.56	were mainly workers in one of the Salt pans there. The
LOAN	25.10.56	name is taken from its close proximity to an ancient
MEDWAY	25.10.56	chapel dedicated to St. Magdalene. The Chapel was
PLACE	25.10.56	situated to the east of the stream in the estate of New
COURT	23. 1.75	Hailes.

See also Magdalene — Part I

MAIDENCRAIG COURT	13.10.55	From Maidencraig Farm, some of the old buildings of
CRESCENT	3. 6.26	which can still be seen as part of Maidencraig garage
GROVE	26. 7.28	at the junction of Maidencraig Crescent, also the old

stone wall dividing the farm from the quarry from which derived the "Craig" although the quarry itself was probably known as Maidencraig quarry.

MAIN STREET — The main street in Davidson Mains formerly called Muttonhole.

MANNERING PLACE 26. 6.32 Corporation Inch Housing. Names taken from the novels of Sir Walter Scott — See "Ashton Grove".

MANSE ROAD	—	Manse Street formerly Hope Street renamed with effect
STREET	14. 4.66	from 1.11.66 because of duplication. The Manse of Corstorphine Old Parish Church exists at 23 Manse Road.

MARCH GROVE	29.11.34	"March" means the boundary line of a property or
ROAD	29. 7.26	farm. March Road was constructed on the northern boundary of Craigcrook Farm fields (also the boundary of Craigcrook estate). The farm was located approximately where Columba Road meets the main Queensferry Road.

MARCHFIELD GROVE	8. 1.25	Marchfield House still in existence next to Marchfield
PARK	14. 3.63	Park.
TERRACE	11. 4.29	

MARDALE CRESCENT	—	Mardale is a small district in Westmoreland 6 miles S.W. of Bamton which is 8 miles south of Penrith. Adjacent is a Roman road of some length running between Windermere and Penrith. For further information see Blantyre Terrace.

MARINE DRIVE	29. 3.56	Named thus because it runs adjacent to the sea.

MARIONVILLE AVENUE	20.12.34	Named from Marionville Road, existing, which was
CRESCENT	—	named from Marionville House built by the Misses
DRIVE	20.12.34	Ramsay, Milliners. Probably named from one of them.
GROVE	20.12.34	*See also Marionville — Part I*
PARK	16. 1.36	

MARISCHAL PLACE	—	This side-name in Blackhall is obviously named from the Keith Family at Ravelston House. One of them was knighted and was created Earl Marischal of the United Kingdom in 1822.

MARITIME LANE	26. 1.67	Formerly Quality Lane and Street renamed with effect
STREET	26. 1.67	from 1.8.67 because of duplication. Name "Maritime" selected simply because of its nautical nature and therefore suitable for use in the Port of Leith.

MARLBOROUGH STREET	13. 7.67	Formerly Wellington Street renamed with effect from 1.2.68 because of duplication. Name taken from Marlborough Mansions which prior to demolition in 1971 was located on the promenade at the foot of this street. Named after Duke of Marlborough of Blenheim fame.

MARMION CRESCENT	26. 6.52	Corporation Inch Housing. Names taken from Sir Walter Scott's Novels — see Ashton Grove.

MARY'S PLACE	—	This side-name in Stockbridge is quite old and first appears in the Edinburgh Street Directory in 1827. The property was owned by the Learmonth family of Dean and the "Mary" concerned was probably a member of this family.

MAURICE PLACE	—	This street was built in 1897 on the estate of the Trotter family of Mortonhall. Maurice Raymond Elton whose father was 2nd Baron Gifford and whose son, Charles Maurice Elton, became 5th Baron Gifford, was the brother of Eva Elton (Eva Place) who married Major Gen. Henry Trotter of Mortonhall.

MAXWELL STREET	—	Built about 1875. Derviation not known but a Herbert Maxwell was a considerable land owner in Morningside around 1700. Street probably constructed on ground inherited from him.

MAYBURY DRIVE	11.10.73	Maybury Road was opened on 21 April 1927 by Sir
ROAD	7. 4.27	Henry Maybury, Direction General of Roads, Ministry of Transport.

MEADOW PLACE ROAD	—	Although named before Meadowhouse Road this street is located to the west of Corstorphine, whereas Meadow House and farm were located to the east of Corstorphine. No houses built prior to 1914 and open fields existed on each side except for a small development in Gylemuir Road. Name probably referes to this open meadow land.
MEADOWFIELD AVENUE DRIVE GARDENS TERRACE	27. 2.36 11.10.56 11.10.56 20.10.38	Named from Meadowfield Farm which existed where Abercorn Court is now situated. The Street, Paisley Drive, was constructed on the access road to the farm.
MEADOWHOUSE ROAD	—	Named from Meadow House and Farm which existed on the south side of Corstorphine Road just west of Downie Grove. The name "Meadow" **descriptive** of the environment. Prior to 1900 open fields existed between Roseburn and Corstorphine, the only building being Meadow House.
MEARENSIDE	11.10.73	Development by Craigs Housing Society who selected name "Mearen", a slip of uncultivated land of various breadths between two corn ridges. The reference is to the farmland that existed prior to the development of the area.
MEGGETLAND TERRACE	25. 2.32	The street was constructed on grounds of, and adjacent to an old house, known as "Meggetland". The area became known by this name.
MELGUND TERRACE	—	From Melgund Castle, Forfarshire, now a ruin 4 miles S.W. of Brechin. It gave a second title of Viscount Melgund to the Earl of Minto. The 2nd Earl, Gilbert Elliot Murray Kynynmound, was ambassador to Berlin 1832—33, 1st Lord of the Admiralty 1835—41, Lord Privy Seal 1846—52.
MENTONE GARDENS TERRACE	— —	These streets were constructed on ground belonging to Duncan McLaren Lord Provost of Edinburgh in 1851 and afterwards Member of Parliament. Mentone is a town in Southern France between Monaco and the Italian frontier. It is well sheltered by mountains and has a very mild climate and is a great holiday resort. See "Ventnor Terrace" which has a definite connection with McLaren. No doubt Duncan McLaren and his family holidayed at Mentone in addition to Ventnor.
MILTON DRIVE CRESCENT GARDENS N GARDENS S GROVE TERRACE	29.11.34 28. 4.32 28. 4.32 28. 4.32 26. 1.67 25. 6.31	Named from Milton Road which was named from the owner of the lands of Figgate, (see Figgate Street) Lord Milton, who sold the lands to Baron Mure in 1762. *See also Milton — Part I*
MOAT DRIVE PLACE STREET TERRACE	— — — —	This name was first introduced when Moat Place, a short line of tenement buildings, was built about 1890. The builder was George Roberts, Haymarket Terrace. No person by the name of "Moat" can be traced. Possibly the idea originated from the location of the Union Cancal to the south and the Water of Leith to the north giving the impression of a moat round this block. In 1890 more open ground existed in the vicinity and the environment then would give rise to this idea more than it would today.

MONKBARNS GARDENS	26. 6.52	Corporation Inch Housing. Names taken from Sir Walter Scott's Novels — See Ashton Grove.
MONKWOOD COURT	21. 8.63	An old house existed on this site called Monkwood.
MONTROSE TERRACE	—	Montrose Terrace existed as a short side name near the junction of London Road. The name did not extend over the entire length of Montrose Terrace today. Comparison might be made with Earlston, Pitlochry, on the opposite side of London Road giving the clue that it was named from the town of Montrose. However, considering the number of streets in the city named from the Peerage it could have been named as a compliment to the Duke of Montrose. All Scottish Dukes names are in use for names of streets in the city.

MOREDUN PARK COURT	26. 1.67	Named from Moredun House and estate, formerly called
DRIVE	27.11.47	Guttaries, later Goodtrees (meaning "ditches"). One
GARDENS	23. 3.33	of the owners Baron Moncrieffe, in the 18th Century
GREEN	17.10.63	changed the name to Moredun, a hill name on his
GROVE	17.10.63	Moncrieffe Estate at Perth.
LOAN	26. 5.66	"Moredun Park" streets were laid out on the Parkland
ROAD	23. 3.33	of the former estate.
STREET	29. 1.48	
VIEW	29. 1.48	
WALK	11. 6.64	
WAY	26. 1.67	

MOREDUNVALE BANK	26. 1.67	The name Moredunval was used as a variation of the
GREEN	26. 1.67	name Moredun to identify areas for easier location.
GROVE	26. 1.67	Moredun House stood opposite 471 Gilmerton Road
LOAN	16. 1.67	between that road and Hyvot Loan.
PARK	26. 1.67	
PLACE	26. 1.67	
ROAD	26. 1.67	
VIEW	26. 1.67	
WAY	26. 1.67	

MOREDUN DYKES ROAD	—	Moredun Dykes is an old road which ran through Gilmerton village down Hyvot Loan (formerly called Moredun Dykes Road) through Ellens Glen to Stenhouse and thence to the City. It was in fact one of the main roads to and from the city on the south side. Also named from Moredun estate.

MORNINGSIDE COURT	—	Reference is made to "Morningside" in 1588 when the
DRIVE	—	Boroughmuir of Edinburgh was feued and the estates
GARDENS	—	of Easter and Wester Morningside were formed.
GROVE	—	The name is older however, it having been a small
PARK	—	village consisting of a row of houses and a smithy. The
PLACE	—	derivation of "Morningside" has never been established.
ROAD	—	
TERRACE	—	

MORTONHALL PARK AVENUE	31.12.70	Development in three phases by three different building
GARDENS	31.12.70	firms.
GROVE	31.12.70	Name "Mortonhall Park" Selected to avoid duplication
WAY	31.12.70	with existing Mortonhall Road in the Grange district.
GREEN	13. 4.72	Streets constructed on the estate of the Trotters
LOAN	13. 4.72	of Mortonhall.
VIEW	13. 4.72	

Cont.

MORTONHALL PARK BANK	8. 3.73	*Derivation on previous page*
CRESCENT	8. 3.73	
DRIVE	8. 3.73	
PLACE	8. 3.73	
TERRACE	8. 3.73	

MORVEN STREET   28. 2.57   Corporation South Clermiston Scheme. Names taken from R.L. Stevenson's "Kidnapped" — see "Alan Breck Gardens".

MOSSGIEL WALK   23. 1.75   Corporation Kirk Brae development where names were selected from associations of Robert Burns. Mossgiel was his farm where "To a mouse" and "Mountain Daisy" were written. See Alloway Loan.

MOUNT LODGE PLACE   28. 1.32   Named from the old house which stood at the point where this street turns sharply south. The street was constructed on the original driveway to the house.

MOUNT VERNON ROAD   24. 4.25   Prior to this date the road was called Liberton Road. New name from Mount Vernon House, formerly called Nellfield. In 1795 it is stated that the ground extended to over 10 acres, well wooded, containing 500 full grown trees. Later the house became the Sacred Heart Home. The site of the house is just to the N.W. of R.C. Church in the cemetery.

MOUNTCASTLE BANK	18. 9.69	James VI in acknowledgement of his loyalty to the
CRESCENT	22.12.32	Stewarts conferred on Lord Claud Hamilton, younger
DRIVE N	22.12.32	son of the Earl of Arran, the Barony of Paisley. In
DRIVE S	28. 4.32	1603 his son was made Baron Abercorn, then Earl of
GARDENS	18. 1.34	Abercorn with the secondary title of Lord Mountcastle.
GREEN	16. 9.71	These streets are constructed on the Abercorn estate.
GROVE	22. 3.34	
LOAN	31. 7.47	
PARK	12. 3.64	
PLACE	16. 9.71	
TERRACE	22.12.32	

MUIRDALE TERRACE   1906   Application to the Dean of Guild Court for Warrent to build these houses was made in 1906 by Mr. A. Muir, Builder, and this is obviously the source of the name.

MUIREND AVENUE   —   The land between the location of this street and Currie was known as the Currie Muir and the part at the junction of Wester Hailes Road (formerly Thieves Road) and Lanark Road was called Curriemuirend. A shortened version was used to name this street.

MUIRHOUSE AVENUE	13. 2.47	Named from the Mansion house of Muirhouse, home of
BANK	12. 2.59	the Davidson family for many years. The Barony of
CRESCENT	9. 4.64	Muirhouse was purchased in 1776 by William Davidson,
DRIVE	9. 2.56	died 1795, buried in Cramond Kirk. It is thought that
GARDENS	9. 2.56	this family gave the name to Davidsons Mains. In a royal
GREEN	12. 2.59	charter of Robert Bruce mention is made of Muirhouse, —
GROVE	9. 2.56	"the King's Meadow and Muir of Cramond".
LOAN	9. 2.56	
MEDWAY	27.11.58	
PARK	12. 2.59	
PARKWAY	9. 2.56	
PLACE E	13. 2.47	

Cont.

MUIRHOUSE PLACE W	13. 2.47	*Derivation on previous page*
TERRACE	9. 2.56	
VIEW	6. 4.61	
WAY	9. 4.64	

MUNRO DRIVE   28.11.35   Application for approval was made by the Merchant
Colinton   Company Charities Board the Chairman of which was
Mr. R.H. Munro, also Master of the Merchant Company
at that time.

MUNRO PLACE   —   Built about 1855 it was owned by Danial Munro who
Cannonmills   owned a Dairy in the vicinity of Cannonmills

MURDOCH TERRACE   —   Built about 1882 the derivation of this name has not
been found

MURRAY COTTAGES   —   Charity Trust of David Murray's Almonry fund.

MURRAYBURN APPROACH	6. 2.69	The Murray Burn flows between Parkhead Drive
DRIVE	6. 2.69	Murrayburn Road.
GARDENS	7. 9.67	
GREEN	7. 9.67	
GROVE	7. 9.67	
PARK	7. 9.67	
PLACE	6. 9.70	
ROAD	7. 9.67	

MUSSELBURGH ROAD   —   Obvious. The road to Musselburgh, where mussels could
be found on the shore.

MYRESIDE ROAD   30. 1.36   Name from the old "lands of Myreside" Myrside Farm
existed where South Gillsland Road is today.

See also Myreside — Part I

NANTWICH DRIVE   22. 9.32   From Nantwich in Cheshire, an estate owned by the
Christiemiller family who also own Craigentinny Estate.
Present occupier Col. Sir. Geoffrey Christie-Miller whose
address is Acton Grange, Nantwich.

NEIDPATH COURT   14. 3.74   From the castle of that name west of Peebles — see
Affleck Court.

NETHER LIBERTON   1927   Formerly part of Penicuik Road. Named from the mill
and community of that name at the junction of Gilmerton
Road and Craigmillar Park. It was included in the
Ancient Barony of Craigmillar. Nether Liberton meaning
Lower Liberton.

NETHERBY ROAD   —   This street was constructed on the Trinity Estate, formerly
owned by the Masters and Mariners of Trinity House.
"Nether" means referring to the lower sited of two
roads, farms etc. such as Netherbow, Nether Mains and
is usually used in place names. Thus Netherby Road is
the lowest or furthest   part of Trinity Estate from Trinity
House.

NEWCRAIGHALL ROAD   —   The road to Newcraighall named from New Craighall
colliery as opposed to Old Craighall, south of Musselburgh .

NEWHAVEN MAIN STREET   14. 9.67   Formerly Main Street renamed with effect from 1.3.68
because of duplication.
Newhaven named thus as the New Haven as opposed to
the Old Haven of Blackness. Consideration should be
cont.

given however to the original intention perhaps being to name the new village, Newhaven, as opposed to the Old Haven of Leith.

See also Newhaven — Part I

NEWKIRKGATE	24. 8.66	Redevelopment of the original old street Kirkgate gave rise to the name New Kirkgate.
NEWPORT STREET	—	Built about 1855 the intention here would be to name this street as the New Port as opposed to the Old Port, Port Hopetoun at the terminus of the Union Canal. Lothian House now occupies the site of Port Hopetoun.
NEWTOFT STREET	26. 1.67	Formerly New Street renamed with effect from 1.8.67 because of duplication. New Street included properties 1 to 10 The Tofts and the new name was an amalgamation of "New Street" and "The Tofts".
NEWTON STREET	—	The derivation of this name has not been found. Construction took place about 1865 and no person of this name is mentioned in old valuation rolls.
NIDDRIE FARM GROVE	14.12.61	Street constructed on the site of the buildings of the Old Niddrie Farm (Niddrie Mains).

NIDDRIE HOUSE AVENUE	2. 4.69	The old mansion house of Niddrie, home for centuries
DRIVE	2. 4.69	of the Wauchope family, stood immediately to the
GARDENS	2. 4.69	north of Tweedsmuir House, Niddrie House Drive. It
GROVE	2. 4.69	lay in a ruinious state for many years following a fire
PARK	2. 4.69	and was finally demolished prior to construction of
SQUARE	2. 4.69	these streets. See also "Niddrie Marischal."

NIDDRIE MAINS COURT	12.12.63	Named from an older Niddrie Mains Road, the road
DRIVE	29. 1.31	leading to Niddrie Mains which was situated where
ROAD	22.12.32	Niddrie Farm Grove is today.

NIDDRIE MARISCHAL CRESCENT	12. 7.51	Niddrie House otherwise known as the mansion house of Niddrie-Marischal. Rebuilt about 1630 by Sir John
DRIVE	—	Wauchope.
GARDENS	10. 6.54	Another member of this family, Gilbert Wauchope
GREEN	—	frequently filled the office of Deputy Marischal in
GROVE	12. 7.51	Parliament from 1527 to 1535.
LOAN	10. 6.54	Lairds of Niddrie were hereitary Bailies to the Keiths,
PLACE	12. 7.51	Earls Marischal and Marischal deputes in Midlothian.
ROAD	12. 7.51	The family had great power in the southern borders.
STREET	10. 6.54	

NIDDRIE MILL AVENUE	9. 2.56	Niddrie Mill was located on the east side of a burn just
CRESCENT	9. 2.56	to the north of where Niddrie Mains Road is situated
DRIVE	9. 2.56	today.
GROVE	11. 3.65	"Niddrie" is of celtic origin. Sometimes spelt Nidrof
PLACE	9. 2.56	and Nidraig in old documents.
TERRACE	9. 2.56	*For Niddrie Road — see Part I*

NIGEL LOAN	26. 6.52	Corporation Inch Housing. Names taken from Sir Walter Scott's Novels — see "Ashton Grove".

NORTH GYLE AVENUE	25. 1.34	When Corstorphine was a separate village the ground to
DRIVE	25. 1.34	to north and west was known as the Gylemuir. North
FARM COURT	10.12.70	Gyle Farm was to the north and South Gyle Farm was
FARM LANE	10.12.70	to the south of this area. The farm buildings of
GROVE	15. 3.56	North Gyle are now incorporated in the development
LOAN	25. 1.34	at North Gyle Farm Court.
PARK	9. 6.66	
ROAD	25. 1.34	
TERRACE	25. 1.34	

NORTHFIELD AVENUE	14. 9.21	From Northfield House and Farm formerly situated where
BROADWAY	14. 9.21	Northfield Park Grove is today. Presumable named thus
CIRCUS	14. 9.21	to differentiate between this farm and Southfield Farm,
CRESCENT	14. 9 21	south of the Figgate Burn.
DRIVE	31. 7.47	
FARM AVENUE	5. 4.29	
FARM ROAD	—	
GARDENS	14. 9.21	
GROVE	31. 7.47	
PARK	21. 8.63	
PARK GROVE	28. 7.73	
ROAD	14. 9.21	
SQUARE	—	
TERRACE	14. 9.21	

NORTHLAWN TERRACE 1. 3.73 Off Easter Park Drive this street was constructed in the grounds of Easter Park House where names were chosen from various parts of the former grounds

OAK LANE 1973 Not officially named by appropriate committee of the Town Council because it was not recognised as a street within the meaning of the 1967 Order. The street was named by residents. There is a large Oak tree at the entrance.

OCHILTREE GARDENS 25. 5.50 Corporation Inch Housing where names were selected from novels of Sir Walter Scott — See Ashton Grove.

OLD BURDIEHOUSE ROAD 21.11.68 Formerly part of Burdiehouse Road renamed with effect from 1.2.69 because this became a separate road after construction of the dual carriageway — see Burdiehouse Road.

OLD CHURCH LANE 14. 4.66 Formerly Church Lane renamed with effect from 1.11.66 because of duplication. Named from the ancient parish church of Duddingston located in this street.

OLD FARM AVENUE 9. 4.70 Named from the farm called "The Old Farm" the
ROAD 9. 4.70 buildings of which were located where these streets are constructed. It was formerly called Colinton Farm on the fields of which Redford Barracks was constructed in 1914.

OLD KIRK ROAD 5. 7.23 This street was constructed on part of an old road which led to Kirk Loan and thence to Corstorphine Parish Church. The road can be traced from Ravelston Dykes Road, up Rest and be Thankful, across Corstorphine Hill, through ground now part of the Zoo. It proceeded to the north of Corstorphine Hill House (now within Zoo) and along where Old Kirk Road is today.

OLD MILL LANE 7. 9.61 This is the old road leading to the community of Nether Liberton where an old mill exists on the banks of the Braid Burn.
Confusion with the street called Nether Liberton required an alternative address for residents.

OLD TOLBOOTH WYND	13. 7.67	Formerly Tolbooth Wynd renamed with effect from 1.2.68 because of duplication.

See Tolbooth Wynd — Part I

ORCHARD BANK	3. 9.27	Named from Orchard Brae, existing, which was the road
CRESCENT	27.10.27	leading to the orchard of Dean House. Dean House,
DRIVE	30. 9.27	demolished 1845, was situated in the ground now Dean
GROVE	19. 9.29	Cemetery.
PLACE	30. 9.27	
ROAD	30. 9.27	
ROAD S	30. 9.27	
TERRACE	30. 9.27	

ORCHARD BRAE AVENUE	13.11.58	
GARDENS	13.11.58	
GARDENS W	9. 7.64	
WEST	17.12.31	*See Orchard Brae — Part I*

ORCHARDFIELD AVENUE	—	An extensive nursery existed to the rear of the ancient
Corstorphine		Dower House in Corstorphine High Street formerly the orchard of this house. This street was constructed on part of the grounds of the orchard .

ORCHARDFIELD LANE		In 1854 the grounds of Pilrig House extended as far
Leith Walk		as Leith Walk where existed a side name "Orchard-field". It seems obvious that this lane led to or from, the orchard of Pilrig House.

ORCHARDHEAD LOAN	28. 3.35	Sixth in line of succession to the estate of Over
ROAD	28. 3.35	Liberton was William Little, died 1685. He left his
Liberton		lands to the 2nd daughter of his sister Sarah who had married Walter Rankin of Orchardhead Stirlingshire. He was succeeded by Gabrial Rankin of Orchardhead who assumed name of Little.

ORMISTON TERRACE	—	One of the older names in Corstorphine and the derivation has not been found.

OSWALD COURT	15. 4.71	Constructed on the estate of the Trotter family of
ROAD	—	Mortonhall. Richard Trotter (1797—1874) 10th in
ROAD S	—	line of succession to the Mortonhall estate, married
TERRACE	—	in 1836 Mary, daughter of Gen. Sir John Oswald of Dunniker.

OXFORD STREET	—	Oxford Street, built about 1861 was constructed on the
STREET S	—	site of Oxford Park which it is said was much frequented
Newington		by gypsies.

OXFORD TERRACE	—	The Earldom of Oxford was not created until 1925 and
Dean		as this street was constructed about 1854 it is no doubt named after the town of that name. More probably however the University. Eton Terrace, adjacent, was to have been called Cambridge Street.

OXGANGS AVENUE	13. 2.47	Named from Oxgangs Farm which was located at the
BANK	11.11.54	southern junction of Oxgangs Road North and Colinton
BRAE	11.11.54	Mains Drive where the police station is now situated.
B'WAY	31.10.57	"Oxgangs" is an old Scots measure of land of approxi-
CRESCENT	13. 2.47	mately 13 acres which was the amount of land that
DRIVE	13. 2.47	could be ploughed by an ox-drawn plough in 1 year.
GARDENS	9. 4.64	
GREEN	11.11.54	
GROVE	9. 4.64	

Cont

OXGANGS HILL	9. 4.64	*Derivation see Previous Page*
LOAN	11.11.54	
MEDWAY	31.10.57	
PARK	11.11.54	
PATH	11.11.54	
PATH E	31.10.57	
PLACE	13. 2.47	
RISE	11.11.54	
ROAD	—	
ROAD N	26. 6.58	
ROW	11.11.54	
STREET	13. 2.47	
TERRACE	15. 4.37	
VIEW	11.11.54	
OXGANGS FARM AVENUE	22.10.53	*As above*
DRIVE	22.10.53	
GARDENS	22.10.53	
GROVE	22.10.53	
LOAN	22.10.53	
TERRACE	22.10.53	

PAISLEY AVENUE	11. 4.29	Paisley Drive was formerly called Meadowfield Farm Road.
CRESCENT	6. 1.27	These Streets were constructed on the estate of the Duke
DRIVE	11. 4.29	of Abercorn who made application for order to construct
GARDENS	26. 4.34	Paisley Avenue and Drive in 1929.
GROVE	1. 5.60	James VI in acknowledgement of his loyalty to the
TERRACE	26. 4.34	Stewarts conferred on Lord Claud Hamilton, youngest

son of the Earl of Arran, the Barony of Paisley.
Later in 1603 the Abercorn title was conferred on his son.

PARK CRESCENT	11. 9.25	Officially named Kirk Crescent, Gardens, and Grove but
GARDENS	11. 9.25	owing to objections by new residents this decision was
GROVE	11. 9.25	rescinded and the streets named "Park" because this

area of ground had previously been known as Park
Gardens for 30 years. The name if obviously associated
with the former Parkland of Mount Vernon House adjacent
now Mount Vernon Cemetery.

PARKER AVENUE	27. 2.36	A Mr. Parker was one of the trustees of the Craigentinny
ROAD	27. 2.36	estate in 1936 on which these streets were constructed.
TERRACE	27. 2.36	

PARKGROVE AVENUE	21. 6.34	The application for street order of 1934 for Parkgrove
BANK	13. 7.61	Avenue and Drive was made by Eastern Counties
CRESCENT	22. 9.38	Properties Limited and described the streets as "at
DRIVE	21. 6.34	Parkneuk" which was a nursery and house at the
GARDENS	21. 9.39	junction of Parkgrove Drive and Drum Brae North.
GREEN	13. 7.61	Probably developers preferred name "Parkgrove" to
LOAN	21. 9.39	"Parkneuk". Name is associated with Barnton Park
NEUK	18. 1.62	opposite (the open parkland prior to house construction
PATH	1959	there).
PLACE	17. 7.52	
ROAD	19. 8.37	
ROW	13. 7.61	

Continued

PARKGROVE STREET	26. 2.53	*Derivation on previous page*
TERRACE	21 9.39	
VIEW	13. 7.61	
PARKHEAD AVENUE	27.10.36	Parkhead Farm was situated to the south of Calder Road
CRESCENT	27.10.36	and just west of where Parkhead Gardens is today. The
DRIVE	27.10.36	streets were constructed on the former farmland.
GARDENS	27.10.36	
GROVE	27.10.36	
LOAN	27.10.36	
PLACE	27.10.36	
STREET	27.10.36	
TERRACE	27.10.36	
VIEW	27.10.36	
PATIE'S ROAD	28.10.36	Patie's Road was constructed on the line of an older road called Pattie's Loan which was an access from the south to Katesmill and Redhall Mill. Origin of "Patie's" is not known.
PEARCE AVENUE	23.10.30	Application for street order to construct streets Pearce
GROVE	10. 3.66	Road and Avenue was made by Edward Pearce, builder,
ROAD	23.10.30	(died in 1947 aged 86).
PEATVILLE GARDENS	23. 2.56	Application was made to construct the street Peatville
TERRACE	28.11.35	Terrace in 1935 by R. Peat, Builder, of Kinnauld, Currie and obviously the street was named after him.
PEFFER BANK	—	Peffer Place formerly Mitchell Street renamed with effect
PLACE	17.11.66	from 15.5.67 because of duplication. Peffer Street
STREET	15. 7.65	formerly Station Road renamed with effect from 1.3.66 because of duplication. Named from Peffermill Road.
PEFFERMILL ROAD	—	Named from Peffer Mill House with mill adjacent on the Braid Burn. In Scoto-Saxon the name means "The Mill on the dark muddy stream". Peffermill House is where the "Laird of Dumbiedykes" lived in Sir Walter Scott's "Heart of Midlothian".
PEGGY'S MILL ROAD	11. 4.30	Previously an un-named road leading to Peggy's Mill officially named on this date.
PEMBROKE PLACE	—	The theme used for naming streets in this area was names of counties or noted residences. Compare Devon, Surrey, Sutherland, and Elgin. See Devon Place.
PENNYWELL COURT	29. 5.69	Named from Pennywell Cottages formerly called simply
GARDENS	25.10.45	"Pennywell" still in existence at the junction of West
GROVE	25.10.45	Granton Road and Marine Drive. In former days pit
MEDWAY	25.10.45	ponies from Orkney and Shetland were unloaded at
PATH	25.10.45	Granton. Drovers from the mining areas around Glasgow
PLACE	14. 3.63	drove the ponies from Granton and the first spot which
ROAD	—	they could water the ponies was at the well at Pennywell
VILLAS	—	for which they paid the sum of one penny.
PENTLAND AVENUE	—	Evident from a view of the Pentland Hills.
ROAD	—	
Colinton		
PENTLAND CRESCENT	18.10.34	As above
DRIVE	28. 1.65	
GARDENS	18.10.34	*See also Pentland — Part I*
GROVE	18.10.34	
VIEW	18.10.34	
Comiston		

PERTH STREET	—	Possibly a name derived from the Earl of Moray's estate in Perthshire. Compare Doune Terrace from Doune also on his Perth estate. The street was constructed shortly after 1825.
PEVERVIL TERRACE	26. 6.52	Corporation Inch Housing. Names taken from Sir Walter Scott's novels — See Ashton Grove.
PIERSHILL LANE	26. 1.67	Piershill Lane formerly Ramsay Lane renamed with
SQUARE E	14. 4.38	effect from 1.8.67 because of duplication.
SQUARE W	14. 4.38	Historians say that the name "Piershill" derives from Col Piers who is reputed to have occupied a villa on high ground overlooking Restalrig, north of Jocks Lodge known as Piershill House (Piershill barracks, built 1793 occupied the site of Piershill Squares E and W). However, no Col. Piers can be traced and it is known that the land was a heritable subject as far back as the 16th century. Reference is made to the "lands of Piershill" in a feu charter dated 20 August 1580. This, therefore, casts doubts about Co. Piers' existence.

See also Piershill, Pursfield — Part I

PILRIG GARDENS	19. 4.34	Name derives from Pilrig House on east side of Pilrig
AVENUE	27. 4.33	Street near Bonnington Road the grounds of which have become Pilrig Public Park. Formerly known as Peilrig and Peilryge named from the ridge (rig) where in the 15th century the Peel Tower stood (Peel rig).

See also Pilrig — Part I

PILTON AVENUE	27. 4.33	Named from East Pilton Farm. The mansion house in the
CRESCENT	27. 4.33	Barony of Piltoun was accidentally burnt down on 8th
DRIVE	27. 4.33	February 1749.
DRIVE N	—	The buildings of East Pilton Farm were located just to the
GARDENS	27. 4.33	west of Pilton Drive and just to the north of the Northern
LOAN	26. 4.33	General Hospital.
PARK	27. 4.33	
PLACE	27. 4.33	

PIRNIEFIELD BANK	26. 8.54	Pirniefield Place existed as an access to Pirniefield House.
GARDENS	29. 4.37	Pirniefield House, of no historical significance, is now
GROVE	29. 4.37	divided into 47 (Laurel Bank) and 49 Pirniefield Place.
TERRACE	15.12.32	

See also Pirniefield — Part I

PITLOCHRY PLACE	—	Built by the Edinburgh Co-op Building Co. Limited and this is probably another of the fanciful names chosen for naming their streets. Compare Earlston Place adjacent. See Earlston Place.
PITTVILLE STREET	21.10.65	Formerly Pitt Street renamed with effect from 4.5.66, because of duplication. Side name "Pittville" also renamed and renumbered. There existed a house in Pitt Street called "Pittville". On 6.9.29 the appropriate committee approved the side-name "Pittville" for Nos. 1—7. The name is derived from William Pitt, Prime Minister in 1783.
PLEYDELL PLACE	26. 6.52	Corporation Inch Housing. Names taken from novels of Sir Walter Scott — See Ashton Grove.

POLWARTH CRESCENT	—	A note exists in the Boog-Watson notes written by other
GARDENS	—	than Boog-Watson "A compliment to Lord Polwarth".
GROVE	—	Proof of this statement lies in the adjacent streets "Harden"
PARK	29.11.34	and "Mertoun" both seats of Lord Polwarth.
PLACE	—	
TERRACE	—	

PORTGOWER PLACE	—	Portgower is a village near Helmsdale Sutherland and no reason can be found for this street being named thus.

PORTLAND STREET	15. 7.65	Formerly Albany Street renamed with effect from 1.3.66 because of duplication. Named from the former Portland Place and Terrace which existed as side-names to Lindsay Road. Said to be named after the Duke of Portland, P.M. in 1807. However as the original Portland Place and Terrace were constructed a number of years after 1807 the name "Portland" may have simply been a made up name from the Port of Leith.

PORTOBELLO HIGH STREET	14. 9.67	Formerly High Street, renamed with effect from 1.3.68 because of duplication.
ROAD	—	Formerly a barren waste called the Figgate Whins or Lands of Figgate ("Figgate" — Saxon for "a common pasture for cattle"). A sailor returned from his ship in a fleet which in 1739 bombarded and captured the important Spanish town of Puerto Bello. He built a house on the lands of Figgate and called it Portobello House, said to be where the Town Hall now is.

PRESTONFIELD AVENUE	30. 9.27	Prestonfield Avenue formerly Hamner Road and Preston-
CRESCENT	30. 9.27	field Gardens formerly Alston Road presumably renamed
GARDENS	30. 9.27	so that all streets in the new scheme should bear the same
ROAD	30. 9 27	name. Named from Prestonfield House; a former owner
TERRACE	30. 9.27	was Sir James Dick who purchased the lands of Priestfield along with lands purchased from the Prestons of Craig-millar, when the area then became known as Prestonfield.

PRIESTFIELD AVENUE	20.12.24	From the lands of Priestfield mentioned as far back as
CRESCENT	18. 2.32	1376. See also above
GARDENS	8.10.64	*See also Priestfield — Part I*
GROVE	18. 2.32	
ROAD N	28. 6.29	

PROMENADE	—	Obvious, Portobello promenade.

PROSPECT BANK CRESCENT	25.10.29	Named from Prospect Bank Road, existing as the access
GARDENS	28. 2.35	to Prospect Bank House, of no historical significance.
GROVE	28. 2.35	Obviously named thus because of the prospect it
PLACE	25. 2.32	commanded before the development of the area.
TERRACE	25. 2.32	*See also Prospect Bank — Part I*

QUALITY STREET	—	Prior to 1890 only three houses existed in this street outside the (then) small village of Davidsons Mains. The suggestion is that the houses built here were of a better quality than in the village.

QUAYSIDE STREET	14. 4.66	Formerly Church Street renamed with effect from 1.11.66 because of duplication. Name chosen simply because the street is near quay and a large works exists here called Quayside Works.
QUEEN CHARLOTTE LANE STREET	13. 7.67 13. 7.67	Formerly Charlotte Lane and Street renamed with effect from 1.2.68 because of duplication. Named after Charlotte — wife of George III.

QUEEN'S AVENUE
     AVENUE S
     GARDENS
     ROAD
	—
	12.10.67
	13. 9.23
	—
		Houses in Queen's Avenue were built about 1900 and the queen perpetuated must have been Queen Victoria.

RAEBURN STREET	12.10.67	Formerly Hermitage Place renamed with effect from 1.4.68 because of duplication. Named from Raeburn Place which obtained its name from Sir Henry Raeburn, the famous painter, who was born in Stockbridge.

See also Raeburn — Part I

RANKIN AVENUE
     DRIVE
     ROAD
	24. 4.52
	24. 4.52
	30. 1.36
		William Little, who built Liberton House had no family and on his death in 1686 the estate passed to his nephew William Rankine who assumed name of Little and married, Helen, daughter of Sir Alex Gilmour of Craigmillar estate on which ground the streets are constructed.

RANNOCH GROVE
     ROAD
     PLACE
     TERRACE
	26. 5.60
	25. 5.60
	6. 6.68
	28. 2.57
		Corporation South Clermiston Housing. Names selected from R.L. Stevenson's novel "Kidnapped" — see Alan Breck Gardens.

RANSOME GARDENS	28. 2.57	As Above
RATCLIFFE TERRACE	—	From Ratcliffe Place a short side-name which existed in 1845 fronting the road running south from Causeway-side. 4 Dwellings existed off Ratcliffe Place called Ratcliffe Terrace access to which was by a pedestrian path. These buildings existed adjacent to where Grange Loan is today and have long since been demolished. No doubt Ratcliffe was a former proprietor but no evidence has been found to prove this.
RAVELSTON DYKES RAVELSTON DYKES LANE	28.11.40 21. 8.63	Ravelston Dykes formerly Ravelston Dykes Road named from Ravelston House now part of Mary Erskine School. House known in 1363 as Raylistoun.

RAVELSTON HOUSE GROVE
     LOAN
     ROAD
     PARK
	13. 4.61
	13. 4.61
	13. 4.61
	13. 4.61
		Development by T. Boland & Co. on the former estate of Ravelston House.

See also Ravelston — Part I

RAVENSCROFT GARDENS
     PLACE
     STREET
	21.11.68
	—
	12.10.67
		Ravenscroft Street formerly Main Street renamed with effect from 1.4.68 because of duplication. Ravenscroft Gardens, development by James Miller and Partners, named because of situation off Ravenscroft Street.
		Ravenscroft Place was the access to Ravenscroft House, of no historical significance, now No. 15 Ravenscroft Place.

RAVENSWOOD AVENUE	25. 5.50	Corporation Inch Housing. Names selected from Sir Walter Scott's novels — See Ashton Grove.
REDBRAES GROVE	13. 7.61	Redbraes House and grounds were situated where Redbraes
PLACE	29. 3.31	Place and Public Park are today.

See also Redbraes — Part I

REDFORD AVENUE	26.11.31	All named from Redford Road formed in 1802 on a
BANK	25. 5.50	much older "road" made in 1747.
CRESCENT	26.11.31	First mention of the "lands of Redford" is made in 1674
DRIVE	4. 7.29	when Sir James Foulis took his seat on the bench as
GARDENS	25. 5.50	Lord Reidford.
GROVE	12. 2.53	The name derives from a ford through the Bonaly Burn
LOAN	26.11.31	prior to the building of the bridge which can still be seen
NEUK	12. 2.53	on the older part of the road on the north side of the
PLACE	12. 2.53	reconstructed carriageway.
ROAD	—	
TERRACE	10. 4.52	
WALK	25. 5.50	

REDGAUNTLET TERRACE	25. 5.50	Corporation Inch Housing. Names selected from Sir Walter Scott's novels — See Ashton Grove.

REDHALL AVENUE	13. 2.47	From the ancient Barony of Redhall which included the
CRESCENT	13. 2.47	estates of Redhall, Oxgangs, Comiston, Swanston,
DRIVE	13. 2.47	Dreghorn, Bonaly, Pilmuir and Baads, Woodhall and
GARDENS	13. 2.47	Colinton.
GROVE	21. 6.51	Redhall Castle was the residence of Sir Simon Otterburn
PLACE	21. 6.51	in 1527. He was a Lord Provost and later M.P.
ROAD	13. 2.47	It was stormed by Cromwell's troops and later fell to
VIEW	26. 6.52	ruins. It stood on the south or south-east bank of the Water of Leith, ¼ mile above the present bridge at Slateford.

REDHALL BANK ROAD	—	As Above
REDHALL HOUSE DRIVE	13.12.73	The original driveway to Redhall House named on this date to give an address to houses attached to new school. See also Redhall Avenue etc.
REGIS COURT	12.12.74	*See after Rutherford Drive.*

RELUGAS GARDENS	15.10.70	Relugas Gardens and Place were a development by James
PLACE	27. 5.71	Miller and Partners named thus because they were off
LANE	26. 2.24	Relugas Road which was constructed on the Grange Estate of Sir Thomas Dick Lauder who married Charlotte, daughter of George Cumin of Relugas.

see also Relugas — Part I

RESTALRIG CIRCUS	—	Named from the ancient village of Restalrig formerly
CRESCENT	—	Lestalrig from the family De Lestalrig settled there
PARK	2. 4.69	between 1128 and 1382.
ROAD S	—	*See also Restalrig — Part I*
SQUARE	—	
TERRACE E	—	

RICHMOND TERRACE	—	Compare other streets in the area named from Dukedoms namely Argyll, Atholl, Breadalbane, and Douglas. No doubt this street was named as a compliment to the Duke of Richmond.
RITCHIE PLACE	—	The Nos 2, 4 and 6 were the first buildings erected in this street about 1880 and all were owned by Mrs. Dorothy Ritchie, 21 Comiston Road.

RISELAW CRESCENT	25. 1.10.	A made up name from "law" — a hill, and the ground
PLACE	25. 1.10	rises quite steeply here being on the lower slope of the
ROAD	25. 5.05	west side of the Braid Hills.
TERRACE	25. 1.10	

RIVERSDALE CRESCENT	21. 5.26	These streets are adjacent to the Water of Leith and
GROVE	21. 9.33	the names are derived from this fact.
ROAD	28.10.13	

| RIVERSIDE | — | At the side of the River Almond at Cramond. |

| RINGWOOD PLACE | 26. 6.52 | Corporation Inch Housing. Names selected from the novels of Sir Walter Scott — See Ashton Grove. |

| ROBB'S LOAN | 30. 1.27 | Robbs Loan was constructed on a very much older Robb's |
| ROBB'S LOAN GROVE | 28. 5.64 | Loan. This Loan led from the Ford's Road/Saughton House area to the east and south of Gorgie Farm (where Robb's Loan Grove is today) then south to Slateford Village. Who "Robb" was is not known. |

| ROBERT BURNS DRIVE | 23. 1.75 | Corporation Kirk Brae Development. See Alloway Loan. |

| ROCHESTER TERRACE | — | Rochester is a small village in Northumberland N.W. of Otterburn. Extensive roman remains can be found here, a camp and a road — See Blantyre Terrace. |

| ROSEBANK GARDENS | 10.11.55 | Named from Rose Park House which had its access off |
| GROVE | 27. 2.36 | Trinity Road now South Trinity Road just past New Bank. The former site was where the west part of Darnell Road is situated today. |

See also Rosebank — Part I

| ROSEFIELD STREET | 14. 4.66 | Formerly Hope Street renamed with effect from 1.11.66 because of duplication. Named from Rosefield Avenue and Place adjacent which were named from Rosefield House. |

See also Rosefield — Part I

| ROSEVALE TERRACE | 12.10.67 | Formerly Hermitage Terrace renamed with effect from 1.4.68 because of duplication. Named from existing Rosevale Place which was built through the rose garden of Lady Fife's house. |

See also Rosevale — Part I

| ROSEVILLE GARDENS | 22. 9.38 | Street constructed on the house and grounds of "Rose Villa", one of the many named houses in Laverockbank Road. |

ROSS GARDENS	6. 3.24	One of the Gilmour family, owners of Liberton and
PLACE	24. 4.52	Craigmillar estate, Sir Alexander Gilmour was created a
ROAD	26. 7.10	baronet in 1678 and he married the Hon. Grizel Ross, eldest daughter of George, 11th Lord Ross.

| ROSSIE PLACE | — | Prior to the buildings on the north side being erected this street served houses built by the Edinburgh Co-op Building Co. Limited who had built several groups of streets in the city, mostly named with fanciful names, or names of directors were used, or places with which these directors were associated (see Glendevon). Compare Glenogle Road. |

Rossie is a place in Angus 1½ miles S.W. of Montrose. Rossie island is included in the burgh of Montrose. Perhaps there is a link in the naming of this street with Montrose Terrace nearby.

ROTHESAY MEWS	—	A note exists in the Boog-Watson notes written other
PLACE	—	than by Boog-Watson "compliment to Kings eldest son?"
TERRACE	—	This statement perhaps should have read the "Queens eldest son", the Queen being Queen Victoria. Edward VIII when born was made Prince of Wales and also Duke of Rothesay, and Duke of Cornwall.

ROULL GROVE	26. 2.48	Roull was a poet who lived in Corstorphine in the 15th
PLACE	13. 7.67	century and was one of the first provosts of Corstorphine
ROAD	—	Church. Little else is known about him.

ROWALLAN COURT	14. 2.74	Named from the castle of that name near Kilmaurs, Ayrshire — See Affleck Court.

ROYSTON MAINS AVENUE	16. 1.36	Royston Mains in 1914 was a small cottage in West
CRESCENT	16. 1.36	Granton Road where house No. 231 stands today.
GARDENS	16. 1.36	The buildings were probably formerly more extensive.
GREEN	16. 1.36	The streets were laid out on the former farm land.
PLACE	16. 1.36	Name derives from the old barony of Royston. Granton
ROAD	16. 1.36	Castle was formerly known as Royston Castle.
STREET	16. 1.36	

RUSTIC COTTAGES	—	From their rustic appearance. "Rustic" means "pertaining to the country", where they used to be prior to the extensive house building in the area.

RUTHERFORD DRIVE	26. 6.52	Corporation Inch Housing. Names selected from the novels of Sir Walter Scott — See Ashton Grove.

REGIS COURT	12.12.74	Development by Bacal Construction Limited on ground formerly Dunvegan House, on Cramond Regis estate. An old house of this name formerly stood nearby — See "Cramond Regis".

SADDLETREE LOAN	25. 5.50	Corporation Inch Housing where names were chosen from the novels of Sir Walter Scott — See "Ashton Grove".

ST. ALBANS ROAD	—	Built about 1880 this street was possibly named as a compliment to the Duke of St. Albans. The peerage at that time was held in high esteem especially of Dukedom Of the 26 Dukedoms in the United Kingdon the names of 19 have been used in naming streets of the city. No evidence has been found however to prove that there is a link between the Duke of St. Albans and this district of Edinburgh.

ST. CATHERINES GARDENS *Corstorphine*	—	The derivation is not known. The street was built in 1898.

ST. CLAIR AVENUE	25. 1.25	In 1878 a yard at 11 Elliot Street was owned by a Thomas
PLACE	—	Watson, 4 St. Clair Street, Aberdeen. By 1894 a printing
ROAD	—	works occupied the site, Dobson Molle & Co. and the
STREET	—	works were known as St. Clair Works. Any connection
TERRACE	—	with the address of the former occupier of the site may be coincidental. The firm Dobson Molle Limited moved from Elliot Street to the north end of what is now St. Clair Street and took the name St. Clair Works with them. As the only occupiers of property in St. Clair Street at that time it is safe to assume that this was the source of the name.

ST. JAMES CENTRE	19.12.68	Built on the site of St. James Square which was said to be named after James VIII by Jacobites attempting to hide the "King" title under the "Saint". A clue is left in the hint which occurs in Little King Street adjacent.

See also St. James — Part I

ST. JOHN'S AVENUE	25. 4.35	St. John's Crescent formerly Chalmers Crescent renamed
CRESCENT	17.11.66	with effect from 18.8.67 because of duplication. The
GARDENS	25. 4.35	ancient parish church of Corstorphine founded in 1429
ROAD	—	was dedicated to St. John the Baptist.
TERRACE	—	

ST. KATHARINE'S BRAE	15. 3.56	Named from the Chapel of St. Catherine now disappeared
CRESCENT	13.10.60	but which stood where the childrens home is. It was the
LOAN	15. 3.56	most ancient place of worship in the parish and the ground around was consecrated for burial. This was prior to '1750.

It is said that some oil of St. Catherine which was being brought from Mount Sinai to St. Margaret was spilt at that spot.

ST. MARY'S PLACE	—	Built at the same time as St. Mark's Place (See Part I) in 1895. No facts have been found about the derivation. It may have been named as simply balancing St. Mark's Place adjacent or a member of Portobello Town Council, Alfred Nicol, may have had an influence in the choice of name. His house was called St. Mary's in 1895.

ST. NINIAN'S DRIVE	20. 4.39	St. Ninian's Church and Manse exists in St. Ninian's
ROAD	—	Road and obviously this is the source of the name.

SALAMANDER PLACE	13. 7.67	Formerly Bath Street renamed with effect from 1.2.68 because of duplication. Named from Salamander Street from the fiery glass and chemical works that existed here, suggesting which single type of creature could live there. The first cones or furnaces were erected by the Bottle House Co. in 1740 on the sands near Salamander Street.

See also Salamander Street — Part I

SALMOND PLACE	—	Built in 1885, all houses were owned by Andrew Paul, Brassfounder, 111 Gilmour Place. The only "Salmond" found in Who's Who of 1885 was the Rev. S.D.F. Salmond M.A. Professor of Theology, United Free Church, Aberdeen. The street was built by the Edinburgh Co-op Building Co. and their usual source of naming streets was in the use of fanciful names or names of Directors. Salmond may have been one of the directors at one time but no evidence has been found to prove this.

SALVESEN CRESCENT	13. 5.48	Application for naming was made by the Scottish Veterans
GARDENS	13. 5.48	Garden City Association the chairman of which had been
GROVE	1950	the Right Hon Lord Salvesen.
TERRACE	13. 5.48	"Muirhouse" as a name had been put forward but "Salvesen" was approved on a 5 to 6 vote by Town Council Committee.

SANDPORT PLACE	13. 7.67	Formerly Bridge Street renamed with effect from 1.2.68 because of duplication. Named from Sandport Street which was named from the old gate opening to the sands where the Custom House now is.

See also Sandport – Part I

SAUGHTON GARDENS	10.12.26
GROVE	10.12.26
LOAN	10.12.26
PARK	10.12.26
ROAD	19. 1.33
ROAD SOUTH	19. 1.33

Saughton Road and Saughton Road North were formerly called Saughton Station Road.

Name derives from the old mansion house of Saughton Hall, home for centuries of the Baird family. The garden and, in particular, the rose garden of Saughton Public Park were the grounds of the old house.

"Saugh" means "The Willow Tree" and the reference is to the willows by the Water of Leith.

SAUGHTONHALL AVENUE	3. 4.24
AVENUE W	3. 6.26
CIRCUS	24. 4.24
CRESCENT	–
GARDENS	24. 4.24
GROVE	24. 4.24
PLACE	24. 4.24
TERRACE	24. 4.24

The name "Saughtonhall" is appropriate for the area in which they are situated. "Saughton" names are further west and are more likely derived from the house of "Old Saughton". The house was situated where Broomhouse Primary School now is to the west of Saughton Road and to the north of Calder Road.

SAUGHTON MAINS AVENUE	26. 2.48
BANK	15.12.55
COTTAGES	12. 6.58
DRIVE	26. 2.48
GARDENS	26. 2.48
GROVE	26. 2.48
LOAN	26. 2.48
PARK	9. 4.64
PLACE	26. 2.48
STREET	25. 6.31
TERRACE	26. 2.48

Named from Saughton Mains Farm formerly situated immediately to the south of St. Salvador's Church in Saughton Mains Street.

SAVILE ROAD EAST	–
ROAD WEST	–
TERRACE	–
TERRACE WEST	–

Possibly named from Sir John Savile (1818–1896), Diplomatist, eldest son of the 8th Earl of Scarborough. He served as a Diplomat, Charge d'Affaires, for many years. In 1883 after 42 years service he became Ambassador to Rome and became a Privy Councilor. In 1887 he retired from the Foreign Service and became the 1st Baron Savile.

The street was the first road to be constructed on the Liberton and Craigmillar estate owned at that time by Brig. Gen. Sir Robert Gordon Gordon Gilmour who succeeded on the death of his grand-uncle, Walter James Little Gilmour in 1887 and was then created 1st Baronet Gilmour.

It could be a coincidence that Sir John Savile and Sir Robert Gilmour were both elevated to the peerage at the same time, on the other hand there could be an association. The streets Savile Road East and West were however, constructed 10 years before this, in 1877.

The name, however, could have been sued because high quality houses were to be erected, the idea being that a similar name in London, Savile Row, is a street where high qualtiy goods can be obtained.

SAXE-COBURG STREET	12.10.67	Formerly West Clarement Street renamed with effect from 1.4.68 because of duplication. Named from Saxe-Coburg Place. For derivation see Part I.
SCHOOL BRAE	—	Formerly Mill Brae. Possibly name change came about because local people would refer to the road as "by the school" or "at the side of the school" and it then became known locally as School Brae.
SCIENNES HOUSE PLACE	13. 7.67	Formerly Braid Place renamed with effect from 1.2.68 because of duplication. The rear of Sciennes House appears as part of the buildings on the north side. One has to pass through to the "back" green to view the front of the house. A plaque is fixed here explaining that Sir Walter Scott and Robert Burns met in the house. "Sciennes" derived from the Convent of St. Catherine of Siena. (See "Sciennes" in Part I).
SCONE GARDENS	—	Compare Lismore, Kenmure and Glenlee, adjacent streets and all noted residences. This street is possibly named from Scone Palace, Scotland's ancient capital in south east Perthshire.
SEAFIELD ROAD EAST	18. 4.68	Formerly Seafield Road renamed because of duplication of numbers at each end. Named from its location.
SEAFORTH DRIVE TERRACE	17.11.66 —	Seaforth Drive formerly Hillview Terrace renamed with effect from 15.5.67 because of duplication. A made up name from the Firth of Forth and the sea — a view of which was more possible from Blackhall prior to the extensive house building that has taken place around the original village.
SEAPORT STREET	15. 7.65	Formerly Bank Street renamed with effect from 1.3.61 because of duplication. A made-up name signifying the character of the Port of Leith.
SEAVIEW CRESCENT	29.11.34	Named from Seaview Terrace. Derivation obvious. *See also Seaview Terrace — Part I*
SHAFTESBURY PARK	—	Shaftesbury Park is adjacent to Ashley Terrace and Ashley is the family name of the Earls of Shaftesbury. The only link with the Merchiston estate on which these streets are constructed appears to be:— 1. Charles 2nd son of the 6th Baron Napier of Merchiston married Grizell daughter of Sir John Warrender (1731). 2. Vice Admiral Sir George Scott Warrender, 7th Baron of Bruntsfield married Lady Ethel Maud Ashley, 4th daughter of the 8th Earl of Shaftesbury (1894). This is however probably not how the street came to be named thus. See "Ashley Terrace".
SHANDON CRESCENT PLACE ROAD STREET TERRACE	— — — — —	Robert Napier (1791–1876) the famous marine engineer built the mansion of West Shandon at Shandon, Dumbartonshire in 1851 situated on the east shore of the Gareloch. The present Napier family is represented by Ian Patrick Robert Napier M.C. of Milton House, Bowling, Dumbartonshire. The family business is shipbuilding and shipowning. There does not seem to be a connection with the Napier family of Merchiston on whose ground these streets were constructed and a mistake could have occurred here in tracing the history of the

Continued

wrong "Napier" in selecting names for these streets.
More detailed study of the family tree of each family,
may, however, establish a link.

SHANTER WAY	23. 1.75	Corporation Kirk Brae Development where names were selected from Associations of Robert Burns. Shanter is from his famous poem "Tam O' Shanter". See Alloway Loan.

SHORE PLACE   14. 4.66

Formerly Queen Street renamed with effect from 1.7.66
because of duplication.
Named thus because street is off Shore which was
obviously named because it was near the seashore.

See also Shore — Part I

SIGHTHILL AVENUE	27.10.36
BANK	26. 5.66
COURT	22.10.53
CRESCENT	29. 4.37
DRIVE	27.10.36
GARDENS	27.10.36
GREEN	26. 5.66
GROVE	27.10.36
LOAN	27.10.36
NEUK	29. 6.44
PARK	27.10.36
PLACE	24. 6.37
RISE	—
ROAD	24. 6.37
STREET	24. 6.37
TERRACE	24. 6.37
VIEW	25. 6.36
WYND	26. 5.66

In bygone days there existed small communities and
farms along Calder Road, such as Gorgie, Saughtonhall,
Stenhouse, Parkhead and Hermiston.
One of these was "Sighthill" which was situated where
Sighthill Health Centre is at Sighthill Court.
No doubt name derives from the fact that travelling
from the west to the City a good view (sight) can be
had from here of either Corstorphine Hill or Arthur's
Seat.

SILVERKNOWES AVENUE	15. 3.34
BANK	27.11.55
BRAE	10. 3.60
COURT	20. 8.52
CRESCENT	15. 3.34
DELL	10.12.70
DRIVE	15. 3.34
EASTWAY	28. 5.53
GARDENS	28. 5.53
GREEN	10. 3.60
GROVE	28. 5.53
HILL	15. 3.34
LOAN	15. 3.34
MIDWAY	10. 3.60
NEUK	9. 6.66
PARKWAY	28. 1.54
PLACE	20. 8.52
ROAD	15. 3.34
ROAD E	10. 3.60
ROAD S	6. 3.24
SOUTHWAY	10. 3.60
TERRACE	20. 9.34
VIEW	10. 3.60

Named from Silverknowes Farm in the estate of Muirhouse
and to the east of the estate of Lauriston. This was farmland
only and it did not appear to be an estate although a fine
house stood at the north end of the old Silverknowes
Road now the Commodore Hotel. There appeared to be
two farms of this name. The buildings of one were located
where the club house of the golf course is at the west end
of Silverknowes Parkway. The old farmhouse of the other
is still is existence on the west side of Silverknowes
Road opposite Silverknowes Court. The other buildings
of this farm were on the east side of the road.

"Silverknowes" is a more modern name, the origin of
which is not known. It was formerly known as Randilstoun
or Rudulf's farm (14th Century).

SLEIGH GARDENS	22. 5.25	From Sleigh Drive existing, named from Sir Wm. Sleigh Lord Provost from 1923 to 1926.

See also Sleigh — Part I

SMITHFIELD STREET	—	Compare adjoining streets Wheatfield, Westfield. All possibly names of fields that existed here in bygone days. Mr. Smith of Smithfield no doubt existed but who he was cannot be traced.
SOMERSET PLACE	21.10.65	Formerly Livingston Place renamed with effect from 4.5.66 because of duplication.

In 1560 at the time of Elizabeth I of England 3000 French troops landed at Leith to help the Scots. The English troops after camping on the Hawkhill and fighting skirmishes from there decided to set up two large mounds on Leith Links and erect guns on them to bombard Leith. One mound was called Mount Pelham, the other Mount Somerset named after the respective captains of artillery, Pelham and Somerset.

SOUTH GYLE GARDENS	15. 6.71	Named from South Gyle Farm and the fact that the lands lay to the south of the Gyle Muir formerly a wide and treacherous swamp N.W. of Corstorphine.
ROAD	—	
SOUTH SLOAN STREET	23. 5.35	From Sloan Street existing named after Bailie Sloan, contractor.

See also Sloan Street — Part I

SOUTHFIELD BANK	26. 5.60	Named from Southfield Farm, the old farmhouse of
GARDENS E	19. 1.33	which still exists at the top of the cul-de-sac Southfield
GARDENS W	19. 1.33	Farm Grove. Other streets were laid out on the former
LOAN	24.11.58	farmland.
ROAD E	17. 1.35	Southfield as opposed to Northfield, north of the Figgate
ROAD W	17. 1.35	Burn.
SQUARE	24.11.38	
TERRACE	17. 1.35	
SOUTHFIELD FARM GROVE	27. 5.54	As Above.
SOUTHHOUSE AVENUE	6. 2.30	Named from Southhouse Farm, the old farmhouse of
BROADWAY	6. 2.30	which is still in existence at the east end of Southhouse
CRESCENT	27. 2.47	Road.
GARDENS	18.10.62	This was the South house of the area.
GROVE	27. 2.47	
MEDWAY	18.10.62	
PATH	18.10.62	
ROAD	6. 2.30	
SQUARE	18.10.62	
TERRACE	6. 2.30	
SPENCER PLACE	—	This street was constructed on the Trinity Estate formerly belonging to the Masters and Mariners of Trinity House and was no doubt named from an elder brother of Trinity House, namely the Rt. Hon Earl Spencer. He was in the Cabinet under Gladstone and served as Lord President of the Council, 1st Lord of the Admiralty and also held many other important posts in the Government of the time. The street was constructed in 1883.

SPENCE STREET	—	Following scrutinisation of the history of Newington and in particular Newington House nothing has been found about anyone called "Spence".

SPENCE STREET — Following scrutinisation of the history of Newington and in particular Newington House nothing has been found about anyone called "Spence".
The street, constructed about 1880, could have been named after James Spence (1812–1882) a noted surgeon who studied at Edinburgh and was appointed Professor of Surgery at Edinburgh. He was a great surgeon of the older school. No evidence exists however to link James Spence with the naming of this street except that Benjamine Bell one of the principal occupiers of Newington House, on which ground Spence Street was built, was also a surgeon by profession.

SPEY TERRACE 21.10.65 Formerly James Street renamed with effect from 4.5.66
STREET — because of duplication.
Named from Spey Street existing. In 1885 it was called Moray Street. No reason has been given in historical records about why the name was altered but presumably because of confusion with Moray Place.
The name "Spey" was probably derived from the fact that this river flows through the county of Moray and into the Moray Firth on the estate of the Earl of Moray.

SPIER'S PLACE — The derivation of this street has not been found. It came into existence in 1875 under a Leith improvement scheme when the new street 50 feet wide and ¾ mile long was made from Junction Street to Tolbooth Wynd, since called Henderson Street. It was made through what was regarded at that time as an unhealthy area and 18 of the most unsanitary closes were cleared away. There may have been a Spiers close here at one time but no evidence exists of this.

SPRING GARDENS — This street probably took its name from St. Margaret's well (Spring) in Holyrood Park adjacent. In Volume I of Leith and its Antiquities (Irons) it is stated on page 300 "not far from the Church of Restalrig stood the beautiful Gothic well dedicated to St. Margaret", and "beside the ancient and little frequented cross-road leading from the Abbey hill to the village of Restalrig". The well was moved to Holyrood Park at a later date.

SPRINGWELL PLACE — The mansion house of Dalry and the parkland adjacent was sold in 1714 to Sir James Nicolson Bt. Sasine was granted "with privilege and use of the spring well of Foull Bridge with power to carry water in pipes". The spring was famous for its volume, purity, and softness of its water. The exact location is not clear but it was near to the Lochrin Burn (the Foull Burn) at Foull Bridge (Fountainbridge) on the lands of Dalry.

SPRINGWOOD PARK 16.10.64 Named from the house "Springwood" located at the junction of this street and Kirk Loan. The street was constructed on the former grounds.

SPYLAW AVENUE —
PARK —
STREET —
BANK ROAD —
Not to be confused with Spylaw Road, Merchiston although the name is derived from the same source. These streets were in the County of Midlothian until 1920 and the date of naming is not known.
Named from the brothers Hames and John Gillespie who owned and worked the Spylaw Snuff Mill by the Water

Continued

178

of Leith. James resided at Spylaw House still in existence in Spylaw Public Park. John attended the snuff shop in the Lawnmarket. They were founders of Gillespie School.

STAFFORD STREET	—	Derivation not known. The Boog-Watson notes state that the street first appears in the Edinburgh Street Directory of 1827, is shown on the Lothian map 1825 and is mentioned partly built in the minutes of the Town Council 8.9.1819.
STANHOPE PLACE	—	Built about 1865 and was probably named from Philip Henry Stanhope, 5th Earl Stanhope (1805–1875). He
PLACE WEST	—	was a member of parliament and held government posts
STREET	26. 5.49	under Sir Robert Peel.
STAPELEY AVENUE	15.12.32	From Stapeley House on the estate of the Christiemiller family who also owned Craigentinny estate. Stapeley is a village in Cheshire two miles S.E. of Nantwich.
STARK'S COTTAGES	—	These cottages were attached to the former Colinton Mains Farm and no doubt housed farm workers at one time. It can only be suggested that Stark was the name of one of the owners of the farm.
STATION ROAD	—	Obvious, the road leading to the local railway station when a suburban line ran to Corstorphine.
STENHOUSE AVENUE	21.10.27	Named from Stenhope Mills Village, a small community
AVENUE W	18. 6.31	where Stenhouse Mill Lane is today. The old Stenhope
COTTAGES	21.10.27	House (Stenhouse Castle) was built 1623 probably by
CRESCENT	21.10.27	one of the Stenhope family who held the land of Stennap
CROSS	21.10.27	Milnes or Stenhouse Mills from 1511 to 1621 and which
DRIVE	21.10.27	was located a few yards further up the Water of Leith.
GARDENS	21.10.27	
GARDENS N	21.10.27	
GROVE	21.10.27	
PLACE E	21.10.27	
PLACE W	21.10.27	
ROAD	24. 6.27	
STREET E	21.10.27	
STREET W	21.10.27	
TERRACE	21.10.27	
STENHOUSE MILL CRESCENT	25. 5.50	As Above.
LANE	25. 5.50	
STEVENSON AVENUE	5. 5.27	Named as a mark of respect for Sir Alexander Stevenson,
DRIVE	21.10.27	Lord Provost when the first street of this name, Stevenson
GROVE	29. 4.37	Road, was constructed. He was Lord Provost from 1926
ROAD	10. 9.26	to 1929.
TERRACE	18.10.34	
STEWART TERRACE	—	Built about 1878 the valuation roll of that year gives the owner of property as Charles Stewart, Boot Manufacturer of North British Leather and Shoe Works, Gorgie Road.
STIRLING ROAD	—	Built about 1889 on the estate of Trinity House. Compare adjacent streets, Lennox, Zetland, and Lomond, all names of ships. Stirling Road is most probably named from "Stirling Castle" built at Leith in 1884. It was sold to Turkish clients in 1898, but formerly had a Leith port of registration.

STRACHAN GARDENS	23. 4.31	In 1698 John Pringle sold Craigcrook Castle and estate
ROAD	29. 7.26	to John Strachan WS who lived there until his death in 1719 after which the estate, on which this street is situated, became a Trust known as the Craigcrook Mortification.
STRAITON ROAD	21.10.27	Prior to this date Straiton Road was known as Penicuik Road. The village of Straiton was in existence as far back as 1447 when a Lady Christian of Straiton is mentioned. Also a family of the name Straton, Stratoun or Straiton is mentioned in a charter of David I.
STRAITON PLACE	—	Portobello. An old street built before 1890. Derivation has not been found.
STRATHALMOND COURT	28. 5.64	Development by T. Boland and Co. Limited. These
GREEN	28. 5.64	streets are located in the Strath of the River Almond.
PARK	28. 5.64	
ROAD	28. 5.64	
SUCCOTH PARK	23.12.65	Named from the Dumbartonshire estate of the Campbells of Succoth also owners of Murrayfield estate.

See also Succoth — Part I

SUFFOLK ROAD	—	See Granby Road.
SUMMER PLACE	—	From the old house formerly on this site called Summer's Place which would possibly indicate that this was from a person called Summer rather than from a season of the year.
SUMMERBANK	—	Derivation has not been found. The 1852 O.S. Sheet shows it as not having been made until a later date when it was constructed as an access from Scotland Street to Bellevue. Possibly it is simply a fanciful name.
SUMMERTREES COURT	25. 5.50	Corporation Inch Housing where names were selected from the novels of Sir Walter Scott — see "Ashton Grove".
SUNNYBANK	27.11.30	Named from Sunnybank Cottage which existed where
PLACE	—	No. 1 Sunnybank is today. Nos 1 and 2 occupy the
TERRACE	—	original grounds of the old house.
SURRAY PLACE	—	From the same source that named Devon Place etc. See Devon Place.
SUTHERLAND STREET	—	As Above.
SWAN SPRING AVENUE	11. 6.59	Natural springs found at Comiston became the first source of water supply when piped to Castlehill. Each spring was marked with a stone image of either a swan, hare, fox or peewit. These can still be seen in a monumental stone structure in a private garden in the area.
SWANSTON AVENUE	19. 9.35	Named from the old village and farm of Swanston still
CRESCENT	16. 9.71	in a state of preservation and one of the few old com-
DRIVE	19. 9.35	munities within the City which has not been obliterated
GARDENS	15.11.56	by housing developments.
GREEN	16. 9.71	Formerly called Swaynystoun or Sweynystoun in 13th
GROVE	15.11.56	century interpreted as Sveinn's Farm of Norse origin.
LOAN	16. 9.71	Originally only Swanston Road existed formerly Swanston
PARK	16. 9.71	Farm Road.
PLACE	15.11.56	
ROAD	—	
ROW	16. 9.71	

Continued

SWANSTON TERRACE	18. 7.35	*Derivation see previous page*
VIEW	15.11.56	
WAY	16. 9.71	

SYCAMORE GARDENS	1. 3.73	The Corstorphine Plane tree, one of the old relics of
TERRACE	–	Corstorphine, is situated opposite Sycamore Terrace. It grew in ground surrounding Corstorphine Castle close to the ancient dovecot, all that remains of the castle.

SYDNEY PARK	25. 5.33	A christian name which appears in the Christiemiller
PLACE	29. 9.32	family of Craigentinny, the owners of the estate on which
TERRACE	5. 2.07	these streets are constructed.

Application for street order for streets Sydney Park and Place was made by Sydney Richardson Christiemiller. The name occurs earlier in the family as shown by Sydney Terrace constructed in 1907.

TELFORD DRIVE	22.10.53	Telford Road was constructed as part of the Edinburgh/
GARDENS	22.10.53	Leith – Glasgow road and was named after Thomas
PLACE	22.10.53	Telford the famous civil engineer who in 1820 was the
ROAD	Jan 1929	first president of the Institute of Civil Engineers. He was born in 1757 at Glendinning in Eskdale, the son of a shepherd. He died in 1834 and was buried in Westminster Abbey.

TEMPLELAND GROVE	10. 8.60	These streets were constructed on ground formerly the
ROAD	7. 2.24	Temple (Church) land or ground within the precincts of Corstorphine Old Parish Church.

THE CAUSEWAY	--	Meaning of "Causeway" Is :—

1. a pathway raised and paved with stone.
2. a raised path through marsh or water
3. a paved or cobbled road

The latter meaning would be a correct description of this old road in Duddingston Village when "causy" stones provided its surface.

THE CRESCENT	9. 4.70	A side name in Morningside Drive where lack of numbers required a new name to be introduced. Development by James Miller and Partners who requested this name for no particular reason other than its possible unique attraction, although Morningside Drive does have a slight crescent shape at this point.

THE EAST WAY	14. 9.21	A pedestrian path in the Northfield housing scheme which ran east from the central section, Northfield Circus.

THE GLEBE	–	The reference is the Glebe or church land of Cramond Parish Church.

THE GREEN	16.12.27	Name suggested by the Housing and Planning Committees. The village green of Davidsons Mains.

THE GREEN WAY	4. 9.70	This wide way was constructed through the Wester Hailes Housing Scheme to facilitate access to houses for pedestrians only. On each side there exists green grass and landscaping, thus the name.

THE HIGH WAY	14. 9.21	A pedestrian path in the Northfield Housing Scheme which climbs to a higher level at Northfield Circus.

THE LIMES	1. 6.72	Named Napier Court but decision rescinded because developers James Miller and Partners Limited wished the name "The Limes". The planting of lime trees was to be carried out in the grounds.
THE NORTH WAY	14. 9.21	A pedestrian path in the Northfield Housing Scheme which runs north from the central area at Northfield Circus.
THE SHOOT	—	An old public way prior to any development of housing outside Colinton Village. Shoot or Shuit meaning "Of banks and walls in danger of bursting into an avalanche" or "a steep bank undermined by a stream". Appropriately named, therefore, by its position on the steep bank by the Water of Leith.
THE SPINNEY	9.12.71	Originally suggested that it be named "Moredun Park Gardens" but developers, James Miller & Partners, insisted that this name be considered by the Committee no doubt because of its more distinctive and unique nature. A spinney or small copse of trees exists at the end of this cul-de-sac.
THE TWIRLIES	—	This path between Woodhall Road and Bridge Road, Colinton does in fact twist or twirl.
THE TURLIES	—	An old public path from Lanark Road near Hailes Grove to Spylaw Bank Road. Turlie or Turkas, Tirl or Turl. Turkas — Pincers or pliers such as used by a blacksmith. Tirl — Part of a mill wheel Turls — The haunch bone of an ox. The reference could be its shape but the present day path is quite straight.
THE WISP	—	A whimsical type name used locally to describe the road between Niddrie Mill and Old Dalkeith Road. The origin is not known.
THOMAS STREET EAST	—	An old street the buildings in which await demolition (1975). The derivation is not known.
THORBURN GROVE ROAD	18.12.30 —	Thorburn Road was in the County of Midlothian prior to 1920 and consisted of a short cul-de-sac about 1890 or 1900. A burn flowed where the back gardens of the houses on the east side are today which was lined with a thorny hedge. Thorburn is a corruption of Thornyburn or Thornburn as the burn used to be known.
TORPHICAN STREET PLACE	— —	The Littlejohn map gives Thomas Street. Shown on O.S. Sheet of 1852. The derivation has not been found.
TORPHIN ROAD	—	The road leading to Torphin Farm which lies at the foot of Torphin Hill.
TORRANCE PARK	28. 2.57	Corporation South Clermiston Housing where all names were selected from R.L. Stevenson's "Kidnapped" see "Alan Breck Gardens".
TOWARD COURT	14. 3.74	From the castle of that name near Dunoon, Argyllshire. See "Affleck Court".

TOWNWOMEN'S GUILD WALK	3. 5.73 —	This guild paid for the trees which line this walk in the Meadows. The planting ceremony took place in May 1973 and the guild requested that the walk be given this name.
TRAQUAIR PARK EAST **WEST**	20. 3.25 20. 3.25	Originally a single cul-de-sac off Station Road called simply Traquair Park when Nos 1 to 37 were built. Extended and divided into East and West on 20.3.25. Proprietors of Corstorphine Estate in 1890 (when Traquair Park was first constructed) were John and W Traquair Dickson.
TRINITY COURT	11. 6.64	Named from the Trinity district but for full derivation see Part I. Trinity Road was divided into East Trinity Road and South Trinity Road on 27.4.28. *See also Trinity — Part I*
TURNHOUSE FARM ROAD	12.10.67	Formerly Turnhouse Road renamed with effect from 1.4.68 to enable name to be applied to section of Turnhouse Road from Maybury roundabout.
TURNHOUSE ROAD	12.10.67	Formerly Stirling Road renamed with effect from 1.4.68 because:— 1. Address of residents was Turnhouse Road in any case. 2. Stirling Road duplicated with street of same name in Trinity district.
TYLER'S ACRE AVENUE **GARDENS** **ROAD**	13.10.55 13.10.55 18.12.30	A corruption of Tailor's Acre Park, a large field to the east of Saughton Road North and to the south of the former Corstorphine House. Obviously this ground (acre) was owned at one time by someone called Tailor.
ULSTER CRESCENT **DRIVE** **GARDENS** **GROVE** **TERRACE**	26. 4.34 11. 4.29 11. 4.29 19. 9.29 11. 4.29	These streets were constructed on the estate of the Dukes of Abercorn, who have also been connected with Ulster since 1634. James 2nd Marquis and 1st Duke of Abercorn was twice Lord Lieutenant of Ireland, 1866—8, and 1874—6. The seat of the present Duke is Barons Court, Co. Tyrone. One of his other titles is Baron of Kilpatrick and these streets were first named Kilpatrick Crescent etc. This decision was rescinded and "Ulster" names substituted. No reason was given by the Committee for the alteration.
UPPER CRAMOND COURT	12.12.74	Development by Bacal Construction Limited on ground formerly Dunvegan House. "Upper Cramond" was the former name of this area and it was suggested by The Cramond Association.
VANDELEUR AVENUE	20.10.32	Constructed on the Craigentinny Estate owned by the Christiemiller family one of whom, Sydney Richardson Christiemiller married in 1904 Evelyn, daughter of Hector Stewart Vandeleur of Kilrush.

VENTNOR TERRACE	—	Ventnor is a watering place in the Isle of Wight which is associated with Duncan McLaren on whose ground the street was built.
		Duncan McLaren was a former Lord Provost and M.P. for Edinburgh. His wife and one of his sons were in poor health and he used to send them to Ventnor for the benefit of their health.
		In a letter to his son Charles Bright McLaren dated 11th May 1862 he states that "I left Ventnor and got home safe having left London at 9 in the morning. I hope you as being the oldest boy at Ventnor will take good care of your Mamma".
VICTOR PARK TERRACE	—	Named from the house known as "Victor Park" at the top of this cul-de-sac.
VIEWCRAIG GARDENS	15. 4.71	Corporation St. Leonard's redevelopment in which there
STREET	15. 4.71	formerly existed a street Upper Viewcraig Row from which these streets derived name. A good view of Salisbury Crags can be obtained.
VIEWFIELD ROAD	18.12.38	Viewfield Farm was formerly situated at the junction of Muirend Avenue and Lanark Road which was probably named thus because of the good view obtained from here of the fields that existed prior to the construction of Wester Hailes housing.
VIVIAN TERRACE	6. 3.24	The owner of the Muirhouse Estate, on which the street is constructed, in 1924 was Mr. Mathew Mather and he named the street after his eldest daughter Vivian Theodora Netta Mather.
WAKEFIELD AVENUE	14. 6.10	This was the first street to be constructed on the Craigentinny Estate owned by the Christiemiller family. The name Wakefield appears as a middle name in this family's history. The owner when the street was constructed in 1910 was Col. Sir Geoffrey Christiemiller whose father's name was Thomas Wakefield Christiemiller. His son, born 1909, was also named Wakefield.
WALTER SCOTT AVENUE	25. 5.50	Corporation Inch Housing where names were selected from the novels of Sir Walter Scott except this street, named after the famous author himself.
WARDIE AVENUE	—	Named from the district and former castle of that name
CRESCENT	—	mentioned 1544. Also known as Weirdie.
GROVE	22.12.32	*See also Wardie — Part I*
PARK	3. 1.24	
WARDIEBURN DRIVE	1.12.32	The Wardie Burn flowed through this area from where
PLACE E	1.12.32	the Northern General Hospital (Wardieburn House was
PLACE N	1.12.32	situated here) is today to Granton Harbour. The track
PLACE S	1.12.32	of the Burn can still be seen between Granton Place and
PLACE W	28.12.33	Wardie Crescent.
ROAD	28.12.33	
STREET E	1.12.32	
STREET W	1.12.32	
TERRACE	1.12.32	

WARDIE HOUSE LANE	15. 3.56	Constructed to serve four new houses built in the grounds of Wardie House now No. 7 Boswell Road.
WARRISTON DRIVE	15.12.55	Named from Warriston House and estate. Warriston
GARDENS	19. 3.26	House stood at the eastern end of Eildon Terrace and was
GROVE	11. 9.30	owned in the 16th century by the Somervilles, in 1581
TERRACE	15.12.55	by the Kincaids. In 1706 the estate was acquired by

Heriots Hospital (now school) which gives a reason for the school's extensive playing fields being located at Goldenacre on the Warriston Estate. Warriston Gardens was formerly called Cemetery Road, renamed in 1926.

See also Warriston — Part I

WASHINGTON LANE	—	This lane led to cottages known as Caledonian cottages also referred to as Washington Cottages, now demolished. The derivation has not been found.
WATERTOUN ROAD	21. 5.31	Application for approval of this name was made by Brig. Gen. Sir Robert Gordon Gordon Gilmour of Liberton and Craigmiller Estate, the owner. No reason was given for the choice of name and the present owner of the estate Sir John Gilmour, Sir Robert's son, was consulted about this but can shed no light on the matter. It might have been one of the field names of West Liberton Mains Farm on the Liberton Estate and which was situated a short distance from where Watertoun Road is today.
WAUCHOPE AVENUE	23. 7.31	Named after the Wauchope family of Niddrie Marischal
CRESCENT	23. 7.31	House and Estate.
PLACE	23. 7.31	The first owner was Gilbert Wauchope who obtained
ROAD	28. 1.32	lands in a charter granted by Robert III in 1390. The
SQUARE	26. 1.33	family were in possession of the estate until 1900 when
TERRACE	23. 7.31	the owner was Col. Andrew Gilbert Wauchope, 17th in succession.
WEST APPROACH ROAD	11.10.74	Known prior to official naming as Temporary Western Approach Road. Name descriptive of its function.
WEST COURT	23. 8.67	Small development on west side of Ravelston House Park.
WEST CRAIGS AVENUE	29. 4.37	West Craigs as opposed to East Craigs, two small district
CRESCENT	29. 4.37	names at the end of Craigs Road. The "Craigs" referred to are small and located on the west side of Maybury Road.
WEST GRANTON CRESCENT	8. 7.65	This development replaced the temporary "Prefab"
DRIVE	8. 7.65	housing the streets in which were named "West Pilton".
GARDENS	8. 7.65	A new name "West Granton" was introduced because of
GREEN	8. 7.65	the already extensive use of the "West Pilton" name.
GROVE	8. 7.65	Named from the much older road "West Granton Road".
LOAN	8. 7.65	
PLACE	8. 7.65	
ROAD	—	
ROW	8. 7.65	
TERRACE	8. 7.65	
VIEW	8. 7.65	
WEST MAINS ROAD	—	The name is derived from West Liberton Mains Farm which existed about halfway along this road on the south road.
WEST MILL ROAD	—	Evident. The road to the West Mill which lay on the west side of the Water of Leith and west of Redhall Mill and Kates Mill. Used up until 1973 for the manufacture of Scotts Porridge Oats.

WEST PARK PLACE	—	Probably referring to the lands of Dalry from Dalry House nearby.
WEST PILTON AVENUE	25.10.45	From West Pilton Farm which was situated where the
BANK	25.10.45	junction of Pennywell Road and West Pilton Avenue is
CIRCUS	25.10.45	today.
CROSSWAY	25.10.45	The name Pilton is from the ancient barony of Piltoun.
GARDENS	25.10.45	The mansion house was accidentally burnt down on 8th
GROVE	25.10.45	February 1749.
PARK	25.10.45	
PLACE	25.10.45	
RISE	25.10.45	
ROAD	25.10.45	
STREET	25.10.45	
TERRACE	25.10.45	
VIEW	25.10.45	
WEST WOODS	4. 4.68	This street was constructed to serve houses of teachers in Fettes College situated adjacent to the woodland to the west of the college.
WESTBURN AVENUE	4. 9.70	Situated in the Wester Hailes housing scheme where
GARDENS	4. 9.70	areas were given different names for easier location.
GROVE	5.11.70	A burn flowed through this area which was to the west
PARK	5.11.70	of the main part of the development.
WESTER BROOM AVENUE	29. 1.59	Wester Broom Place was formerly part of South Gyle
DRIVE	29. 1.59	Road.
GARDENS	29. 1.59	The whole development was by Messrs Mactaggart &
GROVE	29. 1.59	Mickel and was an extension to the west of their Broomhall
PLACE	18.12.58	development. For derivation of "Broom" see Broomhouse.
TERRACE	29. 1.59	
WESTER DRYLAW AVENUE	17. 7.52	Wester Drylaw as opposed to Easter Drylaw. These
DRIVE	17. 7.52	streets were constructed on the west side of Groathill
PLACE	17. 7.52	Road North. The name "Drylaw" is from Drylaw House
ROW	17. 7.52	still situated on Groathill Road North.
WESTER HAILES CENTRE	16.12.71	Wester Hailes Road was formerly Thieves Road renamed
DRIVE	4. 9.70	in 1931. This however was the old road not the present
PARK	4. 9.70	day dual carriageway which was named 4.9.70. Named
ROAD	19. 2.31	from the district and Wester Hailes Farm which was located where block 5 to 8 Clovenstone Gardens is today. See also "Hailes"
WESTERN CORNER	30.11.33	Named from Western Terrace existing which was named
GARDENS	30.11.33	from its western position.
PLACE	30.11.33	*See also Western — Part I*
WESTFIELD AVENUE	—	Compare nearby streets Wheatfield, Smithfield. See
ROAD	—	Smithfield Street.
STREET	—	
WESTGARTH AVENUE	—	In the county of Midlothian prior to 1920 and consisted of a short cul-de-sac (extended 1926) serving a large semi-detached house and "The Rectory" of the Episcopal Church. The second of these houses, now No. 4 Westgarth Avenue, was called "Westgarth" owned by a Miss or Mrs Moncur who ran a private school there.

WESTHALL GARDENS	—	The derivation is not known. See Horne Terrace, there may be a connection.
WESTLAND COTTAGES	—	Named thus simply because they were located in the western part of Old Gilmerton.
WHEATFIELD PLACE	—	Compare Smithfield, Westfield. See Smithfield Street.
ROAD	—	
STREET	—	
TERRACE	—	
WHITEHILL ROAD	—	Named from Whitehill Mains which exists due south
STREET	—	of Newcraighall on Whitehill Road also known as Cairnie — Whitehill Road.
WHITEHOUSE ROAD	—	An old road leading to the White House still in existence opposite Gamekeepers Road and still of the same colour. Formerly no other buildings existed in the area except for Fair-a-Far Farm and cottages.
WHITSON GROVE	10.12.31	Following the pattern of naming streets after Lord
PLACE E	10.12.31	Provosts at that time (Hutchison, Chessar, Sleigh and
PLACE W	10.12.31	Stevenson) these streets were named after Thomas
ROAD	10.12.31	Barnaby Whitson, Lord Provost 1926—1929
TERRACE	10.12.31	
WALK	10.12.31	
WAY	10.12.31	
WILFRED TERRACE	—	A note exists in the original Boog Watson notes written by other than him "Possibly from Sir Wilfred Lawson, temperance advocate".
WILLIAMFIELD SQUARE	4. 2.60	Built on the site of a row of cottages known as "Wiliamfield" most probably named after William Jameson, the "father" of Portobello and who started the brickworks there. These cottages were no doubt built to house his workers.
WILTON ROAD	—	For probable derivation see Granby Road.
WINTON DRIVE	26.11.36	The owner of the Mortonhall Estate, on which these
GROVE	12. 4.73	streets were constructed, in 1936 was Col. Algernon
LOAN	13. 6.63	Richard Trotter. He married Lady Edith Mary Montgomerie,
PLACE	12. 4.73	the younger daughter of the 15th Earl of Eglinton and
TERRACE	26.11.36	Winton.
WISHAW TERRACE	—	Compare Dalziel, Cambusnethan which are adjacent streets and are also places in a district of Lanarkshire. Sir James Steele, a former L.P. also a builder built Cambusnethan Street and it is known that he was associated with the place of this name in Lanarkshire. See Cambusnethan Street.
WOLRIGE ROAD	23. 5.35	The name first appreas in the Gilmour family's history (owners of Liberton and Craigmillar Estate on which this street is constructed) in 1856 when Anne Gordon Gilmour, daughter of William Charles Little Gilmour married Henry Perkens Wolrige, only son of Col. John Wolrige and assumed the name of Gordon-Wolrige then Wolrige- Gordon.
WOODFIELD AVENUE	26. 2.70	Development by James Miller & Partners who bought the ground from the trustees of the Sisters of the Good Shepherd. The Convent is adjacent and is known as Woodfield House.

WOODHALL AVENUE	28. 5.36	Named from Woodhall Road, existing, which originally
BANK	28.11.35	was the road to Woodhall House, former residence of
DRIVE	29. 1.31	the Foulis family owners of the Woodhall Estate.
GROVE	23.12.65	
TERRACE	21. 7.32	

WOODLANDS GROVE 28. 5.59

Named from the former house of Woodlands, which was situated just to the west of where the junction of Woodlands Grove and Duddingston Road West is today. The reference is to the many trees which surround it.

WOODSTOCK PLACE 26. 6.52

Corporation Inch Housing where names were selected from novels of Sir Walter Scott — See "Ashton Grove".

YEWLANDS CRESCENT 13.11.58
GARDENS 13.11.58

From Yewlands House, the entrance gate to which can still be seen at 39/41 Lasswade Road where the name "Yewlands" is inscribed on one of the pillars.
The name is probably a reference to the Yew trees that existed in the grounds of Mount Vernon House adjacent, now Mount Vernon Cemetery.

YORK ROAD —

This street was constructed on the estate of Trinity House about 1845 and was most probably named after the Duke of York brother of George IV. It is stated in "History of Trinity House" page 181 "In the convening room of Trinity House there are models of the "Royal Oak", a 64-Gun Ship of the 18th Century made for the Duke of York, brother of George IV.

ZETLAND PLACE —

Compare Lennox, Stirling, and Lomond, adjacent streets all named from ships with a Leith port of registration. These streets were constructed on the former estate of Trinity House.
Zetland Place was named from the "Earl of Zetland", a Leith Ship.